History of Crime and Criminal Justice
David R. Johnson and Jeffrey S. Adler, Series Editors

Politics of the Sword

*Dueling, Honor, and Masculinity
in Modern Italy*

Steven C. Hughes

THE OHIO STATE UNIVERSITY PRESS
Columbus

Copyright © 2007 by The Ohio State University.
All rights reserved.

Library of Congress Cataloging-in-Publication Data
Hughes, Steven C.
Politics of the sword : dueling, honor, and masculinity in modern Italy / Steven C. Hughes.
  p. cm.—(History of crime and criminal justice)
Includes bibliographical references and index.
ISBN 978–0–8142–1072–7 (cloth : alk. paper)
1. Dueling—Political aspects—Italy—History. 2. Fencing—Political aspects—Italy—History. 3. Nationalism—Italy—History. I. Title.
CR4595.I8H84 2007
945.091—dc22
               2007026537

This book is available in the following editions:
Cloth (ISBN 978–0–8142–1072–7)
CD-ROM (ISBN 978–0–8142–9149–8)

Cover design by James A. Baumann
Text design by Juliet Williams
Type set in Adobe Bembo

9 8 7 6 5 4 3 2 1

To
Sue Cornish
Gwyneth Retta Hughes
and
Curran F. Hughes,
who were all there when Rome was home.
Che bella famiglia!

Contents

List of Illustrations ix
Acknowledgments xi
Abbreviations xv

Introduction 1
Prologue   From Primacy to Paucity 13
Chapter I   Risorgimento del Duello—Duello del Risorgimento 21
Chapter II   Honor and the Nation 53
Chapter III   A Plague of Duels (1860–1914): Dueling and Elites 111
Chapter IV   Institutions of Honor and the Search for Legal Sanction 177
Chapter V   The Great Dueling Debate 213
Chapter VI   The Duel and Fascism 267
Conclusion 315

Works Cited 335
Index 349

Illustrations

Images

Image 1	Cover of Cesare Alberto Blengini's 1864 fencing manual	87
Image 2	*Illustrazione italiana,* duel of the Count of Turin in 1897	108
Image 3	Postcard (1902) from Italy's official fencing academy in Rome	142
Image 4	Cover of Achille Angelini's 1888 dueling manual	143
Image 5	Cover of Cesare Alberto Blengini's 1868 dueling manual	184
Image 6	Cover of Ernesto Salafia Maggio's 1895 dueling manual	185
Image 7	Mussolini's Honor Guard	311
Image 8	Propaganda postcard for Fiume invasion	312
Image 9	Mussolini's office with deathshead symbol	313
Image 10	Postcard, "Befana fascista anno XIX (1941)"	313

Charts

Chart 1	Reported duels in Italy arranged by weapon, 1879–99	89
Chart 2	Reported duels in Italy, 1879–95	261
Chart 3	Yearly averages of reported duels in Italy, 1879–1925	264

Tables

Table 1	Military participants in reported duels arranged by rank, 1890–94	82
Table 2	Reported duels in Italy, 1879–95	115
Table 3	Reported duels in Italy arranged by motive, 1879–95	116
Table 4	Participants in reported duels arranged by profession, 1888–95	117
Table 5	Reported dueling offenses taken to trial, 1880–95	162
Table 6	Reported duels arranged by region, 1887–95	165
Table 7	Fifteen provinces with the lowest number of reported duels, 1887–95	166
Table 8	Percentage of reported duels per 100,000 population, 1887–95	167
Table 9	Fifteen provinces with the highest frequency of reported duels, 1887–95	168
Table 10	Fifteen provinces with the highest number of reported duels per 100,000 population, 1887–95	169
Table 11	Fifteen provinces with the lowest number of reported duels per 100,000 population, 1887–95	170
Table 12	Yearly averages of reported duels in Italy, 1879–1925	261
Table 13	Reported duels per year in the Italian military, 1901–10	263

Acknowledgments

DAUNTING IS THE TASK of recognizing all the people and institutions who made this project possible, for they are many in number and varied in their contributions. First and foremost are the librarians. Dott. Margherita Breccia Fratadocchi and her staff in the rare book and manuscript room at the Biblioteca Nazionale Centrale in Rome were critical in helping me explore the dueling collection of Baron Giorgio Enrico Levi which served as the bibliographic bedrock of what follows. Also of particular assistance at the BNCR were dott. Francesca Niutta, dott. Alda Spotti, and dott. Luisa Jacini. The current director, dott. Osvaldo Avallone, deserves special credit for recognizing the importance of the Levi collection and highlighting it in a spectacular multimedia exhibition at the library in the spring of 2005. Among the staff I also want to thank Lucia Rossi, Rina Niuzzo, Lorella Timpano, Mariolina Benedetti, and Alessandro Giorgetti, with special kudos going to Pino D'Errico for his untiring photographic efforts. Likewise in Rome avv. Claudio M. Mancini offered invaluable information from his private collection and personal knowledge on fencing and dueling history. In Leuven, Belgium, thanks are owed to Chris Coopens and Guido Cloet who facilitated my use of the Katholieke Universiteit Leuven's special collection on fencing originally donated by Archibald H. Corbel. In Sondrio, sign. Pier Carlo Della Ferrara graciously sent to a complete stranger in America some excellent documents from the archives of the Banca Popolare di Sondrio on Vilfredo Pareto's various affairs. Back in Baltimore the interlibrary loan staff, and especially Peggy Feild, tirelessly and cheerfully processed many strange requests in various languages over the years.

For assistance with translations, I thank Pier Massimo Forni, Bill Donovan, Kelly DeVries, Joe Walsh, Will Perkins, Leslie Morgan, and especially Giuliana Risso Robberto. Other forms of valuable help came from Tom McCoog, SJ, Franco della Peruta, Anna Maria Rao, Carlo Pischeda, Renata Ago, Claudio Donati, Mario Da Passano, Silvio Longhi, Francesco Jacinto, Paola Briante, Inge Botteri, Carlo Mozzarelli, Marco Cavina, Ruth Ben Ghiat, Anthony Cardoza, Barbara Ronchetti, Elizabeth and Thomas Cohen, Jane and Peter Schneider, Colin Hamill, Giancarlo Angelozzi, Andrea Branchi, Maria Nadia Covina, Luigi Cajani, Sergio La Salvia, Christel Snels, Marta Petrusewicz, Richard Drake, Gregory Hanlon, Geoffrey Symcox, Ingrid Germani, Sergio Morrara, Antonio Merendoni, Giuseppe Belletti, Antonio Spallino, Silvana Patriarca, Martin Blinkhorn, Richard Boswell, John Woodhouse, Michael Broers, Alessandro Visani, Pietro Del Negro, Oscar di Simplicio, John Davis, David Kertzer, Edward Muir, Raymond Grew, Douglas Hay, Pieter Spierenburg, Robert Nye, and, in memoriam, Filippo Mazzonis and Phil Cannistraro. Andrea Merlotti and Paola Bianchi proved most generous with their expertise and hospitality in Torino, as did Daniele Boschi in Rome. The Monti family of Lecco (Margherita, Antonio, Giacomo, and Nicolò) likewise offered a safe haven for an itinerant scholar, as did Pietro Saraceno in Monte Spaccato before his premature and much-lamented demise.

Financially, the original work for this study resulted from a senior research grant awarded by the Fulbright Program, and follow-up funds were generously provided by Loyola College in Maryland, especially the college of arts and sciences under the direction of Dean Jim Buckley. Particular gratitude also goes to Loyola's Center for the Humanities and Director Claire Mathews McGinnis for helping cover the costs of the photo reproduction. Loyola also twice allowed me sabbatical leave to work on the project, and without that free time this book would not exist.

Many thanks as well go to the history department of Loyola for surrounding me with intelligent and caring colleagues who read and commented on various chapters of the manuscript. Katherine Brennan, Bradley Naranch, Matt Mulcahy, Bill Donovan, Kelly DeVries, Keith Schoppa, Angela Leonard, and Betsy Schmidt participated in two "works in progress" sessions, as did Jack Breihan, Tom Pegram, and Chuck Cheape who further offered helpful written critiques. I offer my appreciation to Joanne Dabney, secretary of the history department, for all she has done over the years. Beyond Loyola, Mary Gibson of the John Jay School of Criminal Justice deserves special thanks for reading the entire manuscript at a critical juncture and making a number of important suggestions. Any remaining shortcomings I jealously regard as my own.

Thanks as well go to The Ohio State University Press, and particularly to Jeff Adler who felt that this book might fit well into Ohio State's series History of Crime and Criminal Justice, which he coedits with David Johnson. A succession of acquisition editors at Ohio State patiently encouraged the project along, and Sandy Crooms calmly helped bring it into being with more focus and less baggage. Gratitude also goes to Ohio State's two anonymous readers, whose encouraging and helpful comments were most appreciated; Maggie Diehl for her excellent copyediting; Juliet Williams for the text design; and James Baumann for the cover design.

Academia aside, many thanks go to friends and family who often suffered the consequences of a seemingly endless project. My father, Whitey Hughes, was always a big fan, and one only wishes he could have lived to see its final form. Thanks to Nancy Hughes for her sisterly support and agricultural comradery. Gwyneth and Curran Hughes both gamely followed their father and mother around Italy and subjected themselves to the travails and opportunities of the Italian public school system without complaint (except for the fact that Italian kids go to school on Saturday). My greatest gratitude, of course, goes to Sue Cornish to whom this book is primarily dedicated. Researcher, lover, wife, mother, proofreader, amusing muse, careful critic—her life along with mine is woven through these pages.

Attributions

Cover art is from *La tribuna illustrata*, June 22, 1902, print and permission from the Biblioteca Nazionale Centrale di Roma. Thanks as well to the BNCR for permission to reproduce images 1, 2, 4, 5, and 6. None of these images may be reproduced without the express permission of the BNCR. Image 3 is from a postcard from the National Fencing Academy kindly given to me by Claudio Mancini, and image

7 is entitled "Genova, Piazza della Vittoria, Mussolini lascia il podio salutato dai Moschettieri del Duce" (May 14, 1938) and was provided by the Istituto Luce in Rome. Image 8 is from www.arpnet.it/arditi/pics/fiume3.jpg. Image 9 is from Renzo de Felice and Luigi Goglia, eds., *Storia fotografica del fascismo,* Bari: Laterza, 1981, p. 11; at the proprietors' disposal. Image 10 is a postcard entitled "Befana fascista anno XIX (1941)" in the possession of the author.

Abbreviations

ACS	Archivio Centrale dello Stato, Roma
AMR	Archivio del Museo del Risorgimento in Rome
ASB	Archivio di Stato di Bologna
ASR	Archivio di Stato di Roma
AST	Archivio di Stato di Torino
BCB	Biblioteca Communale di Bologna
BNCR	Biblioteca Nazionale Centrale di Roma
BNN	Biblioteca Nazionale di Napoli
CDS	*Corriere della sera*
DBI	*Dizionario biografico degli Italiani.* 1960—Roma: Enciclopedia Italiana
DRN	*Dizionario del Risorgimento Nazionale.* 1933–37. Milano: Vallardi.
IRA	Istituto del Risorgimento a Rome
MRM	Museo del Risorgimento di Milano

Introduction

THIS BOOK BEGAN in the State Archive of Bologna where, amidst the papers of the papal police, I stumbled across documents of a duel from the year 1823. According to the dusty documents, two young men, Cesare Arnoaldi, scion of one of Bologna's wealthy bourgeois families, and Federico Francavilla, a marquis of Neapolitan extraction, had exchanged words of "gallantry" at a local theatrical performance on the evening of May 1. They had subsequently arranged to fight a duel early the next morning in a field not far from the city, and they had carried out their plan with the aid of two young aristocrats, Count Luigi Aldrovandi and Count Lataneo di Compignano, who had acted as "witnesses." The duel was short and ended after Francavilla received a serious wound in his arm. Upon returning to Bologna, he quickly sought the attention of a doctor, explaining that he had cut himself while practicing a fancy fencing move at home. Meanwhile, rumors about the duel coursed through the city, and the police started investigating the event that very afternoon.[1] The case rapidly reached the desk of the top political official in the province, Cardinal Legate Giuseppe Spina, who now faced an unhappy predicament: As he soon informed Cardinal Ercole Consalvi, secretary of state of the Papal States, the restoration of power to the pope after the fall of Napoleon had brought

---

1. The relevant documents are in ASB, Ispettorato di Polizia, Atti Riservati, 1823, Busta 27, and attached to Spina-Consalvi, May 3, 1823, #51.

with it a return to the law codes of the *ancien régime*, in this case the 1756 Criminal Statute of Cardinal Legate Serbelloni. According to this venerable legislation, the penalty for dueling—no matter what the consequences of the combat—was death for all involved, including the seconds.[2]

Spina argued that such severity was excessive in this case. The duelists were young; they had been unaware of the penalties beforehand; they had not considered the possible pain to their families; they had no previous criminal records; and finally the charge would be difficult to prove in a court of law. Consequently Spina asked that Consalvi plead with the pope, Pius VII, for permission to allow him to handle the whole matter "economically," that is, outside the normal channels of the judicial system. The pope agreed to this arrangement, and Spina ordered that the perpetrators, who had managed to flee the city, return and be relegated to various monasteries to contemplate their transgressions. Francavilla had requested as well a passport to Lucca where he could take a special cure for his wounded arm, to which Spina agreed but with the stipulation that, because of the marquis' Neapolitan provenance, he not be allowed to return to Bologna. When informed of these provisions, the secretary of state replied rather heatedly that Spina had gone too far in his leniency. This was a serious crime, especially in the Papal States, and an example needed to be set. He therefore ordered extra time for those detained in the monasteries and instructed Spina to announce Francavilla's banishment to the public at large. Yet in the end Aldrovandi and Arnoaldi were released after a little more than two months of relatively cushy confinement; Francavilla was later allowed to return through the intervention of the city's archbishop; and the fourth participant, Count Lataneo, seems to have escaped any sanction whatsoever—certainly a far cry from the blade of the guillotine originally hanging over all their heads.

The narrative power of this episode obviously proved compelling, for here was social/political history at its most piquant. What had prompted the duel? Why had an aristocrat agreed to fight a commoner, albeit a wealthy one? According to the police, a history of bad blood between the duelists had set the stage for the encounter. Had Francavilla, who was described by Spina as insolent and frivolous, found his noble Neapolitan sensibilities affronted by the pretensions of a member of Bologna's more porous urban patriciate? And what about the issues

---

2. Serbelloni 1756, 35–38.

of privilege, rank, and patronage that had quickly taken the case to the highest authority in the land and brought a resolution both reasoned and religious? These considerations were doubly engaging because from the beginning Spina had not been completely honest with his own superiors. Although it may well have been true that the young men did not know the current law regarding dueling, Spina's other affirmation that it would prove a difficult case in court rang rather hollow when one considers that early in the game the police had managed to gather together some 27 pages of extremely telling evidence. Not only did they have people who had seen the duelists leave and return to the city with swords under their cloaks; they also had two eyewitnesses to the very event itself, one of whom had mentioned that after the fighting had stopped, a certain piece of paper had been torn up and dropped on the spot. With an alacrity seldom associated with papal justice, the police had repaired to the scene of the crime and managed to glue together enough scraps of this document to demonstrate that it was a *cartello di sfida* or writ of challenge, proof positive of the nature of the encounter. Still today the pasted-up note sits attached to the relevant police report residing in the archive.

In short, the case was ready-made for an inquisitorial-style court, complete with two eyewitnesses, handwritten validation, and a host of circumstantial detail. Yet the cardinal legate had soft-pedaled the evidence from the beginning and then imposed a penalty so slight as to earn a reprimand from the secretary of state. No doubt he genuinely felt the official penalty inappropriate to the actual offense, and the social prominence of the families involved was mentioned more than once in the dispatches. However, Spina also had to contend with the local political situation. The transition back to papal rule had been arduous. The Bolognesi had experienced some 16 years of Napoleonic rule, and during the Congress of Vienna they had even asked to become part of Austria's empire rather than return to the Papal States. Revolution was in the air, and major uprisings had recently been suppressed in Naples and Piedmont by Austrian intervention. Spina himself had been one of Consalvi's most important liberal allies in the attempt to steer a middle course between clerical reactionaries on one side and radical *carbonari* on the other. Under the circumstances, one can understand that Spina was looking neither to alienate possible allies among Bologna's top families nor to advertise the bloodthirsty attributes of an antiquated law code. Instead he had opted to take a lenient approach, mixing merciful largesse and political acumen.

Such was my introduction to the "politics of the sword," and little did I know in just how many senses that phrase would become relevant in describing the history of the duel in Italy. Frankly, I would never answer all my questions regarding this particular duel; the trail ran cold in that single bundle of papers. But it had served its purpose and alerted me to the duel as a subject that offered a wide variety of perspectives on the past. When I was finally able to devote full-time attention to it, I soon discovered that I was anything but alone in my interests and that social and cultural historians, such as François Billacois (1986) and Robert Nye (1993) for France and Ute Frevert (1991) and Kevin McAleer (1994) for Germany, had begun breathing new intellectual life into a topic that had previously enjoyed an extensive but not very methodical literature.[3] Of these, Billacois was the pathbreaker, and his lengthy tome on the duel in sixteenth- and seventeenth-century France remains a model of originality, industry, and *esprit*. He also captured the breadth of issues that the duel encompasses as a focus of research, defining it as a "total social phenomenon" that is a "touchstone" which offers "an aid to the identification and understanding of a particular period, society and political system, with its moral and aesthetic sensibilities and metaphysical and spiritual background."[4] Since that first wave of books, other works have appeared dealing with the duel in Ireland, America, Russia, and elsewhere, all of which have validated the vitality of the topic.[5]

With the exception of the Renaissance period, however, dueling in modern Italy has for the most part escaped scientific investigation.[6] This lack of study is somewhat strange because following a severe decline in the practice during the eighteenth century, the duel returned with a vengeance during the Risorgimento, and after unification in 1861 it reached levels of frequency that rivaled anything in France or Germany. Commentators talked about the new country as being overcome by a "plague of duels" and a "duellomania" that offered the bloody spectacle of a duel a day. The duel's enduring popularity created constant controversy in liberal Italy as legislators, jurists, and moralists debated whether

3. Also see Kiernan 1989 and Wyatt Brown 1982.
4. Billacois 1990, 5.
5. For example, Kelly 1995; Reyfman 1999; Steward 2000; and Freeman 2001; Shoemaker 2002; Matos E Lemos 1993; Gayol 1999; Piccato 1999; and Parker 2001. For early articles on England see Andrew 1980; Simpson 1988.
6. Aside from my articles (1998, 2001, 2005) see Fozzi and Da Passano 2000; Mazzonis 1989; Cavina 2005, 236–88, and various sections of Banti 2000 and Geltmaker 2002.

and how to bring it under control. Pamphlets with titles such as "Down with the Duel," "War on the Duel," and "The Shame of the Duel" all communicated the passion and concern of those who could not believe that a country that had so recently returned to the path of progress and civilization had also wholeheartedly embraced such a "barbaric" custom. Yet the antiduelists were consistently countered by sober-minded men of rank and influence who felt that the duel was necessary for the health of the nation. Thus Iacopo Gelli, Italy's most esteemed expert on the duel, vaunted its role in 1888 as a guarantor of the very concept of freedom:

> The duel, a result of noble sentiments, of man's strong feeling of esteem, of the profound consciousness of personal dignity, of the moral duty to preserve intact and immaculate one's own honor, even with the sacrifice of one's life, was instituted to vindicate sullied honor, [and] to maintain moral sentiment and civil courage at a high level in the people (*popolazioni*), because otherwise liberty perishes where the one declines or the other is lacking.[7]

Certainly the duel was no passing fancy. As late as 1902 the country's foreign minister, Giulio Prinetti, wounded the honorable deputy Leopoldo Franchetti in a saber duel resulting from angry words exchanged in the antechamber of parliament over colonial policy (see cover image). In fact, the duel remained a common custom in Italy well into the 1930s, whereas most other European countries saw its demise after World War I if not before. Interestingly, its very longevity may help to account in part for the reluctance of Italian scholars to study what was clearly a vital cultural aspect of both liberal and Fascist Italy. Thus, when I approached native historians about this project, they often seemed less interested in discussing dueling as a social phenomenon than launching into a description of how their great-uncle or grandfather had participated in a duel back in the 1920s or even the 1930s. One historian related that he had himself been challenged to a duel after the Second World War (he declined the honor with humor), and one woman commented that when taking catechism in the 1950s, she had still memorized the three great mortal sins as being *omicidio, suicidio, e duello*. As useful and engaging as this all proved to be, it seemed to make the point that the modern duel was not yet "historical" enough for dissection; it

7. Gelli 1888A, 61.

still resided in the common cultural memory as an "obvious" part of Italian life: the realm of anecdote rather than analysis.

Be that as it may, it is my contention that the duel and the code of honor that it disciplined played an important role in the formation, consolidation, and functioning of united Italy. Specifically, it offered a common model and bond of masculine identity for those patriotic elites who, having created a country of great variety and contrast for often contradictory motives, then had to deal with the consequences. As we shall see, dueling became an iconic weapon during the Risorgimento struggle for liberation, with individual honor and courage standing as analogues of the nation's right and need to free itself from the insult of foreign oppression. It maintained that role as it offered a continuing image of martial valor and moral discipline for the liberal state: an affirmation that became particularly important in the face of united Italy's less-than-happy performances as a player on the stage of great power politics both in Europe and abroad. Eventually, the duel fed into the hypernationalism and the cult of violence that marked the early fascist movement, although in the end it would prove too individualistic in its definition of dignity to stand up to the totalitarian regime that would gradually emerge.

Intertwined with these notions of nationalism was an evolving, gendered discourse on Italy's virility as a people and as a nation, and by studying the duel we gain a unique window on the critical role of masculinity in the self-conception and worldview of Italian elites. Dueling was the ultimate mark and test of virility, and it was often defended if not promoted for the sake of the country's biological, psychological, and political future. Conversely, the opponents of the duel would constantly find themselves nonplussed by the need to show that they were no less virile than the other side, and many were the antiduelists who found themselves with sword in hand, defending their right to condemn the practice. Liberal opponents likewise took refuge in the fact that the ancient Romans had never dueled and thus combined manly images of military prowess with a patriotic pride in the nation's classical heritage. Even those groups such as the Socialists and the intransigent Catholics who rejected the nexus of exultant nationalism and chivalric honor had to find ways to protect their masculine credentials with respective proclamations of revolutionary courage and muscular obedience to the pope.

Politically, the duel played an important role in the formative years of the nation. Not only did it allow for the honorable settlement of disputes among men who had had quite different ideas on how the country should be created, but it also eased the transition of various groups of regular and irregular soldiers into a united Italian army. It likewise undergirded the new system of liberal government, buffering the consequences of untrammeled debate and allowing men to vehemently and sometimes violently disagree in word and print, only to return to reasoned relations with honor intact. At the same time, it provided a stage on which politicians could manifest the self-control, respectability, and courage thought necessary to operate in the public sphere, all the while offering the *éclat* of flashing swords and bloody combat for one's constituents. More generally, it reinforced a system based on a highly restrictive suffrage in which the gentlemen who dueled were the same gentlemen who ruled—a powerful projection of privilege and exclusivity based on a supposedly ancient rite. Italy would share these features with other liberal regimes, and this book ends with a comparative analysis of dueling in Ireland, Belgium, and Portugal to illustrate the point. However, Italy's political life was particularly prone to chivalric combat because the system of *trasformismo*, which evolved and then dominated during the liberal period, was based on the deliberate confusion of personal and public power from top to bottom. Lacking political parties as a force of organization and discipline, Italian politics revolved around ever-mutating personal allegiances in which individual honor was constantly at risk and often in need of armed defense.

Socially, the creation of the "gentleman" as a man hyperconscious of his reputation and willing to die (or kill) in its defense offered a psychological and social paradigm of distinction that allowed for the absorption and co-optation of successful newcomers while maintaining critical exclusionary standards against the vast majority of the population. This cultural dimension is important in understanding the ruling elites of Italy, who have consistently evaded easy categorization according to standard economic or ideological definitions of class. Historians such as Raffaelli Romanelli, Anthony Cardoza, Marco Meriggi, and Alberto Maria Banti have stressed the need to look at shared cultural values, life-style choices, and informal symbols of prestige to better grasp the social reality of liberal Italy; and certainly the code of honor provides us with a critical piece of the puzzle in such an enterprise. Particularly important in this regard is how the study of the duel reflects on the growing literature regarding non-economic forms of association and sociability among elite men. One journalist in 1888 complained,

"The country is populated with free associations, in which (particularly for the higher social classes) the laws of honor are a cult and common pact."[8] The duel was the final arbiter of behavior in Italy's many clubs and circles, and in return those institutions enforced the code of honor, threatening expulsion for any member who failed to seek or give satisfaction according to the rules. Deconstructing the dueling code and examining various affairs of honor shed new light on these social spaces which were critical in the development and articulation of "bourgeois" culture.

The political and social importance of the duel in liberal Italy naturally made it difficult to deal with in terms of the law. As we shall see, endless discussion surrounded specific sanctions against it, and the law courts had difficulty dealing with the dilemma of prosecuting and sentencing the best and the brightest, to say nothing of the most powerful, members of society. The issue was particularly prickly because Italy's liberal elites were great believers in law and order, and their own immunity from serious prosecution constantly came back to haunt their own premises of good government. In the end they would opt for a clumsy compromise that injected the fundamental tenets of the dueling code into criminal legislation while indirectly acknowledging the rise of a parallel system of "honorable" adjudication that naturally impinged on the regular judiciary. Meanwhile, the many codes of chivalry and tribunals of honor that appeared after unity would testify to the strength of the dueling ethic among Italy's elites, but they would simultaneously indicate their own doubts about a system in which a man's ability with a sword might trump all other considerations of his character.

This book then is basically about the creation of what one might best call united Italy's "chivalric community"—an elite "honor group" that borrowed the concept of chivalry or knighthood as a lexicon of proper behavior that suited its sensibilities and purposes.[9] One might think that the pervasiveness of the duel after unification mirrored the example of other western European countries where emerging elites directly co-opted the chivalric traditions of their aristocratic forebears. Such co-optation would seem most logical for Italy, which is generally regarded as the birthplace of the modern point-of-honor duel during the Renaissance. Yet such was not the case. Although the modern duel evolved as a caste privilege and obligation on the peninsula during the

8. Indelli 1888.
9. On honor groups and reflexive notions of horizontal honor see Stewart 1994, 54–71.

fifteenth and sixteenth centuries, it had become exceedingly infrequent among the nobility in much of Italy during the eighteenth century, with the important exception of Piedmont. What brought the duel back to Italy was, I contend, the mass experience of Italians fighting under the French, whose military had maintained the dueling tradition. Indeed, prior to the publication of united Italy's first dueling code in 1863, Italians seeking to defend their honor turned to a nineteenth-century French manual rather than one of their homegrown varieties from an earlier epoch. The dueling ethic thus returned to Italy during the course of the Risorgimento as an "invented tradition," and the close identification with the creation of the country itself helps in large part explain its popularity and longevity in Italian society.[10] This historical disjuncture also underlines the fact that as the Renaissance courtiers had recast medieval concepts of chivalry to suit their needs, so too did Italy's liberal elites feel free to create their own version of what being a chivalrous gentleman really meant, and much of what follows seeks to illuminate that conception.

Many men who considered themselves part of the chivalric community never met each other. It was in some ways an "imagined community" that matched the model set out by Benedict Anderson in his influential analysis of modern nationalism, and indeed it derived a large part of its motive force from its reciprocal relationship with Italian patriotism. Yet it was also an exclusive community based on horizontal and reflexive mechanisms of honor, and it spent much of its time and energy vetting and culling a gradually mutating membership. As perhaps befit a system built on individual honor, the center of the chivalric community was dominated by certain personalities, such as Paolo Fambri, Achille Angelini, and Iacopo Gelli, whose careers we shall trace as they came to be viewed as the arbiters of honor for the entire country. They were allied in their efforts with military officers and fencing masters, who enjoyed a special corporate relationship with the dueling ethic that gave them automatic authority over affairs of honor. Surrounding these core groups one finds politicians and journalists for whom the defense of honor was seen as a professional necessity, and beyond them the rest of the "*ceto civile,*" a relatively narrow, yet porous, segment of Italian society for whom the title, rights, and duties of being a "gentleman" were a defining feature. The majority of these men would never fight a duel, but they had to be ready to do so if the occasion should arise, a

10. On the concept of invented traditions see Hobsbawm and Ranger 1983.

contingency contributing to the popularity of dueling manuals by authorities such as Angelini and Gelli. Outside the chivalric community stood the bulk of Italy's population (workers, peasants, and women) although middle- and upper-class women were seen as being capable of understanding "true" honor if they were led in the right direction by their fathers, husbands, and brothers. The larger point, however, is that the chivalric community cast itself in its patriotic imagining as representing the entire Italian nation, while in fact it excluded most of the Italian people: a glaring contradiction which had rather serious ramifications for the liberal regime.

For there is little doubt that honor was also at stake for Italy's lower classes when they clashed one-on-one, knives in hand, with great frequency and often fatal consequences. Scholars such as Pieter Spierenburg (1998), Thomas Gallant (2000), Lyman Johnson (1998), and others have contributed a great deal to our understanding of how important interpersonal violence was among urban and rural working-class men to their status within their communities. Elliott Gorn (1985) has shown how even seemingly irrational behavior, such as eye-gouging matches among American backwoodsmen, made social sense in a frontier world of violent danger, where the one great demarcator at the bottom of society was between free men and slaves, the latter having no freedom over their bodies while the former could risk life and limb, to say nothing of eyes, in defense of their reputations. Thus, as Gorn states in general, "... how men fight—who participates, who observes, which rules are followed, what is at stake, what tactics are allowed—reveals much about past cultures and societies."[11] The present work then really takes on only half the task, for although nineteenth-century Italy was notorious throughout western Europe for its ubiquitous lower-class knife-fighting, relatively little research has been done on the topic, especially of a comparative nature among the different regions.[12] Limited in space, time, and energy, I have restricted myself to discussing this wider world of Italian male violence only as it figured within the narrower context of what I call the "chivalric enterprise" of dueling and honor. But in that context it was vitally important, for, as we shall see, in Italy the demarcation of blood spilled with a knife as opposed to blood spilled with a saber was a resounding leitmotif of the politics of the sword.

11. Gorn 1985, 18.
12. The best work to date is Boschi 1998.

In order to ease the flow of the prose that follows, it is necessary to offer a glossary of terms in Italian that will punctuate the text and whose constant translation would hinder rather than aid the reader's understanding.

> *Vertenza:* An affair of honor arising from an insult that could end in a retraction, an understanding (equivocation), or armed combat.
>
> *Sfida:* A written or oral challenge that constituted the beginning of a *vertenza*.
>
> *La mentita:* "Giving the lie," the basic formulaic challenge of untruth, which derived its totemic power from the fundamentals of chivalric knighthood based on the importance of one's word and fealty to the structures of feudalism.
>
> *Vie di fatto:* Physical acts such as slapping or spitting which automatically occasioned a *vertenza* and most likely a duel.
>
> *Indegnità:* The status of being disqualified from either asking for or receiving satisfaction through a *vertenza*.
>
> *Padrini:* The "seconds" or "witnesses" who attended an encounter on behalf of the duelists or *primi* (singular: *padrino* and *primo*, respectively).
>
> *Direttore:* The person designated to oversee a duel and ensure that it conformed to the laws of chivalry. Usually he was one of the *padrini*, but he could be a third party brought in by mutual consent.
>
> *Terreno:* The dueling "ground" or "field" where the combat occurred.
>
> *Verbale:* A written account of a *vertenza* stipulating as to the specific offense and the nature of the resulting retraction, understanding, or combat. If the combat did occur, a preliminary *verbale* set out the details of the duel (weapons, conditions, and participants), and then a second *verbale di scontro* reported the results, including the number of assaults with swords (or shots with a pistol), the wounds received, and whether the participants were reconciled and shook hands. If one of the duelists lost his courage or failed to follow the rules, it had to be noted in this final *verbale*, along with a condemnation of his actions. In any given *vertenza*, all *verbali* had to be signed by the *padrini*, with copies provided for each side as written evidence for future reference. Not uncommonly, *verbali* were published in the newspapers.

Although it will be reiterated more than once, it bears saying at this juncture that the "perfect" duel as it developed in the nineteenth century did not consist in one man besting another, but rather in having both men demonstrate their courage, according to the rules and with mutual respect for all involved—that is, as "perfect gentlemen."

Prologue

From Primacy to Paucity

LOOKING BACK from the nineteenth century, Italians could either vaunt or lament their country's past ties to the practice of dueling, for it is generally agreed that the modern code of honor, which relied on the rituals of the duel for its enforcement, evolved in Italy's princely courts during the Renaissance and from there gradually spread to the rest of Europe.[1] Brantôme, the great French courtier who fought in the Italian wars, maintained that the point-of-honor duel first developed among the "*grands capitaines italiens,*" and he described dueling as a constant in the garrisons of the peninsula.[2] With the rise of the duel itself, Italy also saw a veritable explosion of books and pamphlets that purported to justify, explicate, and teach the proper defense of one's honor. Lawyers and moralists created and articulated an ethical code that refined and sharpened sensibilities to insult while dictating proper behavior among "gentlemen," a handily ambiguous category that suited the social flux of the period. Print capitalism found this *scienza cavalleresca* or "science of chivalry" to be a tasty topic, and during the sixteenth century, Italian presses would crank out 46 new dueling manuals released in 110 different editions.[3] This massive edifice of paper was reinforced by steel as Italians refined the rapier out of the broadsword and developed scientific fencing techniques to go with it. Such innovations

---

1. Billacois 1986, 70–75; Peltonen 2003, 4–64.
2. Brantôme 1887, 132.
3. Erspamer 1982, 58–61.

spread quickly to the rest of the continent through teachers such as Sanseverino, Lovino, Pompeo, Bonetti, and Fabrizio, as well as instruction manuals by Marozzo, Agrippa, Saviolo, and Capo Ferro.[4] In short, Italy became famous as "dueling central" in theory, practice, and propaganda for more than one hundred years. Even in the early seventeenth century, John Selden still felt comfortable using the Italian term *Duello* to adorn his English treatise (1610) on the topic. Yet, despite its preeminence as the birthplace of the modern duel, Italy eventually lost its pride of place to the French. The actual number of duels fought on Italian soil gradually diminished throughout the seventeenth century and, with the exception of Piedmont, virtually disappeared after the mid-eighteenth century.

Exactly why the point-of-honor duel arose in Italy during the fifteenth and sixteenth centuries is a sufficiently complex question that I have chosen to address it elsewhere.[5] Nevertheless, four general themes emerge from the current literature.[6] First, the rituals of the modern duel derived primarily from the traditional practices, or *lois d'armes*, of the soldier/knights who provided military muscle throughout the states of Italy. These customary laws began to be codified by Italian jurists starting in the 1470s and then spread to other elite sectors of society. Second, and of major importance, the modern duel—despite its later illegality—received substantial support in its infancy from the Renaissance courts, whose princes granted both their "fields" and their good offices to duelists. Many of the early duels of honor were officiated by ruling princes, or judges appointed by them, thus reinforcing the "legalistic" image of the duel being presented by the jurists.[7] The courts offered official sanction to an evolving rite of honor, and in return they gained the prestige attending an ancient but virtually defunct practice—the judicial duel—while introducing new forms of discipline among their elite subjects.

Third, despite its links to medieval precedents—ordeals, jousts, tournaments, *pas d'armes*, melees—the modern duel was something different: it was dependent on a new, private concept of masculine honor that raised men's sensitivity to personal slights but simultaneously limited the field of those immediately involved in the conflict. Hence the appropriateness of the term "point" of honor, because the duel focused

---

4. Anglo 1990, 6–9; Brioist et al. 2002, 63–70; Gelli 1928, 54–58.
5. Hughes, 2007A.
6. For a good bibliography see Cavina 2005, 303–10.
7. Bryson 1938, 178–86.

attention on a particular affront and reduced its resolution to a single point in both time and space. This narrowed the scope of honor from the collective notions of the past, which had extended commitments of vendetta and feud tied to family and friends across generations. Instead the duel placed one's reputation as a gentleman on one's willingness to seek personal satisfaction in a single, ritualized encounter. Birth or office might confer nobility, but it had to be constantly defended on the individual level.

Finally, for all its chivalric trimmings, the dueling code did not arise in France or Spain, where the traditions and structures of feudal knighthood had retained much of their vigor. Instead it came from Italy, where the warrior aristocracy had suffered its greatest competition in both theory and practice during most of the Middle Ages. Thus the duel functioned in part to help redefine the concept of aristocracy or at least demarcate those who should be accorded the attributes of honor in a constantly shifting social landscape. It could "ennoble" talented elites while protecting the position of those traditionally accorded honor because of their rank, or at least who thought they should be. This social function was enhanced by the evolution of the rapier and scientific fencing techniques that allowed courtiers as well as soldiers to participate in a blood ritual that became increasingly divorced from what was happening on the battlefields of Europe. What bound these features of the early duel together was a search for legitimacy and status in the rapidly mutating political and social environments of the Renaissance city-states. That search lead to an affirmation of the myth of medieval chivalry as a model of masculine behavior, but one that served the psychological and social needs of a rather different society. And this pattern would be repeated in the nineteenth century. On the other hand, understanding why and how Italy abandoned the dueling ethic during what later came to be perceived by patriots as a period of political stagnation and foreign oppression helps explain why its return became a keynote for men trying to prompt a resurgence of Italian identity and liberty.

Italy's primacy as creator and promulgator of the modern duel faded rapidly toward the end of the sixteenth century, and the epicenter of chivalric honor shifted to France. Duels seem to have diminished through the next century and (excluding Piedmont) were relatively rare by the 1750s. Thus in 1756 the legate of Bologna, Cardinal Serbelloni, actually apologized in his code of criminal law for even mentioning dueling among the various forms of homicide because it had so completely disappeared from use.[8] Likewise, Paolo Vergani, in his 1776 antidueling tract, *Dell'enormezza del duello,* fully admitted that his arguments were aimed at a practice that had almost disappeared.[9] This view was the same to foreign eyes, and Smollet, who in his *Travels through Italy and France* commented at length on the readiness of French officers in 1764 to fight over even minor affronts to their honor, made no mention of dueling in Italy at all.[10] Samuel Sharpe, in his *Letters from Italy* of 1766, was highly interested in social customs, particularly those regarding relations between men and women. Observant and critical, he chastised the Italians for their system of *cicisbeismo,* in which married women were constantly paid court by a favorite gallant, a practice he found degrading and inappropriate. Gallantry prevailed, women could do what they wanted, and "the word jealousy is become obsolete." Yet he did not once refer to the chivalric code or dueling as part of the Italian scene. On the contrary, he suggested that there was no way for men to "vent their indignation," no "salve for their honor," and hence "[i]t is amazing how many assassinations there are in Italy almost all of them effects of quarrels."[11] Literary tastes mirrored this general trend, and dueling manuals which were still prized possessions in the seventeenth century had become almost worthless by 1750.[12] The extent of this "degradation" of Italy's chivalric expertise would eventually have both indirect confirmation and practical results after the Restoration when, with the gradual return of the dueling ethic, Italian elites would find themselves relying on French dueling manuals rather than on the earlier efforts of their compatriots.

The reasons for this diminution of dueling were complex and varied. The most obvious cause was the impact of the Council of Trent which emphasized, propagated, and enforced the Papacy's prior opposition to the practice.[13] Cast within the Counter Reformation's growing atmosphere of greater moral conformity, the Church's severe condemnation, constant exhortation, and spiritual punishments—such as prohibiting Christian burial for duelists—apparently prompted some nobles to seek alternative means to settling private disputes.[14] The

   8. Serbelloni 1756, 35.
   9. Vergani 1776, 1–2.
   10. Smollett 1979, 135–38, 174.
   11. Sharp 1766, 11, 174.
   12. Erspamer 1982, 18–20; also Cavina 2005, 206–12, Cavina 2003, 333–66.
   13. Angelozzi 1996, 271–308; Donati 2001, 134–62.
   14. Di Simplicio 1994, 49–58.

growing efficiency and declining tolerance of the early modern governments (which started passing antidueling legislation in the 1540s) may also have had an effect, but just as important was the stability (some would say stagnation) brought by Spanish hegemony in the latter half of the sixteenth century, which, for better or worse, reduced the social and political dynamism that had fueled the duel during the Renaissance. In addition, Billacois has suggested that the Italians became absorbed with the punctilious repartee of their own dueling manuals and turned to words rather than swords to adjudicate matters of honor.[15] For the eighteenth century, Francesco Erspamer has added the rationalizing effects of Enlightenment thought and pointed to the enormous publishing success and presumed influence of Scipione Maffei's monumental antidueling treatise, *Della scienza cavalleresca,* which went through some ten editions after its appearance in 1710.[16] All of these factors figure into what Gregory Hanlon has seen as a well-documented tendency toward a more "policed" society in the eighteenth century by which the nobility in particular attempted to solve their quarrels without violence.[17]

Equal in importance to all these causes, however, was the gradual yet certain demilitarization of the Italian nobility after about 1660, which has been carefully analyzed by Gregory Hanlon.[18] The downward trajectory of the military vocation among elites closely matches the gradual disappearance of the duel in Italy. It strongly indicates that, deprived of a military ethos and identity, Italian elites gave way to the aforementioned religious, social, political, and intellectual forces impinging on the dueling ritual. That such was, in fact, the case was evidenced by Piedmont, which was the one clear-cut exception in the general process of demilitarization and which was the only region of Italy to maintain a vibrant and continuous dueling tradition through the eighteenth century. Thus one commentator, Giuseppe Baretti, reported in 1768 that the Piedmontese "are withal so punctilious and so ready to draw the sword, that more duels are fought in Piedmont than in the rest of Italy taken together."[19] The Piedmontese exception is all the more telling because, as Hanlon writes, the House of Savoy was "ferociously Counter-Reformation" in its religious policies, and thus the region's

15. Billacois 1986, 79–81.
16. Erspamer 1982, 19–21.
17. Hanlon 2000, 306–7, 367. Also see Angelozzi and Casanova 2003.
18. Hanlon 1998, especially 303–27.
19. Baretti 1768, vol. 2, 121–22; also see Fougeroux 1835, 294–95, and Bianchi 2002, 71.

continuing tolerance of chivalric combat offers a healthy corrective to any assumption that the Council of Trent automatically tolled the death knell for dueling on the peninsula.[20] It also provides an interesting paradox by which the only early modern Italian state that managed to create a successful absolutist government, complete with a reliable service nobility and a centralized bureaucracy, was also the only area where dueling continued to flourish.

Be that as it may, the evidence indicates that for the rest of Italy the duel had all but disappeared during the eighteenth century.[21] However, its decline proved to be something of a two-edged sword. Foreign commentators often attributed high rates of personal violence in Italy to the fact that gentlemen failed to face each other on the field of honor.[22] Anachronistically underwritten by the popularity of Machiavelli's assertions of princely deception, daggers and poison became the common descriptors of action among Italian men, and one English critic in 1595 inveighed against "O Italy, the Academie of manslaughter, the sporting place of murther, the Apothecary shop of poyson for all Nations: how many kinds of weapons hast thou invented for malice?"[23] Nor had things improved much by the time Rousseau claimed, in his *Nouveau Héloise,* "At Messina or Naples, one waits for his man at the corner of a street and stabs him from behind. That's what they call being brave in that country. . . ."[24] Such unfortunate images could be mixed with foreign misapprehension of *cicisbeismo* to suggest that eighteenth-century Italian nobles were fecklessly unconcerned with protecting the morality of their wives.[25] Certainly travelers other than Boswell must have gone off on the Grand Tour with the explicit hope of availing themselves of supposedly easy women.[26] It was just this perceived combination of sexual nonchalance and dishonorable perfidy in Sharpe's *Letters from Italy* that led Giuseppe Baretti in 1769 to proclaim angrily that, at least in Piedmont, people "mix in intercourse exactly after the manner of

20. Hanlon 1998, 348.
21. Henry Swineburne, an English traveler who visited the south in the late 1770s, tellingly reported that the Neapolitan nobility no longer wore swords as part of their dress. Reported in Davis 2006, 43.
22. For example, Fynes Moryson's comments in Hughes 1967, 402–7, and those of Dallington in Weinstein 1994, 213–15.
23. Nash 1592, 18.
24. Rousseau 1960, 130. Also see Branchi 2005, 51.
25. On the lack of jealousy see Smollett 1979, 230–31; De Brosses 1991, 843–44; Brydone 1901, 211–12.
26. Boswell 1955, 15–17, 30.

the French and the English, and the Piedmontese weapon in deciding sudden quarrels is the sword I say and not the dagger."[27]

The burden of such negative stereotypes might have been relatively light in the eighteenth century, but as Italy became caught up in the greater game of Napoleonic expansion, they would help spark a return to earlier forms of honorable combat. The whole science of chivalry as it developed in Italy had gone on to influence the rest of Europe, much of which would maintain a closer relationship to the duel. As Billacois would say for France, Italy provided two critical components for the development of the cult of honor: "a technique for single combat (fencing) and a juridico-ethical corpus (scienza cavalleresca)."[28] Eventually, France would return the favor as its revolutionary armies brought new concepts of citizenship as well as a mass attempt to militarize the Italians; in so doing, they would reawaken the dueling tradition by both example and provocation. By the same token, Italians after unity would be able to refer with patriotic pride to a time when their country had taught the world how to put honor on the point of a sword.

27. Baretti 1768, vol. 2, 124.
28. Billacois 1990, 18.

I

Risorgimento del Duello– Duello del Risorgimento

IF THE DUEL were dead in much of Italy by the end of the eighteenth century, it would not stay that way for long. Reinvigorated after 1796 by the arrival of French armies, dueling would once again become a regular although infrequent occurrence among Italians: a compelling force that had to be taken into consideration by those aspiring to elite status in the topsy-turvy world of first Napoleonic and then Restoration society. The duel would find constant reinforcement in the popular culture of the day as Romanticism and market forces sent artists burrowing into a mythical past of medieval chivalry to bring forth a barrage of positive dueling images in prose, poetry, and song. Before Italy's unification, Verdi alone produced six operas containing duels of various sorts.[1] Advertised in the real world by spectacular or notorious encounters, many of which were tied to early Italian nationalism, dueling gradually won over the allegiance of a new generation of men who would embrace the sword as a symbol of their manhood, their freedom, and their patriotism. The duel became linked with the Risorgimento, in terms of both its heroes and its tactics, and it would plant seeds of chivalry that would blossom and proliferate once the country had come into its own. At the same time, the return of the duel would be obvious in the attending number of treatises, projects, and laws, all

---

1. The operas include *Oberto* (1839), *Ernani* (1844), *Luisa Miller* (1849), *Stiffellio* (1850), *Il Trovatore* (1854), and *Aroldo* (1857).

of which bemoaned its influence and aimed at its eradication. In contrast, important people began to assert the difficulties of legislating against such a deeply rooted set of beliefs, suggesting instead that the duel had a positive role to play in modern Italian society. In sum, the rhythm of public commentary on the dueling compulsion accelerated through the period, setting the stage for what would become a torrent of debate following unification.

The Rearmament of Honor in Italy: Napoleon and the Restoration[2]

The duel of honor would return to Italy from France where it had thrived since the sixteenth century and where it had remained thoroughly entrenched in the French army even after the Revolution. From 1796 to 1815, the French military in one way or another was actively engaged on the Italian peninsula, and the code *duello* came as part of the package. Internal politics of the different states were constantly subordinated to the grand designs of first the Republic and then the Empire, and the army served as both the goal and the means of the reorganization of Italian society. Accordingly, the French actively recruited Italian elites, established military academies, created legions of honor, and, above all, introduced conscription as each region fell under their power. Exact numbers are lacking of how many Italians eventually served under the auspices of the Empire, but by 1812, the Kingdom of Italy—which included one-third of the peninsula's population—had some 60,000 soldiers commanded by over 3,000 officers, most of whom were of Italian extraction.[3] Just as important, however, was the subtext of inferiority that underlay French attitudes toward their Italian brothers-in-arms, who were seen as lacking masculinity and courage.[4] This went double for elites since, with the notable exception of the Piedmontese, centuries of misrule had purportedly allowed them to degenerate into a parasitic class of do-nothing pacifists who had been emasculated by their priests with the connivance of their mothers. Time and again these assumptions would rise to the surface, and the Italians would react to defend themselves according to the rules of honor recently relearned from their allies. In short, the French

---

2. For a full treatment of this topic see Hughes 2001.
3. Della Peruta 1991, 27.
4. Broers 2001, 258.

brought tens of thousands of Italians into a military machine dominated by the dueling code and then gave them something to fight about.

Consequently, memoirs from the period refer time and again to affairs of honor conducted between French and Italian officers (the latter including important Risorgimento figures such as Carlo Filangieri and Gugliemo Pepe), and many specifically mention the overweening attitude of the French toward the Italians as a major contributing factor.[5] Worse than French haughtiness, however, were the accusations of cowardice or ineptitude, which figured in their general prejudice against Italians as lacking virility or martial mettle.[6] Yet the memoirs also record many duels among Italian officers from all parts of the peninsula that demonstrate how quickly and completely the dueling ethic had been assimilated as they became swept up in the military cyclone of French expansion. Consider the career of Costante Ferrari, a Grenadier from Lombardy, who over time fought a Polish sergeant, a French Dragoon, a Milanese cavalryman, and a Bolognese Scout.[7] His experience affirmed a report from Giuseppe De Lorenzo, a captain from Naples who had himself been wounded in a duel with a French officer. Having been assigned after the battle of Marengo to a special battalion of Italian volunteers in Pavia, he wrote that duels had become a daily ritual: "There is such a martial—or more accurately—a brutal spirit within our battalion that everyday without exception my comrades haul themselves off into the countryside to fight duels among themselves or with some French or Cisalpine soldier with whom they have had even the slightest controversy [...]."[8] Given that both De Lorenzo and Ferrari came from middle-class backgrounds, their stories suggest that the officer corps provided an avenue to increased status, but one that had to be protected by occasional recourse to the duel. Tapping deep-rooted institutional traditions of chivalry, Italians who rose to leadership in the polyglot and polyclass armies of the Empire could now defend their honor with alacrity and courage, and in so doing announce their arrival as elite members of a new society in the making. Moreover, at least some officers who returned to civilian life carried their chivalric concepts of honor

---

5. Filangieri 1902, 62–68; Ulloa 1876, 27–31; Pepe 1847, 206, 311; Zucchi 1861, 9, 15, 28, 34. For an extraordinary mass duel in Spain between French and Italian soldiers see Vigeant 1883, 51–65.

6. For the most famous example see Filangieri 1902, 62–68. Also see Ulloa 1876, 27–31.

7. Ferrari 1942, 12–13, 114, 21–22; for a Piedmontese/Neapolitan duel see Pignatelli 1927, vol. 1, viii–xix.

8. De Lorenzo 1999, 113.

with them. Such was clearly indicated in a papal police report dated December 30, 1819. It seems that two noblemen in Gubbio shared a romantic interest in the same lady, and their rivalry had eventually prompted a clamorous duel in which both were injured. According to the police, however, the immediate catalyst of the encounter had been a disagreement during dinner over the "duels which they had fought under the past government when they were soldiers."[9]

But what of the lasting effect on Italian society? The growing frequency and alarmist tone of antidueling literature during the Restoration forcefully indicated that something fundamental had changed.[10] For instance, in 1827 Giacomo Bossi published a pamphlet in Torino decrying the fact that the duel had returned to favor in Italy. For three centuries after its condemnation by prince and church alike, the duel had been confined to "the repugnant boasting of quarrelsome bullies," but now that had all changed. Instead, "[t]he criminality of the duel is no longer held to be self evident by most men." Popularized and legalized in France and England, the "deadly plague," the "deplorable insanity," was spreading "like a contagious disease" to Italy, and Bossi felt it his solemn duty to lay out the arguments against it.[11] His opinions were shared by a Roman commentator, Ferdinando Malvica, who in 1826 wrote that in current times "the mania of duels grows beyond measure and renders the people deaf to the voices of reason."[12]

Bossi and Malvica would be joined during the next decade by other antidueling authors such as Luca Marcucci (1836), who maintained that support for the duel had become like a massive rock rolling downhill, almost unstoppable in its momentum, or Antonio Cagnano (1837), who complained the compulsion to duel had "conquered the highest classes of society."[13] Moreover, this later literature (nine treatises between 1835 and 1839) was different from that of the 1820s, which had aimed at swaying the literate public against the duel through entreaty, exhortation, and an appeal to sentiment. In contrast, the new treatises, although obviously not short on moral and religious references, unanimously focused on legislation and the need to create criminal sanctions that

   9. ASR, Direzione Generale di Polizia, 1820, Protocollo Ordinario, Busta 49, Title 6, Fascicolo 49, #1708.
   10. Actually one of the most important critics was Alessandro Manzoni, whose justifiably famous novel, *I promessi sposi,* was written in the 1820s and is full of antidueling messages. For more analysis see Hughes 2001, 43–44.
   11. Bossi 1827, 2–4.
   12. Malvica 1826, 6.
   13. Marcucci 1836, 291, 302, 306; Cagnano 1837, 29, 42.

were both appropriate and effective in the fight against the duel.[14] Nor would their voices go unheeded. The Neapolitan government promulgated a harsh antidueling law in July of 1838, while other Italian states devoted substantial technical deliberation to the duel as they worked to overhaul their criminal codes.[15] Obviously, the power of the state had to be brought to bear on what was perceived as a growing problem of public order.

The states were all, however, facing a protean and pernicious opponent. While some blamed the bad example of military men and others the general degradation of elite morality, new cultural factors were operating during the Restoration to spread the dueling compulsion. Thus Pesaro-Maurogonato, a law student writing his dissertation on the problem of the duel in 1838, complained that the practice of dueling vaunted no famous champion or philosopher whom he could attempt to confound directly. Instead, he wrote, "[i]nfinite is the number of writers who write about the duel with a levity particular to those minds which, incapable of thinking for themselves, blindly follow the prejudices of public opinion [. . .]." He was particularly displeased with the authors of comedies and romances who "never miss the opportunity to present the duel in its most noble aspect and always present it as a valid, reasonable, and necessary reparation of every insult."[16] His lament reflected the growth of Romanticism, whose appeal to Italy's literate classes was evident in the success of poets such as Alfieri, Leopardi, and Foscolo.

Particularly important was the invocation of medieval society, and Sir Walter Scott's novels, loaded with duels and chivalry alike, were enormously popular in Italy. Such was the interest in these topics that Melzi in 1838 created a specialized bibliography of over 800 chivalric novels and poems that had been printed earlier in Italy, primarily in the sixteenth century.[17] Likewise, Italian authors, such as Giovan Battista Bazzoni, Tommaso Grossi, and Silvio Pellico, offered their own homegrown historical romances to feed the expanding market for medieval gallantry. They were all clearly eclipsed, however, by Massimo d'Azeglio, whose novel *Ettore Fieramosca* rediscovered and celebrated the triumph of Italian knights over their French counterparts in a duel that had

14. Besides the aforementioned Marcucci and Cagnano these included in chronological order Puoti 1835; Rizzi 1836; anonymous 1837; Pateale 1837; Carrillo 1837; Costi 1839; Pesaro-Maurogonato 1839.
15. Fozzi and Passano 2000, 254–64.
16. Pesaro-Maurogonato 1839, 142.
17. Melzi 1838.

occurred at Barletta in 1503.[18] Combining historical reality, moving presentation, and praise of Italian military prowess, *Fieramosca* was an instant success upon its publication in 1833 and helped feed the growing alliance between dueling and national pride in Italy. Music became equally entranced with such motifs. Starting with *Oberto* in 1839, Verdi would lace his operas with chivalric encounters, and both Rossini and Donizetti used duels and challenges from past ages as dramatic devices. We will return to some of this material in discussing the duel's special relationship to the Risorgimento, but the present point is that during the Restoration, Italian elites were engulfed in images of the duel on stage and in print, often within a glorified medieval context.

All the more potent then were real-life examples of duels fought for the right reason at the right time. Unquestionably the most important of these burst upon the scene in 1826 after the French author Alphonse de Lamartine published a poem containing a number of lines highly insulting to Italians. Weak, obsequious, fawning, and treacherous, they had, he said, betrayed the majesty and courage of their Roman past and now fought only from behind and in the dark. These were fighting words, and Lamartine, who was with the French Legation in Florence, soon found himself facing Gabriele Pepe, a Neapolitan soldier and writer who had sought refuge in Tuscany after serving two harsh years of imprisonment imposed by the restored Bourbon regime for his participation in the recent revolution. In order to avoid Tuscan censors, who hoped to avoid a diplomatic flap with the French, Pepe slipped a backhanded barb against Lamartine as being both weak and cowardly in an analytical article devoted to Dante. Lamartine asked for a personal meeting to try to solve the matter peacefully, but Pepe had no intention of letting that happen. Instead, he received Lamartine at home, and his description of the event, written some weeks later, reveals volumes about his intentions in the affair.

> I received him with all possible courtesy, just as our written correspondence had been genteel and courteous. [. . .] I wanted to use and exaggerate the forms of chivalry. I was dealing with a Frenchman who had depicted the Italians as assassins capable only of treacherously using a dagger in the night. It was thus necessary to demonstrate with facts that the Italians are more chivalrous than the French. Moreover, the Florentines, who shared my estimation of events, were carefully watching

18. On the original incident see Russo 1993.

to see in what ways I would carry out the part of Champion of Italy. And since we Neapolitans, because of past military events, do not have a good reputation, I was simultaneously stimulated by both Italian and patriotic [Neapolitan] feelings.[19]

Here then was a chance to prove that the Italians were as "civilized" as the French, to counteract the image of the perfidious stiletto in the shadows, and finally to redeem the martial valor of his countrymen. Pepe blatantly promoted this "chivalric project" throughout the rest of the affair with a series of gentlemanly gestures, such as accepting French seconds as his own, using a shorter rapier, and binding Lamartine's wounded arm with his own handkerchief after he had bested him in the action.[20]

It would be difficult to overestimate the importance and impact of Pepe's example for dueling in Restoration Italy. It had, in many ways, been a "perfect" duel. Above all, it had been a public event from start to finish, with Lamartine's poetic attack being countered by Pepe's literary retort, leading to a duel that was broadcast throughout the peninsula. The evidence of insult was easily available in print to all, and the injury had transcended personal rancor to reach questions of national character. Also, it had ended well. Not only had Pepe proven himself "more chivalrous" than the Frenchman, not only had he wounded the foreigner "in the hand which had offended," but Lamartine had almost immediately issued an "explanation" of his previous poetic faux pas.[21] Thus the triumph was complete: Italian honor had been defended, restored, and celebrated. In fact Pepe immediately became a hero of the first order, and Antonio Ranieri reported that he was "the most venerated, the most adored of the exiles" to whom "all the Italians, all the foreigners who were in Florence knelt down...."[22] Similar enthusiasm emanated from the rest of Italy. He received letters of congratulation from Milan, Bologna, Rome, and, of course, Naples, and he intimated to his brother that he could not believe how quickly word of the duel had spread.[23]

All in all, the Pepe-Lamartine affair proved a formidable force in promoting the dueling ethic. Carlo Troya in a letter to Pepe excoriated

---

19. Quoted in Pepe 1980, vol. 1, 400.
20. Lamartine's later account was different, but Pepe's description quickly became the Italian version. See Jannone 1912, 56–57.
21. Quoted in Jannone 1912, 69.
22. Quoted in Lucianelli 1994, 98.
23. Pepe 1980, vol. 1, 399. For more detail see Hughes 2001, 45–50.

the few critics of the encounter as poltroons, donkeys, and rogues. He fantasized picking up a stick and punishing such "*mercantantuci*" (gross merchants) and "*dottori degli stivali*" (base hacks) until they repented their weakness.[24] In this regard, although his duel fell clearly into the Napoleonic tradition of Italian soldiers fighting with their French critics, Pepe had now set a public precedent on a grand scale. In fact, he had created a paradigm that could allow almost any duel between an Italian and a foreigner to be read as an analogue of national struggle. Thus in March of 1833, when a tiff during Mardi Gras between a group of Imperial officers and a Milanese engineer led to a duel that left one of the officers dead, it was interpreted as a political event as much as a personal one, leading to the arrest of a number of liberal sympathizers.[25]

Despite the popularity and influence of the Pepe-Lamartine affair, we should be wary of overestimating the frequency with which duels actually occurred during the Restoration period. While contemporaries often bemoaned the growing number of encounters, we must keep their earlier frame of reference in perspective and understand that any increase in a phenomenon that had previously been almost nonexistent was bound to make a major impression. Lacking any consistent statistical record or even a free press to report duels as they occurred, quantitative analysis is impossible, and we are left with subjective estimates based on anecdote and diatribe. Even then the picture is not particularly consistent and appears to have been heavily dependent on one's location on the peninsula. In the Papal States there seems to have been a spate of duels shortly after the Restoration, but it faded quickly. According to Pesaro-Maurogonato, who was writing in 1839, the realm of *Il Papa Re* saw very few duels, and Rome virtually none, except for the odd encounter among foreigners.[26] This general paucity for the Papal States would continue, and a statistical report of crimes committed in the papal provinces of Civitavecchia, Frosinone, Roma, Velletri, and Viterbo between 1854 and 1863 reported only one duel for the entire period, and it included a foreigner.[27]

In contrast, Naples reportedly saw a number of duels, both before and after the law of 1838, and one military commentator in 1848 described the duel as "not a rare occurrence."[28] Piedmont probably led the pack, a

24. Jannone 1912, 64.
25. Gelli 1992, 55–64.
26. Pesaro-Maurogonato 1839, 123.
27. ASR, Miscellanea di Statistica, Busta 42, Fascicolo 1863, note attached to "Tavola IIIa, dei duelli in ordine a ciascuna provincia."
28. Bianco 1848, 22.

result of its continuous practice of the duel from the sixteenth century and its proximity to France. Pesaro-Maurogonato actually claimed in 1839 that the duel in the Kingdom of Sardegna was "very rare," but he then proceeded to describe how officers and students fought "over arguments arising from dances, dinners and rivalries of romance," how soldiers were drummed from the corps if they refused a challenge, and how the *borghesi* went to the border to fight without interference from the government.[29] This would indicate that dueling was hardly as "rare" in Piedmont as he previously suggested, and we see this confirmed in a letter of 1846 from Massimo d'Azeglio to Luisa Blondel in which he referred to an ongoing *vertenza* between Enrico Mayer and the novelist F. D. Guerrazzi: "I was sorry about the Mayer affair. On the other hand, one has to take the world as it is and you can't remake it, and if do not want to fight you should not put yourself in such circumstances."[30] Clearly, he was here referring to the duel as an event that was neither foreign nor uncommon.

Whatever the exact frequency of duels in the various regions, we can ascertain that the Restoration saw the reintroduction of the dueling ethic into Italian public life.[31] Although probably still more prominent among military men, many examples began to appear of duels that included members of both the nobility and the bourgeoisie. Moreover, critics and jurists generally spoke of the duel as a practice in the ascendancy rather than one fading away, and their own growing commentary only confirmed their analysis. On the other hand, actual duels were not a common event and paled in comparison to what came later, after unification, when people spoke frankly of a "duellomania" which prompted a duel a day. Thus Paolo Fambri, himself an avid duelist, would look back from the 1870s and claim, "Today's duel, especially here in Italy, is contemporary rather than modern, and so true is this that the first half of the present century saw not a tenth, but what tenth!, not a hundredth of today's duels."[32] This quantum increase after unity had various causes, but one of the most obvious and important was the bond forged between dueling and patriotism as Italy went through the process of becoming a nation.

29. Pesaro-Maurogonato 1839, 123.
30. D'Azeglio 1987, vol. 3, 202.
31. Carrillo (1837, 33) caught the ambiguity in 1837, when he referred to dueling as a custom but then added, "if in fact a few scarce encounters permit us to speak of custom."
32. ACS, Carte Fambri Busta 21, Fascicolo 18.

Dueling and the Risorgimento

Recalling the duel between Gabriele Pepe and Alphonse Lamartine, one can see how quickly and easily dueling could become a symbol of national struggle and regeneration. That connection would be gradually reinforced as personalities and politics mixed to create icons of Italian identity, some of whom would fight well-publicized duels. A number of early military heroes of the Risorgimento, including Pignatelli, Filangieri, and Gugliemo Pepe, had participated in affairs of honor under the French, and their stories became part of the lore of the movement. Gugliemo Pepe (no relation to Gabriele) also described in his memoirs a duel he fought in 1823 with General Carrascosa, who challenged him over their conflicted participation in the Revolution of 1820 in Naples. According to Pepe, his fellow exile Carrascosa wanted to demonstrate a new-found fealty to the restored absolutist regime by insulting and hopefully defeating a champion of the erstwhile constitutional government. Carrascosa tracked down Pepe in England and sent him an insulting letter reviling the Carbonari and any form of political conspiracy. They fought with sabers, and in short order Pepe severely wounded Carrascosa in the shoulder, effectively ending the duel. Pepe wrote, "In that moment I forgot the problems he had caused our country, and, remembering the days when we had fought together under Murat against the Austrians as well as his brave actions at the battle of Castel di Sangro, I embraced him. By nature and sentiment, I ignore personalities, and hold as enemies only despotism and those foreigners who oppose our independence."[33]

The critical aspect of this one-sided narrative is how well it fit into the political context surrounding the publication date of Pepe's memoirs: 1847, a time of turmoil, hope, and fervor, which focused in large part on the search for an Italian identity. Pepe, the constitutional patriot, acted with both bravery and chivalry in the face of a former comrade's supposed apostasy to the cause. Having proven their mutual courage, and with their differences canceled out by blood, they embraced in testament to past battles fought together against Italy's enemies: literally brothers in arms. Nor did the morality play end there. The duel, at least in Pepe's view, promoted a change of heart in Carrascosa, who dropped his alleged plans of submission to tyranny and pledged his sword to the cause of liberalism. For his part in the duel, Pepe received

33. Pepe 1847, vol. 2, 174–79.

and published a letter from La Fayette praising his "patriotic and generous combat" which he saw as "an explication of the past, as useful for the cause as honorable for you."[34]

Although there was probably no direct connection, one finds many of Pepe's main themes in two treatises on the duel which came out shortly after the establishment of constitutional government in Naples in 1848. Written by a lawyer, Emilio Pascale, and a soldier, Captain N. A. Bianco, these two judicial tracts differed substantially from prior commentary on the duel in Italy. Taking advantage of the new freedom of speech, they attacked the legislation created by Ferdinand II in 1838 as being harsh and inefficient. Given the severity of the penalties, very few duelists had been brought to justice, while "we know that there have been duels whenever there has been need of them."[35] More at issue, however, they both heartily defended the duel as a practice with practical advantages that should not be taken lightly. Like other commentators on the issue, they argued that the duel arose from the inability of the law to protect honor from insult. But their slant was far more positive than previous tracts, and they affirmed the right of the duel to exist, in part because many aspects of personal honor were beyond the reach of the courts. One could and should stiffen laws against calumny and injury, but other offenses would remain to be adjudicated by public opinion through the duel. Besides, the duel did no real damage to society because it was a free choice on the part of the participants, and this same mutual complicity also made it almost impossible to prosecute.

Even more important, however, they argued that the duel could be a positive force in society. It provided an ameliorative function in demanding good behavior from people; it taught and enforced manners; it was, in fact, "a great school of civilization."[36] The counterpart to this didactic force was the duel's demonstration of courage and good actions in the face of evil and abject forces. To punish an honest man who had defended his honor according to the code is, he claimed, not only unjust, but it also "heartens the mean-spirited, it feeds the cowardice of scoundrels, and it encourages those who would disturb the peace of families and the honor of citizens."[37] How could the law equate a man who defends his honor to the murderers, traitors, parricides, and other human trash who got dragged to the scaffold? Such a dichotomy

34. Ibid., 178–79.
35. Pascale 1848, 36.
36. Ibid., 34, Bianco 1848, 18.
37. Pascale 1848, 31.

between honorable and dishonorable crimes perhaps reflected an anxiety among men of substance and education, who in the turmoil of 1848 were looking to distinguish themselves through the mechanisms of chivalry from the vulgar and rambunctious masses as the political landscape offered greater opportunity as well as greater danger.

Be that as it may, neither Pascale nor Bianco went so far as to condone the duel outright, and each in his way offered some palliative condemnation to offset his obvious enthusiasm for the practice. In the same vein, each asked that the law against the duel be completely revised rather than abolished outright. But the fervor of their language belied their hesitations. Pascale spoke of the duel as a "baptism" designed to wipe away any mark of dishonor from an honorable man.[38] Bianco went even further, offering the duel as a mystical moment that dispelled cowardice and bound men together almost as brothers: "After the fight, with their ire laid aside, they embrace each other, and if blood is shed, they offer the gestures of the most heartfelt cordiality. It is a beautiful metamorphosis in truth, a magic effect, poetic in its excellence, which refines behavior."[39] So important was this transfiguration, simultaneously religious and autoerotic in nature, that Bianco saved his greatest disdain, and any real punishment, for men who fought a second duel with each other, having gone through the "beautiful metamorphosis" of honorable combat. They had betrayed the magic moment and thus deserved no leniency.

The attitude and language of Pepe, Pascale, and Bianco betrayed a growing tendency not merely to tolerate or accept the duel but to promote its precepts as a positive force in Italian society. This attitude resonated with a general manifestation of the concepts of chivalry and honor as a cornerstone of Italian nationalist thought in the first half of the century. The importance of such ideas has been deftly revealed by Alberto Banti in a work aimed at discerning the cultural and literary fonts of Italian identity and unity. Rejecting both economic and social causes of the unification movement as secondary, Banti maintains that early Italian nationalists were inspired primarily by the literature they read. Specifically, he points to a "canon" of novels, plays, and operas produced between 1803 and 1848 that created a powerful mythology of patriotic tropes built on "family-ties, sanctity, and honor." Naturally, with regard to the duel, honor was the most important of these, and

38. Ibid., 32.
39. Bianco 1848, 18–19.

Banti demonstrates how patriots could read the resurgence of Italy as an ongoing chivalric challenge designed to redeem the disgraced honor of the land and its people.[40] Dueling thus offered a symbolic means of reasserting Italy's military valor, but even more important was its tie to the chivalrous act, rife through the literature, of defending the purity of Italian women. This image was easily transferred into defending the honor of *Italia* as a woman, which, as Banti effectively demonstrates, was a common poetic and pictorial means of reifying the new nation. Given this cultural baggage, he sees the many duels portrayed in the patriotic canon as expanding the individual notion of honor to a nationalized sense of honor. Likewise, the nationalist canon was full of duels that took place in the medieval past and that recalled a world of grand and selfless gestures attractive to romantic tastes. Celebrating the dueling heroes of yesteryear, the canon helped reinforce an ideal chivalric stereotype, which could then be linked to the ideal of Italian regeneration.[41] In our search for why the duel increased in legitimacy and frequency during the Restoration (although such a search is not Banti's goal), this literature provides an important piece of the puzzle. If the code of chivalry promoted national sentiment, the poets of patriotism championed the dueling ethic across the peninsula.

Other aspects of the nationalist literature studied by Banti reinforce this point, although he perhaps underplays them because of his stress on chivalry being linked to women's honor. For instance, he comments on the importance of references to "blood" as a constant in the canon literature, both as a biological determinant of Italian identity, the purity of which had to be defended, and as a totemic parallel to the redeeming sacrifice of Christ.[42] Obviously the image of blood was a crucial aspect of the dueling ritual, not only in the need to have blood flow to end an affair but also in the common references to a "baptism" by blood (an image reinforced by the use of the term *padrino*, or "godfather," to indicate a duelist's second) and the frequent assertion that "blood washes honor clean."[43] And both of these maxims reinforced the connection between the duel and Christian sanctity, which is Banti's third prepolitical constant of the Italian psyche.

Finally, the patriotic literature virtually teems with images of the sword as an instrument of redemption. Thus in the *Battle di Legnano*,

---

40. Banti 2000, 93, 139.
41. Ibid., 67, 84–85, 105, 140–41, 147, 183, 185.
42. Ibid., 62, 73.
43. For example, Nievo 1973, vol. 2, 783.

which recounts the Lombard League's medieval triumph over the Germanic Empire, Cammarano has the chorus exhorting, "Long live Italy strong and united / With sword and with thought! / May this soil which was our cradle / Be the tomb of the foreigner."[44] And Manzoni in his poem *Marzo 1821* celebrates the conspirator patriots: "They swore: stronger for that oath / And found fraternal response in other regions, / Sharpening their swords in the shadows / Now they lift them to shine in the sun."[45] Alfieri was even more explicit in his image of the sword as a tool for reclaiming lost honor.

> He heard injurious and audacious words
> With which the wicked can wound the good;
> Nor law has he to help him counter.
> Now it is only the sword which
> Offers a healing potion
> Which calms the valorous and silences the rabble.[46]

These references reflected to a certain extent the search through the Risorgimento for the "sword of Italy," a mythical military leader foreshadowed first in Machiavelli's *The Prince* and then in Napoleon, who would redeem the Italian nation and who would eventually become identified by propagandists with both Victor Emmanuel II and Giuseppe Garibaldi. Hence, Marco Minghetti described Victor Emmanuel in 1848 as being a knight of the Middle Ages, who was determined "to not put down his sword as long as a single Austrian remains in Italy."[47] On the other end of the political spectrum, Giuseppe Mazzini reportedly kept in his possession a cavalry saber upon which were inscribed the words, "The fate of Italy is in the sword."[48] Likewise, Garibaldi, in a lifetime replete with portraits, was consistently portrayed with a saber in full view. Symbolically, the sword very clearly carried heavy meaning for Italian elites, well beyond any phallic interpretations one might wish to engage in, and it is not surprising that, as we shall see, the vast majority of duels in nineteenth-century Italy would be fought with the saber, a sword more of the soldier than of the gentleman.[49] In fact the saber

---

44. Banti 2000, 58.
45. Ibid., 57; also see the passage from Verdi's "All'armi" quoted on p. 136.
46. Quoted in Morelli 1904, 252.
47. Quoted in Banti 2000, 188.
48. Mazzini's sword is on display in the Vittoriano in Rome.
49. Even the most literal of interpreters can appreciate the phallic nature of the sword and

later became seen in its management as a uniquely Italian weapon, or, as one commentator claimed, "the true national glory."[50] It hardly seems a coincidence then that the future statesman Giovanni Visconti Venosta described in his memoirs how the patriotic young men of Lombardy would hold meetings in a fencing hall, where they could practice their swordsmanship and plan for the resurgence of Italy.[51]

This emphasis on the sword reinforces the point that early nationalism in Italy was often married to the *remilitarization* of its people and especially its youth.[52] We see this as early as 1815 with Murat's call for Italian unity at Rimini in which he exhorted Italy's young men to return to the martial virtues of ancient Rome and learn to fight anew against the country's oppressors.[53] The underlying assumption of such propaganda was that Italians had once known how to fight—indeed they had ruled the known world—but they had lost both their will and their prowess. That assumption fit into the evolution of a larger political discourse on the Italian character that was heavily inflected by issues of gender. Silvana Patriarca has stressed the importance of understanding that negative foreign stereotypes of the Italians (which we have already seen at the heart of many duels) were critical to the way in which Italy's patriots came to "imagine" their own country and their countrymen. Analyzing the primary tropes and metaphors of the Risorgimento's most important theorists, she reveals how they simultaneously internalized and utilized past portrayals of the Italians as indolent and feminine as they created and promoted a reactive political agenda of revirilization of the people. Significantly, their concern was primarily for the upper classes who were portrayed as lazy, impotent, undisciplined, and sexually lax: a result of a soft and unmasculine education. These idle dandies found their past embodiment in the image of eighteenth-century *cicisbeismo,* which was portrayed by Gioberti as "legal and privileged adultery," a system so dissipated and disorderly that in its acceptance, according to Sismonde de Sismondi, "Italians ceased to be men."[54]

Although Italian nationalists embraced the stereotypes as valid, they generally agreed on the fact that the "emasculation" of Italy's men had

---

its obvious reference to Italy's virility. Certainly there is no need to search for subtext when Marcucci (1836, 317) referred to Italian swords being drawn from their vaginas rather than their scabbards.

50. Morelli 1904, 91.
51. Visconti Venosta 1906, 184–85.
52. Banti 2000, 186–89.
53. Cited in Mack Smith 1968, 17–18.
54. Quoted in Patriarca 2005, 399, 401.

nothing to do with climate or biology but was instead perceived as the result of historical forces: specifically, oppression of foreign occupation, tyrannical absolutism, and—for some—the Counter-Reformation Church. Italians had become servile under despotism, and the unequal power relations of servility had engendered among Italian men a combination of cowardice, dissimulation, and cunning that was also common to women who suffered the parallel subjugation of men. The good news was, of course, that what history had wrought could be undone by political enterprise. What exactly that action should be depended on the ideological proclivities of the patriots, but as Patriarca shows, democrats and moderates alike advocated martial action, be it (respectively) guerrilla insurrection or conventional warfare, as a means of recasting the national character in a more masculine mold. They likewise had in common an overriding belief in sacrificial blood, be it in the streets of revolution or on the battlefields of war, as a necessary source of moral redemption. Moreover, informed and committed individuals could work toward that public redemption by practicing private virtue in their everyday lives, especially with regard to the proper behavior of one's family members. Women were expected to retreat to hearth and home, while primacy was placed on sexual conformity. If *cicisbeismo* had become the icon of Italian dissolution, then marital rectitude was the moral solution that could help reinvigorate the manliness of Italy's upper classes and eventually the country.[55]

Such analysis deepens our understanding of the duel's symbiotic relationship with the Risorgimento. Having in large part accepted the external critiques of Italy's elites, the patriotic enterprise from its inception sought ways to inject virile education into both the public and the private sphere. The duel, which offered the public defense of private honor, was a potent vehicle to help in that project. It offered a personal example of manly prowess and courage, complete with the attending symbolism of a baptism of blood, that could appeal to moderates and democrats alike. It advertised an internalization of martial values and a willingness to bear arms, hopefully with some talent, in the face of perceived insult. It was a perfect foil to the embarrassing and lasting image of *cicisbeismo*, for it showed Italian men active and ready to defend their rights over their women, just as they would defend their other rights as well. Finally, it belied the tradition that married Italian "servility" to feminine dissembling and cowardice by proving that Italian men not

---

55. Patriarca 2005, 403–7.

only spoke the truth but also were willing to risk their lives in support of their words. All told, the chivalric action of a few could be seen as inculcating a masculine sense of self into the entire nation, no matter how it might be defined by its prophets. And this multifaceted symbolism became all the more important when the mass efforts of revolution and war, which had been variously vaunted as regenerative tools in the 1840s, came a cropper in the failures of 1848 and 1849.

A Conspiracy of Duels in Lombardy

The practical results of those failures for the culture of chivalry appeared clearly in the 1850s, commonly called the "decade of preparation," as the duel became a self-conscious means of continuing the national struggle, particularly in Lombardy. As Visconti Venosta recalled in his memoirs: "The thought of duels kept our youthful fantasies burning. Dueling with Austrian officers seemed a patriotic duty; it was individual combat substituted for the war we were unable to fight; and it was certainly a means of keeping alive that continual tension of soul and that moral battle which were our force."[56] The inspiration for these patriotic duels may have come from a fatal incident in 1850 when Luigi della Porta, a young Milanese nobleman and a student of mathematics at Pavia, accidentally trod on the spur of an Austrian officer by the name of Petrus. The latter threatened della Porta with a whip for his clumsiness, and della Porta later accosted him in the theater, provoking a challenge to a duel. Although della Porta had fought in the campaigns of 1848 and 1849, he was, alas, no fencer, and he made the mistake of choosing sabers, a weapon the Austrian handled with great skill. Fighting in the Austrian barracks, Petrus quickly dealt della Porta a heavy blow to the chest from which he died a few hours later. The event shocked Milanese society, and many traveled to Pavia to hear Visconti Venosta's brother, Emilio, offer a stirring eulogy at della Porta's funeral.[57]

With the stage set by this unfortunate example, future and frequent duels between "citizens and officers" took on a more pointedly political purpose. According to Visconti Venosta, after the clashes of 1848–49 the Milanesi totally ostracized the Austrians in a more or less coordinated plan of silent but effective protest. Socially isolated in general, and

---

56. Visconti Venosta 1906, 337.
57. Ibid., 204–5; Barbiera 1919, 178.

specifically shunned by the high society with which they naturally identified, Austrian officers often resorted to hot words and hasty actions as tensions mounted. For their part, Milan's elite youth always acted correctly but ensured that no insult went unanswered and that each *vertenza* was pushed to its logical conclusion. Moreover, at the end of each duel, the Italians were polite to a fault, but they generally refused any form of comradely reconciliation that might be misconstrued as social or political acceptance. Exactly how many such duels actually occurred is unclear. Barbiera mentions at least six of them by name in his book on the patriotic circle of Countess Maffei, and Visconti Venosta certainly implied in his memoirs that it had not been a rare event.[58]

Leaving quantity for quality, the best example of such a "patriotic" encounter remains an account written by Manfredo Camperio of a duel he fought in 1856 with Baron Schönhals, a captain in the Austrian army. Camperio had been one of the most strident anti-Austrian agitators in Milan prior to and during the revolution of 1848, and it is hardly surprising to find him engaged in the "dueling campaign" of the 1850s. The opportunity presented itself when Schönhals accepted an invitation from his landlord, Baron Ciani, to a ball in honor of Camperio's return from a trip to the South Pacific, where he had traveled after the failure of the revolution. Baron Ciani, who was Camperio's uncle, had assumed that the Austrian would not attend in uniform, and when Schönhals showed up in full regalia with medals galore, he brought the party to a screeching halt. A number of the ladies declared that they would prefer to leave rather than support the presence of such a blatant reminder of their country's humiliation. Camperio saved the day by taking Schönhals aside and asking him to leave so as to allow the festivities to continue. When the Austrian understood the problem, he responded that he was only wearing the uniform of their Emperor. "Do you wish to dishonor it?" To which Camperio replied politely, "It's not actually a question of honor, but we all here do not admit that this is the uniform of our Emperor, but rather the uniform of the Austrian army of occupation, which we hope will not stay long in our country."[59] Although shocked at the man's audacity, Schönhals agreed to withdraw, but only after they had exchanged visiting cards in preparation for a duel.

58. Aside from the duel of della Porta, Barbiera includes those of Carcano, Fadini, Battaglia, Viola, Càroli, and Camperio; 179–80. Manfredo Camperio, in a letter written later to Visconti Venosta, adds to these Ropolo and Mancini, which would make at least eight. Visconti Venosta, 1906, 344.

59. Ibid., 344–35.

At this point the public/private nature of such a political action came to the fore. Camperio feared that his action might be reported to the authorities, and indeed Schönfals had proceeded with his wife to a second social engagement, a reception being held by Hungarian General Giulay, who would soon take over military control of the city from the aging General Radetsky. Apprised of the damage done to the prestige of the Austrian army's uniform, to say nothing of the Emperor, Giulay dispatched a squadron of hussars to surround Baron Ciani's house and prevent Camperio's escape, an act that no doubt finally ended the party. Meanwhile, Camperio had fled the area and, being warned that the police were looking for him, managed to escape the city disguised as a peasant. He then crossed over the border into Piedmont where he could stay with friends. However, the intercession of the police and the military had no bearing on the affair as a personal matter between the two men. Before leaving the party, Camperio had asked Carlo Prinetti (later a senator of the realm) and Emilio Dandolo to act as his seconds in the upcoming encounter with Schönhals. They kept in contact with their friend and soon arranged a duel just inside the Lombard territory, because the Austrian officers were not allowed to cross the border with Piedmont.[60] The two adversaries fought with sabers and agreed to end the combat after both had been slightly wounded in the head. Camperio later recalled that he agreed to shake Schönhal's hand afterwards because "I had nothing against him personally but only against his uniform."[61] Camperio subsequently returned to Piedmont, joined the army against the Austrians in 1859, and later served as a deputy in the Italian parliament: another Risorgimento hero who had served the cause on the field of honor.

This deliberate use of the duel as a weapon of propaganda and provocation was not restricted to Austrian officers. It was also employed against Italians who might fraternize with "the enemy." This became particularly important after the Emperor, in hopes of being able to win back the affections of the populace, sent his brother, Archduke Maximillian, to become governor of Lombardy/Venetia in 1857. Glib, intelligent, and well-meaning, the Archduke exerted his considerable charms on Milan's upper echelons, while offering a number of important reforms, including a political amnesty. There was consequently real fear that he might be able, in Visconti Venosta's words, "to open a breach in the rigid and

60. According to Gelli's account, General Giulay allowed the officers to fight and offered Camperio a temporary safe conduct to fight the duel. Gelli 1928, 188.
61. Visconti Venosta 1906, 344.

disciplined patriotism which had hitherto held fast." In order to forestall this threat, something "clamorous" was necessary, so one evening over cigars, Visconti Venosta and his well-heeled compatriots hit upon a strategy to force a duel on anyone willing to socialize at the court of the Archduke: "The idea was accepted with enthusiasm; this bravado seemed beautiful to us, and in fact it indicated the temperature of our heads and of the times in which we lived. That evening we separated with our heads hot with schemes and duels." This was no idle comment, and shortly after helping hatch this conspiracy of honor, Visconti Venosta found himself participating as a second to Alfonso Carcano (who was in on the plan) in a pistol duel aimed at Marchese Luigi d'Adda, who had become too friendly with the Archduke because of their mutual love of horses. D'Adda and Carcano faced off, fired on command, and relaxed as the bullets went astray. The pistols were reloaded, but the seconds agreed that given the political nature of the offense, it would be absurd to continue the duel. The affair soon became the talk of the town, but the police were unable to prosecute because the principals all agreed to deny any involvement.[62]

If publicity for patriotic solidarity was the goal, Visconti Venosta and his friends managed to achieve it by using a personal social compulsion that went beyond mere politics. This worked as well in the duels against Austrian officers, who had to fight because of the equal social status of their challengers.[63] The principle of parity, implicit in having one's challenge honored by an opponent, is critical in understanding the attraction of the duel as a tool of Italian regeneration. We see the same mechanism in the common appearance of dueling terms in the nationalist literature. Thus the revolutionary Settembrini would talk about how the people had challenged the king to a duel during the French revolution and how Palermo had offered a *"cartello di sfida"* to Naples in 1848.[64] Such language automatically raised the level of the challenger to that of the challenged, offering a sort of self-promotion backed up by knowledge of the rules of chivalry and the willingness to shed blood in their observance. The particular success of this strategy, which clearly underlay the "dueling conspiracy" of Lombardy, was totally confirmed by what would become one of the most intriguing patriotic events of the Risorgimento.

The stage would be set by Cavour's intrigues aimed at drawing

62. Ibid., 396–404.
63. Banti 2000, 184.
64. Settembrini 1934, vol. 1, 141, 172–73.

Austria into a war with Piedmont and France. As his plans unfolded in early 1859, tensions in Milan mounted to the breaking point. On January 29, La Scala offered a production of Bellini's *Norma,* an opera well-known for its bellicose libretto. In the first three rows behind the orchestra sat the Austrian officers of the city, while their commander, General Giulay, and his entourage surveyed the scene from one of the boxes. The air, according to Barbiera's reconstruction, was "heavy with storm."

> On the stage, druids, bards, and warriors intoned the impetuous chorus of war: "War! War!" And then the Italians in the audience jumped to their feet yelling: "War! War!" and clapped their hands. "War! War!" they yelled from the loggia and from the pit. Standing erect in their boxes, the women emotionally waved their white handkerchiefs. The Austrian officers for a moment were dumbfounded: but all of a sudden they too jumped to their feet, clapped their hands, and began chanting "War! War!" General Giulay, also standing, revealed his saber a handsbreadth in its scabbard, and then furiously beat it on the floor. And the other officers, all impassioned, beat their sabers on the floor with an air of challenge (*sfida*). "Blood! Blood!" called the chorus from the stage. "Blood! Blood!" responded the crowd still clapping their hands.[65]

What better evidence that the duel had become the signifier of liberation, with the ritual challenge of a partly drawn saber and then the collective sounding of swords upon the floor clearly serving notice that Italian honor had been validated and that the Austrians were ready to redeem en masse the insults and isolation of the last decade? What better spectacle of the tie between chivalry and nationalism? And what better proof of the assertion made years later by the antidueling author Luigi Dossena that the duel drew much of its postunitary popularity from the martial courage that had been released during the drive for independence and its confusion with ideas of personal honor?[66]

We have to look more closely, however, to understand the full psychological and didactic impact of these many patriotic duels. Not only were the young champions proudly manifesting their national status, but they were equally demonstrating their bravery, their *sangfroid,* and their skill with arms in front of foreigners. In short, they were directly

---

65. Barbiera 1919, 195–96.
66. Dossena 1861, 5–6.

combating the unfortunate image of the artistic, poltroonish Italian who, if he should even bother, would protect his honor through hired assassins and a dagger in the dark. By the same token, each of these events became an advertisement for the duel as an appropriate means of settling personal disputes while simultaneously legitimizing it as an intrinsic step in the creation of Italy as a free nation. Yet by Visconti Venosta's own admission, the details of the code of honor were all a bit new to him and his friends. Like Pepe in 1826, they wanted to be particularly assiduous in their observance of the rules of chivalry because it assured their equality as gentlemen with the Austrian officers and protected them from any possible "abuses" on the field of honor. They had to show their command of the ritual as part of their moral authority. But in order to learn those rules, they had to turn to sources outside of Italy: "Thus among us youths who were preparing to act as swashbucklers (*spadaccini*) there circulated a French dueling code, which was said to be very authoritative, and with which we resolved all of the cases with a precision and security that seemed indisputable."[67] While it is important to note that the Italians had to revert to a French manual, further proof that the duel had returned to Italy via Napoleon, the larger point is that these almost pro forma duels between patriots and officers served as a training ground, complete with a foreign textbook, for the proliferation of the dueling ethic among Italy's future elites. Indeed, the names in these accounts are something of a Who's Who of the Lombard elites who soon came to share power in the young country of Italy, and their experiences in the 1850s would inform attitudes toward honor and the duel after the Austrians were long gone.

The Duel in Piedmont

While the Lombards were hacking away at Austrian officers, the Piedmontese were developing a different, albeit equally important, political impetus to the dueling ethic. Here the catalyst was the survival of the *Statuto,* or constitution, following the upheavals of 1848 and 1849. Under the guidance of Victor Emanuale II, the Kingdom of Sardegna had managed to maintain both a functioning parliament and a relatively free press: a unique achievement that contrasted well with the absolutist

---

67. Visconti Venosta 1906, 336–37. Most likely, the code was Chatauvillard's *Essai sur le duel* (1836), which was later published in Italian.

regimes reemerging in the other Italian states. The resulting freedom of discourse, however, often breached the boundaries of honorable etiquette, and already in 1850 Nassau Senior reported that a number of political duels had occurred.[68] This was reflected in the press as well, and an antidueling article in the daily *L'Italia,* also in 1850, complained that journalists from at least four major newspapers across the political spectrum had resorted to the field of honor to settle their differences.[69] Unquestionably, the most important of these various disputes occurred in April of that year between Count Camillo Cavour, future prime minister of united Italy, and Enrico Avigdor, scion of a wealthy Jewish banking family from Nice. Serving as deputies in the subalpine parliament, the two had come to loggerheads over free trade issues, and Cavour's newspaper, *Il Risorgimento,* had run a highly critical account of Avigdor's position. Avigdor responded in kind in his paper, the *Voix de l'Italie,* with the intention of provoking Cavour to a duel. Cavour rose to the bait, later recalling to Émile de la Rüe, "I am no swashbuckler, but there are provocations, which, even when they come from far below, cannot remain unpunished."[70] One assumes that Cavour's comment that the insult had come from "très bas" referred to Avigdor's non-noble status or, more likely, his Jewish heritage. Either way, the fact that Cavour proceeded with the encounter, despite the disparity in their positions, epitomized and advertised the role of the duel as a mechanism of social equality within the new political matrix of parliamentary liberalism. Whether it was the fact that Avigdor was a deputy or that he owned a newspaper, he had reached the critical point of being able to call out a nobleman with long roots in Piedmont's aristocracy. His success in doing so bespoke the brave new world of chivalry and palaver that attended the expansion of political power and influence in the post-1848 period.

Conscious or not of this significance, Cavour played his part in the drama and offered the appropriate challenge. The two fought a bloodless pistol duel at 20 paces and declared their reciprocal honor satisfied. According to Cavour's second, Michelangelo Castelli, the future prime minister had taken the matter very seriously and even declared to Avigdor afterwards that he had made no attempt to miss him.[71] Nonetheless, the two published a mutually agreed-upon account of the affair in

68. Senior 1871, vol. 1, 301.
69. The letter is reproduced in Lorenzini 1852, 351.
70. Cavour 1982, vol. 7, 65–69.
71. Castelli 1888, 131–32.

their respective newspapers, explaining that Avigdor's previous words had been aimed at Cavour's ideas as a politician and not his personal qualities as a man. Such a blatant and public declaration of an illegal act could hardly be overlooked by the authorities, and the attorney general of Turin requested that the parliament rescind the duelists' immunity and allow him to proceed with a criminal prosecution. In a decision that would have a lasting effect well beyond the life of the subalpine parliament, the deputies appointed a commission to study the question and then accepted without discussion its decision not to proceed against the duelists.[72] Given Cavour's growing stature in Piedmontese politics and considering his upcoming role in the unification process, this carte blanche on the part of the parliament set a legal precedent that virtually wedded the dueling ethic to liberal politics through the upcoming decades.

It is worth wondering if the alacrity with which parliamentarians in Piedmont picked up the dueling habit had anything to do with the area's proximity to and affinity for French culture. Italians were well aware that the French favored the duel as a means of settling political disputes, and in 1839 Pesaro Maurogonato ranked France as the top dueling country in Europe—a result, he suggested, of the July Revolution.[73] With easy access to France and a general ability to speak French, Piedmontese political elites may well have found a ready-made model, including the need to duel, for what it meant to be an honorable public figure in a liberal parliamentary world.[74] One might parenthetically note in this regard that Avigdor had recently spent a good deal of time in Paris, and his home base of Nice was an obvious conduit of French customs across the border. Combined with Piedmont's long tradition of military dueling, which remained more or less unbroken, such a model would have been a compelling and ready reference for action as Piedmont evolved into a viable parliamentary monarchy.

Be that as it may, the dueling ethic found a comfortable corner in Piedmont in the 1850s, and the aforementioned legislative largesse that was afforded Cavour and Avigdor soon found its counterpart in the regular courts. A landmark judicial decision came in October 1853, effectively clearing the legal path for the development of the duel on a grander scale. The case in question came from a frivolous but lethal duel that occurred in July of that year in Nice between a young officer,

---

72. DRN, vol. 2, 132.
73. Pesaro-Maurogonato 1839, 107.
74. On France see Nye 1993, 134–47.

Lieutenant Luigi Bottoni, and his long-time acquaintance, Gioacchino Airaudi, a lawyer. The two had bumped into each other downtown on a summer evening, and Airaudi had inquired if Bottoni knew whether people still gambled in a Bistro which was close at hand. Bottoni, who was reputed to have a weakness for games of chance, took the question as a suggestion that he was an inveterate denizen of such establishments. His injudicious response initiated a spiral of fractious words that ended with a challenge and its acceptance. Given the levity of the cause, the seconds worked overtime to find a mutually acceptable exit from the *vertenza,* but as word spread, popular sentiment worked against them. Although it was eventually agreed that they would fight with pistols at the relatively safe distance of 30 paces, Bottoni's bullet still found Airaudi's chest and killed him.

The deadly outcome of such a minor misunderstanding created something of a stir and prompted the government to try to set an example for the future. Bottoni was given a very heavy sentence of 30 years in the galleys, but it was cut to 15 years by the appeals court. This sentence still seemed excessive to the army, which had been forced against its will to drum Bottoni out of the corps, and a vociferous public campaign soon induced the king to grant him a pardon.[75] Even more at issue was the fate of the seconds. Although the courts had declared them not guilty and planned to set them free, the public prosecutor demanded that the case be revisited on the grounds that, as seconds, they had been complicit in Airaudi's homicide. He therefore ignored the court's decision and blocked their release from jail. This conflict between two branches of the judiciary created substantial controversy and brought to the fore the critical question of the culpability of seconds in the criminal code. The 1839 Albertine Code did not specifically mention seconds or *padrini* in its articles, but it condemned anyone "who participated in anyway in the proposal or acceptance of a challenge, or who expressed disparagement of anyone who has attempted to avoid such proposal or acceptance" to 10 years' relegation. Now the justice department wanted to equate any participation in a duel, whether as a second or even as an attending physician, with such complicity and open the way for their prosecution. This was no secondary squabble, because it would have struck at the very essence of the duel, which demanded the intercession of supposedly neutral third parties in the honorable settlement of disputes. Moreover, the willingness of the government to overturn the

75. Gelli 1928, 235–36.

decisions of its own court indicated a new resolve in the desire to bring the duel under control.

The case was argued for the five defendants (four *padrini* and the physician) by P.S. Mancini, one of the bright lights of Neapolitan jurisprudence who had fled to Piedmont after the Revolution of 1848. Mancini had already made his mark in two earlier dueling cases in Piedmont and was generally regarded as an expert in the field. He would go on to become the foremost jurist of united Italy and would serve in a variety of cabinet offices across many administrations, which made his defense of duelists during the Risorgimento particularly relevant with regard to the spread of the practice after unity. That defense would also become especially poignant because, in 1875, his own son would become involved in one of Italy's most notorious fatal duels in which he killed his best friend for having an affair with his wife. That was all far in the future in 1853, but Mancini was well aware that the Bottoni-Airaudi case was going to set precedent for years to come, which is why he agreed to have his arguments immediately published for general consumption. Mancini's defense consisted of two parts. First, the men involved had done all they could to bring about a peaceful settlement to the *vertenza*, and, failing that, they had acted to reduce the amount of bloodshed that might result. They had encouraged Airaudi to adopt swords over pistols. When he balked at that, they had pushed the distance of fire to 30 paces, and they had even chosen the tallest member of the group to measure out the longest distance. True, in the final analysis, these measures had failed, but the accused could hardly be described as promoting a bloodthirsty end to the affair.

These details no doubt carried considerable weight, but his second and more interesting line of argument focused directly on the *sui generis* nature of the duel itself and the special relationship of seconds to that definition. The duel, according to Mancini, occupied a privileged place between the law and personal conscience. It repaired slights that were beyond the regular tribunals and brought "under the aegis of its protection all that is most delicate, and I would say most modest in honor; [...]."[76] Because of this moral function, the duel represented a dangerous and indomitable adversary that had to be treated with respect and care. Its power within society determined that it could not be easily eradicated, and in the meantime it was important to control it as much as possible. This was the role reserved for the *padrini*. They attempted to reconcile

---

76. Mancini 1853, 29.

the parties, they enforced the rules, and "they conserve for the duel its real character and prohibit it from being converted into murder; their presence is a guarantee of loyalty and a safeguard for the social order, which it protects from further disruptions." Consequently, to punish the seconds was to risk losing this moderating influence and thus encourage both the number and the severity of the duels. For this reason, in contrast to the other law codes of the peninsula, the Sardinia Code of 1839 had refused to specifically punish the *padrini*. And in this sagacious clemency it had served as an example for other codes in Europe, including those of Spain, Saxony, Baden, and the Netherlands.[77]

But there was more to Mancini's argument than an enlightened defense of the social fabric. It had a political side as well, for the duel was the arbiter and defender of honor, and the nation needed honor:

> ... the sentiment of honor is the same vital principle of human conventions, it is that which inspires the noblest actions, it is one of the living forces that regulates the social order, and thus it promotes civilization, it improves moral life, and it consolidates political liberty.
>
> If therefore it is important to stop the distortion of this sentiment, it is no less important to maintain its dominance in people's hearts, and its legitimate and salutary influence on our customs.
>
> Thus for a long time a need [for honor] grew in this country, where courage is the glorious tradition of a splendid military history, where it can become the first of the virtues and the first of necessities for the future needs of the common fatherland and for the destinies of those who belong to it.[78]

Obviously, if Piedmont were going to lead the regeneration of Italy, it had to inspire its people to sacrifice and action and not allow itself to be pulled down into the crass materialism of the age. Great deeds lay ahead, and now was not the time to "extinguish the delicate susceptibilities of honor, to dry up the spring from which pour forth courage and contempt of life." Such was the attitude of Mancini—future minister of education and of justice for united Italy—and his oratory did not fall on deaf ears. The appeals court voted unanimously to release the prisoners and uphold the principle that acting as seconds in a duel constituted legitimate, and perhaps even noble, behavior.

77. Ibid., 31, 38–39.
78. Ibid., 58.

This positive attitude toward the duel within the civilian courts reinforced an important pronouncement made by military leaders just the year before. It had long been assumed that officers who refused to duel were not worthy of their rank and should quit the service, but this actually became official policy May 25, 1852, albeit in an indirect way. According to articles 2–7 of the internal regulations of the *Stato Maggiore,* any officer who failed to defend his honor was subject to expulsion from the officer corps.[79] It is important to note here that no specific mention of the duel was contained in the regulations, but it was assumed at the time, and by subsequent generations of officers, that such a failure was in reference to the dictates of the dueling compulsion. Nor were the articles an idle threat, as was immediately demonstrated by the case of Francesco Faà di Bruno, scion of a noble family from Alessandria who had followed his father's and brother's footsteps into the Piedmontese military. In 1853, Faà found himself suffering an insult from another officer, and because of his deep religious convictions he refused to issue a challenge in response or allow any of his friends to take his place. Facing recrimination and expulsion for his lack of action, Faà opted to follow his conscience and quit the service, but not without publishing a forceful tract entitled *Manuale del soldato cristiano,* which unequivocally condemned the duel as a false and sinful test of either honor or courage.[80] Why exactly the Piedmontese chose 1852 to lend de jure support to a de facto practice is unclear, but it is worth pondering whether it was not in reaction to the double defeat at the hands of Austria in 1848 and 1849.[81] Rebuffed in their attempts to redeem Italian honor and independence, it was perhaps thought necessary to at least protect the Piedmontese uniform from any hint of cowardice or weakness.[82]

As if placing the final seal of approval on the chivalric ethic, Piedmont's new criminal code of 1859, which would soon become the law of the land for most of the new Kingdom of Italy, greatly reduced the penalties applied to dueling. What more positive message to men of honor than to reduce the minimum sentence for homicide in a duel from 15 years of hard labor to only one, and even this could be converted to a rather comfortable internal exile somewhere in the

---

79. A copy of the text is in *Rivista penale,* Sept.–Oct. 1884, vol. 20, 242.
80. Faà di Bruno 1854, 5–10; Messori 1998, 89–90; cf. Brachet Contol 1977, 41–43.
81. Another possibility might be the attitude of the new King Victor Emmanuel II of Savoy, who once described the *bonheur* he obtained from securing the release of an officer from prison for having participated in a duel. La Marmora 1881, vol. 1, 192.
82. On the need to redeem the prestige of the Piedmontese army after the defeats of Custoza and Novara see Whittam 1977, 45–48.

realm.[83] All in all then, both the political and the legislative stages were set for the triumph of the dueling compulsion as Piedmont came to share, or rather impose, its laws and assumptions on the rest of the country. Following the failures of 1848 and 1849, Italian exiles had come from all over to partake of the freedoms afforded by the Savoyard monarchy and to work toward unity and independence. At the same time, however, these future leaders of the new Italy would be imbibing the elixir of Piedmont's chivalric traditions, and its heady effects would become readily apparent as they returned to their homes in triumph.

A Transitional Figure: Paolo Fambri

As an antidote to this perhaps overly Piedmontese interpretation, it seems fitting to end this chapter by focusing on Paolo Fambri, a Venetian who came to symbolize the power of the dueling mystique in united Italy. A huge man, he was famous for having broken into a Venetian prison during the Revolution of 1848 and carried the republican leader, Nicolo Tommaseo, on his shoulders into Piazza San Marco, where he presented him with a bar personally ripped from his cell door. It was a dramatic gesture, worthy of remembering, and one which stamped Fambri as daring, patriotic, and bellicose. There is no scholarly biography of Fambri, so one has to be careful in accepting the mythology that grew up around his exploits.[84] Yet it was just the mythic quality of Fambri's life that made him so popular and helped confer a mantle of authority on his shoulders with regard to the duel in Italy. Son of a pottery merchant, he was born in 1827 and began fencing at the age of ten at a military reform school after being expelled from a series of regular schools for unruliness. He claimed in his autobiography that he had fought two duels before he was fourteen (one when he was eleven!), a result perhaps of his precocious size and famous temper.[85] His relationship with the Austrian military ended before it began when he became embroiled in Risorgimento politics in the 1840s. He fought valiantly during the lengthy defense of the Venetian republic in 1849, eventually becoming an officer in the artillery. With the failure of the revolution, he became an engineering student at Padua but was twice expelled for his political

83. Title 10, Heading 1, Section 7, Article, 589. Regno di Sardegna 1859, 177–79.
84. There is a short piece in DRN, vol. 3, 33–34.
85. The autobiography was dictated to his second wife, Rita Levi, in the early 1890s and is with his papers at ACS, Carte Fambri, Busta 28, Fasciolo 27, SottoFascicolo 1.

rabble-rousing. He was eventually forced to emigrate in 1858 to Piedmont in order to avoid arrest. In short, Fambri had all his cards in order as a man who had served the cause of Italian nationalism and suffered for his efforts.

Fambri made his fame as a duelist just as Italy was being forged as a country. He joined the Piedmontese military and rose to become an officer in the infantry during the campaign of 1859 against Austria. Demobilized after the treaty of Villafranca, he started a newspaper in Bologna, where his outlandish behavior (including one duel and an almost-fatal fencing accident) prompted Pinelli, temporary minister of war for the Romagne, to specifically request Fambri's recall to his old regiment in Ferrara. Made a captain in the engineering corps, he moved first to Alessandria and then Torino, and in each city he claimed to have fought a duel, one with serious consequences for his opponent. This seems to have had little effect on his career, and in 1861 he was appointed under General Pozzi to an important defense commission, for which he wrote the first of what would be a lifelong string of reports and articles on Italy's military preparedness.[86] However, his temper and pride finally caught up with him. In a rather amazing admission in his unpublished autobiography, he described how while on an official tour of the South he had set Palermo on its ear by striking down, one assumes with his saber, a "*capo maffioso* [sic]" who had insulted a fellow officer while they were walking down via Toledo. He then refused to put himself under barracks confinement, as ordered by his commander, arguing that he had to maintain the dignity of the corps, "wandering through Palermo challenging the vendettas of the mafia."[87] Backed by other officers, Fambri was allowed to parade through the city in a show of defiance toward local reaction to the event.[88] He was then kicked out of the city by General Calderini, and, having returned to Torino with his compatriots, he was given two months' confinement in the Fenestrelle fortress. According to Fambri, however, the minister of war not only suspended his sentence but offered him words of commendation in the process.[89]

86. Fambri rose from Sottotenente in July of 1859 to Captain in January, 1861! AST, Ministero della Guerra, Ruoli Matricolari, 1 Reggimento Zappatori del Genio, matricola ufficiali, n143.

87. The account is on page 13 of his autobiography in the ACS.

88. In a different account he reportedly threw two "mafiosi" off the city's ramparts when they sought to do him in. Vassallo 1918, 49.

89. No record of this incident appears in the military tribunal's records of the AST or Fambri's matriculation records, so it may have been handled as a simple order and not formal

Nevertheless, Fambri chafed under the strictures of military life, and in 1864, after some of his articles on Italy's defense were criticized by his superiors, he quit the army to dedicate himself to journalism. Moving to Naples, he took over a newspaper, *La Patria,* and again found himself embroiled in furious debate with his political opponents. This led him into an "extreme" (*ad oltranza*) duel with Giorgio Asproni, a deputy of the left, who had referred to him as a paid assassin (*sicario*) in *L'Italia del popolo.* The duel began with pistols and was to continue with swords if no one was injured. In fact, the pistol exchange had no effect, but before switching to swords, Asproni's seconds interceded to say that Asproni had read a testimonial by Tommaseo, whom Fambri had rescued in 1848, and this had convinced him that his opponent was truly an honorable man. Fambri's seconds accepted the explanation and declared the duel over. Peace was made, and, according to Fambri's autobiography, they all became from that moment "the most sincere and cordial friends . . . even in the middle of the most provocative political arguments."

Fambri's prestige only increased with time as his legislative and literary production kept him constantly in the public eye. He wrote successful comedies for the stage, served as a deputy in parliament for four terms, and served on the boards of various cultural societies in the Veneto. He published frequently on hydraulic engineering and kept up a steady stream of articles and books on military issues, including conscription, naval defense, and training techniques. In all of this, Fambri provided a perfect portrait of the transition of the dueling ethic from the revolutionary gestures of the Risorgimento to the more stable parliamentary liberalism of united Italy. Hero, soldier, politico, mathematician, philosopher, and journalist, he combined all the romantic aspects of the age with a certain hardheaded approach to issues of economics, engineering, and national defense. He wrote adventure stories while defending the army's budget and remained a constant and flamboyant participant in public life from one end of the new country to the other.

And he fought duels—36 of them by 1868, according to one author who claimed to know him well.[90] With such credentials he symbolized the new Italian gentleman: daring, caring, and literate. Fambri consolidated this position in 1869 with the publication of a lengthy tome, *La*

---

disciplinary action.
90. Gabelli 1869, 5.

giurisprudenza del duello, in which he offered an impassioned apology for the duel as a civilizing mechanism for a country in need of civility. As we shall see, it would become the foundation document of those who defended the duel in the great national debate that evolved over the next four decades. Combined with other articles in favor of the practice, Fambri became one of the major arbiters of honor in Italy, whose office, according to one admirer, became a sort of Mecca where pilgrims sought chivalric advice.[91] Yet Fambri also represented the exclusivity of the duel as it emerged in the newly united country. The literary nature of his fame underlined the literate nature of the code of chivalry. It was a code, not just as a set of rules but also as a cipher that the uninitiated could not comprehend, and in a country that suffered 70% illiteracy, those who might aspire to Fambri's notions of honor were already small in number. The fact that he had apparently cut down a Sicilian citizen in the streets of Palermo with little reason and even less remorse seems to have had no impact on his career. In retrospect it speaks volumes about both the new regime and the "gentlemen" who created it, to say nothing of the genesis of the "Southern Question." Chivalry and honor were for the new elites, the men who would run the country according to liberal rules and modern precepts. The rest of the country, devoid of honor and the immunity to defend it, would have to be brought along as best as possible.

91. Mariotii 1897.

II

Honor and the Nation

THE PASSIONS and images of the nationalist struggle helped revive the duel as a guarantor of honor among many Italian elites. That stimulus would become even more pronounced as the nation of Italy actually emerged between 1859 and 1870, a period marked by war, revolution, and constant controversy over both the form and the content of the new country. In this crucible of conflict, republicans and monarchists, moderates and radicals, regular and irregular soldiers, all worked as much against each other as they did together in trying to determine the course of unification. The resulting friction of men operating at cross-purposes toward an often-shifting goal made clashes of honor as inevitable as they were numerous. Italy would consequently be born in a baptism of honorable blood as its citizenry sorted themselves out in the new and protean political arrangements taking shape under the aegis of *La Patria*. Witness the following portrait, offered in 1864 by Emilio de Dominicis, a bureaucrat in Piedmont's ministry of war:

> It is astonishing how in the midst of the nineteenth century, and in times of liberty and increasing civility, the mania for dueling, which replaces reason with brute force, instead of slackening has degenerated into a rage. In fact, if ever there was an epoch in which the frequency of these acts became legendary it is precisely the present. There is not a newspaper nor a periodical in whose reading you do not encounter

a similar fact unattended by boasting and outcry. And what is truly saddening is that those, who because of their refinement in knowledge or doctrine, or because of their eminent social position, should be the first in the great work of eradicating the prejudice, instead compete to reinforce and guarantee it through their example.[1]

De Dominicis's amazement at the explosion of dueling among Italy's best and brightest would be echoed five years later by Captain Giuseppe Scaglione, a prosecuting attorney in the Italian army, who in 1869 defined dueling as a "cancerous, incurable plague on society."[2] Paolo Fambri, whose fame as a duelist we have already examined, affirmed that some 3,000 duels had occurred in the first seven years of the country's existence.[3] Other commentators estimated that in the 1860s, Italy saw at least one duel a day, which would actually amount to a surprisingly accurate confirmation of Fambri's assertion.[4] More important in the long run, however, was that this "plague" did not abate after Italy's first tumultuous decade. On the contrary, as the Risorgimento ended and the country settled down to the more mundane matters of economics, education, and justice, the duel remained an everyday part of Italian life. Indeed, it would consistently prove one of the most contentious and difficult issues facing legislators, politicians, and moralists as they attempted to build a society based on the rule of law and equality before that law.

The present chapter seeks to understand the unprecedented increase in dueling after 1860 and to explain its continuity as a dominant theme of Italian society throughout the liberal period. It concentrates on those aspects of the chivalric revival that were tied into the evolution and assertion of Italy as a new nation on the European scene. This evolution entailed the final forging of the boundaries and institutions of the Italian state between 1860 and 1870, a difficult period rife with contradictions and conflicts that found in the code *duello* a manly means of seeking common ground and at least temporary reconciliation. Critical in this creative process was the role of the new Italian military, built primarily on Piedmontese traditions, which would offer practical examples of the dueling ethic in every corner of the country. Italy's officers would remain a constant source of chivalric combat as

1. De Dominicis 1864, 5.
2. Scaglione 1869, 5.
3. Fambri 1869, 13.
4. For example, Dossena 1861, 5–6.

legislators, commanders, and even judges assumed that an effective army was an honorable army, careful to suffer no slight that might weaken its own projection of prowess. Equally important was official and unofficial support of Italy's fencing establishment which evolved through the latter decades of the nineteenth century to become a source of national pride and prestige. Clubs, academies, and *salles d'armes* offered techniques and tournaments for the consumption of the new elite, all the while instilling gentlemanly precepts that insisted on strict adherence to the rules of the dueling code. Finally, those precepts became increasingly tied to Italy's need to find some psychological compensation for the failure of the liberal regime to make good on the primacy promised by Risorgimento propagandists, who had so facilely asserted that great power status would automatically follow unity. Whatever the performance of the country as a whole and however little there was to celebrate in traditional terms of glory, no one could doubt the courage and virility of men who individually were willing to face death on a daily basis in the name of honor.

A Difficult Decade of Honor and Unity

Italian unification was not a pretty process. The efforts of Cavour and the National Society in the 1850s had managed to focus patriotic energies on the twin goals of unity and independence under Piedmontese leadership, while postponing other major issues such as a new constitution, regional autonomy, and popular suffrage for later consideration. Despite this orchestrated effort, however, the pieces of the Italian puzzle did not fall together nicely as they would in Germany, where Bismarck overwhelmed both internal and external opposition with the successes of the Prussian army. Instead, in 1859 Cavour and the Piedmontese military were forced to rely on France to help take Lombardy, and then watched in frustration as the Veneto remained in the grip of Austria after Napoleon III abandoned their alliance. Meanwhile, they had to wait while bloodless revolutions in Parma, Modena, Tuscany, and the Romagna could be slowly and diplomatically transformed into outright annexations to the expanding Kingdom of Sardegna. Worst of all, they had to play catch-up after Garibaldi's Redshirts, most of whom had republican or Mazzinian sympathies, startled the world by conquering first Sicily and then the rest of the Kingdom of Naples. Although Garibaldi managed to avoid civil war by offering this prize to Victor

Emanuel II, both the Veneto and Rome remained outside the fold of united Italy, which was formally created in April of 1861, and efforts to include them kept old divisions over goals and tactics simmering through the decade. Twice, in 1862 and 1867, Garibaldi would raise an irregular army designed to march on Rome, and twice he would run into resistance from the regular army acting on orders from the Italian government.

All the while, republicans and democrats would have to come to terms with a liberal monarchy that they had helped to expand and strengthen, while their hero Mazzini remained under the shadow of a death sentence issued by a united Italy he had inspired but refused to acknowledge. This was the stuff of controversy, and the personal and political animosities that it generated guaranteed that the men who built the new country would have plenty to fight about. It was also the stuff of glory. Acts of courage and audacity abounded; risks were taken and rewarded; heroes arose and cowards retreated as martial prowess was tested in a variety of venues. It was all larger than life and seemed to vindicate the Romantic portrait so eloquently painted by the patriotic literati of the preunitary world. Italy had found its sword in the hands of the *Re Galantuomo*, Vittorio Emmanuele II, and the hero of two continents, Garibaldi, and both were portrayed as acting courageously and chivalrously in the face of adversity.[5] Combining the very real political tensions of the moment with the martial aura of their achievements, Italy's leaders would embrace the duel as a natural and laudable ritual of affirmation and healing.

Nowhere was this clearer than in relations between military men. The conflicts of unification brought an unprecedented number of Italians into uniform, but not always in a disciplined or organized way. Old armies, and especially that of the Kingdom of Naples, had to be absorbed into the Piedmontese military machine while a newly victorious army of revolutionary warriors had to be dealt with. Volunteers, patriotic deserters, civic militias, and regular troops swarmed over the landscape and naturally created confusion in terms of chain of command, precedence of honor, and equivalence of grades. Sometimes, in the early stages of the process, it was just hard to tell who was who, and bruised honor and crossed swords sometimes resulted. We find such a case nicely described in a broadside that appeared on the walls

5. Banti 1996, 223.

of Turin in September of 1861.⁶ The author was Carmello Agnetta, a Neapolitan revolutionary who had been living in exile in Paris until May 1860 when he was called on by the National Society to aid the cause. Arriving in Turin he was granted the rank of captain and asked to escort a large shipment of munitions to Sicily to bolster Garibaldi's efforts. Eventually arriving in Palermo and waiting for the general to review his men, he was ordered by Nino Bixio, Garibaldi's second in command, to lead a burial detail. Agnetta replied that he was sorry, but he did not know from whom he was taking orders. In response, Bixio slapped him across the face. Agnetta pulled out his sword to retaliate but was restrained by onlookers while Bixio disappeared. Informed of the insult by Agnetta, Garibaldi agreed to help him seek out the unknown perpetrator. One can imagine the general's surprise when they suddenly ran into Bixio, who pulled out his revolver as Agnetta sought to throw his visiting card in his face. Garibaldi immediately ordered Bixio to put himself under barracks arrest, and he later informed Agnetta, who had demanded a duel, that he would have to postpone his desire for satisfaction until after the campaign—a judgment confirmed by a hastily convened tribunal of honor of high ranking officers.

Having achieved the rank of major during the ensuing conflict, Agnetta eventually returned to Turin after the Neapolitan surrender and immediately sent his seconds to challenge his adversary who was in Genova. Bixio tried to avoid the issue by accusing Agnetta of having lived off the earnings of a prostitute in Alessandria, an action that would have disqualified him as a gentleman. It was this charge that prompted Agnetta to go public with his broadside, and he denounced Bixio's accusations as those of a coward who had lost his will to fight after becoming a hero. He added that Bixio was a liar and *calumniatore,* thus rounding out the traditional circle of insults leading to combat. Bixio could hardly ignore this public snub—in which Agnetta offered witnesses against the countercharges of unbecoming conduct—and eventually agreed to fight, despite the fact that his wife was in the last stages of pregnancy. They met November 17, 1861, in a saber duel that left Bixio's right hand permanently crippled. Despite the heat of the affair, they were reconciled by the encounter, and, shortly afterwards, Bixio used his influence to help Agnetta, who joined Italy's prefectoral corps and eventually became subprefect of Massa Carrara.⁷

    6. IRA, Busta 722 6/1; "Una riparazione d'onore."
    7. See Agnetta to Bixio, Dec. 16, 1861, and Bixio to Remorino, Oct. 14, 1861, in Bixio 1942, vol. 2, 42. Cf. Staglieno 1973, 197–98.

The affair of Bixio and Agnetta brings to the fore how the muddling of military authority engendered by the upheavals of the Risorgimento could lead to increased dueling. As rank became more fluid and boundaries blurred, chivalrous actions were needed to reestablish status.[8] On the individual level, the affair demonstrated the lengths to which a man like Agnetta, anxious to affirm his position in Italian society, would go to remove any taint of dishonor. More important, however, the very public nature of the preliminaries offered a showcase of the dueling ethic and tied issues of honor to some of the most important names of the moment. Bixio and especially Garibaldi were heroes of unparalleled popularity, and their participation in matters of chivalry naturally advertised and legitimized the code of honor throughout the new country. Garibaldi was reportedly an opponent of the duel, yet he had to acquiesce in the calling of a tribunal of honor and in affording Agnetta a later opportunity for satisfaction.[9] This ambiguity was later manifested in his Romantic novel, *Clelia,* published in 1870, which sported a telling discussion on the issue prior to his *de rigueur* portrayal of a traditional duel with all the trimmings.

> What the devil shall I say about the duel? I was always of the opinion that it was shameful to not understand each other without killing each other, but on the other hand is it up to us—helots of the tyrants of the earth, pariah of Europe—to preach both individual and general peace? Up to us to forgive outrageous insult! Up to us, so insulted by all! Up to us to whom it is prohibited to walk on our own land or proclaim our own glory!? Up to us, whose rights, whose conscience, whose honor are trampled on by the most vile dross of our nation!? Up to us—who in order to live, to be considered, to be protected—have to prostitute ourselves!? Forget it! *(Via!)* No duels when we are established, well governed, and when we enjoy our rights both at home and abroad—but in the face of arrogance, arbitrariness, and privilege—no! one cannot plead for peace.[10]

Obviously, according to Garibaldi, the Italians had much to prove. True, he suggested, the duel should be condemned, but as long as Italy had to suffer the shame of occupation, as long as Italy was weak and dishonored, all insults had to be answered on the point of a sword. On

8. For example, Gelli 1928, 332–33.
9. On his opposition see Abba 1907, 24.
10. Garibaldi 1870, 356–57.

the other hand, the duel was fratricidal, and *Clelia* contains a lengthy speech by an aging Gondolier who chastises the impending duelists for shedding Italian blood between themselves rather than among La Patria's enemies. These pleas go unheeded, and the protagonist, a young Garabaldino, although sorely wounded in the neck, shoots his opponent, a Roman aristocrat, through the heart. Returning to his theme of fratricide, Garibaldi concludes the scene with the Vatican, Italy's most entrenched enemy, smiling "that infernal smile with which it celebrates whenever a holocaust of blood shed by the dagger of discord bathes this unhappy land.—And who spills that Italian blood? An Italian hand, consecrated to the redemption of our country."[11] Like many other Italians then, he was torn between the need to assert the country's virile and honorable image while simultaneously lamenting the bloodshed demanded by the ritual of regeneration. Yet it bears noting, as his readers no doubt did, that when push came to shove his Garabaldino not only fought, but he fought bravely and well.[12]

If Garibaldi had qualms about dueling, many of his followers did not, and in the transition years the Garibaldini found ample opportunity to exercise both their honor and their sabers. Having acquired half of the country for the House of Savoy, they felt entitled to respect, remuneration, and preferment in a new national army. Instead, they received little real support, and in the creation of the Italian army they were often passed over in favor of soldiers from the old regimes, a double insult which—except for Piedmont, of course—rewarded those who had opposed the making of Italy.[13] On the flip side, the Piedmontese army often regarded the Garibaldini as undisciplined upstarts who had managed to parlay participation in a revolution into rapid promotion which they now wanted confirmed without benefit of real military training. Whatever the justice of the two positions, it was a situation bound to create tensions between men who were either soldiers or saw themselves as such, and the ensuing friction—compounded by Garibaldi's renewed recruitment of irregulars for further nationalist adventures in 1862 and 1867—led to some notorious duels.[14] Following the clash of the Garibaldini and regular troops at Aspromente in August of 1862, a Sicilian baron, Turillo di San Malato, who had been

11. Ibid., 360.
12. According to a produeling author, Garibaldi in fact forced one of his followers to fight a duel in the late 1860s. Modugno 1880, 30.
13. Martucci 1999, 8–9.
14. Abba 1907, 22; Gelli 1928, 270–72.

by the great general's side after he was wounded in the ankle, so thoroughly insulted the new Italian army in his newspaper, *Caprera,* that he was challenged by no fewer than 13 officers. The baron, who was considered one of the best fencers in Italy, went on to severely wound Captain Eusebio, who enjoyed the honor of representing his comrades in the collective affront.[15] Such tensions continued, and the *Gazzetta di Milano* carried a story on June 23, 1863, relating how an ex-captain Fazari of the Redshirts had insulted a certain colonel, Dessa, under the porticos of the Po in Turin. They had fought a duel on the Swiss border in which Nino Bixio, now a deputy in parliament, had acted as one of Dessa's seconds.[16]

These incidents, however, paled in comparison to the exploits of the Garabaldino Antonio Riboli, who fought three duels in 1861 for the sake of the honor of the Redshirts and their revolutionary leader. The story began in Parma when an aristocratic lieutenant of the Piedmontese cavalry defenestrated some dinnerware bearing a likeness of Garibaldi, and his regimental compatriots followed suit. The incident raised a furor among the general's followers, who collectively felt the insult inflicted on the face of their duce, and there was fear of violence between the contending groups. An answer arose in Riboli, who had served as a lieutenant in Garibaldi's cavalry and was currently waiting to hear his professional fate in Mondovì, and who now took the liberty of sending a *sfida* through official channels to the entire offending regiment.[17] This was a gesture worthy of a response, and it quickly led to three encounters (two saber and one pistol) with three noble officers, one of whom (the Count di Salasco) was seriously wounded. The notoriety of the affairs soon prompted Riboli to seek a safer judicial climate across the border in Switzerland, where he was joined by a number of the other participants. They were soon allowed to return, and Riboli, who had become acquainted with some of his antagonists during their shared exile, was actually invited to become part of the regiment that he had so publicly challenged. The ministry of war had other ideas, however, and Riboli was eventually attached to another unit.

Nevertheless, the offer had been made, and it was in keeping with the general theme of reconciliation that permeated the entire narrative. Indeed, Giuseppe Abba's account, written years later, stressed the healing properties of the duel on two different levels. First, he commented on

15. Lo Cicero 1929, 3–4.
16. Article reprinted in the Bolognese newspaper *L'Eco,* July 26, 1863.
17. Riboli's duels are in Abba 1907, 19–30. Also see Banti 2000, 143–44.

the obvious social disparity of the principals. Riboli was a commoner, whose bravery, ability, and love of Italy allowed him to compete with dukes and counts on a level playing field. No better statement could be made regarding the honor accorded to the new men who had helped to make Italy alongside the traditional ruling classes. Second, Riboli's duels had brought symbolic resolution to the rift between regular and irregular soldiers, between the Redshirt and the official uniform, between the revolution and the monarchy. The Garabaldino had been worthy of the challenge, the noble officers of Piedmont had recognized his validity both as a man and as a soldier, and a bond of blood had dispelled previous differences. Whatever actual role Riboli's duels played in the creation of a truly national army, the retelling of them was bound to keep the ethic of honor alive and well in the minds of Italians through the following decades.[18]

Meanwhile, similar narratives were unfolding in the more overtly political sphere. Here, dueling would abound, as previously opposing forces and ideologies came to live together under the same institutional roof. A relatively free press and liberal parliament, which had previously existed only in Piedmont—and then only since 1848—suddenly gave vent to all manner of political opinion which earlier would have been the subject of investigation, censorship, or punishment. Within these new showplaces of debate, personal differences abounded, harsh words were exchanged, and honor was offended. Worse, the very real issues of how and when to finish the process of unification made the first years of discourse particularly nasty as radicals and moderates fought hard for their programs and often stretched the bounds of civility and, occasionally, legality. Garibaldi himself was dragged into two chivalric challenges, both with Piedmontese generals, over recriminations following a stillborn expedition to the Trentino in early 1862, and the duels were avoided only after the direct intervention of the king.[19] At the same time, each group was hypersensitive about its legitimate place in the new scheme of things, and each assiduously defended itself against any slight or insult that might demean its respective importance as equal actors in the public eye. This combination of sensitivity and controlled conflict helped fuel the "explosion" of dueling activity that swept through Italy during the first few years of unification.[20]

18. Such encounters would continue through the first decade. For example Gelli 1992, 139–41.
19. Gelli 1928, 92–97.
20. For example, Bottero vs. Botta in Gelli 1934, 17.

The democrats seemed especially prickly about perceived injuries to their reputation or that of their leaders, a result, perhaps, of their subordinate position in the new scheme of things. Consider, for example, the *vertenza* that arose between the novelist and democratic patriot, Francesco Domencio Guerrazzi, and General Agostino Luigi Pettiti, the current minister of war, in June of 1862. Petitti had insulted Guerrazzi during a parliamentary debate on June 10 by saying that his words were "base" and "vile," and Guerazzzi had responded in kind in a Florentine newspaper. A challenge was issued and accepted by Guerrazzi, who immediately wrote to Agostino Bertani and Antonio Mordini, both noted republicans, asking them to be his seconds. They accepted the charge but warned Guerrazzi in no uncertain terms that they would have no truck with a negotiated settlement. Guerrazzi then suggested to them that he would like to submit the case to a court of honor to assure that he would have the choice of weapons, for compared to his military antagonist he had little experience in such matters. In the face of these instructions, Mordini and Bertani now abandoned him, and their rejection letter spoke directly to the larger political issues at hand: "After your acceptance of the *sfida,* we only saw one way possible, that is fight first and discuss later. And gladly we would have assisted you as much on account of that friendship that binds us as for the necessity of our party to show that we do not fear the overbearing insolence or the provocations of our political adversaries."[21] Here we clearly see how Guerrazzi's private honor had become a stalking horse for members of the radical party, and his hesitation regarding the proposed combat was seen as something of a betrayal on the part of his compatriots.[22] "Fight first and discuss later" was a handy shorthand for the bellicose spirit of the times, and it fit the democratic model of Garibaldi and his followers as they geared up for new, irregular adventures in the face of official caution on the part of Italy's ruling moderates. As a frame of context, only a month after Mordini and Bertani had balked at Guerrazzi's trepidations, Garibaldi launched his ill-fated march of volunteers on Rome from Sicily, which ended at Aspromonte in an unfortunate and divisive skirmish with regular Italian troops.

Similar democratic sensibilities can be found in the actions of Baron Giovanni Nicotera, a republican firebrand who had reluctantly accepted the monarchy and who was elected to parliament in June 1861. In

21. BNN, Manoscritti, Carte Ranieri, Busta 13, Fascicolo 131.
22. In fact the affair was eventually pacified by the intervention of the president of the parliament.

October of that year, with controversy swirling in Naples around anniversary celebrations of Garibaldi's entrance into the city, Petruccelli della Gattina published an article declaring that the general's moment in history was over and denouncing any popular demonstrations on his behalf as fetishistic and idolatrous. In response, a group of democratic leaders gathered together to choose by lot who would have the honor of fighting Petruccelli for insulting their hero, and Nicotera drew the short straw. Petruccelli was doing archival research for the novelist Alexander Dumas when Nicotera found him and offered his challenge. At first Petrucelli refused the *sfida,* but he reacted quickly after Nicotera slapped him twice across the face. Dumas offered his services as one of Petrucelli's seconds, and arrangements were made to tie a saber to Nicotera's hand so that he could fight despite a permanent injury to his fingers incurred during Carlo Pisacane's ill-fated democratic insurrection of 1857. This disadvantage notwithstanding, he managed to wound his opponent in both the head and the arm, at which point the duel was declared to be finished.[23] According to the English writer Jessie White Mario, who was in Naples at the time and whose husband Alberto had originally been involved in the *vertenza,* this was Nicotera's second duel of the year.[24] It was soon followed by another affair in June of 1863 occasioned by the publication in *La Nazione* of a highly critical article on Mazzini.[25] Such swashbuckling might have been viewed as over-the-top, except for the reputation and stature of a man like Nicotera who was a genuine hero of the revolution, wounded in patriotic rebellion and long incarcerated in the dankest of Neapolitan prisons. This was a nobleman and a patriot who had paid his debt to unification in time and in blood, and his righteous outrage and chivalric attitude further legitimized the code duello as an intrinsic part of the new political ethos. Like other democrats-turned-monarchists, he would go on to become an important statesman in liberal Italy, serving twice as minister of the interior, and he could be counted on to back up his words with his sword whenever the occasion arose.

Returning to the big picture, it is obvious that the political passions and opportunities unleashed in 1860 by the success of the Garibaldini and the Party of Action in the south created a period of extraordinary tension and often recrimination among the victorious forces of nationalism. Republicans often felt betrayed by the rapid absorption of

23. White Mario 1894, 56–57.
24. Daniels 1972, 100.
25. See *L'Eco,* July 26, 1863.

the Kingdom of the Two Sicilies and the postponement of acquisition of Rome as the capital of Italy, while their moderate opponents saw them as dangerous both to the current successes toward unification as well as to the Piedmontese army and monarchy. The resulting rift between political elites—who all more or less believed in parliamentary procedure, a free press, and a common goal of unity—created an atmosphere that was rife with emotion and anger, but also held in check by a general acceptance of the current regime. The literary myths and romantic images that helped inspire Italian patriotism were by definition holistic, inclusive, and bereft of any grasp of the very real differences obtaining in the different parts of the country.[26] When, in fact, political factions began the very real struggle of dealing with young Italy's many problems, it seemed a betrayal of that fraternal concord which had been central to much of the previous propaganda. The duel flourished in this climate of controlled antagonism, allowing political opponents of extreme views to cover themselves in honor, assert their brotherhood as Italians, and maintain a martial image of virile men who at heart understood one another's motivations and assumptions. Even when *vertenze* did not result in combat, the protocols of challenge, negotiation, and satisfaction offered an alternative venue of pacific conflict bound by rules that stressed commonalities rather than differences among the participants. This emphasis on masculine commonalities helps explain the passion with which both moderates and republicans embraced the dueling code: it reverted back to the chivalric ethos of Risorgimento propaganda and allowed Italians of different parties to affirm their mythopoetic connections through a national dialogue of honor and blood.

Such was obvious in one of the most significant duels of this tumultuous decade. It came in the wake of Garibaldi's failure at Aspromonte in 1862, which led to charges of betrayal on one hand and treason on the other. The ensuing reciprocal recriminations brought down the government of the left/center prime minister, Urbano Rattazzi, in December of 1862. Rattazzi had eventually been replaced as prime minister by Marco Minghetti, a staunch right/center deputy from Bologna who had been one of Cavour's ablest allies. An important political figure, he had already served Piedmont as minister of foreign affairs and minister of the interior. On June 18, 1863, Rattazzi and Minghetti wrangled in parliament over religious policy, among other issues, and Rattazzi cast

26. Banti 2000, 202–3.

aspersions on Minghetti's preunitary service as a counselor to Pius IX, now an inveterate enemy of unified Italy. He further insisted that Minghetti was fickle in his allegiances and had even sought a cabinet post in Rattazzi's left-leaning government during its last few months of tenure until he saw it was doomed to failure. This was too much, and the hall broke into pandemonium as Minghetti defended his record as an Italian patriot and gave the lie—"È falsissimo!"—to the charge of switching parties.[27]

A duel was arranged, and the two men fought with sabers in Turin on June 21, only three days after their exchange in parliament. The written account or *verbale,* signed by the presiding seconds, sharply delineated the dynamics involved in the encounter: "The undersigned declare on their honor: that the honorable Rattazzi and Minghetti, in this morning's encounter with sabers both conducted themselves as one would expect of people of their elevated character: that during the three assaults, which both men sustained with maximum resolve and sangfroid, the honorable Rattazzi was lightly wounded in the right arm."[28] Once again, we have a "perfect" duel. Rattazzi's wound, which ended the conflict, was a minor detail in the greater game of both men demonstrating their courage in the face of immanent danger. In so doing, they were only manifesting the natural superiority of their "elevated character" which set them apart as leaders of a young and vibrant country. The verbale further stated that their shared service both in the past and in the future now dictated that they put aside their differences and declare their delicate sensibilities reciprocally satisfied.

So much for personal and political reconciliation, but for the new Italy this event was an extraordinary advertisement for the duel. It had involved the current prime minister and his immediate predecessor fighting with swords over words in parliament—an act as illegal as it was honorable. The other attributes of the combatants only polished the image of what it meant to be a gentleman in the new order of things. Minghetti came from one of Bologna's non-noble patriciate families, a man of wide learning and great experience and a leading commentator on social, economic, and political issues. A leader of the moderates who pushed the Risorgimento agenda in the Papal States, he would go on to become one of Italy's leading statesmen during the reign of the historic right. Rattazzi, on the other hand, was a

27. Parliamentary debate of June 18, 1863, a copy of which is with other relevant documents in BCB, Manoscritti, Fondo Minghetti, Box 23, #191.
28. Verbale in BCB, ibid.

successful lawyer who had served in various Piedmontese cabinets during the 1850s and represented those democrats willing to back Cavour's monarchical approach to unification. Significantly, he had penned, as part of his revision of the Albertine Code in 1859, the new law that had greatly reduced the penalties for those convicted of dueling. Like Minghetti, he would continue to hold high office in Italian government, and he would become prime minister again for a short while in 1867. The seconds who assisted with the duel also exemplified a broad spectrum of talent, success, and social background. They included General Enrico Cialdini, a double hero of the Risorgimento and arguably the most renowned soldier in Italy's regular army; Sebastiano Tecchio, an accomplished lawyer who had served as royal commissioner of the newly annexed territories in 1859 and who would eventually become an appeals court justice and president of Italy's senate; and Prince Rinaldo Simonetti, a fierce patriot who had fought in 1848, helped organize Garibaldi's expedition to Sicily, and fostered nationalist associations such as the Italian Society for Target Shooting. Like his compatriots in the duel, he had been appointed to the newly expanded senate in 1861.

This mini-prosopography reveals the double-edged importance of Minghetti and Rattazzi's duel. On one hand, it was a high-profile sanction of the duel by people who mattered, a point raised by the *Gazzetta di Milano* which complained that the encounter in Turin had set a bad example for the rest of the country.[29] The diarist Enrico Bottrigari reported from Bologna that the duel was on everyone's lips, and the day afterwards many distinguished visitors had stopped by Minghetti's house and left their visiting cards: obvious approbation of the prime minister's chivalric gesture by his constituency.[30] On the other hand, the very rank and influence of Minghetti, Rattazzi, and their associates meant that they could guarantee dueling's immunity from judicial prosecution as they exercised their prerogatives in the army, the courts, and the parliament. They not only practiced the duel; they also assured its protection from their own laws and thus promulgated the unofficial chivalric code as being both parallel and equal to the official legal code. This paradox was not lost on the new regime's opponents, such as the pro-papal paper *L'Eco* which aptly argued: "While they pretend to make Italy great and render her civil, every day they put themselves

29. Quoted in *L'Eco,* July 26, 1863.
30. Bottrigari 1961, vol. 3, 310.

in the arms of a barbaric custom of those very Middle Ages that the revolutionaries would like to cancel from history. People who create laws every day abandon themselves to the rationale of the sword and of the lead ball and for civility they want to wash their hands in blood."[31] Predictably, the newspaper called for the arrest and trial of Minghetti and Rattazzi, knowing full well that Italy's officials had maintained a studied silence on this flagrant violation of current law. Even Bottrigari, who was a dedicated disciple of Minghetti and his party, bemoaned the poor example set by the highest elected official in the land and suggested that he should have at least postponed the combat until after he had left the cabinet.[32]

The combination of such examples on the part of both radical and moderate politicians, and the obvious immunity afforded those who fought according to the rules of chivalry, helped to make the duel a common occurrence during Italy's first decade of existence.[33] One can see this dynamic at work in the police files of Bologna for the year 1869. On February 14, the Carabinieri informed the prefect that a duel had recently occurred between a captain of the Grenadiers and a lieutenant of the Bersaglieri over words exchanged at a recent dance held by the Felsinea society. Despite the difference in their ranks and the fact that the captain had been seriously wounded in the arm, the prefect passed the report into the archives without further ado.[34] A few weeks later, the police delegate of Pianoro actually apologized to the prefect for bringing to his attention a duel fought between two lieutenants of the Bersaglieri, but he excused his communication by stating that it was his duty to report all events in the area assigned to him. One of the officers had been wounded slightly, but since there had been no public scandal and no further discord, he was sure the military would take the matter no further.[35] The prefect concurred and buried the report in the archives. A similar attitude was taken toward an incident reported by the Carabinieri on September 1. A lawyer, Aristide Venturini, and a landowner, Ernesto Bordoni, had fought with sabers just outside the city gates over a newspaper article critical of one of Venturini's friends. Both had been lightly wounded in the arm, and

31. In *L'Eco,* July 26, 1863.
32. Bottrigari 1961, vol. 3, 310.
33. For example, ibid., vol. 4, 40. One notes that Bottrigari's memoirs did not begin to mention duels in Bologna until after unification.
34. ASB, Prefettura, 1869, Busta 153, report of Feb. 14, 1869, #12.
35. Ibid., report of March 27, 1869, #15 Riservato.

once again the prefect simply passed the case into the archives without any further action.[36]

Such official nonchalance is all the more striking because earlier in the year, Bologna had been rocked by a fatal duel between two of its more prominent young men: Marchese Giovanni Giuseppe Mazzacorati and Marchese Francesco Pizzardi. Having developed a mutual grudge based on old family tensions and certain financial matters, they agreed to fight with rifled pistols at short range. They met on the morning of February 28 on a rural holding of the Minghetti family, and in rapid order Mazzacorati fell dead with a bullet in his head and Pizzardi left for exile in Switzerland.[37] According to the *Monitore*, all of Bologna was shocked by Mazzacorati's death—he had fought bravely under Garibaldi in the recent war against Austria—yet, as witnessed by the previous examples, the incident had done nothing either to curb the penchant for dueling among the city's elites or to prompt the authorities to intervene in a determined manner.

All in all, as the first 10 years of unity ended, the dueling ethic had become the norm rather than the exception, "the order of the day," as one newspaper put it, among soldiers and civilians alike.[38] Its pan-Italian nature was aptly illustrated by a case in December 1869 involving Marco Besso, a mild-mannered agent of the Venetian Assicurazioni Generali who was running the company's office in Messina, Sicily. He had fired an incompetent clerk named Guglielmi who had reacted by physically insulting him (probably with a slap or kick) in the street.[39] Gugliemi was a former Garibaldino, and Besso felt compelled to challenge him to a duel, as opposed, perhaps, to taking him to court. Bereft of any experience with a sword, Besso engaged a fencing master for 24 hours and managed to come out of the ordeal with a light wound to the arm. Besso recounted the affair with surprise that he, being "pacifistic by temperament and choice," should have found himself with a saber in hand, and that he had nevertheless faced the prospect with complete nonchalance. Overall, it seems to have been a positive experience in which he had "formally learned to stand my ground," although he admitted that it would prove to be his first and last encounter. Nevertheless, that a businessman devoid of military training would "measure

36. Ibid., report of Sept. 1, 1869, #58 Confidenziale.
37. ASB, Prefettura, 1869, Busta 153, report of Carabinieri, March 2, 1869, #768; and Gelli 1992, 135–38.
38. *Gazzetta di Milano,* quoted in *L'Eco,* July 26, 1863.
39. Besso 1970, 74–75.

himself" so casually over the consequences of a routine business matter not only showed how rituals of honor might be employed to defend personal interest, in this case Guglielmi's, but also clearly demonstrated the currency carried by the dueling code for certain groups in the young kingdom. It had become, in the words of contemporaries, a "plague": a trope that implied not only dueling's widespread destruction and devastating scope but also its unstoppable nature and its disease-like power which allowed it to pass from infected hosts to uninfected victims. By the time the country was finally united in 1870 with the acquisition of Rome, the duel seemed to have grown into a general infestation of elite society rather than a manifestation of individual human agency.[40]

Officers as Gentlemen

The pattern of elite behavior toward the duel established during the decade of unification would continue up through the fascist period. It would do so not just because of cultural inertia—that is, because the chivalric assumptions of the Risorgimento automatically dominated the actions of the postunitary period—but also because many of the same forces that had inspired the rise of the dueling ethic would retain their influence as the country matured. Particularly important in this regard were the expansion and proliferation of the Italian military as one of the country's key institutions, and the heavy contribution of Italy's officers to the much-lamented "plague" is correspondingly obvious and consistent in the available quantitative evidence. According to statistics compiled by Gelli (which will be more thoroughly discussed in the next chapter), some 3,593 military men fought in duels between 1888 and 1917—an average of over 120 duels a year.[41] The relative importance of that figure becomes clear if one looks at another set of Gelli's statistics (see table 4 in chapter III) which reveals the professions of known duelists between 1888 and 1895.[42] Out of a total of 2,069 men who fought during that period, some 702 or about 34% belonged to some branch of the military.[43] This figure was generally confirmed

---

40. Such epidemiological references would continue. For example, Corsi 1877, 5; Parodi, 1892.
41. Gelli 1926, 243.
42. Gelli n.d. *Statistiche,* 19. For some reason Gelli included only the first six months of 1893 and 1895.
43. For similar figures from a different sample see Meriggi 1989, vol. 1, 280.

in another, overlapping, sample taken between 1890 and 1899 in which Gelli found that out of 1,065 duels, 289 (27%) occurred between soldiers, 153 (14%) included both soldiers and civilians, and another 623 (59%) involved just civilians.[44] Despite the preponderance of civilians in the raw numbers, Gelli rightly pointed out that because there were only about 18,000 men in Italy's officer corps at the time, the per capita proportion of military men in duels was consequently extremely high. This estimate was especially accurate if one considers Gelli's attending assertion that officers—with the presumed aid of the military establishment—actively sought to hide their duels compared to the intrinsically more public affairs of journalists and politicians.[45] Thus one dueling code, written specifically for officers in 1898, recommended that among military men, *only* duels in which one of the participants was actually killed needed to be reported to the regular judiciary.[46] Even with such stratagems in play, however, both the quantitative and the qualitative evidence supports the image of Italian officers as being punctilious, even pugnacious, in defending their honor.[47]

The frequency of *vertenze* and duels involving Italy's officer corps owed much to the overwhelming hegemony of the Piedmontese army, although it no doubt received an extra boost from the absorption of many Neapolitan officers, whose taste for chivalric combat had been awakened during the Napoleonic period and who had much to prove after their humiliating defeats by Garibaldi's irregulars in 1860.[48] Piedmont, however, had maintained a continuous tradition of dueling from the Renaissance compared to the other pre-unitary states, and it had been particularly prevalent among the officer corps. The political ferment of the "decade of preparation" in the 1850s had reinforced this tradition, connecting dynastic military honor to national political honor while influencing the army of exiles who had escaped to Piedmont after the ill-starred adventures of 1848–49. With the successful war against Austria in 1859 and the co-optation of Garibaldi's victories in the south, Piedmont's army gained enormous prestige as an instrument of unification and, equally important, inherited the practical task of creating a new national army. For much of the country, this

---

44. Gelli 1901A, 10. Further discussion of the statistics in Hughes 1998A, 81.
45. Gelli 1901A, 4, 10.
46. Borgatti 1914, 85.
47. On this image in the theater see Menet-Genty 1989, 260–61.
48. There is some evidence that dueling may have been quite popular in the Neapolitan army prior to unification. See Marselli 1984, 30–31.

institution would be created from whole cloth, because, with the exception of Naples and Tuscany, the pre-unitary states had depended on foreign rather than indigenous troops. The idea of a citizen army, and the universal conscription that fed it, were innovations designed to nationalize the masses, reduce regional or local loyalties, and forge an institution capable of both external defense and internal order. This new army was a radical, and often undesirable, shift for many Italians as young men were uprooted from their homes to serve in other areas of the country and as a uniform military presence projected the power of the government throughout the land. In this sense Piero del Negro has argued that in varying degrees Piedmont "militarized" the rest of Italy and, of course, did so in its own likeness and image, including the penchant of its officers to duel.[49]

The main enforcer of such "Piedmontization" was General Manfredo Fanti, who adopted the practice of simply numbering additional units as an extension of Piedmont's original army when different areas were annexed to the realm.[50] As this new/old army of Italy emerged, he pushed a system of mixed brigades recruited from different regions to assure a pan-Italian identity but with the Piedmontese still clearly in the majority, especially among the higher ranks. Even by the end of the century, over one-fourth of the highest officers in the Stato Maggiore were still of Piedmontese extraction, and Piedmont's dialect ruled as the argot of the army in general.[51] From its very inception then, Italy's officer corps was infused with a tradition of dueling that was directly linked to the creation of the country under the auspices of the Savoyard monarchy.[52] The continued liveliness of that tradition among the top officers of the realm, including the king, is probably best illustrated by the career of General Achille Angelini, author of one of Italy's most prestigious dueling codes. Born in Vicenza in 1812, he became an officer in the Austrian cavalry but then immediately joined the Piedmontese army with the revolution of 1848. Having fought in the campaigns of 1848 and 1849, he gained the rank of captain and became an instructor at the military riding academy at Pinerolo. It was here, in 1850, that he was accused, along with his fellow Lombard officers, of profiteering

49. Del Negro 1979, 158–58.
50. De Bono 1931, 20–21.
51. Ceva 1999, 26, 31, 64–66, 86; De Bono 1931, 132–34, 138–40; also see Cardoza 1989.
52. For an early *vertenza* in 1863 involving the king's closest military associates see Della Rocca 1898, 229–30.

on feed for the horses. Having traced the source of the rumor to a Sardinian lieutenant, he called his accuser out and during the resulting duel killed him with a saber blow. Perhaps unhappy over the disparity in the men's ranks, the military tribunal of Turin sentenced Angelini to five years in prison and a fine of 500 lire. However, only four days after the sentence, the king offered him a pardon that reduced the penalty to six months' confinement, vacated the fine, and allowed him to return to active service with his rank of captain intact.[53]

Popular and well-connected, he rose quickly through the ranks and by the early 1860s had become both a major general and an aide-de-camp to Victor Emmanuel II. In the latter position he became known as the "cavalier without fear," willing to meet the slightest offense against the monarchy with sword in hand. His friend and biographer, Countess Adamoli-Castiglioni, claimed that he fought some 25 duels in his eight years of personal service to the king—although modesty led him to acknowledge only six or seven of them. His military career ended abruptly, however, when, having been appointed a high command in Sardinia, his notorious temper got the best of him. Having fallen in love with a young woman in Caglieri, he ran afoul of her brother who resented his attentions and slapped him in public. Maddened by this insult to himself and his uniform, Angelini whipped out a blade from a sword cane he habitually carried and stabbed the young man in the side, almost killing him. The general was eventually absolved of wrong-doing in the courts, but the notoriety of the case forced his early retirement, with full pension, from the army. Nevertheless, Angelini remained a symbol of military honor and an active promoter of the chivalric ethic up until his death in 1889. According to one French newspaper, he participated in at least 70 duels as either a combatant or a *padrino,* a number the good countess thought shy a few. His dueling code, published in 1882, was considered by many to be the most authoritative in Italy, and his long association with the king seemed to lend a royal imprimatur to its precepts. Certainly, his many encounters while under the direct command of Victor Emmanuel II could only feed the notion that Italian officers were expected to defend their honor with alacrity and enthusiasm.[54]

The official translation of that notion was resoundingly obvious in the new regime's refusal to include dueling as a crime in the military

---

53. DBI, vol. 3, p. 209; Adamoli-Castiglioni 1900, 188–90.
54. Adamoli-Castiglioni 1900, 35–36, 252, 490.

penal code.⁵⁵ While murder, theft, and brawling (*rissa*) were all punished with severe sanctions, the rubric *duello* did not even appear in the code's index.⁵⁶ Instead, dueling was relegated to the military's disciplinary regulations regarding insubordination (articles 27–30) and was seen as a violation only if it occurred between men of differing rank.⁵⁷ The message was clear that as long as challenges and duels did not transgress the logical priorities of military efficiency—specifically discipline and the chain of command—then they were seen as acceptable behavior. On the other hand, the disciplinary code immediately specified in article 31 that these provisions did not protect military duelists from the civilian law code—an obvious gesture to the equal rule of law, but one consistently violated in principle and practice because most military duels were intentionally kept within the disciplinary confines of the command structure. Consequently, when in 1881 Eugenio de Rossi put a fellow second lieutenant in the hospital for three months with a saber slash from a duel inspired by a practical joke, he was given only eight days in the brig and forced to pay 50 lire for a dinner of reconciliation, with no negative impact on his career and no mention to the criminal courts. When de Rossi later fought a second duel with similar results, this time as a major in 1907, he apparently received no punishment whatsoever and within a year of the encounter was promoted to lieutenant colonel!⁵⁸ Even more striking, Lieutenant Pietro Cingia dueled with and killed a nobleman in 1887 and a lawyer/journalist in 1891, but he still made captain by the time he had killed a third man and severely scarred a fourth in 1898.⁵⁹ Cases involving insubordination were treated more harshly, but courts could also be lenient depending on the circumstances.⁶⁰ In 1863, for instance, the Military Tribunal of Turin gave one captain two years in prison for simply putting his hand on his sword—a ritual challenge—and calling his major a vile coward who was afraid to fight a duel, but the same year it virtually absolved a

---

55. The Piedmontese military penal code of 1840 did mention the duel as a common crime, but this changed with the new code of 1859. Vico 1886, 427. Cf. Bruchi 1890, 440–45.

56. *Codice penale per L'esercito del Regno d'Italia* of 1869, reprinted in 1882 with an index, and appended to *Ministero della Guerra*, 1899.

57. Regolamento of Dec. 1, 1872, in ibid., 26. If a superior challenged a subordinate, the charge was misuse of authority.

58. De Rossi 1927, 43, 200–201.

59. Gelli 1928, 215–19.

60. For example, Case of Captain Carones and Major Farifoglio in *Rivista penale*, vol. 53, 1901, 236.

sergeant for wounding his superior in a real duel. The difference in the two cases arose from the fact that the sergeant had issued his challenge in a civil and private manner and the cause of the affair had been personal and unrelated to the service.[61] Even if an officer were convicted of gross insubordination for dueling across the boundaries of rank, he could always hope for a royal pardon, as happened in a famous case in 1861 when a Risorgimento hero, Major Stanislao Becchi, fought with and wounded a colonel who he felt had damaged his career out of personal malice.[62]

In contrast to the military's relative silence on dueling as a crime, the ministry of war reputedly offered up the occasional circular designed to limit the practice, but often as not they reinforced rather than lamented dueling's legitimacy, such as when one stated that officers were specifically prohibited from dueling on military property.[63] Even more important, however, the military embraced other regulations that transparently promoted the practice, albeit in an indirect manner. One has to wonder if it were purely accidental that, closely following the articles linking dueling and insubordination, the disciplinary code waxed eloquently on the military's need for *esprit de corps*, the basis of which rested on honor.

> §35. Therefore, every soldier will regard the reputation and honor of his corps as if it were his own reputation and honor: [. . .].
> §36. Whenever some soldier unfortunately fails in his honor, the opinion of his companions will be quick to condemn him and to reject any solidarity with his mistake.[64]

Such exhortation only reinforced the Piedmontese law of May 1852 (mentioned in the previous chapter) prescribing that an officer who failed to defend his honor appropriately would be deprived of his commission and cashiered from the corps. This critical sanction had been automatically adopted by the new Italian army and would remain throughout the liberal and fascist periods the legal justification, used

---

61. AST, Riunite, Tribunale Militare di Turin, Sentenze, 1863, Mazzo 4, vol. 1, Case #62, Pietro Devincenti, and Case #219, Giacomo Batta Caligaris. For other relevant cases see #34 and #58.

62. Gelli 1928, 211–14. For details on the Bruchi case see BNCR, Levi, *Riassunto della difesa detta a favore del Maggiore Stanislao Bechi,* 1861.

63. Marselli 1984, 147–48; Borgatti 1914, 68; Lo Monaco-Aprile 1898, 4–5; Morelli 1904, 39, 41.

64. Regolamento of Dec. 1, 1872, in Ministero della Guerra 1899, 28–29.

time and again in court, to seek exoneration for officers who faced the double bind between the code of honor and the code of law.[65] That this code was more than merely rhetoric was evidenced as late as 1922, when a lieutenant was cashiered by a *consiglio di disciplina* for refusing to fight a duel with a fellow officer because of religious scruples.[66] For all its significance and impact, however, it is important to note that in the law of May 1852, as in the subsequent permutations of the disciplinary code, all chivalric references remained in the theoretical realm of honor. No regulation ever explicitly promoted or demanded dueling per se, for doing so would have put the military establishment in direct confrontation with the law of the land as signed by the sovereign.[67] The official and public face of the Italian military did not much discuss dueling; it was just something officers were expected to do.[68]

This expectation existed in large part because they were defending not only their own private honor as officers but also the honor of their regiment, of their uniform, and, by extension, of their country.[69] Failure to respond to an insult when a man was in uniform both suggested individual cowardice and bordered on treason to the patria.[70] It followed that officers were particularly sensitive to offenses involving *vie di fatto*, such as shoving or slapping, because such acts physically besmirched the dignity of their uniform.[71] To not react immediately and violently—preferably with a blow from the saber that symbolized their rank and occupation—constituted dereliction of duty.[72] Tellingly, when King Umberto I barely escaped an assassin's dagger in 1897, his only regret was that he had not "inflicted summary punishment" on the

---

65. Ettorre 1928, 237; Gelli 1943, 244–48.

66. "Il duello nell'esercito," CDS, Sept. 27, 1922, 5. For another example see Di Giorgio 1938, 121–25. For a general statement on the issue see the opinion of the pubblico ministero, Prampolini, on the Lollini case in *Rivista penale,* Sept.–Oct. 1884, vol. 20, 239n.

67. This fact was used by the Tuscan Court of Cassation in 1884 to disallow any claim on the part of military duelists that they had no choice but to fight or lose their commissions. *Rivista penale,* Sept.–Oct. 1884, vol. XX, p. 242. Nevertheless, the general interpretation of the law was either "duel or dismissal." For example, Longo 1891, 144.

68. On this "silence" see Vico 1886, 428.

69. Morelli 1904, 244; also see Ranzi 1897, 29–30. By the same token, the law considered an officer personally provoked if he responded to a generic insult to his corps. Corte d'appello di Parma, June 12, 1877, *Rivista penale* 1877, vol. 7, 546.

70. On the tie between patriotism and dueling in the military see Marzano 1907, 27–28.

71. On the severity of *vie di fatto* for officers see Crivellari 1884, 141, and Morelli 1904, 266–68.

72. Borgatti 1914, 11; Angelini 1888, 56–57.

perpetrator with the saber normally at his side.[73] Indeed, the saber—which was the only part of an officer's uniform provided gratis by the government[74]—forged a totemic link to the chivalric tradition that clearly marked an officer as a gentleman, with all the attendant obligations that such a designation demanded.[75] The conscious nature of the connection was revealed by Eugenio de Rossi in 1913 when, having recently taken command of the 12th Bersaglieri Regiment in Milan, he administered the oath of allegiance to a freshly arrived group of second lieutenants:

> Thus when the first of the lieutenants called up to swear gave me the saber that I would return to him after the oath, I explained that this was the survival of the ceremony for consecrating a knight, and that therefore they should consider themselves as such and that from that moment they were obligated to strictly observe the laws of honor if they wished to remain worthy of the rank of officer. I explained that returning the naked saber was the symbol of authority that the nation conferred upon them over the other citizens compelled by the law to military service: [...].[76]

This credo of sword and nobility naturally had its practical side, and when the army set up a competition in 1881 to choose its official fencing style, it demanded that the winning entry include instructions on how to fight a proper duel and be inspired by "the most elevated maxims of perfect chivalry."[77] Officers thus learned to fence in part so that they could duel effectively in terms of both protocol and practice. In addition, they were expected to automatically offer their help as representatives and seconds in *vertenze* involving their comrades, even if they did not know them personally, because all officers were assumed to be perfect gentlemen.[78] Such was the strength of this custom that in 1884 the minister of war, General Ferrero, castigated two officers who had refused to represent one of their brethren in an affair of honor.[79]

73. Quoted in Mack Smith 1989, 73.
74. Ceva 1999, 69.
75. For the equation see De Rossi (1927, 84–85) who was pained when his superior officer did not understand the connection. Also see Marselli 1984, 147.
76. De Rossi 1927, 247–48.
77. Morelli 1904, 60.
78. On some of the problems this caused see Lo Monaco-Aprile 1898, 4–5.
79. Morelli 1904, 275.

Honor, then, was the backbone of the army, and the duel was its guardian, as was clearly illustrated in the maxims of General Niccola Marselli whose 1889 treatise, *La vita del reggimento,* was a favorite within the officer corps: "[I]t is a fact that the duel in the army must be judged with rather different criteria than those that can predominate in regular society. The army is a chivalrous society, in which the point-of-honor or touchiness, if you want, must be more alive, and the reparation [of honor] with weapons must have a larger field of action."[80] *Amour propre* and a heightened sense of honor were critical to an officer's character, and one had to be careful not to stifle youthful vitality with overly punctilious regulation.[81] These opinions enjoyed authority as well as popularity. As a teacher of military history at the War College in Turin, general secretary of the ministry of war, and director of both the *Rivista militare italiana* and *Italia Militare,* Marselli was something of a "spiritual father" of the Italian army during the liberal period.[82] As such he simultaneously articulated and promulgated the military's unique identity with the precepts of honor and chivalry.[83]

As part of that identity, Marselli also stressed the duel's relationship to courage, which was taken as being second nature to an officer. Not the slightest hint of fear or hesitation could be shown in the face of a perceived affront, for it indicated a total unsuitability to the profession. Thus, he argued, the complete eradication of the duel from the military was neither possible nor desirable, because its proof of courage was inherent to the calling.[84] Fear was not an option, and it was better to overreact than risk any possible doubt as to one's willingness to fight. All such precepts went beyond a personal sense of physical prowess in the clash of arms on the battlefield. Rather, an officer had to be ready to make life-and-death decisions without hesitation. Qualms in the face of enemy fire or over the shedding of blood were "womanly" character flaws that might mean disaster for comrades and country alike.[85] Courage, according to General Zucchi in 1861, was the most "virile of virtues,"[86] and in addition to upholding personal and corporate honor, the

80. Marselli 1984, 149. At the time he was still a colonel.
81. Ibid., 130.
82. Del Negro 1979, 65.
83. Marselli had tight connections with the dueling world. He was a close friend of General Achille Anglini and inherited the publishing rights for the general's *Codice cavalleresco* after his death. Adamoli-Castiglione 1900, 19.
84. Marselli 1984, 149.
85. De Rossi 1927, 149, 271.
86. Zucchi 1861, 165.

duel offered an opportunity for officers to test their mettle under the threat of death.[87] This institutional function became more important as Italy entered into a long period of peace after 1866 and the duel came to be seen as a substitute theater of bravery.[88]

This primacy of honor and courage in the thinking of Italy's military leaders was a theme with long roots, and John Whittam has pointed out that when the first academies were created in the 1850s, the prevailing sentiment was "[t]he thing of ultimate effect is character—not intellect."[89] The concept was clearly reiterated and tied to the chivalric tradition by General Achille Angelini, who in the wake of the disastrous war of 1866 called for a moral reform in the education of Italy's soldiers. Discipline, he maintained, was important for times of peace, but for war one needed other motive forces, specifically the point of honor and the love of king, country, and corps. That the duel was an imperative piece of this moral universe was obvious to Angelini: "An officer only lives by honor, he must not be insulted by anyone with impunity, otherwise we would have stable flies dressed as officers, who at the first critical moment would demonstrate, with severe shame for the army, the smallness of their characters and the baseness of their feelings."[90] Not surprisingly, Angelini proposed the legalization of the duel among Italy's officers and the establishment of a tribunal of honor to limit and sanction the conflicts.

In the same vein, Marselli's defense of the duel reflected his concern that the *élan vitale* and virile action of Italy's officers might be eroded by the pedagogical trends and technological needs of the modern military, to say nothing of the general "softness" of modern society. Excessive intellectual work, he claimed, "arrests physical development and lowers moral energy," while the real goal of the army was to form a "man of action." Regimental traditions of honor and heroic examples from history had to be employed to enhance a militant, almost unthinking, spirit of action and sacrifice, all the while channeling the resulting ardor and ferocity within the bonds of discipline and respect. The "true soldier" according to Marselli, was a citizen who "loves danger, disdains death and stoically resists pain while carrying out his duties with discipline and modesty."[91] Hypersensitive to issues of honor, real officers

87. For example, De Rossi 1927, 43.
88. See Morelli 1904, 240.
89. Whittam 1977, 46.
90. Angelini 1867, 86–87, 96.
91. Marselli 1984, 16–28, 40–51, 95–120, 130–34, 221.

were instinctively inclined to violence and undeterred by the physical consequences of immediate action.[92]

This aspect of the military's attitude toward the duel was clearly presented by Edoardo de Amicis's short story "A Bunch of Flowers" which appeared in his 1868 collection of anecdotes, *Military Life in Italy: Sketches*. The story includes a description of a duel—recounted in the drawing room of a fashionable lady—that occurs a few years after unification. Nursing a recent wound, a young officer explains that during carnival celebrations on the *Corso* or Main Street, he had overheard a man criticize one of the soldiers maintaining order during the festivities for being oppressive and brutal—a natural result, he added, of the soldier's "education." Confronted by the young officer as to what he meant by such a reference, the man insolently replied, "the military education." In reaction to this generic insult, the officer found himself in the grip of an uncontrollable and blinding impulse: "I neither saw him, the crowd, nor the *corso,* and I do not recollect what I said or he replied; I only remember that the following morning I returned home with a wounded hand, and my friends said that that gentleman had his left cheek laid open. That is all." The hostess to whom the officer relates this story reacts with what de Amicis characterizes as "a genuine woman's question":

> —But why did you provoke him? Would it not have been better to have pretended not to hear?

To which the officer and an accompanying friend burst out laughing and, when queried as to why, he explains his compulsion to duel:

> —Listen my lady, ... Supposing (which could not be the case) that I ought to have pretended that I did not hear, how could I have done so when my blood was boiling and my head in a ferment? Do you suppose I knew what I was doing at that moment? . . .
> —The people all around had heard, ... The insult was one that touched the whole army, and those words were a lie; then just on that occasion the lie was a calumny, the tone of voice in which the calumny had been uttered sounded like a provocation; then the man, as I afterward learned (and it could not have been otherwise, because these are words which reveal a man's soul), was nothing but a . . . .[93]

92. Langella 1989, 207–9, 217–29; for example, De Bono 1931, 117, 157.
93. De Amicis 1887, 129–30.

De Amicis leaves us to wonder who or what this "nothing" man might be, but there is little doubt as to the supposed psychological power of honor over an officer.

That power operates on a variety of levels within his story. On the surface, the insult to the army, the classic invocations of mendacity and calumny, and the public nature of the confrontation, all reflect the stock precepts of the dueling script. Likewise, the woman's comments and the gentle yet scornful dismissal they inspire make clear that matters of honor are for "real" men who understand them instinctively, while women and lesser men might take the easier path of not hearing the insult: a reference to the classic *"orecchie di mercante,"* or ears of a merchant, in which servility and venality take precedence over honor. Digging deeper, however, we find as well a subtle yet powerful image of the warrior *"furioso"*—a man gone blind in a moment of blood lust—who is saved from savage violence in a civilian setting only by the automatic controls supplied by the dueling ritual. By implication the Italian soldier is dangerous and active, ready to fight and sacrifice all in the name of honor, yet disciplined and able to obey the dictates of a higher authority, in this case the strictures of chivalry.[94] The duel thus becomes an analogue and a practicum of the battlefield populated by perfect soldiers. And yet, like the official policy of the Italian military itself—which refused to condemn or comment on the practice—the story offers no details of the duel: it skips the moment of illicit action and thus subliminally avoids the contradiction of the protectors of the state violating the state's own juridical monopoly of violence.

Similar revelations would be important in the works of any author, but de Amicis was much more than a simple writer of stories. As an editor of *L'Italia Militare,* the official propaganda publication of the ministry of war, he was and is still generally regarded as one of the most reliable interpreters of the collective psychology of Italy's officer corps.[95] Ultimately normative as well as descriptive, de Amicis's *Sketches* spread the military ethic of service and honor through the literate classes of Italy, with the definitive edition enjoying 58 printings between 1880 and 1922! According to military historian Piero del Negro, it became a *livres de fond* for Italy's youth and by the turn of the century had been adopted as standard reading throughout the national

---

94. Also see Lo Monaco-Aprile 1898, 28.
95. On De Amicis's own experience with the chivalric ethic see Meriggi 1989, 281, and Gigli 1962, 122.

school system.⁹⁶ Talented, romantic, and engaging, de Amicis appealed to emotions rather than reason and helped assure that the assumptions of the dueling ethic were to be regarded as "automatic" among Italy's officers, both by themselves and by others.

Beyond the conscious ideals of honor, courage, militancy, and camaraderie, the dueling code also reinforced the social gulf that separated the officers from the rank and file. Italy's conscription laws offered a variety of mechanisms designed to allow middle- and upper-class men to buy exemption from service, and in consequence the majority of the regular soldiers included peasants and urban workers, who were generally regarded by elites as belonging to the *infimo ceto,* that is, men bereft of honor. The protection of honor among the officers according to the dueling code added a moral dimension to a social fact and was perhaps seen as a means of reinforcing obedience among men who generally could neither read nor write. In this world, duty and discipline were for soldiers, while honor and glory were for officers, and this view, of course, paralleled the perceived image of society beyond the barracks. The bridge between these two groups in the military was formed by the noncommissioned officers who had administrative powers within their units but were not entitled to any sort of field command.⁹⁷ Theirs was an ambiguous position at the bottom end of the honor totem pole, and, even if they managed to climb into the commissioned ranks, they were generally discriminated against. It was reportedly official policy that they could not rise above the grade of captain no matter what their talents.⁹⁸ This fact perhaps explains the large number of duelists (134, or 27%) listed as noncommissioned officers in a sample Gelli put together of 491 soldiers who fought between 1890 and 1894 (see table 1).⁹⁹ Bestriding the nick point between soldier and officer, it made sense that sergeants and sergeant majors would have been anxious to ascertain their rights to honor and satisfaction.¹⁰⁰

Similar institutional dynamics would help account for the rather startling preponderance of duelists among Italy's lieutenants. Combining

96. Del Negro 1979, 130, 161–63.
97. Ceva 1999, 71–72; Del Negro 1979, 147–53.
98. De Bono 1931, 27, 50–64.
99. Gelli n.d., 23.
100. This heightened sensibility could lead to duels arising from rather trivial confrontations. Consider the case of two furieri or sergeant majors who in 1882 fought over the fact that a local washerwoman had compared the amount of underwear used by the men in their companies unfavorably to each other. Decision of Appeal Court of Perugia in *Rivista penale* 1883, vol. 17, 47.

Table 1
Military participants in reported duels arranged by rank, 1890-94

Participant	Number
Undetermined	2
Soldiers	2
Cadets	4
Noncommissioned officers	134
Second lieutenants	73
First lieutenants	205
Captains	61
Majors and colonels	9
Generals	1
Total	**491**

the two grades of *sottotenente* and *tenente*, they constituted some 56% of Gelli's entire sample. One could blame such an imbalance on either youthful exuberance or demographic distribution, but one could also suggest that a duel was a means of "making one's bones" in the military—a proof of both courage and honor that would aid a young officer's career. Such was the opinion of the sociologist Lino Ferriani who affirmed that "it is a rooted opinion that a young brilliant officer must begin military life with at least a duel or two. He needs a 'baptism of blood' no more and no less than in medieval times."[101] One might argue as well that some young officers needed to duel not only as a *rite de passage* or a steppingstone to advancement but also as a means of confirming their arrival into a more exclusive social sphere. Joining the officer corps was a rapid and effective tool of social mobility, particularly for middle-class youths, and a duel among "equals" could assuage the angst of those less than sure of their claim to gentlemanly status.[102]

Whatever the distribution of combat across the ranks, however, the compulsion to duel was a daunting force in Italy's military. Combining the individual pressures of social and institutional identity with the corporate traditions of a professional mystique, few could resist its dictates. Moreover, the opinion that for Italy's officers, dueling was natural,

101. Ferriani 1897, 431.
102. For example, De Rossi 1927, 32–44. On mobility see Cardoza 1989, 197.

inevitable, and even desirable enjoyed considerable currency beyond the confines of the military establishment. The Anti-dueling League of Italy, created in 1903, reportedly would not allow officers to join because, presumably, it put them in an impossible position vis-à-vis their own institution.[103] On stage, Paolo Ferrari ended his 1868 drama, *Il duello* (which is examined more fully in another chapter), with two encounters, one of which is fatal. Counter to legal logic, the military man who has killed his opponent outright is let off the hook by the authorities, while the civilian participants of the relatively bloodless duel are to be punished by the law. The attending bailiff explains this discrepancy by simply claiming that duels are mandatory for officers: "An officer is expulsed from the army if he does not fight!" he says. "What can you do!"[104] That this was not merely literary license was clear from a number of court cases that began with lower-level judges refusing to indict or convict duelists from the military.[105] For instance, in Asti in 1889, the pretore decided not to move against two lieutenants (who had readily admitted fighting a duel) because of "that serious moral compulsion that deprives them of liberty of action."[106]

Official support for the defense of a corporate compulsion was perhaps most obvious when in 1884 the public prosecutor of Florence, Prampolini, argued that officers simply could not be treated the same way as ordinary citizens when it came to affairs of honor, not only because the regimental councils of discipline had consistently cashiered officers who refused to fight but also because those dismissals had been steadfastly ratified by the ministry of war. Prampolini, however, went well beyond a simple reiteration of the corporate compulsion argument. True, an officer had no choice, but there was an intrinsic tie between dueling and the warrior spirit. That is why armies throughout Europe had long embraced the precepts of the code of honor, and that is why neither the French revolutionaries nor Napoleon had legislated against its bloody outcomes: they had not wanted to weaken the fighting fiber of the nation. Prampolini held up as well the example of Prussia, which had gone even further and installed official courts of honor, thus recognizing the legitimacy of dueling among officers out of respect for its army. Prussia, of course, had become the darling of the Italian military

103. Morelli 1904, 249.
104. Ferrari 1928, act 5, scene 3.
105. For example, Veronesi 1862; cases of Calza/Rivalta in *Rivista penale,* vol. 7, 1877, 546; Virgilio/Selvaggio, *Rivista penale,* vol. 22, 1885.
106. Decision of 1 Feb. 1889, *Rivista penale* 1889, vol. 30, 53.

after its spectacular successes in 1866 and 1870, and his comparison implied that if Italy were going to run with the big dogs of modern nationhood, some sacrifice of equality would have to be made on the altar of legal impunity. Philosophers fight badly, he quoted one of Napoleon III's ministers as saying, and giving up life for honor was the soul of the military life. He did not ask a carte blanche for officers, for doing so would have violated the essential equality of the law, but judges had to ask themselves on a case-by-case basis how the principles of justice might best be served when one considered the special relationship that existed between punctilious chivalry and a successful military.[107]

Despite such debates within the judiciary itself, the higher courts often refused to adopt the argument that an officer's need to defend his honor was beyond his control, although they tended to leniency in punishments.[108] Consequently, officers consistently complained that they were in an impossible position, caught between their corporate compulsion to fight and the dictates of the law. As a military lawyer, Captain Giuseppe Scaglione, put it in 1869, the demands of chivalry put an officer "in a labyrinth" and "[on] an obscure and difficult path" wending between his various obligations of honor and obedience.[109] Nor were such laments limited to military men. Civilian opponents of the duel would consistently use the glaring inconsistency of having the defenders of the state being forced to break the rules of the state in the name of honor as proof of the chivalric code's inherent illogic. The high command, of course, was not unaware of the difficulty. There were repeated attempts to resolve the issue as part of a general reform of the military penal code, but legislative alacrity was not liberal Italy's strong suit, and the long-awaited amendment languished in a perpetual state of preparation. A compromise solution would be attempted with the creation of military courts of honor after the turn of the century, but their story fits more coherently into a later chapter.

Hence we arrive at the more general question of the effect of the military's dueling compulsion on the rest of elite society. In the most practical terms, the expansion of the army through the liberal period and particularly the creation of large territorial reserves after 1870 naturally increased the number of civilians who had been officers or who still had auxiliary status.[110] Both provided a constant leavening of men

---

107. Commentary on the Lollini case, *Rivista penale,* Sept.–Oct. 1884, vol. 20, 239–240n.
108. See the Asti case, just discussed, in *Rivista penale* 1889, vol. 30, 57.
109. Scaglione 1869, 23.
110. Whittam 1977, 108–9; Ceva 1999, 88–98.

who might infuse the military's hypersensitive pretensions of honor back into Italy's upper and middle classes from which the majority were increasingly recruited. Moreover, the military could still put institutional pressure on a retired officer if he were perceived as not meeting his obligations as a gentleman.[111] On a more abstract level, commentators such as F. Ranzi argued that Italy's civilian elites naturally looked to the military in matters of arms and honor, and he urged his fellow officers to consider carefully the portentous example they were setting as they weighed whether or not to fight for their individual satisfaction.[112] Others suggested that because officers offered the most obvious model of sensitive honor and martial spirit, if the government could get them to stop dueling, the rest of society would follow suit. Moreover, as long as military men felt that it was their right and privilege to duel, the rest of civil society would be dragged along into the fray, trying to maintain their own status. Such was the opinion of the jurist Arturo Bruchi, who warned in 1890, "As long as a civilian citizen sees officers who fight he will never understand why he cannot and must not have recourse to the duel as well."[113]

More generally, one must stress the importance of the military establishment at the national level, including how it might act to reinforce the chivalric ideal. From the very beginning, army officers were engaged in Italy's parliamentary politics, providing a constant stream of senators, deputies, and councilors for the new country, including three prime ministers (La Marmora, Menabrea, and Pelloux).[114] Not only did such participation provide them high-profile status within the nation, but it also assured that their special relationship to the code of honor would be constantly represented and protected within the highest circles of power. There was also the close tie between the military and the Italian monarchy. That special relationship had long roots going back to the creation of the Kingdom of Sardinia itself, when the House of Savoy had managed to utilize its small but strategically important army to play for territory and status among the great powers of the day. Likewise, it was the Piedmontese army that had been largely responsible for creating Italy under the aegis of Victor Emmanuel II, and he was portrayed as heir to a lineage of warrior kings who stood in contrast to

---

111. This actually happened to Jacopo Gelli, and he wrote a pamphlet justifying his actions to the ministry of war; *Per l'onore: note e documenti di una vertenza*, Milano, Lombardi, 1895.
112. Ranzi 1897, 20.
113. Bruchi 1890, 444–45.
114. Ceva 1999, 65.

the pusillanimous princes of the other preunitary states.[115] The successful projection of this soldierly self-image was eventually enshrined in the immodest monument erected to his memory in the heart of Rome, where he still sits aside his massive bronze charger, saber by his side.

Patriotism in Italy was thus officially married to the military valor of the king, who could be considered not only the *re galantuomo* (honest king) but also the *re cavalleresco* (chivalrous king).[116] The monarchy was a critical rallying institution of post-Risorgimento society, capable of generating interclass solidarity among elites, and its dynastic traditions offered an important point of reference. According to Bollati, the monarchy was guarantor of the army and internal order, but "it gave another gift to the nation, that of a stylized political/ethical image that expressed itself in a feudal and chivalrous revival of considerable amplitude."[117] Meanwhile, the ascendancy of the royal court as the focus of high society— first in Turin, then in Florence, and finally in Rome—advertised Piedmont's traditions to the rest of elite society, which became embarrassingly brazen in its search for chivalric titles.[118] Significantly, those titles such as Cavaliere or Commendatore were subject to revocation if a man failed to defend his honor properly.[119] Overall, then, the military pretensions of the House of Savoy naturally promoted the general culture of honor among Italy's elites, especially since there was always the reasonable hope that, when blade met flesh and the judiciary chose to prosecute, the king would intervene and pardon the honorable participants.[120]

Swords and Their Masters

Monarchical and military pretensions also reinforced the tie between fencing and dueling in Italy. As one unpacks the official images of Italy's kings, swords and sabers leap immediately to the fore. Victor Emmanuel II was usually portrayed in his dress uniform complete with saber, often

---

115. Marselli 1984, 219–20; also see Mack Smith 1989, 8, 27, 33–34, 44.
116. Banti 1996, 223, 251–53; Carpi 1878, 24.
117. Bollati 1983, 144–45.
118. See Marselli (1984, 152–53) for the *sfrontatezza* with which people sought such honors.
119. See Carpi 1878, 120–21.
120. There are no statistics on how many pardons were granted to duelists during the period, but various examples can be found in the literature.

Image 1
Cover of Cesare Alberto Blengini's 1864 fencing manual

with his hand resting comfortably on the hilt.[121] The same was true for Umberto I, his son and heir, whose official portraits in the Risorgimento museums of both Rome and Turin show him with saber downward directly in front of his crotch, an easy pose to hold for a painter but also one loaded with pointed phallic power. Such projections reemphasize the totemic function of the sword for patriotic Italians and bring to mind the aforementioned role of the saber in the ritual of inducting second lieutenants into their regiments. Further illustration is obvious in the extraordinary melding of officers and swords that adorned the cover of an Italian fencing manual from 1864 (image 1), the center of which holds a temporally distant image of medieval combat under the flying ensign of the House of Savoy. Not surprisingly, when the Count of Turin left as the dynasty's representative to Paris to fight the Prince of Orleans for Italy's good name after the disastrous defeat of Adua in 1896—a case examined in detail later in this chapter—his seconds rejected an offer to use pistols, claiming that the adversaries, because they belonged to two ancient sovereign families of warriors, would naturally use the sword as their weapon, while the pistol was "devoted for the use of betrayed husbands."[122] Blades, not bullets, were what distinguished truly noble warriors, a theme oft repeated in united Italy's many dueling manuals.[123]

This helps in part explain the extraordinary imbalance in the weapons used in duels in Italy as revealed in statistics collected by Gelli between 1879 and 1899, which are demonstrated in chart 1.[124] They clearly indicate that, of the duels fought during those years (and one assumes during the rest of the liberal period), the overwhelming majority, or some 93%, were fought with either swords or sabers, the latter alone accounting for almost 90%.

Such a preponderance of the blade in these encounters reflected a mutually reinforcing relationship between the duel and the art of fencing. The preference of the sword as Italy's weapon of honor may have begun in the patriotic and military clashes of the Risorgimento, but the culture of fencing as it evolved and expanded helped feed the tradition and keep its adepts ready to prove themselves. According to Fambri, fencing was the "mother of chivalry," and Blengini, who wrote

121. For example, Mack Smith 1989, plate 1.
122. Vertenza fra S.A.R. 1897.
123. De Rosis 1868, 84–85; Cesarano 1874, 137; Viti 1884, 58–59; Lo Cicero 1929, 118. For an exception see Ristori 1872, 18.
124. Gelli 1901A, 11.

Chart 1
Reported duels in Italy arranged by weapon, 1879–99

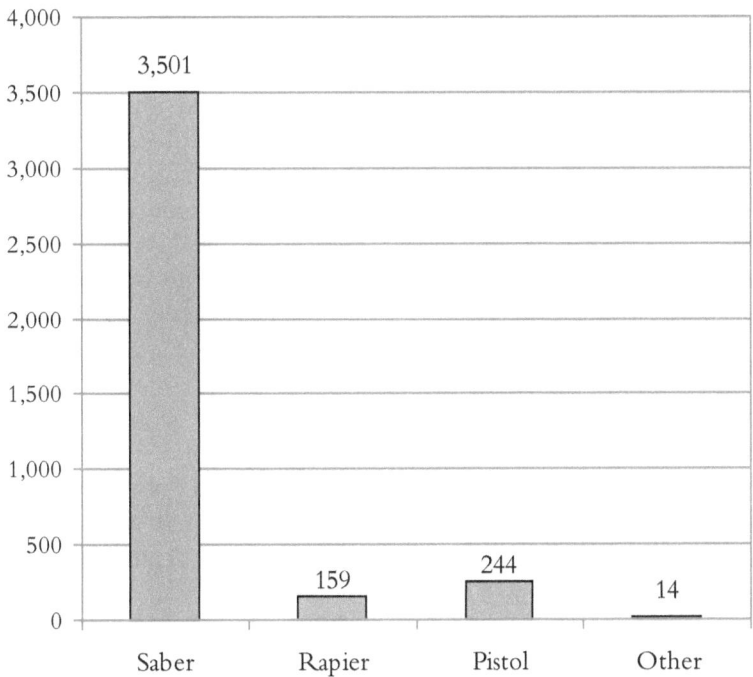

both a fencing and a dueling manual in the 1860s, claimed, "The fencing school must serve primarily the legitimate defense of the individual and the reparation of honor."[125] On the other hand, dueling was in large part the *raison d'être* of fencing in early united Italy. As previously noted, when the ministry of war declared a competition in September of 1882 to create a uniform national system of instruction for officers in both sword and saber techniques, the entrants were expected to include a section on the best way to conduct a duel.[126] Even after the turn of the century, some analysts derided, while others celebrated, the fact that fencing in Italy was still dominated by the psychology and techniques of the *terreno* as opposed to more modern conceptions of exercise and sport.[127]

    125. Fambri quoted in Morelli 1904, 33; Blengini 1864, 16; also see Brunetti 1914, 85.
    126. Parise 1897, 11; Arista 1884, 16, 19–20.
    127. Morelli 1907, 13; Gelli 1901B, 1; Piaggia di S. Marina 1908, 28; Lo Cicero 1929, 21–25, 47–49, 52, 90, 98, 101, 246–47.

Yet fencing as a sport benefited in Italy from these bloody beginnings. As men sought to prepare themselves for "measurement" on the field of honor, the attending proliferation and expansion of *salles des armes* had the effect of inculcating the chivalric ethic into future generations of upper- and middle-class Italians, thus ensuring an ever-expanding clientele for fencing clubs, societies, and academies, where exercise, camaraderie, and enjoyment became the order of the day. This in turn helped promote the popularity of competitive fencing, both professional and amateur, as a spectator sport. By the turn of the century, fencing demonstrations and matches had become elegant affairs, held in stylish venues and even accompanied by musical entertainment and ballroom dancing.[128] Dueling and fencing thus reinforced each other in a variety of ways that would eventually lead to Italy's reemergence as a leader in modern fencing techniques and texts. Suffice it to say, perhaps, that during the Restoration, Italy produced only three fencing treatises of note, whereas 12 appeared between 1860 and the First World War.[129] Nor were these treatises known only in Italy. Luigi Barbasetti's 1898 book on saber fencing was published in German before appearing in Italian.[130] Barbasetti himself was invited to Vienna to oversee the Austrian military's fencing program, just as Italo Santelli went to Budapest and Giuseppe Magrini went to London to teach the latest techniques in saber, which was regarded as Italy's special weapon.[131] Overall, by the turn of the century, Italians could take patriotic pride that their country had come to rival France as an international fencing powerhouse, both in the demand for its masters and in the achievements of its champions.[132] Fencing, nationalism, and dueling became bound up in a self-reinforcing nexus of honor that consistently primed ritual combat with blood drawn by blades.

As mentioned, the military played a key role in this equation by officially promoting the growth of the fencing establishment in Italy. Immediately after unification, officers were expected to obtain fencing instruction as best they could from local academies and experts.[133] However, that expectation changed dramatically with the unfortunate

---

128. See the advertising flyer for such an affair held in the Casino of the Bagni di Montecatini in 1908 in Santini 1989, 19.
129. See the table of contents in Gaugler 1998, vii–viii.
130. Ibid., 276.
131. Morton 1988, 156–57, 162; Evangelista 1995, 516.
132. Coelli claimed in 1904 (102) that there were at least 42 Italian fencing masters teaching outside Italy. Also see De Simone 1921, 28–37, 43–54.
133. De Simone 1921, 14.

war of 1866 against Austria. Following the humiliating defeats of Custoza and Lissa, Italy embarked on a massive restructuring of its army, and one of the earliest reforms was to provide each regiment with its own fencing equipment and master of arms. The purpose of this measure, introduced in 1868 by the new minister of war, Bertolé-Viale, seems to have been to engender confidence, honor, and "fiber" among Italy's officers, whose lack of "character" had been cited by those seeking explanations for the military's poor performance.[134] Likewise, officer morale was dangerously low as a wave of "self-castigation" swept the country, and reinforcing the "most virile exercise" of fencing could be seen as means of boosting the various regiments' self-esteem.[135] The plan apparently originated with the aforementioned General Angelini, fencing expert and duelist *par excellence,* who published a set of reforms in 1867 designed in large part to increase the sense of honor within the army and "inculcate in the officer those chivalric ideas that characterize the officer corps of the best armies of Europe."[136] The army's new commitment to fencing skills entailed a substantial investment in resources, and it also created an obvious need for trained instructors. Official schools for fencing masters were founded in Modena and Parma, but these schools were eventually absorbed by a new, larger school in Milan.[137]

It was a bitter debate over the techniques being taught in this new establishment that forced the defense ministry in 1882 to set up a nationwide competition to select an official fencing style. Ten treatises were submitted, and the prize went to a program that embraced the "classical" Neapolitan style, in part because of its verisimilitude to actual dueling combat, a factor specifically mentioned by Paolo Fambri who reported the results.[138] The winner, Masiniello Parise, was an accomplished fencing master from Naples, whose family had suffered under the Bourbons for their patriotic politics, and he was given command of a new national academy of fencing masters in Rome. The existing school in Milan had to close its doors, and teachers throughout the army had 40 days to adopt the new official style. The resulting controversy would

134. Also, some of the few successes of the war may have involved cavalry and sabers. See Cesarano 1874, 10–11.
135. On the effect of the war see Whittam 1977, 99–103. On the virility of fencing see Gandolfi 1876, preface.
136. Angelini 1867, 31, 92. Also see Morelli 1904, 58; Adamoli-Castiglioni Branda 1900, 269, 438–39.
137. Arista 1884, 5–9; Gaugler 1998, 167.
138. Gaugler 1998, 78; Piaggia di S. Marina 1908, 28, 41.

drag on throughout the rest of the century, but the key point is that following the defeat of 1866, the government had intervened and made fencing a national concern. Texts, techniques, and teachers were openly discussed and publicly funded, while the official academies, eventually concentrated in one *Scuola Magistrale* in the capital, continually cranked out instructors who would often end up selling their skills on the open market.[139]

Meanwhile, that market was growing as upper- and middle-class men sought to prepare themselves for the eventual possibility of having to defend their honor. In such a case one had to be ready to fight with only a few days' notice, and it made sense that prior training offered the best guarantee of surviving such an encounter with minimal damage. This pressure was reinforced by etiquette books for men, which, along with details on proper dining and theater attendance, advised would-be gentlemen of their obligation to defend their honor, with the understanding that they would be able to do so when the time came.[140] Not that everyone who fought a duel already knew what he was doing. Despite all the advice and prohibitions of the dueling "authorities" against postponing a duel in order to seek instruction, people did just that, and one fencing master from the 1930s related how desperate men would show up on his doorstep and beg to be prepared in a certain number of days.[141] Correspondingly, one fencing expert complained that the reason Italy saw mostly saber duels after unity was that the saber was an easier weapon to manage in a short period of time compared to the rapier.[142] But whether driven by short-term panic or long-term planning, such training took time and money, which naturally acted to maintain the exclusivity of those who could claim the rights of honor (this as opposed to the pistol which was seen as easy, egalitarian, and pedestrian). Besides engaging a private fencing master or attending his studio, a man could also join one of the fencing societies that arose in various cities and that combined expert instruction with conspicuous sociability. By 1889, Florence had two such societies, which exacted entrance fees of 10 lire and monthly dues of between 4 and 8 lire, sums

---

139. Indeed, one of the complaints against the Milanese style was that it allowed men to gain a certificate in a few months which they could then use to find work as *Maestri* after their stint in the army. Forte 1878, 15–16.
140. For example, Bergando 1888, 86–93.
141. Conversation with Maestro Greco, Rome, 1992. Also see Mancini 1986, 212.
142. Morelli 1904, 91.

that made them accessible but still exclusive.[143] Whichever path one chose, however, it all fed into the expansion of the fencing establishment which increasingly combined sports, business, and dueling.

There is, unfortunately, no systematic study of the spread of fencing schools across united Italy, but it is obvious from anecdotal evidence that they became increasingly popular through the century, and some rose from the most humble roots to national stature rather quickly.[144] It is equally obvious that they actively promoted the cult of dueling, with fencing masters acting as something akin to high priests. Often assiduous in defense of their own honor, some were notoriously pugnacious, such as Agesilao Greco who once fought a duel with a man in Naples for throwing snail shells at two girls in a café.[145] Characteristically, Agesilao's last encounter occurred in 1927 when he was almost 60.[146] Eugenio Pini, one of the best fencers of the liberal period, was also a famous *bretailleur* who specialized in fighting well-publicized duels with other experts over the merits of their techniques.[147] Equally notorious was the aptly named Athos di San Malato whose exploits brought him fame as a modern-day musketeer. Having designed his own sword and developed a revolutionary style of fencing, he fought duels in France, Spain, Argentina, and Italy as an advertisement of his skill, bravery, and technical innovations.[148] Such controversy helped inject energy into the world of competitive fencing and prompted one master to complain, "One struggles hard to persuade people that fencing is pure art and has nothing to do with the duel, and then here spring forth masters, who I would say almost unconsciously preach fencing of the *terreno.*"[149]

Besides leading by example, Italy's masters saw themselves as uniquely qualified to set the rules and regulations of honorable combat for the new country. This assumption was most blatantly illustrated by the fact that of the 22 dueling codes published in Italy between 1860 and 1914,

---

143. Romanelli 1994, 842.
144. See, for example, the history of Circolo Fides of Livorno in Santini 1989, 12–15; 40–88. For an interesting view of fencing schools in Rome in the 1920s see Mancini 1986.
145. Cohen 2002, 368. Gaugler (1998, 339) reports a very similar incident involving Agesilao's brother, Aurelio Greco, which leads one to question the details. However, it was just such mythic motifs that permeated the fencing halls, and the repetition of such lore constantly reinforced the reality.
146. CDS, April 15, 1927, 5.
147. See, for instance, his duels with Agesilao Greco, Athos di San Malato, and Henri Thomagueux in Santini 1989, 26.
148. Lo Cicero 1929, 31–33, 54, 101, 151.
149. Morelli 1904, 71.

no fewer than 13 were written by fencing masters.[150] Of these chivalric "experts," six also authored fencing books, including Masaniello Parise, who had won the military's competition of 1882 and whose winning treatise has been called the "bible" of Italian fencers.[151] Parise's home institution, the National Fencing Academy in Naples, would eventually formalize this special relationship between fencing and chivalry by creating a Permanent Court of Honor for its members, and the Venetian Fencing Club would do the same under Paolo Fambri's direction in 1888.[152] Giovanni Gandolfi, a fencing master from Turin, went so far as to suggest that the fencing schools of each major city should organize themselves into regional centers of chivalry which could provide juries of honor to potential duelists while organizing exhibition matches on the side.[153] In Rome, the participants of the Grand National Fencing Tournament of 1889 nominated a commission to set up a National Congress of Chivalry which would create a pan-Italian dueling code.[154] Although the commission failed to meet a second time, a similar tournament three years later helped sanction Iacopo Gelli's recently published *Codice cavalleresco Italiano* by awarding him a gold medal of recognition.[155] As late as 1913, the Italian Fencing Association—well-known for its emphasis on fencing as sport rather than combat—felt compelled to offer yet another gold medal to Athos di San Malato for his *Partita d'onore*, a particularly bellicose code of honor that argued for the legalization of the duel in Italy.[156] On a more practical note, one can assume that the many details regarding who should be able to duel and over what issues that filled the fencing masters' various dueling manuals also permeated the lessons and attitudes that they provided their students on a daily basis.[157] This was certainly the opinion of some Italian jurists who blamed the popularity of the fencing schools for promoting the practice.[158]

The fencing community, like the chivalric community, was pan-

150. For a list see Hughes 2005A, 54–56.
151. Gaugler 1998, 217.
152. See chapter 4.
153. Gandolfi 1876, 57.
154. Salafia-Maggio 1895, 17–19.
155. Levi and Gelli 1903, 191.
156. Lo Cicero 1929, 123.
157. Fencing masters were well aware of their reputation as purveyors of chivalric chaos, and some felt it necessary to rebuff the charges in print. For example, Cicirelli 1873, preface.
158. For example, *Rivista penale* 1884, vol. 17, 481; *Rivista penale* 1882, vol. 17, 44.

Italian in nature, and it was likewise charged with nationalistic themes.[159] Indeed the regeneration of Italian fencing came to be seen in and of itself as a political act.[160] On one hand, this view was tied to military preparedness. One fencing hall in Padova in 1872 was opened with the proclamation, "'We Italians must not forget that we were the best swordsmen in the world; but if we should do it again it will not be to succeed as captains of adventure, as in the Middle Ages, or to go as masters of arms to the courts of Europe, but we will have prepared so many individual forces that we will feel them multiplied by the hundreds on that day that the patria needs them.'"[161] On the other hand, prowess in swordplay could be an advertisement of Italy's new virile place in the world. Accordingly, Cesare Enrichetti, future head of one of the military's fencing schools and coauthor of united Italy's first dueling code (1863), lamented in the introduction of an 1871 fencing manual that Italian fencing was still in sad shape because the country's youth had been consciously prohibited from the martial arts by the tyrants of the preunitary regimes. They had instead been forced against their will to engage in silly games and "vile effeminacies." With the country having shrugged off the yoke of oppression, the new regime had consciously chosen to return fencing to its rightful place of honor, and his fervent hope was that his fencing manual would help move Italy back to its previous glory as *maestro di armi* to the world. That this expertise included dueling as well was made obvious when Enrichetti began the next paragraph by emphasizing the advantage of studying fencing as a means of bringing courage and *sang-froid* to the field of honor.[162]

By the turn of the century, Enrichetti's nationalist fencing aspirations were well on the road to being realized. The Italian saber and its attending techniques were growing in popularity throughout Europe and South America, with Italian teachers correspondingly in demand.[163]

---

159. The rivalry in the 1880s over what would become the military's official style included competing claims of unique patriotic legitimacy, with Neapolitans vaunting their classical Renaissance roots and the Milanesi stressing their modern use of the saber as an Italian invention. For example, Melina 1888, 10; Forte 1878, 5–7; Besenzanica 1886, 11; Gelli 1890, 6, 20–29; Arista 1884, 11, 21, 29.

160. This was particularly true for Athos di San Malato, whose father had been a Garibaldino as well as an advocate of Italian fencing over all others. See Lo Cicero 1929, 3, 14, 21, 85, 224–25.

161. Quoted in Cesarano 1874, 16.

162. Enrichetti 1871, 37–38. As this related to the Risorgimento see Fambri 1884; for a literary form of propaganda for Italian fencing see *Tre volte cid* in Fambri, 1888B.

163. See, for instance, Nedo and Aldo Nadi (1955), both Olympic champions and both employed as masters abroad, with Nedo in Buenos Aires and Aldo in New York.

Italians were winning international competitions in all three weapons (saber, rapier, and foil), including two gold and two silver medals at the 1900 Olympic Games, and Italian masters were holding their own in a series of exhibition grudge matches with the French. Occasionally, however, such friendly rivalry turned nasty, prompting duels designed to defend both national and individual pride.[164] In 1902, four fencing masters—two Italian and two French—defended their respective schools in a double duel in Nice, which was proclaimed in the Italian parliament as a new "*sfida* di Barletta."[165] Attended by reporters and photographers, these bouts offered a titillating combination of patriotism and bloodsport, which guaranteed circulation for the periodicals, fame for the contestants, and patriotic legitimacy for the chivalric ethic.[166] Unafraid and sensible to insult, Italians thus fought with swords to maintain their respect in the world of sport and the world of honorable men.

Virility, Honor, and Nationalism

In 1863 Enrichetti and another of Italy's most famous fencing masters, A. Marchionni, published the new country's first dueling code in Florence. While their book, *Norme sui duelli,* did not fare very well compared to rival codes over the coming years, it did contain a passionate conclusion that tied together many of the themes already current in this study.

> In a time in which bellicose tendencies are dominating and in which every citizen of Italy is, or is becoming, a soldier, we thought it more than necessary to fill a void and bring to light some theories that prove how noble is the art of fencing, and what means must be adopted in order to impede or diminish the shedding of blood, and do so in such a way that every duel can proceed with all fairness and all justice possible.
>
> We are no longer a weak and inert people. Recently emerging

Parenthetically, both fought duels while still in Italy. Santini 1989, 12–15, 40–88, 103. Also see Aldo's autobiography (Nadi 1995).

164. See, for instance, the duel between Athos San Malato and Baron Damotte in Santini 1989, 23–26.

165. *Rivista penale* 1903, vol. 57, 117. Cf. Italian and French accounts in Coelli 1904, 109–14, and Andre 1903.

166. For example, "L'eternamente '*sfidato*'" in *Scherma Italiana,* Jan. 25, 1892, #25, 6. More generally see Gelli 1902.

from gigantic battles we are preparing ourselves for the next fight and the final redemption. In our august and adored King we have the first soldier of Italy. It is necessary then to be ready for everything, to know the laws that form the basis of affairs of honor, to have force to oppose force, rights to oppose rights, and not appear inferior in anything to the foreigner.[167]

The king, the sword, and the wars of liberation all figure prominently in this proclamation of national honor, but equally obvious is the idea that dueling as a practice symbolized for these two swordsmen the overcoming of past weakness on the part of Italy's people. Paolo Fambri, in his lengthy defense of the duel in 1869, struck a similar note, saying that Italians had to duel so that foreigners could not return home to report that Italians had no fiber and "that in our salons, in our theaters and clubs the best of gentlemen meet each other, insult each other and then leave as if nothing had happened."[168] For Fambri, knowing the laws of chivalry and applying them bravely, forthrightly, and reasonably would somehow raise the country into equality with the rest of Europe.

In the same manner, dueling also continued, albeit in an individual way, the drama and heroism of the Risorgimento itself. As Italian politicians settled into the often banal business of running a large country, the duel offered an exciting though temporary return to the dash and élan of the revolutionary period. It also allowed those same politicians to virilely combat the evolving image of parliament as a den of inefficient, venal poltroons who cared only for their own special interests. Chivalric bravado was particularly important for members of the left, whose romantic republicanism had had to give way to moderate compromise with the monarchy and who now had to make the difficult shift, to paraphrase Carducci, from the poetry of revolution to the prose of administration. The party of Garibaldi and Mazzini had been the "party of action," and somehow that energy had to be channeled into the framework of parliamentary palaver and reasoned, some might say picayune, negotiation. Such a transformation was aided by infusing public discourse with a passion of conviction and a potential of conflict that occasionally forced politicians and journalists to take armed action once again in defense of their ideals. The duel thus attracted opposite poles of the political spectrum by offering chivalry and tradition to monarchical purists and dangerous deeds to radical democrats.

167. Marchionni and Enrichetti 1863, 49.
168. Fambri 1869, 27.

One might further argue that as Italy remained a small fish in the big pond of European diplomacy, and as its military failed to function efficiently, much less gloriously, the duel offered an individual antidote to possible accusations of a lack of martial spirit or courage at the national level. In fact, the 1860s had failed in many ways to meet the tumescent expectations of Italian patriots. Double defeat—on land at Custoza and on sea at Lissa—had marked the war against Austria in 1866, and failure to support Garibaldi against the French at Mentana in 1867 had led the radical Achille Bizzoni to accuse the government of "dragging the nation's honor in the mud."[169] The same spirit affected the poet Giosue Carducci, who (after the lackluster taking of Rome in September 1870) closed a funerary ode to the patriot Giovanni Cairoli with the lines, "Sad news I bring you: our fatherland is cowardly."[170] Even a stalwart military man like General Eugenio de Rossi, whose allegiance to the monarchy was unimpeachable, complained in his memoirs that Italians were generally held to be "pusillanimous" by the other nations of Europe.[171] The duel naturally thrived in such an atmosphere, because against these accusations of collective cowardice the Italians could offer the almost daily spectacle of men risking their lives in defense of their personal honor.[172]

Unfortunately, Italian adventures abroad made these issues all the more sensitive. Italy came away from the Treaty of Berlin in 1875 with "clean but empty hands" and then saw France carry away the prize of Tunisia, an area of assumed Italian influence, in 1882. Nor did it help matters when Bismarck quipped that "Italy had a big appetite but small teeth" during a trip to Vienna. Worse, it seemed to be true as Italy blundered into colonial expansion without proper preparation or capable leadership. A bloody and embarrassing loss to native forces in Africa at Dogali in 1887 brought no end of recrimination tinged with inferiority compared to other European exploits. The nationalist "prophet" Alfredo Oriani attempted to assuage the humiliation of Dogali by claiming that the 500 soldiers killed had sacrificed themselves as heroes to redeem Italy's long history of military defeats reaching back to the revolutions of 1821, 1831, 1848, and the war against Austria in 1866.[173]

169. Galante Garrone 1976, 35.
170. Ibid., 215.
171. De Rossi 1927.
172. For example, Fambri 1869, 27.
173. Oriani (1889) 1943, 315; Whittam 1977, 124. Also on Dogali see De Rossi 1927, 62, and Marselli 1984, 233.

Yet Dogali weighed on the national conscience, and, combined with an even worse defeat at Adua in 1896, exacerbated a sense that Italy faced a crisis of virility as it entered into the Darwinian "struggle for life," a phrase that became increasingly common through the rest of the century and beyond.[174]

How this inferiority played out in chivalric terms was already readily apparent during debate over the revision of the criminal code in 1875. Digging into the details of the dueling law, Senator Angioletti argued that legislators should be careful in penalizing the *provocatore* more than the *provocato*, because sometimes public opinion demanded that a person act provocatively. Suppose, he said, that an Italian finds himself among foreigners who insult the patria, the government, or the king. Is he not duty bound to react, and if the person continues his insults, does he not have the duty to challenge him to a duel? And if he kills him, then, according to the law under consideration, he might get three to four years in jail—and did this not seem too much for a man who was defending his country's honor?[175] Similar questions applied to discussion of whether Italians should be prosecuted for fighting duels outside their own country. Such a provision, it was suggested, would hamper Italians abroad where they might need to defend their honor— or more specifically the honor of the patria. "A thousand circumstances can occur," claimed another senator, "a thousand occasions, of which it is perhaps more prudent to remain silent, in which an Italian must either issue a challenge or resort to *vie di fatto* in order to reclaim our dignity. At least in the face of foreigners let us show ourselves to be chivalrous."[176] In other words, Italians expected to encounter disdainful barbs from contemptuous foreigners when they traveled, and they had to feel free to react without hesitation, even with a slap or a shove, in order to force the issue into the ritualized arena of combat. To do less would only reinforce the stereotype of national weakness. It does not seem superfluous to point out that the dueling sections of the resulting criminal code of 1889 in fact contained various hedges concerning penalties for "provokers" of duels and made no mention at all of Italian duelists abroad.

Fighting haughty foreigners was obvious in its nationalist overtones, but fighting fellow Italians was important as well, for it inculcated and projected a virile stance toward life that left no doubt as to the "fiber" of

---

174. Bonetta 1990, 171.
175. Angioletti in Crivellari 1884, 176.
176. Gallotti in Crivellari 1884, 181–82.

Italy's elites. Not surprisingly, it was Paolo Fambri who best articulated this attitude, and he wrote in 1869 that the country needed the duel to combat the image abroad of Italian cowardice and to deal with the sad fact that many Italians were indeed poltroonish in their behavior. Chivalry forced men to assert themselves, and the elites had to use it both to distinguish themselves from the pusillanimous mass of Italians and simultaneously to lead them by example to a more evolved and braver society. Making Italy was one thing, but making Italians that were worthy of the effort was another, and he offered the duel as an antidote to the disappointment attached to the first decade of unification. Fambri was well aware that the dueling "plague" had only begun after unification, and thus it stood as something particularly Italian; to defend it was almost a patriotic act that stood in defiance of the individual and national cowardice of the past.[177]

Fambri's arguments lost none of their energy as the heroic moments of unification faded into the past and as it appeared that Italy was in danger of slipping from resurgence into degeneration. In 1888, one year after Dogali, Fambri warned the Italian Press Association that the spirit of struggle inherent in the duel had served Italy well and had to be respected if the momentum were to be maintained:

> Fifty years ago the duel did not exist in Italy, or almost not. [...] It was an age in which the highest [aspects] of man, fierceness and dignity, had been brought low; pitiable was he who was content with it. *Ubi solitudinem faciunt, pacem appellant.* Not even peace, indolence one should say. The Greeks had a beautiful and efficacious word to indicate such a state of consciousness: *anandria,* deficiency of virility. At that point the country suffered from *anandria;* and I guarantee that slaughter in any measure is better.

Through the martial spirit intrinsic to the duel, Italians constantly manifested their will to defend their private honor and, by extension, to defend their country's honor. True, said Fambri, the Italians had become touchy about their honor, perhaps even overly sensitive—but better this virile and aggressive approach to one's dignity than a poltroonish lack of patriotic energy. Woe, he warned, to those who would suggest that it was better to avoid trouble rather than assert one's manhood. "Do you prefer a society with only ordinary and busybodyish

---

177. Fambri 1869, 11.

(*pettegola*) sensitivities and without any virile sensibility? In that case I tell you that you will not find in the deepest depths of some black torrent the mud comparable to the human mud that would derive from such a state of things." Such images implied almost a biological threat and suggested that Italy's men had to promote and protect the pride of their masculinity or else all of society could slip into the androgynous mud of sexual confusion.[178]

Fambri's fears revealed the continuing and evolving concern with virility among the Italians as the high-blown hopes of Italy acting, if not as the civilizing "Third Rome" of the Mazzinian or Giobertian paradigms, at least as a great power, faded in comparison with other European states. There is certainly no mistaking the fixation of the eminent economist Leone Carpi on the issue when in 1878 he praised the Piedmontese aristocracy and ruling house for being "among the most virile of Europe," but then harshly condemned the rest of Italy's elites for failing to bring the country the economic progress that it deserved and needed.[179] His analysis of this stagnation however, focused much more on character and moral fiber than production or trade data. He criticized the non-Piedmontese aristocrats whom he saw as corrupted by the church, manipulated by their women, and dedicated to leisure. The bourgeoisie, instead of acting like an entrepreneurial middle class, dedicated itself to seeking sinecures and milking the expanding bureaucracy, with no stomach for the risks and energy needed to create a truly productive economy. Like Fambri, he worried that Italy's elites were sinking into *poltrooneria* and small-minded self-interest. The antidote he offered was to inculcate in the youth a sentiment of individual and national dignity—"the sentiment of that Italian I, *civis Romanus sum,* the only thing capable of transforming a conglomeration of men into a virile people." Like a tocsin he hammered this adjective through his book: virile works, virile proposals, virile education, virile economics. He called on the aristocrats to break their enervating ties to the clergy and redeem themselves with exercises, especially those with weapons, which "ennoble the soul and reinvigorate the body." He further stressed that they should embrace military service and thus restore nobility to its real roots—the sword. For the bourgeoisie, he also recommended gymnastics, swimming, fencing, and target practice, for they were intrinsic to the physical and spiritual health of the nation, in large part because

178. Fambri 1888C, 1–2.
179. Carpi 1878, 21.

they inspired "that point-of-honor and that respect for personal dignity" which the Italians so sorely needed.[180]

Like Fambri, Carpi had a historical perspective, and he recalled with sadness the "bitter and famous apostrophe" of Italy serving as a whorehouse for its Spanish conquerors: "Ah Italy servant of a sad hostel / Not a woman of the provinces but of the bordello." He further invoked the image of the old eighteenth-century aristocracy which had failed to properly defend female honor and allowed the institution of *cicisbeismo* to weaken the rule of husbands and the sanctity of the family. Only Piedmont had maintained its military dignity, and, tellingly, only Piedmontese men had maintained their personal honor with the openness of the sword rather than with indifference or perfidious treachery:

> And I have mightily grieved of it [*cicisbeismo*], though the strength of soul that is inseparable from military habits and education is a powerful antidote against this evil custom erected as a system and repugnant to every sentiment of honor. Nor could I more objectively and concisely state my thought than Baretti when he said "The piedmontese decide their questions with the sword and not the dagger." And the sword and the dagger have their counterparts *under a thousand other forms* in order to characterize the magnanimity or the baseness of purposes in the social life of peoples [Carpi's emphasis].

The combination of images here is forceful in delimiting Carpi's fears and hopes for Italy. Individual honor is taken as an analogue of national honor throughout his discourse, and the sword, be it of the army or of the duelist, offered the antidote to sexual corruption, cowardly revenge, and a "thousand other" problems.[181]

Unfortunately, he asserted, those failures of preunitary society continued to plague the new country: "one cannot pretend," he lamented, "that the Italian people have a character, a masculine type through which it renders itself distinguished and respected among other peoples." The Italians had banded together during the Risorgimento to create the "masculine act" of unity, but many had fallen back into their previous indolence and did not sufficiently respect themselves and hence were not respected by others. While other countries virilely collected colonies in Africa and elsewhere, the Italians let their productive people

---

180. Carpi 1878, 10, 67, 74, 106–7, 123, 230 348, 305, 536.
181. Ibid., 48, 101–2.

be siphoned off by emigration, a critical failure on the competitive world stage. Such a weak showing would not do. Italy's elites had to regenerate themselves, harden themselves to "male deeds," and embrace Montalembert's adage that the only life worth living is the virile life, full of danger and perpetual effort.[182]

Carpi's concerns and assumptions were hardly the isolated musings of a hypercritical economist; rather, they harmonized with a growing chorus of gendered criticism that portrayed united Italy as effeminate and weak and that arose from some of the most energetic and influential writers of the time. The intellectual godfather of this "cultural despair" was the poet Giosuè Carducci, whose popularity was undisputed, and perhaps unmatched, in the post-Risorgimento era. His disillusion with the "prosaic" and materialistic Italy that seemed so at odds with the heroic vision and actions of Mazzini and Garibaldi, to say nothing of the past glories of Rome, found increasingly shrill interpreters in Angelo Sommaruga, Edoardo Scarfoglio, Pietro Sbarbaro, Alfredo Oriani, and Gabrielle d'Annunzio, all of whom combined trenchant and sometimes outlandish diatribes against Italy's leading politicians with the marketing strategies of modern journalism.[183] An engendered imagery of lost virility continued to punctuate this discourse, and Carducci would talk about the "emasculation" of Italy since the sixteenth century and the need to reinvigorate the "old Italian people" made up of "friars, brigands, *ciceroni* and *cicisbei*."[184] Sbarbaro would attack the parliament as being the seat of "uterine" government, and Scarfoglio would later refer to colonial disaster in Africa as a venereal disease infecting the body politic.[185]

Anxieties over Italy's strength and masculinity were mirrored in the growth of the physical fitness movement in united Italy. Focusing primarily on the teaching of gymnastic exercises inspired by German examples, the movement began under the influence of a Swiss instructor, Rudolfo Obermann, who was brought to Turin in the 1830s to train members of the Piedmontese artillery corps. Immediately following unity, the new government embarked on a plan to introduce Obermann's gymnastics to some schools in Italy, and Turin became the epicenter for the training and certification of instructors throughout the country. The obvious relationship between the growing success of

182. Ibid., 237–39, 256–57, 519.
183. In general see Drake 1980.
184. Lanaro 1988, 166.
185. Drake 1980, 21, 136, 144; for Scarfoglio see Murialdi 1996, 114.

the gymnastics movement and that of the patriotic push for unification and independence—both of which emanated from Piedmont—was not lost on later commentators, and the minister of education, Emilio Broglio, wrote to the prefect of Turin in 1869, "From his free country Obermann brought to Italy the art which is only for free men; and familiarizing the Italians with virile exercises of the body he preceded and almost divined the times of our redemption, conquered through the virtues of intelligence and through the force of souls and arms (*membra*)."[186] Liberty and virility thus walked hand in hand, and Broglio's comment echoed what would become a growing emphasis in united Italy to effect a "virile education" as indispensable to the creation of a dynamic and respected country.[187]

But what did they mean by "virility," and how was it to be taught? On one hand, it clearly implied inherent sexual prowess and an active regenerative capacity. On the other hand, it more specifically focused on the physical aspects of what George Mosse has identified as the Western stereotype of male beauty (lithe, powerful, and proportioned bodies radiating restraint and self-control) which developed from classical models in the last half of the eighteenth century.[188] "Virile education" was, however, also very much about character, which became coterminous with the physical attributes of the ideal male as was made clear by Italy's minister of education, Francesco de Sanctis, in an address delivered at the University of Naples in 1872: "Remake the blood, reconstitute the fiber, increase anew the living force, is the motto not only of medicine but also of pedagogy, not only of history, but of art, raise again the vital forces, retemper [men's] characters and with the sentiment of force regenerate moral courage, sincerity, initiative, discipline, the virile man and therefore the free man."[189] Strength, endurance, virtue, and courage all emanated from the disciplined conditioning of mind and body together.

Yet these traits only fed into the larger organizing principle of a "virile education" which was preparation for successful combat. Truly virile men were dangerous men, men anxious to fight well when the time came. Fencing, javelin practice, target shooting, riding: these were considered the most virile exercises, but they had to be undergirded by

186. Ferrara 1992, 29–37.
187. Bonetta 1990, 84, 167–69. Also see Marselli 1984, 103; Capone 2000, 205–7; Petrosino 2000, 318.
188. Mosse 1996, 29.
189. De Sanctis 1872, last paragraph.

the general fitness and fiber (a favorite word of the period) of Italy's youth. Consequently, the whole slant of Italy's physical fitness programs, no matter how fierce the debates may have been over specific techniques or organizational details, was informed by a desire to produce an effective military machine for the state.[190] In this search to inculcate Italy's young men with a *spirito militare* aimed specifically at "warrior regeneration," it is hardly surprising that the army, the government, and society in general were overwhelmingly indulgent toward the aggressive agenda of the dueling code which manifested the elites' own virility. Italy might long for a virile education for its youth, but surely part of that education was already happening in the almost daily clash of swords of men unafraid to risk lives and laws to protect their honor.

Other remedies for Italian "decadence" also overlapped with the dueling ethos, particularly in the continuing images of sacrificial blood, which had become common patriotic currency during the Risorgimento period. Thus the populist deputy Rocco de Zerbi demanded in 1882 that a "bath of blood" was necessary to invigorate the Italians, and Francesco Crispi was applauded in parliament for exhorting a "baptism of blood" prior to the war of 1866.[191] The radical democrat Felice Cavallotti, who would die fighting his thirty-third duel in 1898, would later echo Crispi, calling for a "bloody baptism" to wash away the sins of Italy's poor military record and the insult of Dogali.[192] Such invective paralleled the belief that much of Italy's unification—in 1859, 1866, and 1870—had been achieved too easily or with the help of foreigners and that not enough Italian blood had been shed to truly bind the nation into a patriotic community. Combining social Darwinism and fanciful aesthetics, the radical nationalist Oriani exalted war and blood as Italy's only answer to weakness: "War is an inevitable form of struggle for existence, and blood will always be the best warm rain for great ideas."[193] Redeeming blood, mortal dangers, and unflinching strength in the face of insult: these were also the tropes of the dueling field, and not only would they promote the chivalric ethic of honor, but, as we shall see later, they would also make it difficult for Italian legislators to pass or enforce laws against the practice.

190. Bonetta 1990, 82–92, 167–80.
191. Mack Smith 1989, 32, 78; also see Drake 1980, 25.
192. Gallante Garrone 1976, 421, 499–500.
193. Quoted in Thayer 1964, 137.

A Perfect Patriotic Affair

The apotheosis of the virile duel which would conflate many of the metaphors of national and individual honor came in August 1897 when the Piedmontese Count of Turin fought the French Prince of Orleans in reaction to Italy's stunning defeat the previous year by the Ethiopians at Adua. Underfunded and overencouraged by the government, General Baratieri blundered into an untenable position against Ethiopian emperor Menelik's vastly superior forces. Some 4,000 Italian troops were killed and another 1,500 taken prisoner on March 1, 1896, in one of the greatest losses of a European army to native forces on record. Coming less than 10 years after the humiliation of Dogali, the shock of Adua to the self-esteem of Italy's elites, and particularly of its literate young men, would be difficult to overstate. Nino Valeri in his memoirs, wrote: "It is almost incalculable the influence that event had on the mental formation of our generation."[194] Enrico Corradini attributed his conversion to radical nationalism to the African defeat and would later use it as a literary platform upon which to chastise the liberal government and exhort imperialist adventures.[195] Giovanni Papini remembered Florence after Adua as being in mourning and described how "I a precocious Italian adolescent felt in me almost the responsibility and the remorse of that shameful defeat of my fatherland. What could I do to expiate it? What could I do to restore honor to my nation?"[196]

Many other Italians were asking themselves the same question, and it did not help that some in the European press chastised their country for cowardice and incompetence on the world stage. One such attack came from Prince Henri d'Orleans, scion of an ex-royal house of France and foreign correspondent to the Parisian daily Le Figaro, who, in a series of articles dispatched from Ethiopia, portrayed Italy's soldiers as lacking the spirit and grit necessary to deal with the Africans. The prominence of the newspaper, the status of the reporter, and the repetition of the charges all demanded action. Various challenges were issued to the prince, but the one that took precedence came from the Count of Turin, a young but prominent member of the House of Savoy and an officer in the Italian cavalry. Having alerted King Umberto I of his intentions and having taken the resulting royal silence as approval, the count and his seconds proceeded to Paris on August 12, 1897. After

---
194. Valeri 1975, 59.
195. Corradini 1923, 8, 251–64.
196. Papini 1994, 47.

intense negotiations over weapons and conditions, the duel occurred early on the morning of the 15th in the Bois des Maréchaux just outside the city. Fought with rapiers rather than sabers, the combat continued for 26 minutes (with both sides drawing minor blood) when the count lunged to deal a deep thrust to the prince's abdomen. Following examination by the doctors, he was declared to be in a clear state of inferiority, and the duel was halted. In the end, the prince was able to stand and offer his hand to the count, who accepted the ritual act of reconciliation.

As with the famous Lamartine-Pepe duel of 1826, Italian honor had been redeemed with blood in the face of a French insult, and once again the official account of the affair offers an important window into the manipulative mechanisms of the dueling ethic. The Italian report of the encounter, which was written by the count's seconds, was a masterpiece of chivalric one-upmanship. The French were portrayed as having hesitated throughout the negotiations, and only the constant and forthright pressure of the Italians had brought them to task. Meanwhile, the Italians proved themselves consummate gentlemen. They knew the rules of the game better than their opponents and referred to both French and Italian dueling manuals to bring their points home. They proved more generous, and, having established the count's rights as the offended party, they gave way on the choice of arms, allowing the duel to proceed with the épée rather than the saber, which they considered Italy's national weapon. Finally, it was made absolutely clear that after the duel it was the Frenchman who had sought reconciliation, for the inverse would have impugned the seriousness of the original offense. Throughout, the report shows the legalistic and punctilious care taken in each phase and in each phrase of the negotiations. The men involved felt that they were writing for posterity, and they knew that Italian dignity was at stake in a variety of ways.[197]

And they were right. Italy's newspapers rejoiced in the count's "triumph" which not only rebuffed the insults of the French but also helped take some of the sting out of Adua as well. Extrapolating from the individual to the national, it was manifest that Italians would defend their honor, had the knowledge and courage to do so, and, when it came down to it, gave the French a lesson with their own weapon. According to one report Italy erupted in joy at the news. "National sentiment vibrated with one throb. [. . .] And the people applauded

197. Vertenza fra S.A.R. 1969.

Image 2
Illustrazione italiana, duel of the Count of Turin in 1897

with an ardor so profound, so universal, so conscious, as is rarely seen in our country [...]."[198] An exhaustive account appeared in various papers, and the *Illustrazione italiana* offered up a double-page drawing of the prince as he was stabbed in the bowels (image 2).

Naturally, this event and its attendant publicity spoke quite well of the duel as well as the nation, and advocates thereafter could point to the count's encounter as an example of how certain situations simply could not be dealt with in any other way. Opponents of the duel, on the other hand, had to work overtime to combat such a popular advertisement for the practice. Some socialists, for instance, emphasized the purely aristocratic nature of the encounter, portraying it as an affair of the House of Savoy rather than of the people, brought on by an arrogant and ill-favored foreign policy. Others, such as Gianni Casati at an antidueling conference in 1911, readily accepted the appropriateness, and the popularity, of the event: "It is a duel that we Italians can be proud of, and that moves not only those who love the fatherland, but the whole civil world. . . ."[199] He then turned to the purpose at hand by

198. "Per il duello," March 13, 1898, no author cited, BNCR Duello C.7.I bis. 1.
199. Casati 1914, 19–20.

stating that the exalted nature of the count's encounter clearly placed the everyday duels of Italy in a negative light because, in contrast, they arose from "a false and unjust concept of honor." The less-than-happy logic of this approach only served to underline how the "Prince's duel" had galvanized popular opinion and reaffirmed the matrix of connections between chivalry and nationalism.

Those connections reflected the frustrations of men who had hoped to overcome images of weakness, effeminacy, and cowardice dating back to the eighteenth century. Frequent dueling and superior fencing cast an honorable gauntlet in the face of those unfortunate traditions, just as they provided an edifying prod to those "poltroons" who seemed to perpetuate them. Meanwhile, the "miracle" of unification had appeared to offer a virile national response to past failings, and hopes had run high that Italy would take its place among the great nations of the world. Consequently, in the 1870s, a rational economist like Leone Carpi could call for "masculine" actions overseas to make way for Italian colonists; but the plan had backfired, and first Dogali and then Adua had called into question the country's prowess. Insulted by the accusation of being less than European—for even tiny Belgium knew how to handle the Africans—the Italians had needed honorable blood, extracted with a sword, according to the rules, by a gallant soldier, and from a worthy opponent, to help wash the stain away.

III

A Plague of Duels (1860–1914)

Dueling and Elites

IN 1864 THE antidueling author Jacopo Nicoletti expressed his shock over the growth of the duel since unification: "But in these recent times the mania of the duel is resurgent, and the abuse spreads like a flood. Even today we are constrained to recognize that we have this iniquitous means to define questions of offended honor as a principle of social affirmation.... Thus the student, the literato, the officer, the nobles, the deputies, and the representatives of the nation and the government, the ministers, all fight in turn and thus give proof of themselves."[1] Nicoletti's list of participants and his definition of the duel as a guarantor of social relations take us beyond the patriotic impulses of honor examined in the previous chapter to see how dueling was crucial in identifying and affirming the new ruling class of Italy. The duel thus owed much of its vivacity and continuity to the fact that it provided a variety of political and social functions inherent to the arrival of a liberal, constitutional regime on the peninsula. Free speech, parliamentary debate, and relatively relaxed press laws created new forms of interchange with which Italians had had little social or legal experience. In this new public sphere, the code of chivalry offered a means of adjudicating disputes that might result from the often acrimonious exchanges between journalists and politicians. It further reinforced in a reciprocal fashion the highly personal nature of politics in liberal Italy, where

1. Nicoletti 1864, 26.

individual power brokers rather than organized parties came to dominate the scene. Within Italy's evolving social structure, the duel acted as a touchstone of "gentlemanly" status, not only standing as the final arbiter of honor but also proving that a man had the "right stuff" in terms of education, sensibility, and courage. Looking at the available statistics and other sources regarding who dueled and why, one can appreciate how the practice aided in the creation, legitimization, and empowerment of a new elite that self-consciously set itself apart from the rest of society by using exclusive chivalric concepts of honor and its defense. If dueling had been useful in creating the new Italy, it was equally important in creating the new Italians, or at least those who counted in society.

Quantifying the "Plague"

Any systematic study of dueling in Italy must begin with the work of Iacopo Gelli, a Tuscan journalist who eventually became the country's primary authority on the practice. Gelli began his quantitative analysis of the duel at the request of Luigi Bodio, head of Italy's official statistics bureau. Because challenges and swords had continued to fly through the 1870s with no sign of abatement, Bodio felt that the time had come to study the problem in a scientific fashion, and he offered the job to Gelli, who already had a reputation as an expert on both fencing and the lore of chivalry. Gelli collected data of various sorts from 1879 up through 1925, and his results provide a substantial numerical portrait of Italian dueling through and beyond the life of the liberal regime.

But how good are Gelli's statistics? Naturally they are limited by the problems inherent in the quantification of illicit activities and, in particular, the "dark figure" of unreported crime which always haunts the cliometrician. Moreover, dueling provides special difficulties in that the perpetrators were often the elites of the land whose power and position would tend to discourage the authorities from prosecution. In other words, formal police and court records can tell us little of what was happening on the ground. Gelli himself was aware of the problem of under-reporting, and, as previously noted, he felt that military duels were particularly difficult to track down because the officers involved preferred to keep such matters out of the public eye.[2]

2. Gelli 1901A, 4.

Likewise, as Robert Nye has suggested for France, duels dealing with highly personal family matters or the honor of women were often surrounded in secrecy so as to protect the privacy of the principals. Indeed, Nye would suggest that, given such problems, duels in France were seriously under-reported, and, although an "expert" such as the French criminologist Gabriel Tarde could find only about 60 duels a year in the 1880s, the real number probably ranged between 200 and 300.[3] As with most crime then, one must accept that, even at their very best, statistics reflect more the visibility than the reality of dueling.

But there are reasons to believe that Gelli's statistics do at least offer a consistent portrait of that visibility. First, he approached their collection with a certain amount of methodological rigor. Either he or one of his associates would systematically scan Italy's major newspapers for evidence of duels, and, upon finding such evidence (or hearing from rumor or some other source), he would send off a printed questionnaire to a contact in the area to be completed and (he hoped) returned. This technique was more effective than one might initially think because, in general, dueling was a semipublic practice. Defined as a crime, it was naturally hidden from the authorities, yet the concept of individual honor involved the opinion of others and was consequently dependent on the community's knowledge of one's willingness to fight—a willingness best validated by the reporting of duels through the "public voice" or even in print. The very fact that in order to have a "legal" duel there had to be a requisite number of "witnesses" (seconds, physicians, and the like) virtually guaranteed some form of public knowledge. Gelli was also aware of some of the pitfalls of data collection, and he was careful to take note of changing laws and jurisdictions that might create reporting errors. Finally, we have an independent check on Gelli's numbers by the forensic psychologist Lino Ferriani. Like Gelli, he attempted to put together a compendium of duels based on newspaper accounts and private reports. He carried out this study for 10 years, between 1886 and 1895, but his results indicate that although his data were in the same ballpark as Gelli's, Gelli had a more efficient system of collection. Thus Gelli found 1,682 duels during the sample years in contrast to the 1,052 discovered by Ferriani.[4] All in all, the quality of Gelli's statistics was such that Bodio felt it safe to include them in Italy's official *Statistica delle cause delle morti* published by his office in 1891.

3. Nye 1993, 185.
4. Ferriani 1897, 434–35.

Unfortunately, whatever rigor Gelli may have used to collect his statistics, their publication can only be called erratic, a result perhaps of his economic need as a journalist to spread his material across a variety of articles rather than produce a single, definitive piece. Also, he published his findings more or less as they changed from year to year, often appending them to other publications about dueling. Consequently, one must deal with different sets of data, which, although usually consistent among themselves, do not always cover all variables for the entire period. Moreover, Gelli was not above making simple mistakes in calculation, and occasionally his published figures simply do not add up they way they should. In sum, Gelli's statistics are hardly perfect—nor given the "dark figure" could they be—but they do open a number of quantitative windows that allow us to look at the causes, participants, and outcomes of most reported duels, and thus they provide important insights into why dueling found such a comfortable niche in the political and social ethos of liberal Italy.

In his best run of material, Gelli analyzed 3,513 duels which occurred between 1879 and 1895.[5] As revealed in table 2, the majority of these duels took place in the 1880s, and on average there were 269 reported duels a year.[6] Although this figure falls somewhat short of the "duel a day" claims of observers in the 1860s and 1870s, it still seems very high. If for fun one were to apply Robert Nye's aforementioned formula from France, it would suggest that Italy actually saw about 900 duels a year, which really would have constituted an epidemic. Whatever the case, aside from the generally high number of reported duels, Gelli's statistics also demonstrate a noticeable drop after 1890 which was apparently linked to the adoption of the new Zanardelli Penal Code of 1889. The code, which levied harsher penalties against duelists and their seconds, took effect in 1890 and is carefully discussed in chapter VI. Nevertheless, even with the decline of the 1890s, it is easy to see why people considered dueling a very real problem, especially if one considers that for every duel fought a large number were avoided through various forms of mediation. It would have been difficult for a "gentleman" to ignore the possibility that he too might someday be caught up in one of these chivalric disputes or *vertenze* and called on to defend his honor.

---

5. Gelli n.d., *Statistiche*. Also on his statistics see Hughes 1998, 80n12.
6. Appendix A from Gelli n.d., 9.

Table 2
Reported duels in Italy, 1879–95

Year	Number	Year	Number
1879	203[a]	1888	269
1880	282	1889	132[b]
1881	271	1890	177
1882	268	1891	138
1883	259	1892	122
1884	287	1893	146
1885	261	1894	98
1886	249	1895	73[a]
1887	278		

[a]Represents only six months.
[b]Represents only five months.

Journalism and Politics

But why so many *vertenze* and hence so many duels? We have already noted the primacy of the military in answering that question, but Gelli's statistics suggest as well that the advent of liberal politics and a free press had a lot to do with it. Breaking down his reported duels by "motive," as seen in table 3, he found that journalistic polemics constituted by far the largest catalyst of duels, and politics followed in third place, with unspecified oral arguments falling in between.[7] Indeed, over one-third (34%) of all duels fought between 1879 and 1889 were over insults published in newspapers.[8] In addition, Gelli's numbers, as shown in table 4, demonstrate that journalists ranked as the most likely people to fight duels except for members of the military.

Gelli's conclusions were supported by other voices, such as Ferriani, who in 1897 commented, "The journalist theoretically combats the duel, but he is the first to provoke it or accept it as soon as the occasion

---

7. It is perhaps superfluous to add that such disputes might well have contained elements of either politics or journalism. Thus Gelli (n.d.) listed some 97 more causes than duels because in some cases he felt it necessary to place a single incident into two categories.

8. Ibid., 11. For confirmation on a limited sample see the statistics section of the *Rivista penale* 1885 (vols. 22, 140, 276, 280, 502).

Table 3
Reported duels in Italy arranged by motive, 1879–95

Motive	Number
Journalism	1,125
Oral dispute without specific cause	875
Politics	431
Insults and scuffles	392
Matters of intimacy	279
Unknown causes	242
Physical aggression	184
Gambling	36
Religion	31
Private interests (money?)	14
Hunting	1
Total	3,610

presents itself."[9] Dueling, in fact, very quickly became an intrinsic part of Italy's early print culture, to the extent that some editors felt that a newspaper had not really "arrived" until it was "baptized in blood" by a duel.[10] Paolo Fambri charged in 1869 that a paper he knew of kept a professional swordsman or *spadaccino* on retainer just to defend its articles.[11] One editor, Gaston Banti, later claimed that he paid his journalists for defending the paper in duels and that there seemed to be an increase in duels toward the end of the month, when their salaries began to run thin. This was the same Gaston Banti who put a fencing runway in his newspaper offices to keep his men fit for such duty.[12] Likewise, the Press Association of Rome had its own *sala d'armi* in the 1920s, complete with professional instructors.[13]

This obvious overlap between pen and sword can be explained in part by the dramatic nature of dueling itself. Chivalric controversy could provide copy for weeks, as it did regarding the deadly duel between Cesare Parrini and Eugenio DeWitt in 1884. The cause of the duel had

9. Ferriani 1897, 431.
10. Cesana 1874, 141–60.
11. Fambri 1869, 132.
12. Santini 1989, 22, 25.
13. Mancini 1986, 212.

Table 4
Participants in reported duels arranged by profession, 1888–95

Profession	Number
Members of the military	702
Journalists	425
Lawyers and notaries	246
Profession unknown	133
Students	117
Property owners★ and independently wealthy	110
Politicians (excluding senators)	107
Engineers	34
Professors	32
Merchants	29
Medical doctors	27
Fencing masters	24
Clerks in public administration	19
Bankers	18
Judges	8
Actors	6
Diplomats	5
Industrialists	4
Workers	4
Music teachers	3
Private clerks	3
Accountants	3
Senators	2
Pensioners	2
Other	6
Total	**2,069**

★*Capitalisti*

been journalistic in nature, with Parrini reporting unflattering news about DeWitt in an article concerning a local trial. DeWitt tracked Parrini down, slapped him in the face, and eventually killed him in a saber duel. Carlo Pancrazi, editor of the *Gazzetta d'Italia* which had published the original offending story, took umbrage at these events and accused DeWitt of cheating during the duel: an offense tantamount to homicide. Charges of murder and countercharges of calumny mounted in the press over the fairness of the duel, eventually leading the *padrini* involved in the encounter to attack Pancrazi in a rival paper: "The *Gazzetta d'Italia* published an untruthful, calumnious, and cowardly article today. We will not respond to *signor* Pancrazi, who is the author; he is only worth being spit in the face; prison would be infected by his presence."[14] Inflammatory and exciting, such obvious sensationalism led one exasperated criminal prosecutor in 1877 to accuse the quotidian press as being both the "promoter and procuress" of the duel.[15] In various ways, then, journalists used *vertenze* and duels to create their own piquant news for an ever-appreciative audience, which could flatter itself for being "in the know" regarding both the game of chivalry and its present-day paladins.

And paladins of the press there were aplenty, as certain newspapers, editors, and journalists became notorious for their chivalrous exploits. Achille Bizzoni, for instance, was a Lombard democrat who founded *Il Gazzettino Rosa* with Felice Cavallotti in 1867 and who claimed to have fought some 50 duels in defense of his articles, including two in one day![16] Another battling journalist was Giacomo Belcredi, a correspondent of the *Tribuna,* who reportedly fought his twenty-fourth duel in Rome in 1892.[17] Equally assiduous in defending his words was Ferruccio Macola, editor of the Gazzetta di Venezia. He would become famous for killing Cavallotti, head of the radical left (and veteran of over 30 duels), in an encounter in 1898, but Macola had fought plenty of times prior to that.[18] Such was Macola's faith in the dueling code that when a *vertenza* between himself and some students was derailed by the publication of a new antidueling tract in 1894, he publicly insulted the author, Filippo Abignente, to such an extent that Abignente was forced to fight despite his recent condemnation of the practice.[19] For the sake of veracity one must wonder whether we should take the large number of duels claimed by such characters as Bizzoni, Belcredi, and Macola at face value, but the actual tally is perhaps less

14. Relevant documents are in Gelli 1992, 177–94.
15. "Duello Selmi/Sciacca," *Gazzetta d'Italia,* Nov. 7, 1877, 3.
16. DRN, vol. 2, 308.
17. Gelli 1928, 203n1.
18. He almost crossed swords with Paolo Fambri. See ACS, Carte Fambri, Busta 21, Fascicolo 19, Cantelli/Tiepolo to Fambri, July 7, 1891.
19. Gelli 1928, 208–9.

important than the need to assert them as part of their public persona as men of the press.

Certainly, the dueling imperative ran much deeper among journalists than a simple scramble for notoriety and subscriptions. Rather, it was connected to the very nature of the journalistic profession. The "truth-claims" intrinsic to the journalistic enterprise automatically put the authors of conflicting accounts of events, accusations, or even statistics into an antagonistic position which called into question their reciprocal veracity. Such truth-claims went to the heart of the traditional dueling etiquette which had relied on "giving the lie" as the defining moment leading to challenge. In many cases, either one side or the other simply had to be wrong, and unless care was taken to soften the language of confrontation, it was natural that articles on even the most innocuous subjects could ultimately lead to a *vertenza* or even a duel.

Yet such care was often in short supply because editors realized that controversy, innuendo, and sarcasm added spice to their copy, and they did not hesitate to push the limits of taste and manners in their search for a larger readership. In other cases, journalists simply lost their tempers and resorted to epithets which begged a chivalrous response. Thus in 1872 Ernesto Teodoro Moneta—editor of the Milanese daily *Il Secolo* and later winner of the 1907 Nobel Peace Prize—found himself calling Carlo Righetti, director of the *Cronaca Grigia*, a *lurida canaglia* (filthy scoundrel) and *rettile schifoso* (repugnant reptile) for impugning the courage and veracity of his newspaper.[20] In these exchanges, the duel was seen first as a palliative and second as a remedy for such invective. Thus Enrico Bottrigari, a Bolognese lawyer who generally condemned the duel, could sing its praises in 1870 because it helped control "the abuse of the press to vilify everybody and torture people's reputations" which had become "shamefully established of recent."[21] With the arrival of constitutional government, journalists might say pretty much what they wanted to about private individuals, but they also might have to answer with sword in hand and life at risk.[22]

These problems were exacerbated by Italy's lack of effective libel laws, a result perhaps of the country's long history of strict press controls. Under the absolutist regimes there had been little need to adjudicate printed insult or calumny because virtually nothing reached the public without first passing through the finely knit filter of the

---

20. MRM Library, "Agli Onorevoli Membri del Giurì d'Onore," Aug. 3, 1872.
21. Bottrigari, vol. 4, 129. For related details see 40, 43, and 222.
22. Murialdi 1996, 46.

government censor. After unity, judicial recourse to libel was further hampered because newspapers by law had to have an *editore gerente,* a person who in theory was responsible for any legal infractions, but who in practice often became something of a straw dog, designed to divert attention and action away from those actually setting editorial policy or composing articles.[23] One famous example occurred when Giovanni Nicotera sued the *Gazzetta d'Italia* for libel in 1877. Seeking to derail Nicotera's political career (he had recently held the post of minister of the interior), the newspaper published an "autobiography" that falsely attacked his credentials as a hero of the Risorgimento. Nicotera reportedly spent a lot of money on a lengthy trial that did not always turn to his credit. In the end he managed to win the case, but the penalty fell not on the director of the *Gazzetta,* Carlo Pancrazi, who had arranged publication of the libelous document, but rather on Sebastiano Visconti, the *editore gerente,* who was essentially innocent in the matter. As an ultimate irony, Nicotera agreed to spend even more money helping Visconti, whose family was suffering while he was in prison for a crime he did not commit.[24]

Uninhibited by the law, journalistic prose was also often inflammatory because Italian newspapermen had little experience, especially in the 1860s and 1870s, in dealing with their new-found freedom, and it was always easier to err on the side of sensation and allegation rather than caution. Paolo Ferrari, a playwright who had participated in numerous *vertenze,* recalled that in the late 1860s, "[t]o every free citizen it could happen to wake up in the morning and find oneself esteemed on one of the [newspaper] pages as a thief, a spy, a ruffian, or some other qualification. And so duels here and duels there. Oh what a life it was."[25] Time did not, however, improve matters a whole lot, and in 1897 the sociologist Ferriani referred to libelists as Italy's new bandits. "Today the brigand wears different clothes, speaks another language: gloved hands do not handle a weapon that can kill with a blow, but the weapon of the pen which brings down the enemy slowly, killing his reputation."[26] With personal attacks nasty and frequent, and judicial alternatives expensive and clumsy, men were forced to fight in order to clear their reputations; and refusing to demand an "explanation" or

23. For example, Ferriani 1897, 437.
24. "I duelli politici del nostro tempo," *La Folla,* June 29, 1902, 24. Gelli 1928, 98–99; White Mario 1894, 103–20.
25. Ferrari 1928 (1868), "Cenni storici."
26. Ferriani 1897, 295.

"satisfaction" for such slights was tantamount to admitting either guilt or cowardice. In consequence, as we shall see later, few of the debates that raged over dueling through the liberal period would fail to include some impassioned call for more practical laws regarding both libel and defamation.

Unbridled in their speech, journalists also had much to prove regarding their place in the new scheme of things. Journalism, in fact, was a relatively new occupation, at least on the scale to which it grew immediately after unification. Newspapers had multiplied rapidly with the arrival of liberal institutions, and the period 1858–73 saw the number of periodicals jump from 278 to 555: a 100% increase in only 15 years, with a corresponding growth in those engaged in the profession.[27] In this world of expanding public communications, the honor and prestige conferred by the dueling code were particularly precious to Italy's journalists, who often fit what might be called the minimal criteria of gentlemen—literacy and white-collar employment—but whose income and status were not particularly high. Public esteem for newspapermen did not gain a great deal from the advent of unity, largely because they quickly became so dependent on external funding to make ends meet.[28] Illiteracy rates of over 75% greatly reduced the potential market for the many newspapers that had sprung up during the first decade of unification, and consequently their primary means of survival was to seek subventions from government organs, political factions, or individuals with special interests.[29] Such attachments did little for the general reputation of newspapermen, and Ruggero Bonghi, editor of the *Perseveranza,* would complain, "It is absurd to suppose that one can remain an honest man while doing the job of a journalist. The more miserable the salary, the more he is disposed and constrained to sell himself and re-sell himself."[30] This venality reportedly extended to underhanded acts of blackmail in which an editor would threaten publication of some unfortunate fact or scurrilous semifiction in hopes of extorting money in exchange for silence. Even if they avoided such obvious iniquities, editors were reportedly willing to spread rumors, stir up trouble, and cast aspersions, all for the sake of generating interest in their pages.[31]

27. Murialdi 1996, 54, 70.
28. Barbèra 1930, 412.
29. For example, Castronovo 1973, 81.
30. Murialdi 1996, 64.
31. Barbèra 1930, 409–11, 296–97. For a later example of editorial blackmail see Toeplitz 1963, 168–69.

So much greater, then, was the need for journalists to be ready to defend their honor against any besmirching of their veracity or honesty, because many tended to have an inflated view of their role in society, perceiving themselves as intellectuals and literati working out grand ideas rather than simply reporting events of importance or interest to their constituents. Not unjustly, Italy's newspapermen considered themselves as part of a literary continuum that placed them in the same group, if not at the same level, as Italy's poets, playwrights, and philosophers, who did indeed often contribute articles to their favorite periodicals.[32] Giuseppe Prezzolini, for instance, would assert in 1909 that three-quarters of all Italy's literary criticism appeared in its newspapers.[33] Consequently, Carducci, Croce, d'Annunzio, and other literati carried out their intellectual and aesthetic debates in a print environment that occasionally meant having to take sword in hand to defend one's view. Meanwhile, in the light of Risorgmento liberalism, newspapermen offered an image of paladins of the press, constant symbols of the advent of a new political arrangement which allowed free discussion and promoted dissent, albeit within a limited range. One combative journalist, Attilio Valentini, who would eventually die in a duel in Buenos Aires, reportedly defined journalism as "a school, a mission, and, above all, a tribunal in which there reign courage and sincerity."[34] Fine words, but, in contrast, journalists were often perceived as always ready to print gossip, innuendo, or propaganda for a price. The tension between these two opposing images made journalists highly susceptible to the dueling ethic in that it promised a means of legitimizing their words as worthy of note and at the same time reinforced their identity as gentlemen, despite the prejudices surrounding their profession.

Nothing so effectively demonstrated the underlying connections between journalism and chivalry as the founding in August 1877 of the Press Association of Italy in Rome. Its inspiration came from the perceived need to establish a permanent jury of honor capable of adjudicating *vertenze* among its members and thus reducing the number of duels between them. The catalyst for its creation was a rather nasty duel precipitated by an article in the semisatirical newspaper *La Fanfulla*. The article had made fun of a deputy, Augusto Pierantoni, for beating the bushes in his search for a district to represent. Pierantoni, a highly

32. Murialdi 1996, 79–80, 103.
33. "Caccia all'uomo," *La Voce,* June 3, 1909, 101.
34. Palanca 2001. On his death see Gelli 1992, 233–42.

successful lawyer with a healthy ego, did not find the references humorous and defended his honor by slapping the author, Fedele Albanese, in public. A duel ensued a few days later in which Albanese was wounded in the arm. Pierantoni's overweening response to a rather innocuous comment, well within the conventions of the *Fanfulla*'s jocular style, galvanized the parliamentary press corps. They protested to the quaestor of Rome as well as the president of the Camera, Francesco Crispi, that such actions represented a hindrance to the freedom of the press in its ability to report honestly on individuals in the public sphere.[35] Protest aside, they also got organized. On May 20—only four days after the duel in question—some 60 editors and reporters from Rome's various newspapers gathered together in the offices of *Il Diritto* and voted to establish a jury of honor "with the express and well-determined goal of protecting the public interest with the morality and dignity of the Press."[36] A committee of seven members (including one foreign journalist) was appointed to draw up guidelines for such an institution. By the time the committee offered its recommendations in August, however, the project had expanded considerably, and its rapid evolution from a simple jury of honor into a general press association (which is still in existence) reveals reams about the problems, conceits, and aspirations of Italy's journalists.

While the new organization would still be very involved in adjudicating *vertenze* between members, its main focus was now to bolster the self-esteem of journalists as professionals and build respect in the eyes of the public. The committee's report affirmed: "Certainly no one has it in mind to limit the full independence and absolute liberty of the opinions of each newspaper and of each party. But in the field of courtesy and aid the Press also must have its obligations and its amour propre and it is for these obligations and for this amour propre that we wish to provide [...]."[37] This reference to "courtesy and aid" was not an abstract one, because along with a jury of honor the association would also act as a mutual aid society, providing funds for those members who risked destitution because of unemployment, disability, or old age. The new plan thus affirmed the precarious—and notorious—financial position of Italy's journalists and offered a dignified and communal means for their support. Simultaneously, however, it affirmed the honor and dignity of all journalists as bona fide gentlemen who deserved each

35. Pesci 1907, 487–89.
36. Associazione della Stampa 1877, 3–4.
37. Ibid., 9.

other's high regard and that of the general public. They thus took as their motto "loyalty and honest manliness (*galantuomismo*)."[38]

As for affairs of honor, the association went beyond the original concept of a jury and created a court of honor consisting of 20 active members to be elected at regular intervals. The court's goal was clearcut: "to prevent insolent impositions (*soverchierie*) and to give a good example limiting duels and withdrawing personal questions from agitation and from individual arbiters." In order for this to occur, all members of the Association agreed to bring their personal disputes of honor before the court, which would then appoint five of its "jurors" to hear the case. The members also promised, on pain of expulsion, to not fight duels among themselves without first requesting such a jury; they could also call on the court for consultation in *vertenze* involving nonmembers. Likewise, anyone could bring disputes to the court if he felt he had been unjustly treated in print by a participating journalist. Journalists who continually used insulting language or who engaged in character assassination regarding other writers would be warned, then censured, and eventually condemned by this court with a corresponding notice in all of Italy's newspapers.

The interlocking themes of professional prestige and personal honor for Italy's press corps resounded mightily in the selection of the first members of this newly established court of honor. The president, or more precisely the head judge, was Benedetto Cairoli, and the association would have been hard-pressed to find a more eloquent choice to exalt the new court's credentials and connections. Cairoli was a hero of the Risorgimento, a Garibaldino who was wounded at Palermo in 1860 and who had gone on to political success as a leading member of the historic left. Elected as a deputy in 1860, Cairoli remained a member of parliament until his death in 1889, and in his lifetime he served as minister of the interior, minister of justice, and three times (between 1878 and 1881) as prime minister. In November of 1878, he was awarded the Gold Medal of Military Valor for taking a bullet in the hip as he threw himself between King Umberto I and a would-be assassin during a royal visit to Naples.[39] In short, he was everything the association needed to sanction the resolution of its members' disputes and then provide legitimacy to those remaining affairs which could be resolved only with the shedding of honorable blood. Hardly less impressive were his compatriots on the court. They included the

38. Ibid., 17.
39. DRN, vol. 2, 472–75.

ubiquitous Paolo Fambri, as well as an admiral, a count, a professor, a senator, and five deputies (including Silvio Spaventa, one of the country's foremost administrators) and Luigi Zanardelli, future prime minister and architect of the unified Italian Law Code of 1889.[40]

This stellar cast of dignitaries on the court of honor pointed up the extraordinary role that the chivalric ethic had come to play in the new liberal regime, and their participation undoubtedly reinforced the viability of the dueling mystique in the eyes of their fellow citizens and legitimized its special importance among Italy's journalists. Moreover, the presence of so many polished politicians and estimable jurists emphasized the "legal" nature of the new institution, which took itself quite seriously in matters of protocol, procedure, and, of course, adherence to the code of honor as a parallel system of judicial authority. Conversely, their own self-importance could only gain from their promotion to be the arbiters of honor for so many of Italy's public figures who looked to them to protect their rights as "gentlemen." Why exactly the court failed to function very effectively (or so it seems from Gelli's statistics) remains a mystery because its archive still remains to be found. For all we know, it may have solved a majority of *vertenze* before they could draw blood.

Be that as it may, the composition of the association's court of honor once again underscored the inextricable tangle of ties between politics and the press in the new nation. A free press had been part and parcel of the battle of liberalism against the *ancien régime*. Consequently, journalism was bound to liberal politics both in a formal and an informal sense. To comment and criticize in print had previously been political acts because doing so defied the traditions of censorship inherent to absolute rule. To publish freely was, in and of itself, an informal exercise of newly acquired political power. More formally, the press represented the many voices that had emerged from the Risorgimento charged with all the zeal of the different factions which had created the new Italy as much in mutual opposition as in mutual cooperation. Combined with economic necessity, which forced editors to seek extramural funding, the press was thoroughly in thrall to politics, and vice versa. Such a system was naturally exacerbated by the personal nature of Italian politics and the lack of formal political organizations to coordinate and mediate policies—all of which prompted Antonio Gramsci's oft-quoted truism that instead of parties Italy had newspapers.[41]

40. For a complete list see Pesci 1907, 490.
41. Cited in Castronovo 1973, 76.

Politics as Reputation

Partisan newspapers, however, were only the most obvious manifestation of a general political ethos in which character, prestige, and reputation were the organizing principles of power. The advent of representative government greatly enhanced the connection between one's private and public persona, and the code *duello* automatically became the arbiter of personal relations in the new parliament. Already in May 1864, when the minister of war felt he had to comment on increased dueling among the military, he affirmed, "As for duels, it is a topic that I don't know how to discuss in this Chamber, because every direction I look I find duelists."[42] Certainly a duel could benefit a deputy by affirming both his position as a man of honor and the strength of his convictions, to say nothing of gaining easy and sensational access to the press, which dutifully reported such encounters. In fact, it became expected for deputies to duel, and, as we shall see later, Felice Cavallotti, head of the parliamentary "historic left," died in 1898 fighting his thirty-third such encounter.[43]

But the roots of political dueling went deeper than press reports or grandstanding. Rather, they were embedded in the evolution of the liberal regime itself. Prior to unification, few Italian elites had had much experience with parliamentary politics, and except for Piedmont after 1848 the idea of a "loyal opposition" had been tantamount to treason under the old regimes. Especially in a public forum, urbane discourse and polite disagreement are social skills that evolve, and Italy's early *Camera dei deputati* was known for its rough-and-tumble debates in which deputies spoke "without hair on their tongues," as the Italians say. "Madman," "imbecile," "bawd," "beast," and "pigs" were just some of the epithets thrown around by deputies as they dealt with the nation's problems, and they could raise the level of personal animosity to fighting pitch.[44] As late as 1910, a bitter yelling match broke out in parliament during which the republican deputy Eugenio Chiesa excoriated the undersecretary of defense, General Prudente, for refusing to answer questions about a possible sex and espionage scandal involving a fellow officer. In the face of Prudente's silence, Chiesa cut loose with "It is a shame. You protect spies. Shame on you. You should not hold that position." The president of the Consiglio, Giuseppe Marcora, yelled at

42. Nicoletti 1864, 27.
43. Gelli 1928, 332.
44. For epithets and citations see Parodi 1892, 35–36.

Chiesa to come to order and added for good measure, "You are an ass, an ass." Uncowed, Chiesa continued to rant about prostitutes and spies and called Prudente "face of a drunk." Despite a temporary recess to let tempers cool, more insults ensued (with Chiesa accusing the army of being packed with "generals of the Merry Widow") which later led to blows being exchanged in the antechamber. All of this, of course, remained to be settled out in a gentlemanly fashion, and Chiesa ended up in a Gordian knot of five overlapping *vertenze,* two of which ended in duels.[45]

We must be careful, however, in seeing these outbursts as irrational or purely the result of unrestrained emotions and prickly pettifogging. On the contrary, the basis for such truculence lay in the constant meshing of public and private identities in an open arena of debate, where disagreement over facts or issues naturally impugned the veracity and character of one's opponents. The division between the political and the personal had scarcely developed in Italy, and the lines were blurred even more by the very nature of the Risorgimento itself which had been carried out by a small number of elites led by romantic personalities such as Mazzini, Cavour, and Garibaldi. Indeed, a number of senators and deputies had made their political bones in the revolutionary upheavals of unification when violent and even illegal action had been a backhanded virtue. Political passion could be regarded as a positive attribute of the new system, even if it entailed offending one's fellow lawmakers. The oft-mentioned Cavallotti, as head of the radical left, argued at one point that harsh words were necessary in Parliament as an antidote to the pacifism and servility of the preunitary past. Censured by the president for calling other members of the chamber perfidious and venal, he retorted: "History, honorable president, teaches that those parliaments where the exuberance of life became tempestuous never caused the decadence of institutions, but those parliaments where servility dominated, were those stigmatized by ugly epithets and marked by the politics of decadence."[46] In addition, as we have seen, the heroic exploits of 1859 and 1860 had given way to acrimonious and armed confrontation over how to complete the unification process. The final solution, which made Rome the new capital in 1870, threw large numbers of elites (and especially the ultra-Catholic nobility) into intransigent opposition. In consequence, Italian politics consisted of a muddy

---

45. CDS, March 5, 7, 9, and 10, 1. *Avanti,* March 5, 1.
46. Galante Garrone 1976, 576.

middle of powerful personages with extremists on both the left and the right who fundamentally disagreed with the system itself. This environment was hardly fertile ground for consensus, and the duel reflected in its stylized violence the heat of Italy's early political discord. Indeed, the pugnacity of debate and the bellicose response of punctilious honor were part and parcel of a society coming to grips with the daunting task of building a nation based on liberal principles.

In order to understand this process better, we can turn to Joanne Freeman's analysis of how honor and dueling were intrinsic to the politics of postrevolutionary America. As in Italy, the question of treating and dealing with political enemies and allies created consternation as the new country faced an uncertain future. Unable to trust past patterns of provenance or partisanship, American elites relied on personal character and reputation as a means of orienting themselves and their actions. Gentlemanly honor provided a traditional moral compass by which to navigate these new politics, and the code *duello* set forth rituals and boundaries to regulate the combat inherent to the "chaos of national public life." Such rules were clearly necessary because, in this highly personalized political struggle, opponents often attacked each other's probity, reliability, and veracity as much as their policies. Consequently, politicians resorted to gossip, innuendo, and rumor in order to discredit their enemies and support their allies.[47] They engaged as well in a constant "paper war," which utilized broadsides, pamphlets, newspaper articles, published memoirs, and private letters carefully designed to either besmirch or defend individual statesmen.[48] Despite the seemingly petty issues sometimes at hand, these interchanges went to the heart of the politics of reputation and hence must be understood as actual arbiters of power. Unanswered gossip or ignored slights in the press could weaken a man's position and eventually ruin his career. All of these traits ran parallel to Italy's postunitary political culture. Historians may find it tempting to trivialize the overly personal, pettifogging, and irascible nature of much of the discourse and polemics of this culture, not realizing how important these issues were to the political process of the day.

Consider, for instance, the 1886 case of lawyer Carlo Panettoni and Commendatore Ranieri Simonelli, both of Pisa. In the wake of electoral defeat in May of that year, Panattoni had heard that Simonelli, who ran on the same ticket, had publicly accused him of having betrayed the

---

47. Freeman 2001, xvii, xx, 62–104.
48. Ibid., 105–58.

party. Panettoni confirmed Simonelli's "slander" with three witnesses, and he immediately sent his representatives to open a *vertenza*. The rapidity of his response was important because any delay might be misinterpreted as moral hesitation or, worse, physical cowardice. Simonelli replied via his representatives that "he accepted the challenge unconditionally" but then demanded the choice of weapons. This demand was at odds, according to Panettone's representatives, with chivalric practice because their man, as the offended party, maintained that prerogative. When Simonelli's representatives persisted in this presumption, Panattoni "posted" him by publishing the documents of the *vertenza* in a pamphlet at his own expense, including quotations from dueling authorities such as Angelini and Gelli to back up his position. The chivalric niceties here are less important than the extraordinarily public nature of the affair. The negotiations gradually dragged various people into the fray, and it soon became the talk of the town. Eventually, newspaper articles in Pisa and Florence questioned whether the original offending words had even been spoken. In reaction, Panettoni published a lengthy pamphlet that included three affidavits attesting to his original charges. We do not know whether or how Simonelli responded, but the case shows how important the game of honor was to a politician.[49] By pushing the affair, Panettoni had redeemed any doubt about his character—he was ready to fight and maybe die over a few words spoken against him. When his opponent seemed to balk at such combat, he threw the moral force of dueling experts in his face, thus affirming his own position as a true gentleman. Following defeat at the polls, he had managed to grasp a personal victory in the public arena by affirming his courage, demonstrating his lawyerly grasp of the rules of honor, and attacking his detractors as unworthy.

Such chivalric skirmishing often remained relegated to paper, but it could quickly turn bloody. In 1883, for instance, Giovanni Nicotera was having a tough battle during his bid for reelection in the college of Salerno. During the campaign, a vitriolic pamphlet written by Calabritto dei Tirreni accused Nicotera of having used his time in office as minister of the interior (1876–77) to enrich himself. The pamphlet failed in its efforts to defame Nicotera, and he won the election. However, returning to parliament, he soon learned that the "libelous" author had been rewarded by the government with a knighthood and

---

49. Details with Panettoni's bias in *Questione d'Onore: Panettoni-Simonelli*, Pisa: Valenti 1886 (copy in MRM).

his father had received a cushy sinecure in Catania. Storming through the parliament building, he cursed the current prime minister, Agostino Depretis, whom he blamed for this calculated attack on his character, and lamented Depretis's advanced age of 78 which blocked the avenue of honor. He stumbled instead on the Honorable Francesco Lovito, a fellow deputy currently serving as secretary general of the ministry of the interior and a man who proved to be in the wrong place at the wrong time. Fixating on Lovito as the source of his woes, Nicotera unleashed his fury, proclaiming, "*Massaro* (farmer), *vigliacco* (coward), *pecoraro* (sheepherder)! I will not lay my hand on your face for fear of sullying myself, but I will spit on you, I will spit on you!" and he proceeded to do just that. Turning completely pale at these insults, Lovito managed to control himself and immediately sent his representatives to arrange satisfaction.

Both men were attended by fellow deputies at the duel. The arrangements had, in fact, been made in the restaurant of the parliament building, and it was determined that the fight would be with sabers and would continue until one of the men was seriously incapacitated—thus eliminating the palliative of *primo sangue*. Bare-chested, the duelists faced each other and were reminded by the *direttore* of the rules incumbent on them as gentlemen. The fight began, and on the first assault Nicotera wounded Lovito in the arm. The *direttore* commanded the men to drop the points of their swords, which Nicotera did, but Lovito, for whatever reason, continued the combat and slashed Nicotera severely across the face. This was a serious breach of the rules, and Nicotera reacted with understandable anger. Screaming "cowardly assassin," he came after Lovito, who—in another breech of etiquette—grabbed his opponent's saber by the blade, severely cutting his hand. He then stumbled or fainted and had to be protected from the furious Nicotera by the *padrini*. Order was soon restored, the men were patched up by the attending physicians, and they returned to town for further medical help. The *padrini* from both sides quickly put together a *verbale di scontro* in which they condemned Lovito for his failure to obey the laws of chivalry and generally deplored the irregularity of the encounter. According to Gelli, Lovito never completely recovered his reputation as a gentleman, and the duel damaged his political career.[50]

The Nicotera/Lovito duel combined many of the elements of the politics of reputation. It began during an election and was inspired by

50. Details in Gelli 1928, 98–101.

a published pamphlet, one of the most powerful weapons in the arsenal of paper combat. Rumor and innuendo surrounded the provenance and intentions of the pamphlet, and Nicotera attacked not the main suspect in the affair but a man closely associated with him. He insulted him publicly in the parliament building in such a way as to assure a duel and then used the rules of the game to discredit him. Lovito would probably have been fine had he managed to control himself during the combat—a critical aspect of the dueling ritual—but his failure to act in a gentlemanly fashion worked to his disadvantage and possibly kept him from higher office. Rather than take the libelist to court, which would have entailed substantial expense and possibly an unfortunate outcome, Nicotera had gone to the public arena of honor to restore his name and attack his enemies. This was all seen as appropriate by parliament, and when asked by the judiciary to proceed against the duelists—who were in clear violation of the law—the deputies voted overwhelmingly to maintain their immunity from prosecution.[51]

Thus duels or potential duels were used to arbitrate disputes engendered by political discourse, but they could also be timed in a tactical fashion—sometimes before or after critical elections or votes—toward specific goals. At the same time, it is important to understand that, despite the political purposes of their affairs, the combatants never lost their sense of real personal injury. It was this very tension of public and private that, for Freeman, explains the role of the duel in the American political system that was in flux between "deference and democracy" and was as yet bereft of the stability and anonymity offered by disciplined political parties. Affairs of honor in America offered "a grammar of political combat that politicians recognized and manipulated as a means of conducting politics in the early republic."[52] This "grammar" would have been very familiar to the elites of united Italy, where the weakness of formal parties and the dominance of key personalities were prominent features of parliamentary life all the way up to the advent of fascism.

In the early decades after unity, these patterns of power were due primarily to Italy's restricted franchise which limited voting rights to an exclusive group of men coming from a limited social sphere. This included literate men over age 25 who paid over 40 lire in direct taxes, as well as certain professional groups including notaries, civil servants, professors, surveyors, pharmacists, physicians, and veterinarians. All in all,

51. "I duelli politici del nostro tempo," in *La Folla,* June 29, 1902, 24. Also see White Mario 1894, 201–3.
52. Freeman 1996, 293.

this amounted to only about 8% of the male population of age and 2% of all Italians.[53] In 1870 only 529,000 men had the right to vote, and, as a result, in some constituencies active politics were the prerogative of only a few hundred people.[54] Even then many of the franchised did not vote or participate, especially "intransigent" Catholics who took seriously Pius IX's refusal to recognize the Kingdom of Italy and his dictum "neither elector nor elected be." Politicians and voters constituted a very small group indeed, thus weakening larger and more formal efforts at organization which might have helped depersonalize political issues.

Reputation and image were critical, then, in bolstering one's prestige among the local electorate, while the proven ability to secure advantages for the province from the central government became the key measure of political success.[55] These "pork barrel" priorities were exacerbated by Italy's prefectoral system which gave the central government extraordinary power in provincial affairs and allowed for the creation of majorities by pandering to the interests of local elites. Thus, despite its centralized bureaucracy, Italian political life was intensely tied to provincial patterns of privilege allocation.[56] The key to this system was personal contact within the parliament and the administration, while networks of friends and clients assured both acclaim at home and influence in the capital. There was, as we have seen, partisanship aplenty, but after unity was achieved in 1870, Left and Right became handy but fuzzy terms of categorization in a rapidly mutating political matrix where friendship, ideology, and interest all blurred together.[57] In this small world, where one's personal and political identities were indistinguishable, the code of honor helped set boundaries for just how aggressive men could be in their political struggles.

Given this situation, logic would dictate that when more-formal mechanisms and organizations of political action had developed, the duel would lose much of its efficacy. But this is exactly what did *not* happen in Italy, as Luigi Luzzatti complained in 1874:

> In Italy political parties in the true sense do not exist as one understands them in the great constitutional countries.... Unfortunately ... we define ourselves through personal loves and rancors, and, God forbid,

53. Romanelli 1979, 46–47.
54. Seton-Watson 1967, 16.
55. Banti 1926, 30, 191–212.
56. Romanelli 1998, 178.
57. For a grassroots practical example see Fontana and Subacchi 1991, especially 508–9.

also regional [loves and rancors]; [or] through revolutionary or royalist origins, and too often our parliaments screech with individual fights; too little do the calm and grand controversies of thought shine there.[58]

Even with the rise of greater electoral participation, Italian political life remained intensely personal and maintained all the assumptions and rituals of its early turbulent years. Indeed, rather than develop disciplined parties, the anonymity of which would have blunted the personal asperity of debate, Italy's leaders came to elucidate and embrace the system known as *trasformismo,* thus further muddying the already murky currents of liberal politics. In some ways, *trasformismo,* as it was labeled by prime minister Agostino Depretis in 1882, simply recognized a system already in operation by which prime ministers sought support from a wide spectrum of politicians and attempted to "transform" previous opponents into allies by offering a variety of posts, perks, and favors. Depretis, however, not only named this system of constantly mutating alliances; he also sanctioned it, claiming what was generally seen as a political vice to actually be a political virtue capable of assuring parliamentary majorities and providing better government.

The positive and negative effects of *trasformismo* have often been debated, but there seems little doubt as to its effect on the style of Italian politics and its integral ties to the code of honor and dueling.[59] Above all it blocked the development of parties which would have helped depersonalize political struggle. Combined with the continuing intransigence of Catholic elites, who might have offered a loyal conservative opposition had they participated in government, *trasformismo* led to a series of "parliamentary dictatorships" that reinforced the tradition of individual power brokers in the liberal regime, creating what Galante Garrone has called a system of *"persone e personalismi."*[60] Rising to the top, prestigious and authoritative notables created "combinations" of clients who jockeyed for influence and favors. Transformism thus obscured political differences and sanctioned shifting alliances as new rivals were co-opted into the established patterns of patronage. Yesterday's friend might be tomorrow's foe, creating just the kind of personal insecurity and political tension that would lead to frequent *vertenze* and occasional duels. On the other hand, as clientelism and patronage became the political coin of the realm, they often broached the threshold of legality.

58. Quoted in Banti 1996, 44
59. On *trasformismo* in general see Bollati 1983, IX–XVIII.
60. Galante Garrone 1976, 409.

Crispi, who eventually became one of the major notables himself, would complain that when there was an important vote on the floor, parliament became pandemonium, a market of "subsidies, decorations, canals, bridges, streets, everything" as the government sought support.[61] Such constant barter easily led to reciprocal charges of malfeasance and corruption among opponents, who then often resorted to *vertenze* to sort matters out in the public eye.

In this environment a politician had to constantly be on his guard to protect his reputation as a man of honor, for failure to do so meant a decline in the personal influence which determined one's career. Such a system explains as well the constant overlap of honor and politics with journalism, for newspapers gave voice to individual politicians or their factions, and it was in their columns of print that much of the bickering, innuendo, and mudslinging took place. A man had to challenge every charge in order to maintain his credibility, and it was easy to slip into a spiral of invective that would force an affair to clear the air. These dynamics of honor swept across the political spectrum from conservative to socialist alike, although one senses that radical republicans, such as Bizzoni and Cavallotti, may have been the most ready to bring out the swords. Nor did just deputies duel. Provincial counselors, town councilmen, and other local officials had to be wary of their reputations as well, and all of this created a positive portrait of honorable disputation that naturally served as a model, or at least an excuse, for the rest of civil society. Significantly, the elites most immune to the sirens of chivalry were the intransigent Catholics, but they were generally prohibited from participating in the political process by the papacy, which refused to even recognize the new country. Their abstention in both spheres—honor and politics—only emphasized the integral identity that tied the dueling ethic to the evolution of Italy as a sovereign state.

Defining the "Civil Class"

The frequency of the duel among journalists, politicians, and officers reveals only the most obvious aspect of how the culture of honor helped define and legitimize Italy's elites following unification. As revealed by Gelli's statistics, many other people from different professions felt that it was their prerogative to demand and receive armed satisfaction. In

---

61. Quoted in Montanelli 1973, 181.

fact, some 40% of the duelists listed by Gelli came from categories other than the aforementioned top three (soldiers, journalists, and politicians), including lawyers and notaries (12%); students (6%); capitalists and the independently wealthy (5%); engineers, professors, merchants, and physicians (6%); fencing masters, public clerks, bankers, judges, actors, diplomats, industrialists, workers, music teachers, private clerks, accountants, senators, and pensioners (5%). Taken together, these categories rather effectively indicate that the dueling ethic went deeper than political skirmishing or military posturing. Rather, it provided a general and critical component of the social/psychological matrix of Italy's new "bourgeois" society.

One uses this term with some trepidation. Just as Medieval and Renaissance Italy have always eluded categorization as "feudal," so too has the term *borghese* been fraught with difficulties when applied to nineteenth-century Italy. The Risorgimento has often been portrayed as a bourgeois revolution in that it enshrined notions of private property and brought forth an individualistic/liberal political ethos in the place of the juridically confirmed corporate systems of the old regimes. Consequently, both the term and the concept of *borghese* are commonly applied and accepted in Italy's historical literature. On the other hand, as Raffaele Romanelli has pointed out, just what constituted Italy's *borghesia* and what made it *borghese* has been a constant problem for Italian historians, especially given the centrality of the term to ideological and political debate in both the past and the present. Originally conceived in terms of political economy, it implied a dichotomy between conservative landed aristocrats and innovative capitalistic urbanites, with the latter portrayed as the forces of modernity. Such a definition, however, has consistently foundered on the fact that many of Italy's noble landowners led the charge in pushing for both economic and political change, while wealthy commoners often owned considerable amounts of land, remained chiefly agricultural in their interests, and generally failed to fit the model of a capitalist entrepreneurial class.[62] This muddle was compounded by the importance of an "educational" bourgeoisie, whose titles as physicians, professors, and lawyers assured their consideration as part of the new ruling elite, a fact attested to by their specific inclusion in the electoral franchise of first Piedmont and then Italy even if they failed to meet the strict property requirements.[63]

62. Banti 1996, 65–97.
63. In general see Romanelli 1991.

This confusing contrast between theory and reality has led Marco Meriggi to argue that Italy had multiple *borghesie* rather than a single *borghesia* and that at the time people were more concerned about being considered members of the *ceto civile*. For a man, one's place was defined by an "auto-perception" of oneself "in terms of an adhesion to certain rules of civilization, rather than the enjoyment of a definitive social and professional collation." Having good food and wine on a daily basis, being able to hire a servant in the home, marrying a woman of "some culture"—all constituted, along with the right to vote, a "metaphor of living civilly" which marked one's status as a person who counted.[64] By definition this group was not a static one, yet it viewed itself as exclusive despite the lack of precise criteria of who might actually belong. As Banti has argued, the boundaries of elite status were fluid in both time and space and served as the "object of a daily social construction on the part of whoever wanted to distinguish themselves from the others."[65] Consequently, as the country developed economically and institutionally, greater numbers of people would eventually gain the education or finances to qualify for elite status, but they also had to act as part of the "moral and cultural *milieu*." It was in this normative comportment that the code *duello* would come to play a dominant role in united Italy as men affirmed their right to be considered part of this select group. In fact, the code offered an almost ready-made nationwide notion of masculinity and respectability that could transcend the differing regional and professional backgrounds of the recently empowered "bourgeois" elites.[66]

The political aspects of this process were particularly important. The unification of Italy created a new political structure in a surprisingly short period of time. Although the electoral law of 1861, which was based on that of 1848, has rightly been noted for its exclusivity compared to the overall population, it also suddenly enfranchised a diverse group of people, many of whom had not previously held political power and who were unknown to each other at the national level. In doing so, it endowed a new set of elites with "full citizen" status which made them legally equal among themselves, whatever differences of profession or region might separate them, while setting them

---

64. Meriggi 1996, 74.
65. Banti 1996, viii.
66. As one prefect complained about a deadly duel in his jurisdiction, "[U]n qualsiasi mascalzone ben vestito crede lecito di affermarsi gentiluomo" ("[A]ny well-dressed rascal believes justified in calling himself a gentleman"); Nasalli Rocca 1946, 112.

off from the rest of society. Hence the Italian constitution destroyed the old juridical notion of aristocracy by birth but created a new, juridically sanctioned elite based on the "money or brains" necessary to qualify for the suffrage. However, because the "natural" criterion of birth had been set aside, the new elite was rife with its own intrinsic, albeit porous, hierarchies and strata that ranged over a considerable social and financial topography.[67] In consequence, a wealthy urban proprietor, a landed aristocrat, a prominent commercial lawyer, a hardscrabble pettifogger, a poorly remunerated judge, and a just-comfortable professor all qualified for elite status. Within this world of legal equality, however, social distinctions and ranks had to be constantly asserted, maintained, and rejected, especially through exclusionary membership in the explosion of clubs and associations that proliferated through Italy after unification.

Given the differences and tensions between the various *borghesie* included in the *ceto civile,* to say nothing of the almost automatic inclusion of the old line nobility, symbolic modes of reinforcement were obviously critical in forging individual identities, especially for those who had just barely made it over the threshold of "full citizenship" or those who aspired to such elevation in the near future. Such social symbolism was particularly important for men whose income was not particularly high but whose pretensions were fed by their cultural or professional accomplishments, such as many lawyers or, as we have seen, most journalists. Their need was all the greater because of the considerable ambiguity at the bottom of the middle class where clerks, teachers, surveyors, and the like might see their education and white-collar status as sufficient to membership in the growing elite.[68] In fact, one senses that the real target of the excluding function of the duel was not so much the popular masses, who were automatically considered to be without a refined sense of honor, but rather this liminal group of literate yet "servile" men who might be tempted to assume the mantle of a gentleman. Given the prevailing precepts of chivalry, such an assertion would necessarily need blood to back it up, and it was assumed that men who had "ears of a merchant," that is, a willingness to ignore slights for the sake of gain, would balk at such a challenge. And such distinction became all the more pressing after the electoral law of 1882 opened the suffrage and its attending status to all literate men, a requirement that

---

67. Luigia Caglioti 1996, 141; Banti 1996, 115–37.
68. On aspirations of the lower middle classes, see Lyttleton 1991, 232–33.

still excluded some 70% of the active male population. In the face of these social and political pressures, the culture of honor, enforced by ritualized violence, provided just such a symbolic identity and helped men of the *ceto civile* affirm their equal status as "gentlemen," recognize and affirm new members in the group, and distinguish themselves from the rest of society.

At the top end of the scale, *vertenze* and duels allowed these new elites to test their metal, both literal and figurative, against members of the aristocracy. While dueling could directly enhance the career of a journalist or politician, it could also indirectly legitimize any gentleman's social status as being on a level with counts and barons. Although juridical differences of birth were eliminated by the Piedmontese constitution of 1848, and consequently also that of Italy in 1861, the presence and mystique of the nobility continued to carry great weight after unification. While some nobles had followed their preunitary rulers into obscurity, and others had followed Pius IX into Catholic intransigence, their absence in public life had been more than compensated for by the advent of a national court organized around the king, the extended use of Piedmont's "service" aristocracy during the period of transition, and the gradual acceptance of the new regime by an expanding "liberal" nobility. Aristocrats were thus consistently over-represented in parliament, in the cabinet, in the diplomatic corps, and in certain sectors of the army, although the imbalance shrank throughout the liberal period.[69] If, as Carpi argued in the 1870s, the tendency of the "middle class" was "to make disappear, or at least compensate the difference with the rich and noble classes," then chivalric honor and its defense offered an excellent mechanism for doing so.[70] The potential of the duel in this regard was probably best demonstrated by Gelli's punctilious refusal to categorize differences of birth as opposed to profession in his statistics. "Noble" did not appear among his categories of participants, nor did he bother to set the aristocracy apart when distinguishing between military and bourgeois duels. This approach made perfect sense for Gelli, the son of a coppersmith who made his living by writing, but it also reflected the equalizing function of the duel for the upper strata of Italian society.

Nor could the nobility do much about it, trapped as they were by their own adherence to the chivalric code. As one Piedmontese marquis

---

69. Cardoza 1997, 64–88.
70. Carpi 1878, 129–30.

wrote in his memoirs, "One fought among the *signori*, that is among recognized and accredited members of the only social category which then 'counted': officers and people living off rents. Sometimes, however, it was necessary to fight with professionals or politicians [who were] obviously not signori: or even with parliamentarians of the left. . . ."[71] Those who refused to fight such social inferiors, he continued, would be accused of cowardice and hence be socially disqualified. Not surprisingly then, "mixed" *vertenze* and duels abounded throughout the liberal period. For instance, examining the participants listed in Gelli's 1899 book *Duelli mortali,* which included noble titles along with the names of the participants, 21% or six of the twenty-nine fatal duels recorded between 1860 and 1899 in Italy matched commoners against aristocrats. Such social homogenization becomes even more obvious when one considers the many "mixed" representatives and *padrini* who attended these and other encounters.[72] In the final analysis then, according to the "liberal" rules of the new *ceto civile,* the status of "gentleman"—which automatically subsumed the titled nobility—was at least in part a matter of auto-definition and depended on a man's willingness to know and embrace the rituals of chivalry and, if necessary, to risk his life to protect his honor.[73]

Creating a Spiritual Aristocracy: Honesty, Courage, and Courtesy

These social dynamics were perfectly clear to most practitioners and defenders of the duel. Paolo Fambri, who generally shunned the terms "aristocracy" and "nobility" in his writings, argued in 1869 that the relatively recent resurgence of the *codice duello* had created a new class of gentlemen who had helped promote a new civil society.[74] Some 20 years later, and reprising his role as a mathematician, he would reaffirm this assertion and offer a clever social calculus explaining the historical necessity of honor as a means of identifying new elites: "Gentlemanliness = honesty x courtesy x courage." Note well, he added "that the sign is that of multiplication not addition; and the reason is this: that

---

71. Marchese Mario Incisa della Rocchetta, *Impressioni e ricordi di 'altri tempi,'* typescript in possession of the family. Thanks to Anthony Cardoza for sharing this document.
72. Gelli 1992, 122–86.
73. Gelli 1894, 3, 6.
74. Fambri 1869, 32.

if any of the three factors is reduced to zero it destroys gentlemanliness."[75] The man who could put together this combination naturally demanded respect for his position, and he had to be willing to show both his courtesy and his courage in dealing with his social equals.

Honesty, however, was the critical first component of this equation, as befit a society anxious to excel in liberal self-governance, open politics, and free-market capitalism. Actions that might disqualify a man included usury, theft, fraud, and cheating at cards, to say nothing of perjury. In fact, the alter-ego of honesty was veracity. Speaking the truth was the touchstone of a true gentleman, just as "giving the lie" had always been the most definitive step toward the field of honor since the duel's Renaissance genesis. Nowhere was the value of truth-telling better illustrated than in a letter written in 1886 by the soon-to-be famous social scientist Vilfredo Pareto regarding a rumor in circulation that he did not share the same family lineage as the Marquis of Pareto. The purveyor of this gossip turned out to be a friend of his, Count Carlo Alessandri, and Pareto immediately sent his representatives to demand armed satisfaction. "Finally," he wrote to a friend, "I found the one who is responsible for the infamous calumnies said against me years ago in Pistoia and I will not let him escape me. I want to fight in any way." Aside from preparing to duel, however, Pareto also took substantial pains to secure evidence, both verbal and written, of his proper "civil state," that is, as a legitimate member of the Genovese nobility. What made his efforts in this direction so interesting was his assurance to Ubaldino Peruzzi that it was not the issue of being connected to the marquis that counted but rather the need to prove that he had made no false assertions in this regard: "It is ridiculous that I, a democrat, would fight over the title Marquis for which I don't give a dried fig! But that is not what's in play, if it were I would let it go, but my veracity, that's something else again."[76]

Despite their disdain for past caste distinctions, such sentiments clearly fit an image of a new nobility beyond birth, not just of talent but also of temperament, and it was this same image that prompted Italy's most prestigious philosopher, Benedetto Croce, to characterize Italy's early ruling elites as "a spiritual aristocracy of upright and loyal gentlemen . . . a permanent source of moral and political education."[77] The attending icon of this spiritual aristocracy was the medieval knight,

75. Fambri 1888C, 1.
76. Letter of Sept. 22, 1886, in Busimo 1977, 793–94.
77. Croce 1963, 5.

whose symbolic devices often appeared in both fencing and dueling manuals. Such references could be subtle, as when Costantino Cacchione attached knightly spurs to the simple blazon adorning his *Scherma e codice per duello* of 1895; or they could be more blatant, as evidenced by the lance, helmet, shield, and heraldic trumpet (complete with the cross of Savoy) appearing on the cover of Masaniello Parise's *Trattato teorico-pratico della scherma* of 1884.[78] Many of these same devices are obvious in a 1902 print celebrating the military's official fencing academy in Rome, although the presence of the swashbuckling Musketeer offers an extra layer of anachronism to the mixture (see image 3).[79] However, it was one of Italy's most prestigious codes, written by General Achille Angelini, whose career we have traced in the previous chapter, that pulled out all the stops (see image 4). Here the General's illustrator has gone beyond the symbols of helmet, lance, and heraldic trumpet to actually personify a peacock-plumed knight on horseback, complete with his own herald, whose trumpet proudly sports the she-wolf on the ensign of Rome, thus tying the capital city to a host of Savoyard crosses and eagles. The latter symbols cleverly underline the pan-Italian nature of chivalry while liminally suggesting royal, if not state, approval. Such iconography directly linked Italy's *gentiluomini* to ancient attributes of knighthood—courage, loyalty, and gallantry—while simultaneously recalling ancient rituals of individual combat that reinforced the duel as the touchstone of elite status.

As a young man, Croce himself became caught up in the *oblige* of this new *noblesse* when he fought a duel in April 1895 against one of his own friends, Duke Riccardo Carafa d'Andria, and the circumstances of the affair clearly reinforce Fambri's aforementioned equation linking physical courage and personal prestige in liberal Italy. Croce asked Carafa to represent him in a *vertenza* over an article he had written criticizing the sad state of Italian literature. However, given the rarified nature of the "insults," the negotiators decided that no duel need ensue. Unfortunately, Carafa let it be known that the reason he had proffered the olive branch was that he feared that Croce's lack of experience in the martial arts, combined with a gimpy leg from an old injury, might ultimately prove dangerous in a duel. This unintended insult was too much for Croce, who wrote a letter angrily chastising his maladroit representative for automatically assuming both weakness and cowardice

78. For another example see Ristori 1872, cover.
79. Print kindly provided by Claudio Mancini. Also see the cover of Iviglia 1907, a vade mecum for military cadets.

Image 3
Postcard (1902) from Italy's official fencing academy in Rome

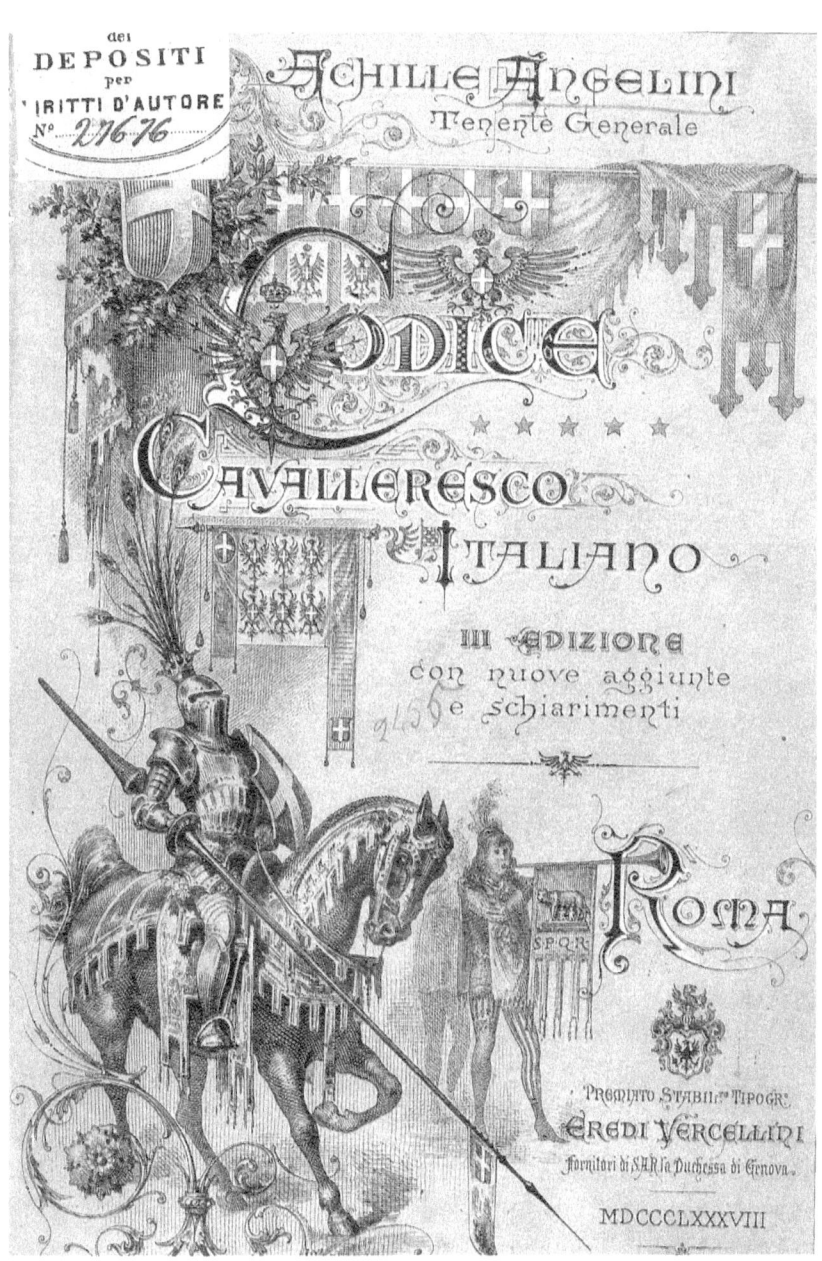

Image 4
Cover of Achille Angelini's 1888 dueling manual

on his part. Carafa had no choice at this point but to challenge Croce and then try, as an expert fencer and seasoned duelist, to do him as little damage as possible. The participants in the actual duel constituted a virtual advertisement for the pretensions of the new "aristocracy," with the commoner Croce and his two *borghesi* seconds facing off against the good duke and no fewer than two princes.[80] In the end, Croce was lightly wounded, despite (or maybe because of) a brave effort to take some fencing lessons, but he described the event in what can only be called affectionate terms: "at dawn, in a beautiful villa of Portici, I had the pleasure of seeing my friend Carafa as my enemy and receiving from him a gentile little wound on the cheek: which was a natural thing on the part of an old cavalry officer toward a litterato aspiring to be a philosopher."[81] The journalistic antagonism in this case had obviously ceded primacy to the greater issue of mental and physical mettle, and once Croce's blood had stained his cheek, he and Carafa resumed their previous amity. He had stood his ground and ritually declared his equality with an aristocratic cavalry officer in terms of bravery if not swordsmanship.

As we have seen for officers, the importance of courage permeated the code *duello* at a variety of levels. First, one had to respond to even a hint of insult with alacrity. Failure to act within 24 hours implied either cowardice or a lack of regard for one's own honor—both equally devastating to one's standing as a gentleman. For this reason, a dated copy of all correspondence regarding a *vertenza* had to be scrupulously maintained so as to be able to prove the timing of one's actions. Having arrived on the field of honor, it was critical to demonstrate resolve, calm, and *sang-froid*. A man had to stand his ground in the face of his opponent's bullet or saber without any sign of fear or misgiving. While it was obviously better to emerge from a duel unscathed, the crucial issue was not who won but that both men had faced danger undaunted in defense of their honor. As one pundit put it, "Winner or loser matters little, from the baptism of blood and fire comes the baptism of honor."[82] It is important to note that courage for a gentleman was not thought to be learned, acquired, or intermittent. It was natural, essential, and constant. Consequently, once a man's courage had failed him, either in the preliminaries or in the execution of an affair of honor, he was held to have demonstrated his true nature and to have disqualified himself

80. Artieri 1957, 133–39.
81. Quoted in Nicolini 1962, 158–59.
82. Di Menza e Vella 1875, 2.

from demanding or offering satisfaction in the future. True courage was never really gained or lost; it was simply part of being a real man.[83]

Fambri's gentlemanly attributes of honesty and courage might apply, at least in theory, across a broad social spectrum. In contrast, however, his concept of *cortesia* was naturally more exclusive precisely because it had to be learned. Decorum, bearing, and style came with exposure to and "embodiment" of prevailing elite norms, and being a gentleman required knowing how to behave correctly in polite society. This definition was and still is manifest in the Italians' use of the term *educazione*, which does not relate to matters academic (generally categorized as *istruzione*) but refers instead to social *savoir faire*. Good table manners, proper personal comportment (e.g., covering one's mouth during a yawn or when using a toothpick) and civil behavior toward others, all added up to make a person *educato*. Conversely, *maleducato* was one of the most serious epithets that could be directed at a gentleman. The need to learn and internalize such standardized behavior on the part of Italian elites, and especially those newly arrived to the *ceto civile*, was reflected in the extraordinary growth of etiquette manuals and self-improvement books during the nineteenth century, particularly after unity.[84]

Courtesy for a gentleman, however, went well beyond how to hold one's fork or handle a handkerchief. Chivalrous sensitivity to what was proper and improper in mixed company reflected a dichotomy of gender identities which was tied to growing middle-class concerns of respectability.[85] Men had to know how to treat ladies as befit their distinct nature and protected (not to say subordinate) status. Equally important, however, was how courtesy helped regulate behavior among men themselves, both in traditional public areas such as theaters and cafes and in the fast-growing number of clubs and associations which offered semi-public spaces of male-only culture. These male-only domains derived their original impetus from the fact that the late eighteenth and early nineteenth centuries saw the advent of increasingly gendered views of reality and society which radically altered notions of masculinity and femininity. This change has been variously attributed to a mania for biological categorization during the Enlightenment, to the propagation of a "male aesthetic" from classical Greek models, and to the fact that middle-class men worked more and more outside of the home and

83. For pan-European aspects of "courage" see Nye 1995, 74.
84. Botteri 1999, 188–89. Lyttleton (1991, 232) suggests that the main market was probably the lower middle classes.
85. In general see Mosse 1985.

needed a refuge of domestic security to escape the pressures of early capitalism.[86] It was also tied to the evolution of liberalism which embraced an ideology of "separate spheres" that relegated upper- and middle-class women to the privacy of the home while their male counterparts handled the public arena of work and politics.[87] In Italy the institutional analogue of this socially and sexually exclusive public realm was the comfortable world of men's clubs and associations, which had evolved right along with liberal politics and which Meriggi has argued acted as a "gymnasium of civil education" where men learned to respect themselves as they respected others, normalizing useful regulatory behaviors while enhancing their social status.[88] In the end, men who could handle themselves and their associations effectively felt that they could just as readily be trusted with public power.

The associative movement in Italy was clearly connected to the contemporaneous proliferation of the dueling ethic through the peninsula after unity. Above all, the clubs and societies offered "extra-familia" all-male enclaves of sociability, which were theoretically open to all, but both exclusive and hierarchical in practice.[89] To meet the financial and personal requisites of entry was in and of itself an honor and confirmed one's position in the *ceto civile* as a gentleman, especially for non-noble elites who now entered a social geography (although not always the same spaces) that had generically been dominated by aristocrats and *rentiers*.[90] Within the associations, and especially in the recreational clubs based on the English model, men could meet and socialize in a masculine world clearly distinct from the old salon tradition which had been within a family setting and had allowed for the active participation of women. The new approach, which almost universally excluded women, reflected, according to Raffaele Romanelli, "the affirmation of a modern bourgeois society, individualistic and egalitarian, and therefore virile and politicized."[91] It was within this virile, political ethos, where men could read newspapers, drink coffee, play cards, and gamble, that the masculinity of chivalric honor was constantly reinforced among Italy's new elites.[92] For a man to fail to defend his status as a gentleman against

86. Mosse 1996; Tosh 1999, 11–26.
87. Clark 1995, 2.
88. Meriggi 1992, 95–101.
89. Romanelli 1994, 814.
90. Meriggi 1992, 137.
91. Romanelli 1994, 820.
92. On the importance of social clubs in the transmission of notions of honor in France see Nye 2000.

insult or injury meant almost sure expulsion from whatever club or circle to which he had managed to gain access: a symbolic shaming that would reverberate through all of his social relations.

Beyond membership, however, behavior within the clubs and circles was equally important in reinforcing the code of honor.[93] Punctilious rules abounded designed to maintain a calm and dignified atmosphere which reflected well on the members. Feet were to be kept off the furniture, umbrellas should be placed just so, and newspapers should be replaced on their racks. Inspectors were assigned from the membership on a rotating basis to assure compliance with such regulations, and it was assumed that rules of play would be scrupulously observed and all gambling debts would be acquitted immediately.[94] Equal within the confines of the club, members should treat each other with the utmost respect, and conflicts should be adjudicated quickly and quietly without recourse to bravado or brouhaha. The boundaries of such polite behavior, however, were ultimately policed by the mechanisms of honor, which offered a controlled and ritualized response for a gentleman who felt he had not been granted due respect. In this case a *vertenza* might allow representatives to sort out a solution, or, if not, a duel would act to restore both men's honor without either having to admit fault.[95] This was the lovely logic of the system: it allowed a redress of grievances without either man having to act in an obsequious or culpable way, all the while asserting the privileged identity of the group as a whole.

The emphasis on equality and self-control among gentlemen in the club setting reinforced parallel compulsions throughout the entire *ceto civile*. By demanding equal treatment within a self-proclaimed elite, gentlemen set themselves apart from the rest of society as a group. But given the highly stratified and competitive nature of that group, men had to be on constant guard against slights and insults that might impinge on their honor and lead to derogation. A heightened sense of honor resulted, for which one might risk life and limb over the most trivial offenses such as staring too long into a man's eyes, reading his newspaper without permission, or failing to return his greeting on the street. Angelini, grand doyen of Italy's dueling community, talked about a true gentleman having a refined "chivalrous instinct" that would force him to react to an

---

93. For example, ACS, Biblioteca, *"Vertenza* Conte Ivan de Vargas Machuca—Principe Altieri, Roma: Columbo, 1930, 4.
94. Romanelli 1994, 832–34.
95. Nye 1993, 128–29.

insult without thought of the consequences.[96] This distinction explains the frequent use of the word *squisitissimo*—an adjective which implied taste, discrimination, and excellence—to describe not only proper behavior but also proper feelings regarding honor.[97] Such definitions did not automatically exclude any groups or classes in society, but they did imply education, etiquette, and social contacts that were far beyond the reach of most Italian men. In the final analysis, a gentleman was a man willing to fight a duel over personal honor according to the regulations laid out by other gentlemen. There was a certain egalitarianism in this definition, but it worked primarily for the upper-middle classes and had its obvious limits at the bottom, especially since a duel could be an expensive proposition, including fees for the doctors, gifts for the seconds, and—in a pinch—money for emergency fencing lessons.[98]

Once on the field of honor, one had to demonstrate the same self-control expected of a gentleman in all of his affairs. This implied courage, of course, in the face of immediate danger, but it also meant that one had internalized the rules of the game and could play accordingly. Advantage should never be pushed unfairly, strict attention should be paid to the presiding director, and a touch should never be celebrated just as a wound should never be lamented. Losing control of one's emotions or actions during combat was infinitely worse than being wounded and could bar a man from requesting satisfaction in the future. It could also open him up to heavy legal sanctions, because failure to abide by the rules meant that the lenient penalties reserved for proper duelists gave way to the full weight of the criminal code.

For instance, in 1889 an ex-deputato, Giuseppe Bonajuto, was fighting a saber duel with a lawyer, Enrico Fongi, over a mutually insulting exchange of letters, when he was stabbed in the chest. The director of combat called "Alt" and Fongi began to obey, but Bonajuto grabbed the offending blade with his left hand and drove his own sword deep into Fongi's neck, an action that narrowly missed killing the man. The *padrini* of *both* parties were shocked by such an egregious infringement of the regulations, and they published a scathing denunciation of Bonajuto in the newspapers. More to the point, the *procuratore del re* indicted Bonajuto for attempted murder. Evidence was collected from all the participants, and Bonajuto's lawyer was able to substantiate that his client was hard

---

96. Angelini 1888, 211.
97. For example, Associazione della Stampa 1877, 18.
98. One might add expenses for travel, for a director, for weapons, and even for lookouts for the police. See Mussolini 1974, 35; Nadi 1955, 149; and Gelli 1912, 8.

of hearing and thus might not have heard the command to stop. The court consequently dropped the homicide charge but still convicted Bonajuto for personal assault and sentenced him to 18 months in jail plus disqualification from public office—the latter being a punishment reserved only for dishonorable crimes. In stark contrast, Fongi, who had followed the rules of chivalry, got off with only 16 days in jail, despite the fact that he had wounded Bonajuto first.[99] Such was the legal and social power inherent in the dueling code, the details of which were supposed to be second nature to true gentlemen.[100] Consequently, the best notice that could appear in a newspaper regarding a duel was that both men had acquitted themselves as "perfect" gentlemen and that they had mutually affirmed and reconciled their honor. Graphic, almost scientific, descriptions of what wounds were received were included as well, but they were designed to demonstrate that the flow of blood had sanctioned the end of the conflict rather than designate a winner. *Sangfroid* mixed with real blood was what really counted.

Respectability, Self-Control, and Countertypes

At heart, the defining element of both courtesy and courage for the *ceto civile* was self-control, and this control necessarily extended to a gentleman's family. George Mosse has argued, along with others, that the early nineteenth century saw an increase in concern over respectability in both sexual and domestic matters. He attributes the new emphasis to a variety of factors, including the rise of Pietism and Evangelicalism, a romantic longing for the supposed moral purity of the Middle Ages, and the need for people to find stability in a rapidly changing world. Respectability also lent itself handily to the forces of nationalism which used a dichotomy of normal and abnormal sexuality to direct men's "lower passions" to higher patriotic purposes and emphasized the solid family as a surrogate for the nation.[101] As previously noted, the protection of women's purity and sensibilities became a defining trope of the nationalist movement during the Risorgimento, and the pressure toward social and sexual conformity only increased as Italy sought its place as a

---

99. *Rivista penale* 1899, vol. 50, 122–23.
100. For a good example of legal intervention in the face of "ungentlemanly behavior" on the field of honor see *Cavalleria* 1889.
101. Mosse 1985, 9–25.

"real" nation in Europe and the world.[102] Thus Menet Genty has pointed out that the Italian theater consistently pushed an extremely prudish stereotype for women, especially when compared to their French counterparts.[103] Increasingly relegated to the private sphere of the home, elite women in public spaces were expected to be accompanied by a man and screened from coarse or rude behavior.[104] Conversely, women had to watch their own language, especially in public, because chivalry dictated that a husband be prepared to fight over any offensive words on the part of his wife.[105]

Even more important, a gentleman had to assure the sexual discipline of the female members of his household. Daughters were expected to remain chaste until marriage, and wives to remain faithful to their husbands. Women's honor tended to be unidimensionally sexual and derived its importance by reflecting on the men in the family. Illicit sexual relations went beyond propriety and sentiment to issues of property, inheritance, and marriage strategies, and so carried a special economic weight that could render them all the more devastating to a man's status as a gentleman.[106] A wife's honor, according to one dueling advocate, was a gentleman's "first and inestimable treasure, which surpasses the worth of his own life."[107] If a man were violated in this most sacrosanct notion of respectability, he automatically had to challenge and fight the seducer who had trespassed against him or else he would remain ostracized and ridiculed. As we shall later see in the discussion of the debate over the duel, proponents of the chivalric ethic would effectively argue that there was simply no other recourse in these matters. They struck at the heart of a man's domestic world and were too private to take to any other forum of adjudication. On the contrary, there could be no negotiation, no explanation, and no satisfaction granted in such cases—blood had to flow in order to redeem the honor of the *talamo,* or marriage bed.

As befit the gravity of sexual relations, duels stemming from such matters of family intimacy were generally reported to be more dangerous in their consequences. One journalist, for instance, recounted that a certain Baron Compagna, famous for his bellicose, not to say blood-

102. Patriarca 2005, 41, 42. More generally see De Grazia 1992, 6.
103. Menet Genty 1989, 271.
104. On the associational life of women especially in Naples see Luigia Caglioti 1996, 137–50.
105. For example, Corte d'Onore Permanente Firenze, "Lodo *vertenza* Vaccari-Gatti," Firenze: Ricci, 1926, 36–37. BNR, Levi.
106. On legal aspects of "family discipline" see Rizzo 2004.
107. Modugno 1880, 50.

thirsty, approach to directing duels, was brought in to assure the severity of those encounters pertaining to the heart.[108] There is, unfortunately, no reliable quantitative method to determine the greater risk involved in such affairs because Gelli never cross-referenced his statistics on causes of duels with those on the physical damages incurred, which are discussed below. However, if one examines the 29 fatal duels listed between 1860 and 1899 in Gelli's book *Duelli mortali del XIX secolo,* eight or 28% arose from *cause intime,* or affairs of the heart. This number stands in contrast to only 8% of duels (279 out of 3,610) arising from such causes as reported in Gelli's general statistics and suggests that indeed the emotions tied to adultery or family honor tended to make matters more serious. On the other hand, the 21 fatal duels not associated with intimacy also do not justify the idea that other types of duels were necessarily without their dangers.

Whatever the case, the difficulties of dealing with adultery without recourse to the duel were amply illustrated by the case of Vilfredo Pareto, who in 1901 suffered the indignity of having his wife, Alessandrina Bakounine, run off with his cook while he was away in France. Already a respected professor of political economy at the University of Lausanne, Pareto was saddened and embarrassed by the loss of his wife, but he was positively mortified by the social status of her lover. "One cannot fight a duel with one's own cook," he complained to Maffeo Pantaleoni, and this unfortunate chivalric fact threw him into a quandary as to how to proceed. Unable to defend his honor in the standard way and anxious to protect his finances against any claim by "the lover of my ex-cook," he would have to resort to the courts, which would incur both expense and scandal. Such was his concern for the latter that he considered moving to the border town of Domo d'Ossola for a couple of months and thus avoid the notoriety that a trial might provoke in Florence, his legal residence in Italy. These issues may have been less galling if he had been able to fight his offender, but the servile status of the cook—especially a man in his own service—forbade such recourse. The social implication was that the cook had no honor to defend, and to challenge him would have put Pareto's own status as a gentleman in question.[109]

Pareto's dilemma points to the general insensitivity of Italian elites to conceptions of lower-class honor. Workers and peasants provided ready countertypes against which gentlemen could compare themselves and

---

108. For example, Maurano 1973, 77.
109. Pareto to Pantaleone, Céligny, Nov. 29, 1901. Fondo Pareto, Banca Popolare di Sondrio.

their actions.¹¹⁰ This reaction was partly due to the poverty and illiteracy of Italy's working classes, 62% of which were still engaged in tilling the soil in 1881, a figure that would change little by the turn of the century.¹¹¹ From today's standpoint it is difficult to fathom just how abject conditions were among many Italian workers and peasants during the nineteenth century, and in some areas unification brought even more misery rather than less. Often hungry, ill-clothed, and poorly housed, the masses, most of whom spoke only local dialect rather than Italian, seemed to stand totally at odds with the sensibilities and niceties of honor common to the urban upper and middle classes. Although there was a strong literary/political tradition of portraying the peasantry and rural life as sources of healthy, unspoiled "energy" for the new country, it was counterbalanced by an underlying fear of the *popolo minuto* who lived unfortunate and unruly lives, constantly threatening the good order of society.¹¹² Suffice it to say that in a monumental treatise on crime published in 1870, Italy's foremost police authority, Giovanni Bolis, generically described workers as a "dangerous class" along with prostitutes, pimps, and thieves.¹¹³ Such a designation was then given a patina of positivistic legitimacy by Lombroso, who created "scientific" subcategories of delinquency that included most of the population.¹¹⁴

There seemed little hope of raising the bulk of this *volgo* up to the standards of polite society, and Botteri has shown how even etiquette manuals written for the *popolo* were actually aimed at the lower middle classes and not the *popolaccio*, that is, not the "mob, the rabble, the vile multitude, the poor people, the low people, the bestial, filthy people," to which one of her authors referred.¹¹⁵ One might have added *facchini* as well, in reference to Italy's ubiquitous urban porters and carters, whose rough manners were so notorious that applying the term to a gentleman would have brought an immediate demand for satisfaction. There was also a particular disrespect attached to peasants, which we have already seen in the remarks of Giovanni Nicotera when he was attempting to insult a political rival. For him, "farmer" and "sheepherder" were epithets synonymous with *vigliacco* or coward, implying baseness of spirit as well as of work.¹¹⁶ And this came from a Mazzinian democrat proud of his

110. On countertypes see Mosse 1996, 56–76.
111. Meriggi 1993.
112. Bollati 1983, 62–105.
113. Bolis 1871, 394–96.
114. Bollatti 1983, 157.
115. Botteri 1999, 330, 359–62.
116. Also note the term *bifolco,* or ploughman, to indicate a lout, churl, or boor.

revolutionary credentials. Plebes of the *infimo ceto* (lower class) were portrayed as insensitive to insult, and one of Italy's most influential dueling manuals maintained that neither peasants nor artisans felt any dishonor in being slapped in the face.[117] Although Italy's gentlemen might be willing to grant a certain *cavalleria rusticana* to the working classes (e.g., mitigating penalties for crimes of passion), they regarded honor and the duel as a defining feature and obvious prerogative of "civil" society, quite beyond the comprehension of the *volgo* or general populace.[118] As one positivist deputy proclaimed in parliament in 1898, the duel "occurs for reasons of an elevated moral order, that is for offenses of such a high level that the *volgo* cannot feel them." He reiterated the point later in the speech: "The common people do not have the duel because they do not arrive at the high sensibility to have it."[119]

As with the other attributes of a gentleman, the fundamental issue here was one of self-control. In a sort of chivalrous sleight of hand, the fact that plebeians settled their personal differences without benefit of refined rituals was blamed on their robust passions, quick irritability, and lack of emotional restraint.[120] They also used the wrong tools! Constant contrast was made between the violent and uncontrolled passions of working men, who fought on a moment's notice with their hands or knives, as opposed to the calm adjudication and respectable rituals of dueling gentlemen and their refined weapons.[121] Thus a distinction between the plebeian knife and the civil-class sword was a recurring theme among those defending the dueling ethic.[122] Consider, for instance, the assertion of Cesare Alberto Blengini di San Grato, a fencing master who published a dueling code in 1868: "The common people and lowly plebes will perhaps use their fists or a club; they will also use a knife; but all of these—even if used without faithlessness, without treachery, without surprise behind one's back, are weapons of a scoundrel, worse than an assassin, from whom an educated man flees as he flees from tolerating his own shame."[123] As the crude peasant or the rough worker offered a countertype to the cultured gentleman, so, conversely, did the sword stand in contrast to the work-a-day knife, used

---

117. Angelini 1888, 4. Also see Crivellari 1884, 39.
118. For example, Modugno 1880, 49–52.
119. Venturi 1898, 4, 7.
120. Gambarella 1898, 8.
121. This distinction is more throughly examined in Hughes 2007B.
122. For example, Fambri 1869, 90; De Rosis 1868, 85; Cesarano 1874, 137; and Di Menza e Vella 1875, 12.
123. Blengini 1868, 12.

for a variety of manual tasks, and the perfidious dagger, a corrupt and sordid weapon, the very nature of which prevented its use for noble purposes.

Although some writers and poets of the period talked about the importance of knife fighting as a key to a man's status among the lower classes, legislators, jurists, and chivalric commentators generally portrayed such conflict as outside the bounds of "real" honor. This assumption on the part of Italy's liberal leaders came out in the continuous debate regarding the duel's legal status that began shortly after unification. Dealing with fine distinctions of definition and punishment, the discussion often focused on whether there was something fundamentally different between a duel between gentlemen and a lower-class street fight or *rissa*. This was a sore point for Italy's liberals because the new country would rather quickly gain a "sad primacy" for having the highest murder rate in Europe, a result of frequent and deadly knife fights among the lower classes.[124] The tension formed part of the cultural baggage of Italy's liberal leaders as they wrestled with how to square lenient treatment of the duel with heavy penalties for plebian *risse*. Thus one legislative commission in 1870 argued that it was important to avoid that those accused of "crimes committed during a duel be equated with vulgar assassins."[125]

The basic difference, as another commission would argue in 1875, was one of deferred gratification and rational self-control. "The *rissa* is an impetuous event, an event in which passion plays a greater role than reason; the duel in contrast is a mediated event, an event preorganized with mature counsel; it is an event regulated by customs so that it is almost elevated to the level of an institution."[126] Carrara, one of Italy's greatest legal commentators, put it another way: "In the *rissa* there operates a concept of disdain: in the duel there operates a concept of honor, of common danger, and of reciprocal consensus."[127] Crivellari, who studied the problem more closely than anyone else, offered a parallel argument, which at least took into account the attributes of *educazione:* "Among people of the other [lower] class, one responds to a terrible insult with the impetuousness of anger, with a knife blow that kills the adversary; no other objective do they have than to offend the offender

---

124. Boschi 1998, 129–30.
125. Parliamentary Commission on Codice Penale, session of Jan. 14–15, 1870, in Crivellari 1884, 119.
126. Parliamentary Commission on Codice Penale, session of 26 April, 1875; ibid., 162.
127. Quoted in ibid., 49. This argument would be echoed by the Rome's Court of Cassazione in 1881 (*Rivista penale* 1881, vol. 15, 208) and later by Brunetti 1914, 124.

in life and limb. Among people civilized by education the need runs in the opposite direction; one lets anger disappear, one sends a written challenge."[128] This emphasis on self-control helps explain as well the fixation that Italian gentlemen had on the seriousness of physical contact in prompting duels. *Vie di fatto,* such as slapping, hitting, or kicking, were among the most serious insults and often beyond the repair of any chivalric negotiations that might occur among the representatives in an affair. To strike someone was to lose control of one's temper and one's body, just as to suffer such a slight without immediate reaction implied subservient status. A duel was doubly necessary in this case as much to resurrect and reinforce the offending gentleman's assertions of equanimity, far from the brawling images of the savage plebes, as it was to assuage the aggrieved honor of the injured party.

The issue of self-control went to another common assumption about lower-class quarrels, which was that the participants were quite often portrayed as drunk.[129] Consider Crivellari's reaction to a court decision in Florence which threatened to loosen the rules as to what constituted a "legal" duel.

> I cite an example: an argument breaks out between two peasants (*villani*) in a pub: the one says to the other: come outside with me, take your knife out of your pocket and to this [the knife] we will entrust our fortune. The adversary accepts; the two knives are the same; the two exit; the one is before the other; they fight; they wound each other. According to the maxim of the Florentine court, this would be nothing more and nothing less than a duel. But if those French gentlemen who over past centuries fought while scorning the severe edicts of their Kings; if those Italian gentlemen, who went down to the closed field to sustain the fatherland's honor, could take off their winding sheets, they would rise up out of the sepulchre and make heard their voice, oh! Without doubt they would find a word of reproach against a modern jurisprudence which with its judgement wants to confuse them with drunken peasants, who of chivalrous procedure know not even the name.[130]

Here Crivellari's image of drunk peasants underlines the lower classes' lack of control over their drinking habits while placing them in stark

128. Crivellari 1884, 49.
129. Bolis (1871, 394, 417) saw abuse of alcohol and lack of sexual control as the fundamental problems of the working classes.
130. Crivellari 1884, 257.

contrast to Italy's sober patriotic gentlemen, an effect enhanced by his choice of the term *villano* for "peasant," with its implications of ill-breeding and boorishness, rather than the more neutral *contadino*. By conflating issues of class, comportment, and nationalism, Crivellari unconsciously leads us through the underlying logic that connected chivalry and Italy's *ceto civile*. Only men who could truly control their emotions and their bodies were fit to rule the nation.

Women, of course, were automatically excluded from this definition, and they offered another handy, albeit more complex, countertype to the true gentleman. The complexity arose from the fact that upper- and middle-class women could, unlike peasants and workers, eventually understand notions of chivalry and even participate in their regeneration. But women's nature was often portrayed as being antithetical to the dueling code: their unrestrained emotions and maternal instincts supposedly balked at the courage and risk necessary to the defense of honor. Consequently, a number of cautionary tales in the dueling literature describe the need for women to be brought away from their natural pacifist tendencies and to be educated to the social necessity of embracing the code *duello* for their sons and husbands.[131]

The best example of this theme is undoubtedly contained in Francesco Garzes' play *Bianca D'Oria*, published in 1892. The central character, Bianca, the daughter of Duke Fabrizio d'Oria, is betrothed to a dashing young marquis and ex-cavalry officer, Giorgio d'Arbia, whom she loves desperately. When, during a fox hunt, Bianca is secretly accosted and violently kissed by a family friend, Count Maurizio di Sangro, she reluctantly relates the incident to Giorgio. He immediately declares his intention to kill or be killed in a duel with Maurizio, but Bianca says she loves him too much and cannot bear the thought of losing him. She suggests escaping, to which Giorgio retorts, "Would you have me a coward?" She responds:

> I love you. I am a poor girl who knows nothing of life; but I understand through instinct that which is grand and generous. I know that you men have inexorable laws; I know that to these laws you are obligated to sacrifice mind, heart, passion, life.—And yet, to the man who says he loves me, I ask a terrible trial; but a secure one. Put my love up against the prejudices, the laws, the customs, and habits. I will recompense you

---

131. For example, Tomei 1898; Praga 1926; Ferrari 1928; "I bimbi" in Fambri 1888B. Cf. De Simone 1906.

for the sacrifice you make for me, and in my affection you will find such sweetness to make you forget past bitterness.[132]

When Giorgio still balks, she swears on her mother's memory that if he fights Maurizio, she will never marry him. This drastic oath has the desired effect, and he promises to hold his peace even if insulted, but he bluntly warns Bianca that she will come to regret her actions.

Sure enough, Giorgio is unable to control his anger and immediately confronts Maurizio who publicly threatens him with a horsewhip. Caught up in his promise to Bianca, Giorgio cannot respond appropriately to this "extremely grave insult" and even has to reject an on-the-spot offer from a friend to be his *padrino*. Everything goes downhill from there. Rumors soon circulate about his personal courage and, worse, about Bianca's own chastity. Giorgio's club begins procedures to have him expelled for conduct unbecoming a gentleman, and his closest friend—the Marquis Giuliano Riva—has to fight a derivative duel with a mutual acquaintance in defense of Giorgio's good name. Bianca observes all of this with increasing concern and indeed begins to doubt her actions as well as Giorgio's character. "But if I did badly, why then did he capitulate [to me] accepting that which he should not have accepted? Was I mistaken in imposing myself on a man, or was he wrong in having obeyed a young lady [*fanciulla*]?" She also finds herself in a double bind: She cannot tell anyone that Giorgio's lack of action comes from his promise to her, because this would portray him as being under the thumb of his fiancée and hence add "the ridiculous to cowardice...."[133] Thus as the play progresses, public impressions are becoming increasingly important to the heroine.

Meanwhile, Maurizio, who had originally insulted her, comes to tell her that he is leaving forever, but that he appreciates her discretion regarding the "incident." He adds that he feels Giorgio, who has shared that discretion, to be a true gentleman. She soon shares this message with Giorgio, who mysteriously departs immediately upon hearing it. Shortly thereafter she is informed that there has been an accident with a pistol and Maurizio has been killed. All of this sets up the final scene in which Bianca and Giorgio are to sign their wedding contract. Guests are scarce because Giorgio's supposed cowardice has soiled the family's reputation. By this point, Bianca's feelings for Giorgio have

132. Garzes 1892, 50.
133. Ibid., 140.

deteriorated to the point that she scorns his celebratory gift of flowers. She confides to a friend that she does not love him but will go through with the ceremony because everything is actually her fault—she forced him to prove his love by dishonoring himself. At the last minute she receives a posthumous note from Maurizio which leads her to believe that he truly loved her and that his death was no accident but a suicide caused by his remorse for having insulted her.

Somehow this seems to change everything: her vile assailant turns out be noble and her betrothed a coward who could not stand up to her own girlish dictates. She approaches the table to sign the marriage contract, but when she is handed the pen, she can't go through with it; she throws the pen to the side and shouts, "No, No!" She then explains to Giorgio:

> I should have lied, I know; but in the supreme moment my soul rebelled. That which you should have done, I have done. You are a man, used to fighting. It was up to you to let me know that which you can concede to passion without dishonoring yourself. You should have broken your promise to me. It would have given me great pain at first, but great pride in you afterwards. You should have shown me that in love there is all the savage poetry of life.[134]

She then relates that in the confrontation between the two men, it had been Maurizio who had taken honorable action in suicide. She cannot marry a man she does not respect.

But there are revelations still to come! Giorgio publicly declares that Bianca has been doubly deceived and that he actually killed Maurizio in a legitimate duel. The "accident" had been invented to cover the crime of chivalry, and the "suicide" was her own misunderstanding of Maurizio's note. Bianca falls to her knees knowing now that Giorgio had been right all along. But he stops her and says she deserves to stand on her own two feet, for she had learned her lesson on her own: "If you had not seen in yourself that slow and ferocious reaction, it would have been I Giorgio d'Arbia who would no longer marry Bianca d'Oria." Hearing that she has successfully passed this unknown ordeal of honor, she collapses in his arms, and the curtain falls.

Bianca's collapse at the dramatic denouement signifies her ultimate reliance on her man, but it also further underlines the overall impor-

---

134. Ibid., 148.

tance of self-control in the chivalric equation. As countertypes, women, workers, and peasants all lacked this essential ingredient in one way or another, and this lack impinged not only on the mechanisms of honor but also on the political criteria of rationality and judgment. Power should be allocated only to those capable of controlling their feelings, their bodies, and, of course, their words. As recently pointed out by Madeleine Hurd, this theme was common in liberal regimes. Refining Habermas's ideas on the bourgeois public sphere, Hurd examines how manners, mores, and masculinity became critically important markers in the new ethos of liberalism which stressed probity, openness, and rationality as hallmarks of discussion and action. Liberal public debate was supposed to be universally inclusive, but, of course, it was not: it ringed itself with defenses to exclude various groups who were seen as unfit for political discourse. Thus "those unable to govern their passions or themselves—criminals, women, children, cult members, paupers, drunkards,—remained suspect."[135] Public discussion among "rational" people became an essential part of sovereignty which was now invested in a "transparent" state, the actions of which were constantly under public scrutiny. Newspapers, political associations, demonstrations, and speeches all became part of the public sphere of power relations. In consequence, participants in this system had to demonstrate good manners, which assured reasonable debate and discourse, while maintaining a new "public masculinity" that stressed responsibility, respectability, sobriety, and a concern for one's family.

Hurd's desire in delineating the rules of liberal manhood is to discuss how workers and socialists tried to break into the system with a "sort of hyperrespectability, a demonstrative and public display of manly self-discipline," but her analysis applies handily to the importance of the dueling code among Italy's elites. First, the duel was used to police behavior within public debate, either oral or written. If one transcended the boundaries of propriety—especially with one's comments—a duel (or simply a *vertenza*) might ensue that would restore the balance of honor. On the other hand, the very nature of the duel with its own legislation and rules aided in the process of creating civility, but more important it allowed members of the *ceto civile* to demonstrate a reasoned composure which they felt set them off from the rest of society. Understanding and embracing the code of chivalry allowed a restricted number of new men to join the political and social elite while

135. Hurd 2000, 76–77.

protecting their privileged identity (and the right to vote) from the masses as well as from their own women.[136]

Legal and Physical Impunity

The social and political functions, both direct and indirect, of dueling in Italy were enhanced by the fact that men of honor actually faced little real danger from either the law or the sword. As previously suggested, the Piedmontese Criminal Code of 1859, which was quickly adopted throughout united Italy (with the exception of Tuscany), was notoriously lenient with regard to the duel compared to those of the other preunitary regimes, some of which still prescribed the death penalty for the simple act of crossing swords. Even compared to the earlier Piedmontese Code of 1839, the 1859 law substantially reduced sanctions for convicted duelists. It set the minimum penalty for homicide in a duel at one year in prison instead of three, abandoned automatic exclusion from public office as a penalty, and allowed the transmutation of hard labor to simple confinement depending on the circumstances. Whereas seriously wounding an opponent in 1839 could bring seven years of hard labor, in 1859 the maximum was set at two years. All in all, then, the 1859 code represented a more positive attitude toward the duel, which, one might suggest, reflected once again the integral relationship of the chivalric ethic and Piedmont's leadership in the unitary movement. And even with these lighter penalties at hand, judges and juries alike seldom sentenced duelists to anywhere near the maximums allowed.

Take, for instance, the case of Pier Alberto Selmi, a provincial administrator in Milazzo, Sicily, who killed one of his acquaintances, Salvatore Sciacca, in a saber duel in 1877. Their *vertenza* had started innocently enough in a swimming pool in the town of Patti, where Sciacca could not restrain himself from splashing and dunking Selmi, who repeatedly asked and then demanded that he halt his aquatic jests. Harsh words ensued, and Sciacca took the affair to the next level by slapping Selmi, who immediately challenged him to a duel. Because the local police got wind of the dust-up, actual combat had to be postponed for over a month, but the men eventually managed to fight outside Milazzo, and Sciacca died almost instantaneously from a wound to the chest. The

---

136. As I have argued elsewhere, one group for whom the rituals of chivalry seemed particularly important was Italy's Jews as they sought to take advantage of the opportunities of equality offered by the new liberal Italy. See Hughes 2005B, 27–29.

prosecutor, after a spirited denunciation of dueling as an "arbitrary enemy of order," asked that Selmi and his seconds be given one year's imprisonment, the minimum penalty for homicide in a duel. The tribunal, however, felt differently. The seconds were completely exonerated, and Selmi suffered only three months *confino,* or urban confinement, plus court costs of 51 lire.[137] For less deadly combat, penalties became almost risible, especially after it was established by the courts that in a duel that occasioned a wound, only the wounding party was subject to sanction. The actual crime of dueling could thus be applied to the principles only if no one was wounded—a rare case indeed given the "first blood" rules of the ritual under the liberal regime.[138]

If the provocation to duel was powerful enough, all penalties could be avoided even if one of the principles died as a result. Such was the case when Eugenio Mancini, son of P. S. Mancini, killed his wife's lover (who was also his best friend) in a pistol duel in 1875, a case so notorious and romantic that the offending spouse went on to write a successful novel about it.[139] Yet such clemency was not necessarily restricted to affairs of the heart. In one of the most sensational cases of the period, in which the lawyer Eugenio de Witt killed the professor and journalist Cesare Parrini in 1884 for supposedly slanderous accusations made against him in print, de Witt was absolved by the jury because the charges had so inveighed against his reputation that he had had "no liberty of election" in choosing to duel.[140] Courts could be surprisingly liberal in deciding what constituted such compelling circumstances, as was illustrated in 1882 by a young fellow who was completely exonerated for killing a man in a duel because he had been "horribly and bloodily" provoked when his opponent had called him "scoundrel" *(canaglia)* to his face.[141]

All of these decisions fit the general pattern of legal action against duelists, which was consistently sparse and lenient in its execution. Fozzi and Da Passano have found, for instance, that the number of cases actually brought to trial reflected only a small portion of the duels known to have occurred.[142] Extending their quantitative analysis, as shown in

137. "Tribunali: Il *duello* Selmi-Sciacca" in *Gazzetta d'Italia,* Nov. 7, 1877, 3.
138. For example, "Ferito/Feritore," *Rivista penale* 1883, vol. 17, 44–45. The Zanardelli code attempted to close this loophole by making the duel a crime against the administration of justice as opposed to one against persons.
139. The wife was Evelina Kattermol, and the novel Princess Lara; see Gelli 1992, 148–50.
140. Gelli 1928, 191–93.
141. *Scherma italiana,* #13, July 15, 1891, 1.
142. Fozzi and Da Passano 2000, 291.

Table 5
Reported dueling offenses taken to trial, 1880-95

Year	Duels	Trials	Percent
1880	282	23	8
1881	271	28	10
1882	268	24	9
1883	259	38	15
1884	287	37	13
1885	261	35	13
1886	249	9	3
1887	278	—	—
1888	269	—	—
1889	132[a]	—	—
1890	177	20	11
1891	138	25	18
1892	122	32	26
1893	145	26	18
1894	98	—	—
1895	73[b]	17	14

[a]Reported at 5 months.
[b]Reported at 6 months.

table 5, on average, prior to the new provisions of the Zanardelli Code of 1890 (which will be discussed later), a duelist had roughly a one in ten chance (10.29%) of facing a tribunal for his actions. With the sterner penalties in force, after 1890 this rose closer to a two in ten chance (17.43%), but it should be pointed out that the actual number of prosecutions did not rise, and the rate change was due primarily to a smaller number of reported duels.

Nor did going to trial necessarily entail punishment. Excuses could be found, motives could be probed, and, if one were convicted, prosecutors and judges tended toward minimum penalties or even less. In one of his many works on dueling, Gelli gave an overview of sentences handed out for dueling from 1891 to 1893, and almost all ranged between three to ten days confinement, with a few fines along the way.[143] Moreover,

143. The longest sentence was five months, which went to a municipal clerk who had

one gets the sense that even paltry convictions were routinely appealed and often led to lesser punishments.[144]

The very fact, however, that so few duelists came to trial, despite the open reporting of their exploits in the local and national press, suggests that the legal establishment had a difficult time dealing with a crime which seemed so much in tune with public sentiment, including that of its own members. There is no way to deduce exactly which duels came to be prosecuted or why. The temptation is to suggest that duels involving serious injury, death, or extraordinary circumstances were more likely to end up before the courts, but a quick glance at the cases listed for 1885 in the juridical statistics of the *Rivista penale* demonstrates that others showed up in greater number. Of the 35 duels brought to trial that year, only five resulted in death or serious wounds, while the rest involved wounds, light injuries, or even "scratches." It is probably safe to say that duels ending in death always came under investigation, but for the rest, prosecutorial caprice seems to have dictated who ended up in court.[145]

If duelists had little to fear from the law, the same was relatively true of their opponents, because, quite frankly, Italian duels were simply not terribly dangerous. According to Gelli, in the 3,918 duels reported between 1879 and 1899, only 20, or substantially less than 1%, actually ended in death.[146] Likewise, of the 5,090 wounds received in these duels, only 1,475 (29%) were considered "grave" or worse. The others were judged as light (2,026) or very light (1,589). These results were driven by a variety of mechanisms. First and foremost was the choice of weapons. As indicated in the previous chapter, almost 90% of Italian duels were fought with sabers, the sharpened blade of which caused lighter wounds more quickly than the single, more lethal point of an épée. Incidentally, as medical science progressed, the blades were sterilized just before the encounter to avoid possible infection. Second, surrounding the conflict were many rules which were designed to keep the duelists at absolute parity in terms of position and stamina and which purposefully worked to keep the opponents from getting seriously hurt. Should a duelist fall, trip, or drop his sword, the action was suspended so as to let him regain both balance and composure. It was also said that certain directors of duels could be engaged who were particularly proficient at limiting the

killed a lieutenant in a pistol duel in Messina. Gelli 1894, 16–20.
144. See, for instance, *Cavalleria* 1889, 39.
145. "Statistica," *Rivista penale* 1885, vol. 22, 140, 276, 280, 401, 503.
146. Gelli 1901A, 11.

164 / Chapter III

damage done to the duelists: a handy resource in those *vertenze* arising more from social conformity than from personal wrath.[147]

Doctors were always on hand to ensure minimal complications from wounds and also to judge whether parity was being maintained in a physical sense. Doctors could even override the wishes of the combatants and, in the case of a seemingly debilitating wound, could refuse to countenance further fighting—thus leaving the rest of the participants to face the higher penalties of an "illegal duel" should they continue the encounter.[148] Because it did not generally matter who won the duel, there was seldom a need to go beyond "first blood" to satisfy either society or the participants. In fact, the perfect Italian duel was probably typified by the frontispiece of Blengini's 1869 dueling code in which two men gladly shook hands while one had his left arm bandaged by the attending physician (see image 7 in chapter VI). This is not to belittle the courage of men who risked their appendages if not their lives in the pursuit of honor, but it does make their willingness to take on a duel over seemingly trivial matters more understandable. In short, the prestige, position, and publicity to be gained from a duel greatly outweighed its risks, whereas to refuse a challenge could ruin a man's social and even professional life.

A Geography of Honor in Italy

The intimate relationship between Italy's elite political culture and its code of honor clearly emerges when one attempts to gage geographic differences in the frequency of duels. Luckily, Gelli's statistics allow for such an analysis, although only for the period between 1887 and 1895. His approach in this endeavor was rather straightforward: he simply collected the number of duels reported province by province and listed the results year by year in alphabetical order without any attempt at aggregate analysis.[149] To make the numbers more approachable for my study, it seemed best to consolidate the years into a single figure for each province and then rank them starting with the highest number of total duels. I then separated the numbers into the three regional groups of

---

147. For example, Colonel Albertini, in Mancini 1986, 212.
148. For example, Toeplitz 1963, 168–76.
149. Gelli n.d., 16–17. For 1895 he provided figures only for the first semester. He also made a couple of errors in addition which resulted in two of his totals being different than the sum of the parts. I have used the raw data to recalculate the totals.

Table 6
Reported duels arranged by region, 1887–95

Region	Total Number	Percent	Number of Provinces	Duels per Province
North	415 (479)	43 (50)	27 (29)	15.4 (16.5)
Center	305 (241)	32 (25)	18 (16)	16.9 (15.1)
South	230	24	24	9.6
Foreign	11	1	—	—
Total	961	100	69 (69)	—

Note: Only the first semester of 1895 was counted.

North, Center, and South for comparison, a relatively easy task, with the exception of two provinces, Bologna and Forlì, whose placement has been debated by Italian social and administrative historians. In contrast to the current vogue of placing these two provinces in the North, I decided to leave them in the Center so as not to skew the total number of provinces for each region. Unfortunately, however, Bologna had the fifth largest number of duels in all of Italy, and so this decision had a substantial impact on the final results. Consequently, for purposes of contrast, the results have been calculated and displayed according to both definitions, with bracketed figures referring to Bologna and Forlì as being in the North.

The reason for dividing the data into these three regional groups derived from my original hypothesis, which was that there might be less dueling in the South of Italy because of its stronger traditions of family vendetta and blood-feud, which would seem to contradict the individualized notions of honor connected with the dueling ritual. At first glance, this assumption would appear correct, as is demonstrated in table 6 which reports the frequency of reported duels in each of the three regions, as well as those which occurred abroad.

The data would suggest that dueling was indeed lower in the South than in the other two areas, with only 24% of the total duels occurring in that region. This pattern holds true even if we account for the number of provinces in each area, with the South accounting for only 9.6 duels per province as opposed to 16.9 for the Center and 15.4 for the North. Likewise, among the 15 provinces that have the *fewest* number of duels (see table 7), the South figures prominently, with 9 provinces at

Table 7
Fifteen provinces with the lowest number of reported duels, 1887–95

Province	Region	Number of Duels
Campobasso	South	0
Ascoli-Piceno	South	0
Arezzo	Center	0
Teramo	Center	1
Siena	Center	1
Sassari	South	1
Potenza	South	1
Cosenza	South	1
Caltanisetta	South	1
Cagliari	South	1
Trapani	South	2
Salerno	South	2
Padova	North	2
Massa Carrara	Center	2
Chieti	Center	2

the lower end of the scale compared to 5 for the Center and 1 for the North. This tendency, as illustrated in table 8, still holds true even when the figures are adjusted for population in the various regions, with the South having a ratio of 2.15 duels per 100,000 people versus 4.97 for the Center and 3.45 for the North. Naturally, the figures for the Center and the North would be different if Bologna and Forlì were counted in the latter. Given these results, one could fairly argue that dueling was less commonly practiced in the South of Italy, and one might suggest that the difference depended on the persistence of older forms of social consciousness which demanded a collective response to dishonor and thus tended to lead to long-term vendetta rather than the focused individualized rituals of the duel.[150]

However, such a conclusion is seriously weakened by other aspects of the data. First, three southern provinces (Messina, Napoli, and Catania)

---

150. See, for instance, Muir 1993, 247–72.

Table 8
Percentage of reported duels per 100,000 population, 1887-95

Region	Total Number	Percent	Population	Duels per Population
North	415 (479)	43 (50)	12,013,889	3.45 (3.99)
Center	305 (241)	32 (25)	6,142,974	4.97 (3.92)
South	230	24	10,698,677	2.15
Foreign	11	1	—	—
Total	961	100	28,855,540	3.33

had a relatively large number of duels and appear among the top 10 provinces listed in table 9, with Palermo closely following as number 11. Indeed, when adjusted for population, as is done in table 10, Messina with 10.3 per 100,000 comes very close to a tie with Bologna, with 10.4 per 100,000 for the number 2 position for all of Italy. On the other hand, a number of Northern and Central provinces demonstrated rather low frequencies of dueling, with 13 provinces or 29% reporting an average of 1 duel or less per year.

Considering these results, it is clear that any regional stereotype of honor is too clumsy to accurately account for the distribution of dueling in Italy, and thus alternative explanations are in order. Looking at the data from a fresh perspective, one might argue that one of the key variables has to do with urban and rural percentages of the population. Dueling tended to be an urban phenomenon, and one would like to know just how many people in each province lived in large cities. Unfortunately, such demographic precision for every province would require prohibitive endeavor and may, in fact, be impossible. However, it should be obvious from table 9 that, in terms of raw numbers, the provinces with the greatest number of duels tended to be those with large, dominant cities. In fact, one is struck by the number of preunitary capitals among the top 10 provinces of table 10, and this becomes even more evident if one considers Genova, Bologna, and Palermo (number 11), all of which had a history of being independent political capitals at one time or another. These considerations would seem to emphasize the important political role that dueling played during the liberal period, a role that fits the major theme of this work quite handily. But the point here is social in the sense that those cities with politically

Table 9
Fifteen provinces with the highest frequency of reported duels, 1887–95

Province	Region	Number of Duels
Milano	North	100
Roma	Center	85
Genova	North	78
Firenze	Center	49
Bologna	Center	48
Messina	South	48
Napoli	South	46
Livorno	Center	40
Torino	North	40
Catania	South	36
Palermo	South	20
Alessandria	North	16
Forli	Center	16
Verona	North	14
Pavia	North	14

active urban elites were more likely to demonstrate substantially higher rates of dueling, at least in raw numbers, than other areas.[151]

Yet the picture changes somewhat when we examine table 10, which demonstrates the 15 provinces with the highest number of duels when adjusted by population. One has to wonder why Livorno, Messina, Porto Maurizio, Grosseto, and Catania have such high percentages of dueling per 100,000 when compared to other provinces. Did it have to do with the fact that four of the five were seaports, or was it perhaps the effect of large military garrisons in these areas? As already noted, officers tended to be over-represented among those participating in duels, and thus a large army or navy base could skew the normal distribution of a province—especially perhaps by bringing in people who were foreign to local customs and who were thus more likely to cross the lines of accepted etiquette. A combination of factors might also be involved.

151. One also has to consider the possibility of a bias in Gelli's reporting system, which was based primarily on newspapers. More politically active towns might have had a wider press arena for such reporting.

Table 10
Fifteen provinces with the highest number of reported duels per 100,000 population, 1887–95

Province	Region	Duels per 100,000 Population
Livorno	Center	33.0
Bologna	Center	10.4
Messina	South	10.3
Genova	North	9.9
Roma	Center	9.8
Milano	North	8.9
Porto Maurizio	North	7.2
Grosseto	Center	6.7
Catania	South	6.4
Forli	Center	6.3
Firenze	Center	6.1
Ancona	Center	4.7
Napoli	South	4.6
Piacenza	North	4.3
Pisa	Center	4.2

Livorno, after 1885, had Italy's sole naval academy, but it was also famous for its fencing academy and masters, and one wonders if they were not as important in creating a demand for technical dueling skills as they were in offering a supply of them. Consider, for instance, the description of the city's most famous fencing master, Eugenio Pini, who was vaunted as exemplifying "the fighting character of whoever wants to be considered a good *livornese*, intolerant of tyranny and ready to match up with audacity, which sometimes seems like impudence to whoever tries to impose himself on others."[152] This was an attitude designed to elicit confrontation, and it is perhaps not insignificant that one of the very last recorded duels in Italy took place in Livorno.[153]

Just as interesting are the cases of provinces where one might expect to have more duels. Padova, for instance, had a famous university which,

152. Quoted in Gelli 1927, 83.
153. See Santini 1985, 121–52.

Table 11
Fifteen provinces with the lowest number of reported duels per 100,000 population, 1887–95

Province	Region	Duels per 100,000 Population
Campobasso	South	0
Ascoli-Piceno	South	0
Arezzo	Center	0
Potenza	South	0.18
Cosenza	South	0.21
Cagliari	South	0.23
Salerno	South	0.34
Caltanisetta	South	0.37
Teramo	Center	0.38
Sassari	South	0.38
Siena	Center	0.48
Padova	North	0.50
Avellino	South	0.50
Chieti	Center	0.56
Trapani	South	0.70

as a training ground of elites, might be expected to generate a number of duels. However, as can be seen in table 11 it reported only two in five years and thus had one of the lowest rates in Italy.[154] Was there some other cultural variable, perhaps the strength of the Catholic movement—which was critical both of liberal politics and dueling— that worked against the practice, or was it just the accidental effect of random variation?

Such questions lie beyond the reach of the present work, but the statistics taken as a whole still obviously allow some reasonably secure assertions. First, dueling was a pan-Italian phenomenon. Although the South had fewer reported duels in both real and adjusted terms, it still accounted for almost one-fourth of the total number. This fact clearly

---

154. In fact, Italian students tended not to duel with the same alacrity as their German counterparts. See Laven 1992.

indicates the weakness of any global cultural model when speaking of either the South or the North and suggests that other variables, such as the presence of large cities or military bases, were probably more important in determining levels of dueling. That the dueling "mania" of united Italy was not restricted to a single region of the country says something about the creation and communication of a distinctly Italian political culture in the decades after unification. The "cult of honor" clearly provided a common ground of understanding for Italian elites which could help bridge regional and provincial differences. Those areas with the greatest political activity and concomitant journalistic debate naturally led the pack. On the other hand, we can see that although widespread, the distribution of dueling in Italy was anything but balanced. Indeed, the top 10 provinces (or 15%) listed in table 9 accounted for 570 of the reported duels, or almost 60%. Thus in certain towns, such as Bologna, Milan, or Livorno, a "gentleman" might have faced the possibility of getting caught up in a duel on a daily basis, while in Padova, Arezzo, or Cagliari it may have been an issue of less concern. Nevertheless, the widespread acclaim accorded by various newspapers to the many duels occurring through the period suggests that it would have been difficult as a member of the *ceto civile* or at least the reading public to have ignored the very real pressure of the code of honor.

An Ideal Duelist: Felice Cavallotti

It seems fitting to conclude this chapter with a minibiography of Felice Cavallotti who acted as both archetype and advertisement for the duel during the liberal period and who died during his thirty-third encounter in 1898.[155] Born to a humble clerk in Milan, Cavallotti got caught up in the student politics of the day and became a fervent Italian patriot. Overwhelmed by the charisma of Giuseppe Garibaldi, he lied about his age in order to join the second wave of volunteers leaving for Sicily in June of 1860 and saw action at Milazzo, where his commander was killed at his side by a musket ball. His experience as a Redshirt confirmed his democratic affinities and influenced his style of politics which stressed action over caution and courage over compromise.[156]

---

155. One journalist put the number at 39 duels. Lega 1930, 330.
156. Galante Garrone 1976, 19–36, 43–60, 87.

Asked later in the century to define his political philosophy, he replied simply that he was, and had always been, a *Garibaldino*.[157]

It was, however, his literary abilities that determined his success in life and his influence in Italy. These talents came to the fore with his "War Hymn," written en route to Sicily, which became an unofficial anthem of Garibaldi's expedition. Other patriotic poetry would follow, and eventually he would garner the title of Italy's "bard of democracy." He wrote a number of successful plays (often based on patriotic themes) which, although he was never wealthy, allowed him to indulge his passion of journalism.[158] Eventually he became coeditor of Milan's *Il gazzettino rosa* with Achille Bizzoni, another firebrand of democracy, and they became famous for their unbridled language and biting satire, as well as their willingness to back up their words with their swords. On one occasion Cavallotti challenged the entire directorship of the prestigious Felsineo club in Bologna, because they had removed one of his books of poetry, which had proven offensive to a member, from their library. He took on the first three of 21 directors in consecutive duels, but a wound put an early end to the escapade.[159] Like many of his contemporaries, he justified the duel as a useful, albeit illegal, tool for society because it allowed for the quick and cordial reconciliation of "those disputes and questions that through another route would go on forever, becoming poisonous and leaving behind them a sad aftereffect of new disputes and rancors and profound irreconcilable hatreds."[160] Nevertheless, according to his biographer Galante Garrone, Cavallotti's love of the duel went beyond any excuse that it was a necessary evil; rather, it fit his personality, combining courage, militancy, and a love of public display. Not that he was particularly proficient at it; hampered as he was by short stature, bad eyesight, and a surprising lack of training. Nevertheless, by 1880 he had already fought some 20 duels, many of which had ended with his blood rather than that of his opponent on the ground.[161]

Impetuous, impulsive, and committed to the cause of republicanism, his unrelenting, sometimes scurrilous, criticisms of the monarchy and the "historic right" often prompted sequestration of his articles and occasionally landed him in jail—all of which only enhanced his

157. *Avanti*, March 8, 1898, 1.
158. He was never well off. At one point he published a couple of books on dancing for young gentlemen to make ends meet. Galante Garrone 1976, 200.
159. Ibid., 455–56.
160. Letter of Feb. 12, 1888, in *Cavalleria* 1889, 19–24. Cavallotti dramatized his support of the duel in the stage play *Agatodemon* published in 1889.
161. Galante Garrone 1976, 174–75, 381–86, 391.

popularity on the radical left. Such dramatic confrontations with the law became less frequent after the taking of Rome in 1870, and he eventually agreed to serve in the national parliament in 1873. Having come to uneasy terms with the monarchy, however, Cavallotti lost neither his fire-eating rhetoric nor his petulant attitude. On the contrary: having compromised on the issue of the monarchy, he was almost dutybound to maintain a fierce and unaccommodating independence vis-à-vis the ruling majority, including the historic Left after 1876. Unafraid of losing office, he constantly berated other politicians for their lack of probity, their willingness to trade conscience for votes, and their utilization of high-handed techniques in manipulating elections. His behavior and rhetoric added up to a recipe for chivalrous combat, as he consistently had to prove that, in accepting his seat in parliament, he had lost none of the "combative vigor" of the Garibaldian moment. His many *vertenze* and duels enhanced his public presence as an extraordinary man of courage and conviction, all the while maintaining his reputation as a man of the people who literally "fought" to expand the electorate, promote civil liberties, and assure the rights of workers.

His battling spirit and many duels made him as well an analogue for a vigorous and vibrant Italy, an Italy of action and élan. Ironically, Count Ferruccio Macola, the man who would kill him in a duel 14 years later, praised him in 1884 as a model for the youth of the nation: "I admire you because of your strong character, which stands out in these times of weakness, in this effeminate and queer epoch, that destroys the fiber of our youth, that obscures their ideals, that slackens the love of the fatherland in their hearts."[162] His radical intransigence and his Garibaldian romanticism no doubt contributed to this portrait, but it was his chivalrous gallantry, his constant willingness to face death for the sake of his convictions, which kept the image of patriotic virility alive in a political environment that had necessarily shifted from the heroic to the prosaic.

For all his panache and prestige, however, it was his spectacular death while fighting a duel with Macola that secured his place in history. The events leading up to the tragedy were hardly extraordinary; rather, they almost mundanely fit the pattern of political duels established after unity. Macola, a fellow deputy and newspaper editor, had idolized Cavallotti as a young man, but he had become increasingly conservative during the turbulent 1890s. Having first backed the authoritarian government

162. Quoted in ibid., 708.

of Francesco Crispi, whom Cavallotti despised for betraying his Garibaldian roots, Macola aligned himself with those calling for the curtailment of civil liberties in order to deal with the growing power of the socialist and anarchist "menace." Such, in itself would have put Macola at odds with the "bard of democracy," but he hoped to use his personal acquaintance with Cavallotti to boost his own prestige, and he suggested in a series of articles that, in private, Cavallotti had confided his support for such draconian measures. Cavallotti consistently repudiated these claims, and when Macola wrote him an angry letter accusing him of malfeasance, Cavallotti published a response calling him "a professional liar."[163]

This assured a bitter *vertenza,* and during the negotiations Macola reportedly demanded use of the *guantone*—a large glove designed to raise the risk of serious injury by protecting the fencer's arm. Cavallotti's representatives protested the *guantone,* not least because it favored Macola's longer reach. However, knowing that Cavallotti wanted to end the affair quickly and that he would reject any condition that might even hint at trepidation, they eventually agreed to the conditions of combat. With the preliminaries out of the way, the duelists met with their respective entourages outside Rome in the villa of Countess Cellere on the afternoon of March 4, 1898. Macola was younger, taller, and the better fencer, but it was Cavallotti's own impetuousness that would prove fatal. Charging with his usual sound and fury, he quickly managed to impale himself on his opponent's sword, which entered his mouth and cut the carotid artery at the back of his throat. He died in minutes suffocating on his own blood.

Cavallotti's final duel was a perfect microcosm of Italy's politics of the sword. Both of the duelists and all of their seconds were deputies in parliament. The duel was hosted at the villa of Countess Cellere who oversaw all of the physical preparations and seemed to put an aristocratic stamp on the proceedings. At least three of the participants were also journalists, and the root cause of the conflict had come from a series of published charges and countercharges. Moreover, those charges had resulted from the personal political rapport between Macola and Cavallotti as Italy once again went through political realignment during the turbulent decade of the 1890s. With the fall of Crispi after Adowa and the ongoing instability occasioned by the rise of the socialists, the violence of the anarchists, and the repressive tactics of the government,

---

163. Other factors contributing to the duel can be found in Lega 1930, 326–29.

previous arrangements of power were in play. Cavallotti's prestige on the extreme left made him an arbiter of possible solutions. Overstepping the bounds of presumption in his efforts to effect such a solution through public pressure, Macola ran afoul of Cavallotti's personal sensibilities and brought the matter to a point of honor. In fact, some would later say that he intentionally provoked the duel and then demanded possibly lethal conditions in the hopes of getting Cavallotti out of the way.[164]

Such a conspiracy seems highly unlikely, especially considering what happened to Macola after the encounter. Contrary to popular perception, the Italian parliament did not offer him immunity, and he was prosecuted for murder during a duel.[165] In part, the government's decision derived simply from the notoriety of the encounter as well as from Cavallotti's prominence as a political figure and friend of the people. Enormous public mourning attended his death, and crowds of weeping peasants and workers lined up early to pay homage to him as the train carried his body from Rome to Milan.[166] Nor did Macola's reputation fare well at the trial. Witnesses testified as to the manner in which he had provoked Cavallotti beyond normal limits, while "experts" in chivalry were brought in to comment on the legitimacy of the *vertenza* and especially on Macola's insistence on using the danger-inducing *guantone*, despite the early protests of Cavallotti's representatives. Found guilty, he was originally sentenced to 13 months in prison but then managed on appeal to get a reduction to 7 months.[167] While the sentence fit the general pattern of leniency in Italy—after all he had killed a man and had been portrayed as the aggressor—the real penalty came from public opinion and his own conscience. Generally shunned by his fellow deputies, he never fully recovered from the traumatic event or its aftermath. Although he managed to remain in parliament, he eventually killed himself on August 18, 1910.[168] Much like Aaron Burr who killed Alexander Hamilton in 1804, he had, whether by design or by accident, broken the unspoken rules of political dueling. Killing one's opponent upset the balance of honor, it implied subterfuge, and it ran counter to the many safeguards designed to keep affairs bloody but not

---

164. See Premuti 1924.
165. *Rivista penale* 1898, vol. 47, 625.
166. For a report on such a scene in Grossetto see *La Risveglia quadrimestrale di varia umanità*, nn7–8/Maggio–Agosto 2001/Settembre–Dicembre 2001, ARCHIVIO.
167. *Rivista penale* 1899, vol. 49, 558.
168. Lega 1930, 338.

lethal. The many political purposes of the duel were best served when both combatants lived to tell the tale.

Thus Felice Cavallotti stands as the apotheosis of Italian dueling. Born into the petit bourgeois, he combined patriotism and talent to become one of the leading lights of the liberal period, and he died dueling with a member of the nobility. A convinced democrat and republican, he saw no paradox between his populist notions of power and his chivalrous assumptions of honor. In challenging Aldo Aldini to a duel for insulting his poetry, he celebrated the "maxim that every citizen is the first and best custodian of his own honor."[169] The key word here is perhaps "citizen," for it held out hope to each Italian that he could become an active member of the *ceto civile* and thus could share in the personal empowerment offered by the dueling code. Unafraid of titles, honors, and pedigrees, Cavallotti once simultaneously challenged a prince, a count, and a *commendatore* for insults to his artistry, and all three accepted his invitation to combat. The son of a nobody, who lived much of his life on the edge of poverty, he used his abilities, his brio, and his sword to carve a prominent place in the politics of united Italy and died surrounded by fellow deputies in the drawing room of a countess. A massive demonstration of shock and grief followed his demise, and Turati, head of the socialist party, eulogized him as not just a man, but as "a generation of men, and of that which in it was beautiful, exalted, proud."[170] Such was his stature that when he died by the sword, a wave of indignation rose up against the duel which, as we shall see in chapter VI, set in motion new forces that would seek to undercut the chivalric axioms that had dominated his worldview.[171]

---

169. Galante Garrone 1976, 456.
170. Quoted in ibid., 723.
171. See Vassallo 1918, 112–18.

IV

Institutions of Honor and the Search for Legal Sanction

BEFORE DIGGING too deeply into the protracted debate that surrounded the duel in liberal Italy, one must examine the elaborate complex of codes, juries, and courts that began to grow around the practice after unification. This was an ongoing project that would last well into the fascist period, and the constant renewal of such regulation testified to both the pretensions and the apprehensions of the chivalric community. On the one hand, the production of new dueling manuals and the well-publicized operation of juries of honor testified to the vibrancy and constancy of the dueling ethic in Italian society. They further provided the framework for a parallel code of privileged justice that worked to enhance the influence and stature of its adherents. Real gentlemen were held to have special sensibilities of honor, and it only made sense (at least to them) that there should be pan-Italian mechanisms to recognize and regulate their needs and deeds. On the other hand, the large number of competing dueling manuals and the persistent demand for better-organized and more-formal institutions of honor betrayed an underlying uncertainty as to the efficacy and the legitimacy of the whole chivalric enterprise. Gentlemen might be gentlemen, but they needed a great deal of help validating each other and disciplining themselves as they wrangled over their honor.

On a practical level, the dueling manuals and courts of honor promised solutions to a variety of problems arising around the ritual. Some of these dealt with the mechanics of how, when, and where one should seek satisfaction. But the overarching issues were about the "why" and above all the "who" of honorable combat, and these questions derived from the open-ended nature of the *ceto civile*. If a willingness to fight duels in a proper fashion helped determine the definition of a gentleman, what was to stop some unprincipled character from using the code of honor to cover his less-than-savory background or dishonest actions? This problem was compounded by the powerful social/psychological compulsion to duel that weighed on members of polite society. An unscrupulous but talented swordsman, or *spadaccino*, could use his martial abilities to blackmail or extort patronage from victims who, because of the dictates of honor, could not refuse to do battle if he challenged or insulted them. Interestingly, some of the most dramatic examples of such abuses of honor came from Paolo Fambri's lengthy 1869 defense of the duel, *La giurisprudenza del duello*. In one case, he recounted how an enterprising fencing expert cleverly provoked a young man into challenging him after a gambling session and then demanded a large sum of money from his mother in order to allow himself to be lightly wounded instead of killing her son. Naturally, Fambri decried this "brigandage in white gloves," but with his usual brio he claimed he could make a list of 150 paladins who would gladly hire out their sword for a thousand lire. Even nonexperts, according to Fambri, could use the dueling compulsion for improper purposes, with professors being challenged for giving bad grades or bankers called out for refusing loans to bad credit risks.[1] Both proponents and opponents of the duel talked about such abuses but, of course, with completely different purposes. For opponents it was patently obvious that they demonstrated the moral bankruptcy of dueling in general, while proponents argued that they made the creation of efficient courts of honor imperative so as to bring them under control.

This chapter looks at the chivalric community's attempts to regulate itself as the dueling ethic came to dominate the new country. It examines the various dueling manuals that appeared after unity and explains why one of them, Iacopo Gelli's 1892 *Codice cavalleresco italiano*, so thoroughly prevailed over its many competitors. Specifically, it argues that Gelli came to dominate the scene because, along with other factors, he understood the need to make his code part of a larger matrix of chivalric justice, which allowed gentlemen greater leeway in settling their *vertenze* while mimicking the style and authority of the regular legal

1. Fambri 1869, 5–7, 120–26, 132–35.

system. Such efforts, then, fit into a conscious campaign to force the state to recognize the special dictates of elite honor, even though such a move ran counter to the basic principles of the liberal regime. In the end, the long battle to win government sanction for the courts of honor reflected a fundamental desire to gain greater legitimacy for the chivalric ethic, all the while coming to grips with the unsettling paradox that Italy's elites owed allegiance to two codes of comportment that were at heart mutually exclusive: one legal and the other illegal. Italian gentlemen certainly embraced the duel as a part of their personal and national identity, but they were not always at ease with the relationship or its consequences. Men of private honor and public order, they needed the "jurisprudence of the duel," as Fambri correctly called it, to ease their consciences and to finesse the logic of their actions.

The Search for a National Dueling Code

One of the most obvious affirmations of the chivalric ethic in Italy was the continuous publication of dueling codes during the liberal regime. Between 1860 and 1914, some 22 such codes appeared, most written, as we have seen, by fencing masters but others penned by military men, lawyers, and journalists. Some of the codes were short pamphlets or appendices designed to enhance the sale of technical fencing manuals, but others were full-blown tomes running to hundreds of pages. Whatever their length, however, the codes kept appearing and thus constantly reiterated to the male reading public that society expected them to "do the right thing," and that they should know what they were about should the occasion arise. As a reviewer tellingly said of General Achille Angelini's popular code, "it is indispensable for whoever belongs to the caste of gentlemen and for anyone who believes and can belong to it."[2] The codes simultaneously reinforced the link between patriotism and chivalry because each in its own way maintained that it was the *real* Italian code which faithfully interpreted the traditions and customs of Italy in the face of foreign imports. Finally, and perhaps of greatest significance, the codes consistently offered substantial legal legitimacy to what was technically a crime.[3] According to this logic, dueling was no random act; rather, it had rules codified from time-honored consensus

---

2. From the *Unione liberale di Terni*, in Angelini 1888, 9.
3. See Morelli 1904, 254.

derived from ancient judicial practices. The fact that experts and their codes sometimes wrangled over the details only enhanced the illusion of a living jurisprudence that offered a parallel legal system to those men who qualified for its protection.

That a specifically Italian code was necessary seemed obvious to all involved in the chivalric community. First of all, potential duelists needed a homegrown reference work that they could employ as a hedge against the Italian legal system. Unlike France, Italy's penal codes of 1859 and 1889 defined dueling as a crime in and of itself, but they also generously mitigated sentences against assault, mutilation, and murder if these acts were committed during a "legal" duel. In consequence, murder usually carried a sentence of over 20 years' imprisonment, but conviction of murder during a duel after 1889 brought a penalty of between only six months and five years in prison—and that constituted an increase compared to the old law of 1859.[4] The trouble, of course, was how to determine whether such deeds had actually been committed during a "real" duel. Enter the dueling codes, which offered the combined authority of chivalric experts, adherence to which could assure duelists the much more lenient penalties attached to the practice.[5] Correct notification of a *sfida,* the presence of a doctor to care for the wounded, exact equality of weapons, proper preparation of the *terreno,* a carefully worded account of the combat signed by the padrini—all guaranteed the "legality" of this blatantly illegal act. Attention to such details became even more important after the code of 1889 spelled out very harsh punishments for people caught cheating during a duel.

A dueling code was also seen as necessary to help stem the flood of duels that followed unity, or at least to limit their consequences. A book of rules governing affairs of honor, it was argued, would define who was allowed to duel and who was not. It would exempt certain people from having to fight, and it would prioritize offenses of honor so that people would avoid dueling over trivial matters. Likewise, it would set careful rules of protocol designed to eliminate the possibility that unscrupulous people would use duels as a form of extortion or for other dishonorable purposes. Especially important were strict rules for the actual conduct of the duel and the responsibilities of the seconds, which worked to make the encounters fairer and less bloody. Pistols could not be rifled and thus more accurate. Swords had to be of equal

4. Article 239 (1889) vs. article 589 (1859).
5. For a courtroom example see *Cavalleria* 1889.

length, and no advantage could be drawn from a broken weapon or an accidental fall. Each wound inflicted had to be examined by attending physicians and seconds to determine whether the combatants were still equal in their faculties and whether honor had been sufficiently served in balance of the damage done. In general, then, most dueling codes worked hard to protect the participants from excessive danger or pain, although there were a few later exceptions which are discussed below. A good dueling manual might even be a source of comfort and advice to some neophyte who inadvertently found both his honor and his life on the line. Finally, and perhaps of greatest importance, it was hoped that a code would provide the legislative basis for the juries and courts of honor that would attempt to adjudicate offenses between gentlemen and bring most encounters of honor to a peaceable resolution. Given the perceived need for a code and the well-heeled pool of potential duelists, there was a strong market force at work as well. The author who could pen the generally accepted code not only would accrue considerable honor, prestige, and status within Italian society but would also stand to make a substantial profit.

Each of the competing codes naturally vaunted its special expertise in settling affairs of honor as each sought to carve a niche in the growing opus of dueling lore and increase its own credence and audience. However, given the codes' normative function, it is not surprising that they differed little in their basic precepts. They happily wrangled over whether the *offeso* (offended party) or the *sfidato* (challenged party) should be allowed the choice of weapons (most opted for the *offeso*); or whether a representative who had taken over from another representative in mid-*vertenza* had to honor the agreements already established by his predecessor; or whether one should wait 15 or 20 minutes for a tardy opponent on the field. Such issues were certainly considered important to the adherents of this new *scienza cavalleresca*. Yet for the most part, they represented minor tweakings of a system already set in place by the French, who in turn had built their own system on that of the Italian experts of the sixteenth century.

If there was one serious difference among the codes, it was how much blood needed to flow for a "real" duel. Many authorities rejected frivolous "first blood" duels, and most felt that certain offenses, such as being slapped or having one's woman meddled with, automatically demanded a duel *ad oltranza,* in which one of the participants had to be so badly wounded that he could not continue the combat. A few, however, argued that virtually all duels should end in serious bloodshed.

Such was the opinion of Luigi Barbasetti, whose *Codice cavalleresco* of 1898 demanded that every *vertenza* be put before a jury of honor, and if it was deemed worthy of action the seconds should insist that the duel result in wounds so severe that one of the duelists be unable to stand on his feet. Putting real teeth in the dueling ethic would, he argued, eliminate the many "silly" duels which ended with a scratch and would discourage those who attempted to use the ritual for the wrong reasons. This would, of course, greatly reduce the number of duels in Italy, and Barbasetti justified his violent demands with the motto "one fights the duel with the duel itself." Perhaps to avoid legal problems for his book, Barbasetti did waffle a bit, offering a gradation of offenses that might determine less serious conditions, but on the whole his code was aimed at making duels life-threatening occasions that truly tested men's resolve and promised pain and suffering to at least one of the participants.[6]

Barbasetti may have been influenced by the greater harshness of Germanic dueling practices, for he wrote his book in Vienna (where he taught fencing) and he dedicated it to a Prince of Thurn and Taxis. However, in Italy he represented a minority position on a spectrum of opinion that generally tended to keep duels less than deadly. His view did become increasingly popular after the turn of the century as dueling codes became more bloodthirsty. San di Malato Staiti (1913), Borgatti (1914), and especially Brunetti (1914) all excoriated the degrading influence of frivolous duels fought without danger, and they all argued for greater rigor in their execution. The reasons for this trend are unclear, but it may have been a testy reaction to a gradual decline in duels after 1890 (examined in the next chapter) or to the growing criticism of the practice on the part of the Socialists and Catholics. In Brunetti's case (see chapter VI) it was clearly linked to a hypernationalist despair over the supposed feminization and weakening of Italian society. Whatever the case, none of Italy's dueling codes, Barbasetti's included, permitted the arrangement of a duel that could only end in *ultimo sangue,* or the death of one of the principles, for such encounters were considered both unchivalric and tantamount to either suicide or premeditated homicide. Likewise, none of Italy's codes, with the notable exception of Brunetti's, claimed to actively promote the proliferation of dueling. Rather, they all portrayed themselves as working to discipline and limit an unstoppable activity demanded by society.

6. Barbasetti 1898, 15, 21, 51–65.

With few actual differences in important details of challenge or combat, authors of dueling codes resorted to various gimmicks to try to attract a larger audience. One author offered a series of "do-it-yourself" photographic plates illustrating each stage of the duel, from arriving at the *terreno* to writing up the *verbale*.[7] Another technique was to induce any number of officers, politicians, and masters of arms to affix their names at the end of the code as testament to the legitimacy and authority of its contents. One early author, Luigi de Rosis, offered 83 such signatures in his code of 1868, including all 15 professors of the Neapolitan Fencing Society.[8] He was clearly outdone, however, by Pasquale Cicirelli, who five years later offered a code signed by no fewer than 270 southern fencing masters.[9] Another author, A. d'Amico Franz, had only 55 such signatories for his code of 1894, but they included 12 parliamentary deputies, 5 titled aristocrats, and an honorary fencing master of the royal household.[10] The idea was not just that these worthies supported the author's claims of expertise but that they pledged themselves to conduct their own affairs of honor according to his precepts. Having prestigious men in positions of power lead by example in their *vertenze* was obviously considered a powerful and, one might add, inexpensive form of advertising.

Another weapon in the battle for popularity was the use of ornate and enticing book covers and frontispieces. Some, as we have seen, dripped with medieval icons of knights, swords, spurs, and lances. Others, such as that of Blengini (see image 5), stressed the fraternal and bonding nature of the duel as a means of healing honorable disputes between true gentlemen.[11] But the prize for creative (and sensationalistic) artwork goes to Ernesto Salafia Maggio's *Codice cavalleresco nazionale*, which was published in Palermo in 1895. His cover (see image 6) sported a bare-breasted *Italia* who is wearing a turreted crown and whose torso is twisted to titillating advantage as her right hand grasps a massive two-handed medieval sword, the phallic overtones of which need no explication. The blade carries the inscription, "don't use (*impugnar*) me without reason," a clear caveat that chivalric combat should not be entered lightly. In her left hand rests a *caduceus*, an ancient symbol of healing and a ready reference to the pacifying power of the

---

7. Salafia Maggio 1895.
8. De Rosis 1868, 89–95.
9. Cicirelli 1873, appendix 1.
10. D'Amico 1894, 30–32.
11. Blengini 1868.

Image 5
Cover of Cesare Alberto Blengini's 1868 dueling manual

Image 6
Cover of Ernesto Salafia Maggio's 1895 dueling manual

duel among gentlemen. At her feet lies a motley pile of law books and dueling weapons, from the bottom of which there protrudes a two-handed sword that is also very obviously a crucifix! Here the image is ambiguous. Is Salafia Maggio trying to suggest that his national code will finally cut through the current mess of chivalrous legislation? Or, more likely, does the image argue that both the law (as designated by the book *Lex*) and the church fall before the feet of Italian honor? Less obscure are the strength and the energy of *Italia* herself, whose swashbuckling leather belt hangs just low enough to demonstrate her fertile female midriff while simultaneously creating an aura of virile combat. The whole enterprise succeeds in capturing the essential icons of Italy's need for national honor while appealing to the sexual tastes and market motivators of Italian males. Alas, the brilliance of Salafia Maggio's artwork did him little good in the end, and his much-vaunted *Codice* would fail to capture the hearts and minds of Italy's gentlemen.[12]

That honor would eventually go to Iacopo Gelli, whose career as a chivalric statistician we have already examined, and his triumph tells us much about the evolution of the duel during the liberal period. First appearing in 1886, his *Codice cavalleresco* quickly became the standard handbook of "honorable" behavior, and by 1926, the year of its fifteenth edition, it had sold over 55,000 copies and could be found in Austrian, Spanish, and Portuguese translations.[13] Other editions would follow in 1932, 1935, and 1943, and a reprint of the 1926 version would appear in 1981 and 1990. In addition to guiding potential duelists, his book was used as expert testimony during criminal trials dealing with duels and was cited in published debates of gentlemen seeking to discredit their adversaries with erudite arguments over points of honor.[14] In both 1933 and 1937 it was confirmed by the fascist Consiglio di Stato as the most authoritative guide to chivalric "legislation."[15] Gelli's stature was no less impressive among the military, and already in 1901 his book was off-handedly referred to by one jurist as the *jus receptum* of officers.[16] In 1920 it was adopted by Italy's War College and was recommended to its students as basic reading, a policy also instituted at the

---

12. Salafia Maggio 1895. Cover illustration by S. Turati.
13. Athos Gastone Banti, preface to Gelli 1926, xiv, xix.
14. For example, "*Vertenza* Fecia di Cossato-Chiesa," in CDS, March 7, 1910, 1; and *Procedimento penale contro Giulio Moroni e Rodolfo Terlizzi,* Florence, Dec. 26, 1925, typescript, BNR, Levi (K.2.I.2), 2.
15. Specific decisions cited in Gelli 1943, 243, 247.
16. La Manna 1901, 9.

military's official fencing academy in Rome.[17] Despite an almost constant stream of newly published dueling codes by rival experts, Gelli and his *Codice* maintained their position as the primary arbiters of honor in Italy, a fact bolstered by his tenure first as secretary and then president of Florence's *Corte permanente d'onore,* which made decisions on cases from all over Italy. By 1920 Gelli claimed to have personally intervened in more than 4,000 *vertenze,* and by 1926 that number reportedly had risen to over 7,000.[18]

But who was Iacopo Gelli that he could claim the right to adjudicate matters of such public and private import for gentlemen, whether aristocrat or commoner, colonel or corporal? The answer is a provocative one because Gelli, at least in a sociological sense, was nobody: the son of a coppersmith from a small town in Tuscany whose active military career stopped as a second lieutenant and who eventually came to make his living as a sports journalist. Thus besides writing on dueling, he also published books on stamp collecting, bocce ball, billiards, and how to write elegant letters. In the larger context of Italy's search for a national code, it is important to understand how it is that such an unlikely character came to such prominence among Italy's elites and why his *Codice* enjoyed so much success against so many contenders. His triumph reveals once again the legitimizing social functions provided by dueling in postunitary Italy, for no clearer example of "careers open to talent" can be found than Gelli's own story, and it illustrates the intensely personal nature of power in Italy and how a person like Gelli could combine his abilities with his connections to gain status and honor on a national scale.

Looking at Gelli's competition, his success seems somewhat unlikely. As previously noted, some of the most prestigious fencers of the period produced dueling manuals, as did some lawyers, who could vaunt their juridical training as necessary to sanction what was in effect a parallel code of law. Yet only two other codes managed to go beyond a single edition, and only one of these would offer Gelli any serious trouble.[19] This was the *Codice cavalleresco Italiano* of General Achille Angelini, which went through three printings between 1883 and 1888. Angelini's code enjoyed a number of important advantages over its rivals. First, as

17. Comando della Scuola di Guerra, *Norme riguardanti le vertenze cavalleresche ed i giurì d'onore,* 1920. Typescript copy. BNR, Levi (O.9.I.2). On the Scuola Magistrale see Minuzzi 1998, 112.
18. Gelli 1920, xx; and Gelli 1926, preface by Banti, xxii.
19. De Rosis's code appeared in 1865, 1868, and 1869.

we have seen, the author had been a high ranking officer in the Piedmontese army with close ties to the royal family. He thus utilized the prestige of the military and the monarchy—both national institutions—in order to create a specifically "Italian" code of honor that attempted to reconcile differences in dueling practices throughout the new country.[20] Second, he not only was recognized as a formidable fencer but had been the head of the 1882 commission to choose an official fencing style for the instruction of Italy's armed forces. Third, he had initiated and then presided over an important national conference that had met in the new capital, Florence, in May 1868, to discuss the creation of a nationwide system of courts of honor.[21] Based on the proceedings of that commission (examined later in this chapter), Angelini could argue that he had received a sanction to write a national code, and when it appeared, it included the adherence and signatures of over 80 honorable gentlemen, most of whom were officers, aristocrats, or deputies.[22] Thus Angelini could claim patriotism, expertise, and consensus for his code. In addition, he had plenty of field experience, including participation in over 70 *vertenze* and the rather rare distinction of having killed a man in a duel only to be pardoned by the king.[23]

Why, then, did Gelli's code come to dominate? One reason had to do with a fatal flaw in Angelini's own assertion of communal authority, which he claimed to be its greatest strength.[24] Shortly after the general's death in 1889, Paolo Fambri wrote a devastating article in *La Venezia* which maintained that although Angelini had consulted some of his prestigious signatories, he had actually never obtained their approval of the final version, which consequently contained some rather serious mistakes and lacunae.[25] Given Fambri's unassailable position as an authority on dueling and the fact that he was among Angelini's supposed underwriters, this attack carried a great deal of weight, especially since no one else rose to dispute his accusation.[26] In fact, Angelini's code never recovered, and although some would later refer to

20. Angelini 1888, xii–xiv.
21. An account is in Fambri 1869, 192–200.
22. Angelini 1888, 231–42.
23. Morelli 1904, 257.
24. Angelini 1888, xxix, xxxiv.
25. Paolo Fambri, "Il codice cavalleresco," in *La Venezia,* Dec. 5, 1889, 1.
26. For a more detailed but biased analysis of the controversy over Angelini's code see Iacopo Gelli, "Anomalie e codici cavallereschi," in *Scherma italiana,* June 29, 1891, #11, 85–86.

it, especially within the military, his book was never printed again.[27] Combined with Angelini's death, Fambri's attack clearly left the door open for a new authority on dueling, and Iacopo Gelli was more than ready to take advantage of the opportunity.

Yet even without Fambri's deprecation of Angelini's code, Gelli would probably have risen to the top, for he was a man of energy, talent, and ambition. He was also erudite, and one cannot account for his success without recognizing his mastery over the literature of dueling. In particular, he prided himself on his knowledge of the history of dueling and of the many early treatises concerning protocol and points of honor. As one friend commented, "Gelli is not a man: he is a living archive: a human file cabinet."[28] Particularly important in this regard was Gelli's familiarity with Italy's Renaissance dueling literature. Reinvigorated by Napoleon's troops, the resurgence of the duel during the Risorgimento had generally been based on French models, specifically on Chatauvillard's famous code of 1836, an Italian version of which appeared in 1864. In contrast, it was clearly to Gelli's advantage in the competition to create a national code that he could easily and accurately refer to the Italian ur-texts which had established the code *duello* for the rest of Europe. To reinforce this connection, Gelli occasionally wrote under the pseudonym of famous sixteenth-century "doctors" of chivalry, such as Attendoli and Mutio, and he repeatedly affirmed his expertise with a steady stream of books and articles devoted to dueling in both the past and the present. He likewise constantly corresponded with other gentlemen, including Paolo Fambri, who sought his opinion over various points of honor.[29] Finally, as an accomplished swordsman who authored his own popular treatise on Italian fencing (1901), he was well ensconced in the professional network of masters who ran schools, organized competitions, and participated in exhibitions. His two fencing magazines, *Cappa e spada* (*Cloak and Sword*) and *Scherma Italiana* (*Italian Fencing*), offered a perfect mixture of articles on both sports and chivalry.

Erudition and expertise aside, Gelli's code contained a number of important changes compared to that of General Angelini, despite the latter's claim shortly before his death that they were essentially identical.[30] First, Gelli made his book look more like an actual legal code.

27. See Morelli 1904, 260.
28. Banti 1996, xxi.
29. For example, Fambri to Gelli, Jan. 1, 1892, in ACS, Carte Fambri, Busta 31.
30. Adamoli-Castiglioni 1900, 498–99.

Indeed, the 493 articles of his 1892 edition numerically mirrored the 498 articles of Italy's first uniform penal code of 1889! Divided into six sections complete with technical glosses and precedent-setting decisions by juries and courts of honor, his *Codice* virtually dripped legislative authority in the grand Napoleonic tradition. Its detailed categorization and lengthy index made it a ready reference, just as its juridical tone made it seem the letter of the law. Such similarity was important for those attempting to argue their way into or out of a challenge, and it became even more important in the tribunals of Italy as people sought to demonstrate the "legality" of their duels. Some authorities found Gelli too precious and nitpicking to serve real men of action, but it was, in fact, Gelli's penchant for pettifogging details that made his code so useful to men who might prefer to debate the fine points of their *vertenze* rather than face the sword points of their adversaries.[31]

Gelli differed from Angelini in other respects as well. In terms of authority, Angelini had relied on the signatures of worthy gentleman (in fact, it had been his downfall), but Gelli rejected the logic of borrowed gravitas and stood on his own, arguing that a dueling code had to be "in perfect correspondence with the tendencies of the public consciousness and customs, and not impose, like dogmas, the views of just one or of a few."[32] He viewed himself as an informed interpreter of current culture—a claim backed up by his experience on Florence's Permanent Court of Honor—rather than the purveyor of a static table of laws, and he did not hesitate to change important parts of the code over the years.[33] By the same logic, Gelli was less specific about defining aspects of honor itself. Unlike Angelini, he made little attempt to list the offenses—from staring too long in another man's eyes to reading a man's newspaper without permission—that might give rise to a duel. Thus he left the definition of honor to the sensitivity of the individual gentleman, and in doing so he broadened the parameters of the practice of dueling to a wider range of behaviors. Gelli was also more inclusive in his target audience and would eventually claim a gentleman to be a person of "refined moral sensibility" who found the laws of the state inadequate to the defense of his honor *and* who followed the rules of chivalry.[34] Hence a gentleman was a man willing to fight a duel over

31. For example, Morelli 1904, 261.
32. Gelli 1892, 13–14.
33. For example, compare duels *ad oltranza* for grave insults in Gelli 1892, 33, 115–16, and Gelli 1926, 76.
34. Gelli 1926, 1.

personal honor according to the regulations currently codified by Gelli. All of this amounted to an autodefinition of honor that opened up the benefits of chivalry to ever-larger groups. Gelli would therefore affirm that it was impossible for someone to avoid a legitimate duel with a Jew on the pretext that no Jew could be a gentleman.[35] On the contrary, such a tactic was counter to the laws of chivalry, and anyone attempting to employ it would himself be denied the prerogatives of a gentleman. Using such arguments, Gelli proclaimed that he was trying to reconcile the duel with modern society "which would like to see democracy associated with the noble traditions of chivalry."[36]

Equal to his content and presentation, however, was the way he reached his audience. As a journalist, Gelli understood distribution, and he eventually selected a publisher that targeted a mass market[37]—the Casa Editrice Hoepli, of Milan, which in 1872 had started publishing a series of relatively inexpensive "how to do it" books. By 1912 the list of Hoepli "Manuals," as they were called, amounted to some 1,200 titles on virtually every conceivable topic, from spiritualism to seismology. Gelli himself wrote the Hoepli Manual on billiards and fencing, as well as the *Codice cavalleresco,* which found a comfortable niche on the publisher's list right above the *Codice civile del Regno* (the actual civil law of the Kingdom of Italy). Despite such an august neighbor, it is difficult to deny the somewhat banal appearance of Italy's national dueling code among so many other reference books promising mastery out of literacy, especially with palm reading, tattooing, cycling, guitar, and cinematography all on the same page.[38] Nevertheless, listing the *Codice cavalleresco* provided Gelli with real advantages over his competitors. Above all, he had a national network of both advertising and distribution that really made his the first "Italian" code. Second, his very selection by Hoepli as Italy's "authority" on dueling automatically conveyed a confidence that made it difficult for others to overcome. This status was reinforced as more and more people bought the book, and thus its own success created a self-fulfilling form of validation throughout the land.

That validation was further bolstered by Gelli's intimate relationship with the institutional alter-ego of the dueling codes: the juries and tribunals of honor. His code succeeded because he was an intelligent

35. Ibid., 5.
36. Gelli 1892, 13.
37. The first edition with Hoepli was published in 1896.
38. This particular list appeared at the back (page 249) of the 1910 Hoepli Manual entitled *Spiritismo* by Armando Pappalardo.

man who made himself an expert on dueling and then used his abilities and connections as a journalist to promote his own legitimacy. But one doubts that this would have sufficed if he had not placed himself at the very center of those groups that defined themselves as the arbiters of chivalry in Italy. He was secretary and then president of the Permanent Court of Honor in Florence, which was one of the most active in Italy, first for a short while in the 1890s and then for a long time after World War I. In that role he made contacts throughout the country, established his "juridical" credentials—even though he had no legal training—and rapidly created a clever, legitimizing circle of personal expertise and authority leading from his *Codice* to the court and back to the *Codice*. He consequently figured among the most vociferous advocates for state recognition of such courts, and in doing so he helped shape one of the most controversial and complex arguments regarding the duel during the liberal period.

Juries and Courts of Honor

No idea excited the imagination of the chivalric community more than the state sanction of tribunals of honor to deal with the many *vertenze* arising among Italian gentlemen. The courts were seen as a panacea for a variety of problems arising from the dueling code itself. These included the frivolous duels that seemed to make a mockery of the ritual; the fear of extortion by unprincipled *spadaccini;* the suspicion inherent in facing a "gentleman" of unknown or shady background; and the need to settle disputes of chivalric negotiation such as who should be considered the offended party and hence have choice of weapon and conditions. Courts of honor could further offer censure or condemnation of a gentleman who failed to meet his obligations of honesty, fair play, or courage. Ultimately, it was argued, the courts would help reconcile, pacify, and mediate many misunderstandings and contretemps that had hitherto ended up on the field of honor. Dueling would gradually be restricted to an ever-shrinking set of *vertenze* arising from only the most serious insults, and with society's own evolution it might eventually disappear entirely. Equally attractive was the idea that such institutions would work hand in hand with the regular courts of the realm, advising them on points and procedures of honor that might impact their decisions in dueling cases and adding a much-needed arena of semilegal adjudication for certain insults or offenses that were considered inappropriate for a regular courtroom. Given these lofty goals, it is hardly surprising that many of the dueling manuals praised the concept of the courts and occasionally provided lengthy sections on how they should operate. Even some opponents of the duel, including Italy's Anti-dueling League, argued for their official establishment, although, in stark contrast to the "doctors" of honor, they obviously rejected the notion that certain select cases had to eventually end in bloodshed.[39]

Yet for all this support, the tribunals of honor had a difficult time during the liberal period and failed to achieve the potential promised by so many. The reason was primarily one of legitimacy, for the Italian state understandably balked at granting its imprimatur to an institution whose ultimate sanction was an illegal act. There was also the difficulty of turning juridical power over to "gentlemen," a category whose definition and recruitment tended to be lacking in academic or professional rigor. In the final analysis, the gentlemen who assumed that they would run the new courts could claim authority based only on status, reputation, and self-assertion: not the kind of criteria designed for a system of law that throughout the century had rejected privilege for equality. Consequently, except for the military which adopted official juries of honor in 1908, the tribunals either would remain attached to voluntary associations, such as the Press Association in Rome and the Fencing Academy in Naples, or, like the Permanent Court of Honor in Florence, would try to stand alone, confident that the gravitas and expertise of its members carried sufficient social clout to make a difference in men's lives.

Yet even without official government recognition, the courts, like the less formal juries, played an important role in liberal Italy, allowing for the adjudication of a variety of *vertenze* over the years, offering advice to men stuck in tricky situations, and, above all, providing a forum in which gentlemen could assert their special, albeit unofficial, status in society. In this respect, the courts and juries, like the dueling manuals, offered a constant propaganda of deed that publicly reaffirmed the principles of the code of honor as the key to being a man of respect and power. Their complex and sometimes convoluted history clearly deserves our attention because it offers an important window into the assumptions and pretensions of Italy's chivalric community, just as it brings into focus the critical antimony of an essentially private

39. For a summary (and a condemnation) of this "bloodless" approach see Brunetti 1916.

system of justice operating successfully within the matrix of a modern state.

Approaching the daunting literature that dealt with this topic, one must differentiate between "permanent" courts of honor and "contingency" (*eventuale*) juries of honor, although even the experts sometimes muddled the terms during discussion.[40] Contingency juries had been around at least since the Napoleonic period and were ad hoc organs of chivalric clarification and potential reconciliation made up of three or five members selected by the participants in a *vertenza*.[41] (We have already seen one in operation in the Agnetta/Bixio case in the first chapter.) They arose primarily when the representatives could not agree on some critical aspect of a *vertenza*, such as a dispute over who was the offended party, what degree of offense had been given, or whether both men were qualified to seek or give satisfaction. If both parties could not agree to submit a case to a jury, a man might call for a "unilateral" jury of his own choosing: an expedient usually adopted for cases in which one man felt his opponent unworthy of treatment as a gentleman.[42] Of greatest relevance to the long and complicated debate surrounding them, these juries could also rule on the overall validity of a *vertenza*, and if there were insufficient cause for combat, they could attempt to reconcile the parties. Contingency juries thus offered discipline and legitimacy to duels on one hand and the possibility of pacification on the other.

As an institution, however, such juries were flawed in that they had little formal organization or accountability and could be difficult to arrange. Moreover, they were often recruited along partisan lines, and, although the theory remained that all gentlemen would act according to accepted traditions of chivalry, the truth was that the jurors would on occasion act more as advocates for the rights of their principals.[43] Some could actually do more harm than good. Such was the case in 1898 when a jury took a relatively minor encounter in a Trapani theater between an officer and a gentleman (for which the latter actually offered to publicly apologize) and defined the offense as "extremely serious with disrespect," a designation that consequently called for a dangerous pistol duel which resulted in the death of the officer.[44]

40. Gelli 1892, 162–66; Barbasetti 1898, 21, 26, 151–57.
41. For a good description see D'Amico 1894, 27–29.
42. For specifics see "Giurì unilaterali," *Scherma italiana*, May 8, 1893, #44.
43. Fambri 1888A, 262–63; also Fambri 1874, 898.
44. Case of Sacco and Serraino, in Gelli 1992, 260–64.

Despite such problems, however, their potential for pacification and their projection of calm adjudication made contingency juries popular with Italy's dueling mavens, some of whom argued that **all** *vertenze* should be subject to such scrutiny. In order to force compliance, they advocated changes in the law that would deprive duelists of the lenient penalties currently accorded "legal" duels if they failed to submit their *vertenza* to a jury for consideration before proceeding to the *terreno*.[45] As we shall see, much of the ensuing debate would focus on approving this form of legal encouragement of contingency juries, which would have entailed at least indirect state recognition of their authority.

Fambri's Paradigm: National Tribunals of Honor

That debate, however, was continuously complicated by the call from important voices within the chivalric community, including various members of parliament, to completely replace the old contingency juries with a more uniform and better regulated system of adjudication, sanctioned or even organized by the government. These "permanent" courts would be composed of distinguished gentlemen who would volunteer their good offices for a given period of time, and their status, expertise, and probity would overcome personal interests and connections for the sake of both truth and honor. The most ambitious and influential architect of such a project was Paolo Fambri who saw in such tribunals nothing less than a mechanism for the moral regeneration of all of Italy.

Fambri took both inspiration and justification from the aforementioned Congress of Chivalry presided over by General Angelini in Florence in May of 1868 (only four years after the city had become the new capital of Italy). Angelini called the conference to deal with the frequent abuses surrounding the duel since unification, a point made clear in a letter he sent to Nino Bixio soliciting his participation: "We have in the front line and masters of the field unworthy men for whom grabbing a sword is a means of aggression no different than a dagger, if not for the material fact that it has a longer blade. Many of us have agreed to finish it and Nino Bixio must help us with all his great heart."[46] Bixio did indeed join Angelini, and along with some 30 other luminaries,

---

45. *Digesto italiano,* Torino: Torinese, 1899–1902, vol. 9, 1206–12.
46. Paolo Fambri, "Il codice cavalleresco," *La Venezia,* Dec. 5, 1889, 1.

including two ex–prime ministers of Italy, they sent out an invitation to select gentlemen asking them to help create a national system of tribunals of honor that would "put an end to the frequent encounters over petty causes, and whose authoritative verdict would be enough to reinstate the honor of whoever was attacked unjustly or who was offended by a person unworthy of wielding a sword." They met in a private hall, and their comments were recorded by the official stenographer of the parliament, a shorthand symbol of the semiofficial nature of the enterprise. They eventually voted to create a commission of 10 experts, with Angelini as president and Fambri as secretary, to write a statute establishing the new tribunals and a *codice cavallersco* to inform their proceedings.[47] For all its gravitas and good intentions, however, the actions of the conference came to naught, a result perhaps of the rapid and unexpected translation of the capital of Italy from Florence to Rome in 1870. Whatever the reason, the 10 experts never met again as a statutory body, and no collective proposal was ever created.

Nevertheless, the "Congress" had important residual effects. Angelini, as we have seen, went on to write his famous dueling code in partial fulfillment of its original charge. More to the point, in the second half of his appropriately named *Giurisprudenza del duello* (1869), Fambri took it upon himself to lay out a detailed blueprint for the creation of the proposed courts of honor. Fambri's scheme matched both his bravado and his faith in the chivalric ethic. As with most other proponents of the institution, he touted the success of the Prussian military courts of honor, established in 1843, but he found them too restrictive and wanted to create a uniquely Italian system which would find its roots in the country's history. The courts were thus best understood as a "reinstitution" of Italian traditions rather than "an innovation or reform," and he larded his text with references to medieval and especially Renaissance doctors of chivalry."[48] The goals of the courts were appropriately broad and ambitious: "The purpose of the institution of the courts of honor is to protect social morality as well as individual honor and liberty; to substitute for the impassioned judgement of the interested parties or their friends the unimpassioned decision of the judges; to limit the use of the duel according to the requirements of justice and the spirit and traditions of chivalry."[49] To achieve these ends, Italy's gentlemen would have to swear to submit their own *vertenze* to

47. Fambri 1869, 192, 194–98.
48. Ibid., 199, 215–17, 241–43.
49. Ibid., 202.

the new courts and to refuse participation in any disputes outside their jurisdiction. Duelists who fought without gaining a court's consent and a license of *campo franco*—a direct and intentional reference to the legitimate duels sanctioned by princes during the Renaissance—would be denounced to the legal authorities as common criminals. To make this work, Fambri argued, the regular justice system would eventually have to somehow recognize the new courts of honor, although he carefully skirted around the details of such an implication.

Fambri's plan envisaged a permanent "Assembly of Honor" (recruited from Angelini's original congress) in the capital. This voluntary association would then oversee a system of provincial courts located in the army's divisional headquarters and run by the ranking general of the territorial militia. In theory the system would handle all chivalric disputes arising in Italy. Judges would decide on the merits of each *vertenze*, seek reconciliation of the parties if appropriate, and invoke a hierarchical series of social punishments (such as temporary or permanent loss of the right to seek satisfaction) against men who acted counter to the laws of chivalry. Notification of these punishments would appear in a regularly published bulletin of the assembly. If a duel was seen as appropriate, the assembly would send representatives to oversee the combat, thus assuring both its chivalric validity and its "juridical" legality. Anyone failing to follow the proper rules of combat would be "disqualified" and turned over to the regular courts on charges of attempted homicide.[50] Such a system, according to Fambri, would eliminate the charlatans and rascals who might abuse the concept of honor; it would protect people's rights of free speech from armed extortion; and it would help reconcile many minor conflicts which currently led to unnecessary duels—all of which would have a civilizing effect on society. Thus, Fambri predicted that shortly after the tribunals' introduction, dueling would fall off by 60%.[51]

Aside from its grandiose goals and proportions, which rather handily sidestepped the question of who was going to pay for it all, Fambri's proposal was stunning in its assumptions regarding the mixing of public and private power in Italy. Beginning with a small coterie of influential people, he hoped to create a national institution that would co-opt the structure and prestige of the military while impinging on the prerogatives of the judicial system. The motive force of such pretense was his

50. Ibid., 200–210.
51. Ibid., x, 93.

faith that he had the backing of some of Italy's most honorable and prestigious men, who felt that they had the right to create a parallel system of adjudication, which was necessary because the regular courts could not satisfy their sensitivities or protect them from their own rituals of violence. Perhaps more impressive, these men claimed the power to decide who in the new scheme of things could consider himself a gentleman, and in this sense Fambri's tribunals would have been the greatest if not the grandest of all of Italy's new and exclusive men's clubs. It was, of course, an extreme plan drawn up by one of the country's more flamboyant characters, but it fit the worldview of the chivalric community and helped set the terms of the debate over how much official recognition should be given to gentlemen who wanted to regulate their own conflicts with the blessing of the state.

The Campaign for State Recognition

Considering its scope and complexity, it is hardly surprising that Fambri's system failed to come to fruition. Yet it helped promote the idea of permanent tribunals of honor, and within 10 years, as we have seen, the Press Association of Rome would create a working model, albeit for a limited community of professionals. To the south, the National Fencing Academy in Naples would also eventually establish a permanent Jury of Honor in order to serve the needs of its members.[52] Interest in the juries and courts would be further promoted by the ongoing discussion among Italy's legislators as they wrestled with how to handle the thorny issue of the duel in the construction of the country's first comprehensive penal code, which would only be finished in 1889. As early as January 1870, a parliamentary commission adopted a suggestion from the Appeals Court of Naples that for a duel to be "legal" and hence enjoy lesser penalties, it had to have been preceded by a review of the *vertenza* by a jury of honor.[53] The idea was later backed by Minister of Justice Paolo Onorato Vigliani, who deemed it an important innovation and included it in his proposed penal code of 1874.[54] After the senate approved the provision and sent it on to the chamber, confidence rose

---

52. The Academy's Web site lists the foundation date of its jury as 1880 (www.accademianazionalescherma.it/documenti).
53. Crivellari 1884, 119. The Court of Appeals of Messina independently made the same suggestion.
54. Crivellari 1884, 128–29. For other plans see Fambri 1874, 893–99.

that it would become law, and during its national competition on fencing techniques (discussed in chapter II), the military related its enthusiasm for the proposal's passage to the minister of war, predicting: "The tribunals of honor will have a legal existence; chivalric jury members will not be able to evade their delicate but necessary office any more than regular jury members evade theirs today; every affair (*querela*) will be placed under their adjudication and consequently under their investigation. Any armed solution of a personal affair that has not traversed this stadium of even handed research and attempted reconciliation [...] will involve ordinary [criminal] responsibility."[55] Headed up by Angelini and Fambri, the Fencing Commission naturally failed to see that some legislators might see the matter rather differently.

In fact, opposition to the proposal both in and out of the chamber was fierce, primarily because recognizing the juries or courts of honor could be construed as a legal acceptance of the duel itself.[56] As one commentator on the revision of the penal code explained, it would constitute "a type of indirect consecration of the duel, making it impossible to punish a duel fought after having permission granted by a jury organized and made mandatory by the state."[57] As befit such a controversial proposal, references to the courts bounced into and out of subsequent drafts of the penal code as commissions and experts debated their merits. As with the other issues regarding dueling and the law, the courts and juries of honor constituted a difficult issue for Italian legislators, with informed and heartfelt opinion on both sides.

The key player in this drama was Minister of Justice Giuseppe Zanardelli, whose name is still attached to united Italy's first comprehensive penal code, approved in 1889. Zanardelli was quite familiar with juries of honor, for he had been one of the founding members of the Press Association's court of honor in 1879. What that experience had taught him is unclear, but when he presented the new code for final comment late in 1887, he specifically rejected the proposal, popular in earlier drafts of the law, that greater leniency should be granted duelists who had sought the judgment of a jury of honor. Such latitude, he claimed, ran contrary to the logic of the law by legitimizing the mechanisms of an illegal practice.[58] He did declare himself willing to

---

55. "Relazione della commission," in Parise 1884, xxxi.
56. For example, *Digesto Italiano*, vol. 9, 1899–1902, 1206–7, 1210–11; Crivellari 1884, 84–86; Brusa 1871, 398–400.
57. Facchinetti 1890, 21.
58. Zanardelli 1888, 391–92.

promote the *unofficial* spread of such juries through Italy as a means of resolving *vertenze* peacefully, but he fundamentally rejected the idea that they could or should allow some affairs to proceed to combat; to do so would only feed the pretensions of the dueling establishment.

Zanardelli's expunging of all mention of the juries from the code's penultimate draft brought forth a rapid reaction from the chivalric community, which began a vigorous campaign to bring the juries back in January of 1888. Lectures were arranged, articles were written, and Gelli published a 40-page pamphlet taking Zanardelli to task for not grasping the basic issues at hand.[59] The exact influence of such propaganda is hard to measure, but by March rumors were coming from parliament that legal acknowledgment of the juries had finally been assured.[60] This apparent victory galvanized Italy's chivalric paladins into action: finally the government had realized the critical function of the juries. Surely, this created a need for their greater organization and coordination.

To get the ball rolling, Fambri wrote to Gelli from Venice announcing the creation of a Permanent Court of Honor under the auspices of the Venetian Fencing Society. He exhorted Gelli to establish a similar institution in Florence (something Gelli had already considered) and then to go with him to Rome to start a new tribunal, perhaps building on the one attached to the Press Association. Gelli declined the trip to Rome, but that did not stop Fambri from going to the capital to hold a conference on the topic. Meanwhile, Gelli had received similar encouragement to start a Florentine court in letters from Baron Ottavio Anzani, who was working to set one up in Naples, and from his friend Francesco Spirito in Rome, who had been chiefly responsible for the inclusion of the juries of honor in the revised legislation. To top it off, Gelli claimed that Zanardelli himself had written to him to push such a project.[61] In an article in his fencing magazine, *Cappa e spada,* in April 1888, he challenged the gentlemen of Italy to seize the moment and prove themselves no less chivalrous than their neighbors to the north, who already had such institutions: "Considering that the law promises us its moral support, let me flatter myself with the hope of seeing the juries of honor arise in Italy, and the day that we have achieved our goal we will be able to boast that we have marked a new era of moral civilization for the nation and one well worthy of humanity. [. . .]. So what are we waiting for? Perhaps to be prompted by France or Germany?

59. Gelli 1888C, 22–23.
60. In fact Gelli claimed a "triumph" of his ideas. Gelli 1888B, 6–7; 1888A, 62.
61. Gelli 1888B, 7, 10–11.

Gentlemen, let us do it ourselves, like our fathers!"[62] Venice, Rome, Naples, Florence—suddenly a nationwide system of chivalric courts did not seem so far away. Since the new penal code reportedly provided an official role for the juries of honor, they should be governed by permanent institutions throughout the realm manned by disinterested gentlemen/jurors and overseen by Italy's chivalric experts: this as opposed to letting the exciting new legal responsibility fall to the old, unregulated system of "contingency" juries, an unhappy alternative that Fambri vigorously criticized in the July 1888 issue of *Nuova Antologia*.[63]

No one could ever accuse Iacopo Gelli of missing an opportunity. Armed with his letters of encouragement from around Italy, he assembled 32 other "eminent gentlemen" of Florence on May 28, 1888, to create a permanent court of honor for the city. It was an impressive group that included 5 aristocratic officers, 5 noblemen, 10 non-noble officers, 8 *commendatori* or *cavalieri*, 3 senators, and 2 current deputies in parliament. Gelli started with a short speech laying out the need for such courts, their historic pedigree back to Louis XIV, and the official juridical function soon to be bestowed on them by the new penal code. This impending sanction, he said, had led other cities to move toward their creation, and he appealed to regional pride by suggesting that Florence should not play second fiddle to anyone in "this rush of civil progress." The group responded with a resolution proclaiming that the necessity of the courts was "universally understood" and that the new penal code "cries out for the help of all gentlemen to limit the abuse of the duel and mitigate penal action through the juries of honor [...]." They proceeded to establish a permanent court of honor open to all gentlemen willing to swear to its authority and elected a president and secretary to oversee its operations. The first president was Count Eugenio Giacomini, and the secretary was, as one might expect, Iacopo Gelli. Thus was born the Permanent Court of Honor of Florence, which for a time would become Italy's most active and best-known chivalric institution.[64]

Unfortunately, Gelli's triumph and the "national" project of which it was a part suffered an immediate setback from Italy's lawmakers. Contrary to the information and assumptions that had inspired the creation of the courts, Zanardelli ultimately rejected the modifications adopted by the chamber's commission. Instead he again stripped all references to

62. Gelli 1888A, 62. "Do it ourselves" was a patriotic reference to the Risorgimento.
63. Fambri 1888A, 262–63.
64. Gelli 1888B, 14–17.

the juries of honor from the final version of the code, which became law in 1889 and went into effect in 1890. In explaining this decision, he reiterated his original conviction that "the law cannot, without contradicting itself recognize in any way the jury of honor." Moreover, he claimed to have been influenced by the senate, which had criticized the untested novelty, lack of uniformity, and inherent instability of the juries, all of which were bound to create abuses.[65] No doubt aware of the feathers his decision would ruffle among the champions of chivalry, he was quick to praise the basic concept of the juries as well as their participants:

> It is truly desirable that the intervention of the juries of honor have an ever-greater application in duels, and those generous people who, in such a way, vigorously contribute to the diminution of dueling cases, are to be highly praised; but the law that would offer public recognition to the juries would only discredit itself and at the same time also discredit the institution of the jury of honor, when it incriminated, even with a minor penalty, a duel that the jury itself had declared imperative and necessary.[66]

These carefully chosen words were designed to encourage the peacemaking functions of the juries and the newly established courts while gently reminding them of their ambiguous position before the law. If they wanted to keep their essential character as effective arbiters of honor, complete with the right to sanction duels, they should keep out of the limelight of juridical rigor.

Words of praise notwithstanding, this was a harsh blow to the chivalric community and probably to Gelli personally, although he never seems to have publicly lamented the decision.[67] The failure to gain even indirect legal sanction of the juries or the courts from the state naturally shook the prestige of the fledgling institutions and deprived them of the coercive force that would have helped bring a majority of *vertenze* under their purview. The Zanardelli code, according to one of Fambri's eulogists in 1897, had betrayed Fambri's "ardent apostolate" of a national jurisprudence of the duel. As a consequence, the much-heralded permanent courts, which had previously seemed to be taking root, had already

---

65. Zanardelli 1889, 107. Also see *Il digesto italiano*, vol. 9, 1899–1902, 1211; Facchinetti 1890, 20–21.
66. Zanardelli 1889, 107.
67. Indeed, he praised the code; e.g., Gelli 1891, 131; 1894, 10.

been forgotten when Fambri died.[68] Gelli himself admitted in 1903 that the courts had by then become almost useless, and a year later, produeling commentator Ercole Morelli analyzed their fatal flaw.[69]

> [. . .] the Italian Courts of Honor are anchored to nothing; and I believe that there are few people who at present remember the Courts of Honor of Rome, of Venice, or maybe just that of Florence, which was however the one that showed the greatest practical action.
> And it was fated to be so: those tribunals of honor had no other support than the platonic approval of the citizens; they lacked therefore the force necessary to make their judgements respected. Hence, those people who did not find it in their favor [*comodo*] to adhere to them laughed at them: while the pusillanimous found in them a shield of their cowardice, and they could, under the aegis of that assembly of gentlemen, bluster with impunity.[70]

Once again, the grand scheme had foundered, hamstrung by the basic inconsistency of having privately established courts, even those populated by gentlemen, crossing the line into the business of the state. Zanardelli had encouraged the private creation of the courts to help restrict the duel, but he could not square the circle of legalizing a mechanism that at heart was based on a crime. Without some official sanction, the courts lacked any central reference or juridical clout, which made it more difficult to recruit men willing to put themselves in the role of judges over their compatriots in matters of delicacy and controversy.[71] Indeed, Gelli would later complain about the abuse he personally had to withstand from certain "brigands in tailcoats" whom he had "unmasked" in *vertenze* which he had been asked to adjudicate.[72] A truly effective permanent system of honor simply needed more than private good will and personal credentials to make it work.

We should not, however, underestimate the importance of the campaign of 1888 and its results within Italy's dueling culture. The Permanent Court in Florence, to which it served as midwife, resolved several hundred *vertenze* during its first three years of activity and, in so doing, created a baseline of chivalric "legislation" that found its official registrar

68. Mariotii 1897, 12–13.
69. See Gelli 1903, 2.
70. Morelli 1904, 247–48.
71. Gelli had warned people of this problem during the campaign. Gelli 1888A, 62.
72. Gelli 1912, XII.

in Gelli and his *Codice*. In the long run, these precedents would prove useful after the First World War when the Florentine Court was revivified in October of 1922 to deal with a new onslaught of duels during the advent of fascism.[73] Even in the short run, Gelli maintained that despite its brief lifespan the Court had promoted greater use of unofficial juries of honor: "Thus it is that while in 1889 these represented a laudable utopia, in 1890 they peacefully resolved twenty-five percent of the *vertenze;* in 1900 this percentage hit fifty percent, and in 1910 seventy-five percent."[74] There is, unfortunately, no way to check the veracity of this assertion, and frankly his statistics seem rather off-the-cuff. Yet as we shall see in the next chapter, the average number of duels began to decline after 1890, and Gelli would suggest that it was due in part to increased participation in juries of honor. Meanwhile, Gelli kept the image of a nationwide system of honor alive by tracking important decisions made by various contingency, fencing club, and press association juries. Later versions of his *Codice* would cite these precedents from Milan, Torino, Bologna, Genova, Rome, and, of course, Florence.

New Attempts at Legalization

Despite its failure, the campaign surrounding the Zanardelli code only whetted the appetite of those who wanted the government to offer its authority to the chivalric tradition, and this would quickly lead to yet more proposals for some form of official recognition. Already in 1889, in disappointed reaction to the final version of the penal code, the executive committee of the National Fencing Tournament in Rome proposed a new chivalric congress, similar to that of 1868, to create a truly national code, and it called on five parliamentary deputies, including Paolo Fambri, to help organize the event. The congress was never convened, but one of the committee, Professor Ernesto Salafia Maggio from Palermo, was sufficiently inspired by the concept to publish a new dueling code in 1895 that dedicated over 30 pages to a new pan-Italian court of honor, sanctioned and paid for by the government.[75] Unencumbered by false modesty, he suggested that his own code would serve as the basis for this august body's adjudication's.

Salafia Maggio's ambitious program, which owed a great deal to

73. See Ettorre 1928, 174.
74. Gelli 1920, xix.
75. Salafia Maggio 1895, iii–vi, 17–21, 141–67.

Fambri's earlier example, had little if any chance of affecting policy. More proposals, however, soon came to the fore in response to Cavallotti's death on March 23, 1898. His dramatic end unleashed a wave of antidueling commentary across Italy, including demands for tougher laws and more-efficient enforcement. Amid the growing clamor for increased action toward abolition, defenders of the duel reacted by revivifying the call for national courts of honor as a means of reducing the number and severity of encounters. In fact, in 1898 the produeling camp provided a bumper crop of schemes devoted to chivalric tribunals, including proposals by an army officer, a fencing master, a lawyer, and a politician.[76] The latter, Deputy De Martino, argued in parliament (only one month after Cavallotti died) that the duel arose from a deeply rooted prejudice in Italian society and was consequently impervious to the normal sanctions of the law. Taking this fact into account, the state should limit the damage done by authorizing a nationwide magistracy of chivalry that would allow gentlemen to regulate their affairs of honor according to their own time-tested rules.[77] De Martino's project, which blatantly offered official judicial sanction to the entire dueling ritual, found little favor in a parliament that was still reeling from the violent death of one of its members, and it was immediately voted into the legislative limbo of "further study."

Nevertheless, the idea of chivalric courts would not die and even gained support from the other side of the dueling controversy. The Italian Anti-Dueling League, founded in 1902, adopted as part of its original statute a commitment to foster and support tribunals of honor throughout Italy.[78] Their plan, which was laid out in detail in 1905, was to create regional juries of honor run by members of the league and designed to mediate questions of honor, but without recourse to the duel. As with the other schemes over the years, the league was long on details and short on results, but the promulgation of the courts as a tool of pacification remained a key part of the association's propaganda prior to World War I. That in and of itself would prove important, because the league's advocacy of the courts only added to the clamor coming for them from the champions of the duel after Cavallotti's deadly

---

76. Respectively, Lo Monaco-Aprile (1898); Barbasetti (1898); Modugno (revised edition, 1898); and De Martino (see note 77 below).

77. *Atti parlamentari,* Leg. XX, 1st session, vol. 574, 5076–77, with discussion on 5800–19: April 10 and 16, 1898, respectively. Also see Venturi 1898, 5–17.

78. *Statuto per la Lega Italiana contro il duello,* BNR, Levi (P.4.I bis, I, p. 1); also see Brunetti 1916, 611.

encounter. Albeit in radically different guises, the courts were becoming increasingly acceptable across a broad spectrum of public opinion, thus setting the stage for new attempts to gain official recognition.

As mentioned in chapter II, the military was the first to respond, and on October 4, 1908, a decree demanded that all *vertenze* between officers be adjudicated by a jury of honor composed of three officers superior in rank and selected by the divisional commander.[79] Within the long-standing controversy over the state's sanction of courts or juries of honor, the military had an easier time of making such a move. First, there was no parliamentary review of the process: the decree came from the ministry of war more or less as an executive order. Also, as already noted, the military penal code did not contain any references to the duel, and so, at least regarding its own internal legislation, there was no obvious conflict of purpose. Equally important, the chain of command already provided a clear-cut and legal mechanism to recruit the juries, whereas civilian juries were notoriously ambiguous in their selection criteria. Draped in the mantle of hierarchy, the military's juries simply added an extra dimension to existing obligations of obedience and provided a pan-Italian structure of enforcement with little or no extra expense to the state. Still, it was a big step, and one that had been avoided for years because it seemed to sanction the duel itself, an impression that the decree clearly tried to dispel by making no specific references to either dueling or chivalry. Significantly, that step had to be taken by a person who was free of the military's corporate ethos. Senator Severino Casana, who signed the law and whose name it came to bear, was the first civilian minister of war since Baron Ricasoli in 1861, and his bold innovation inversely reflected the previous intransigence of chivalry among the officer class.

The immediate consequences of this decree depended on one's point of view. One Buenos Aires newspaper quipped that in the five months following its implementation, there were at least five duels among officers in Italy.[80] This figure would no doubt have been appalling to a strict abolitionist, but five duels in five months actually worked out to an average of only 12 duels a year, and within the military this number would have represented a significant decline. Gelli, writing in 1920, recalled that in the long run the legislation was a "well-adjusted blow

---

79. Decreto di 4 ottobre, 1908, in *Rivista penale* 1908, vol. 48, 629.
80. "Il duello e i medici," *La patria degli Italiani*, Oct. 19, 1910. Cited in Capretz 1926, 71.

of a club to the tradition."[81] In fact, the available statistics, which are examined at the end of the next chapter, suggest that the decree of 1908 probably did help reduce the number of duels among officers prior to the First World War.

The decree also paved the way for the most ambitious plan yet for official recognition of the courts, and it came from no less a personage than V. E. Orlando, Italy's Minister of Justice. On December 1, 1908, less than two months after the creation of the military juries, he presented parliament with a proposal to establish official tribunals of honor attached to each of Italy's courts of appeal. Orlando adopted a novel approach to the problem by focusing the new institution on changes to the laws regarding defamation rather than dueling. He acknowledged that there was a realm of honor-insults that was poorly served by the regular courts, and as a result many men chose to avoid legal redress in favor of the ease and acclaim of personal combat. He further noted that public opinion had come to support the idea of special courts that could handle the tricky issues of honor while freeing the regular courts for more-concrete offenses. Acknowledging the power of the current culture of chivalry, Orlando's courts were to be hybrids of public and private power. Every appellate court would have one of its members act as a magistrate of honor who would organize a special tribunal for each case. The tribunal would consist of two volunteer "judges" (selected by each of the litigants from a list proposed by their opponents) working together under the magistrate's professional supervision. Orlando argued that such a system would combine the attributes of the private juries of honor, which were growing in popularity in Italy, with the gravitas and expertise of a regular judge. The tribunal would consider the evidence in a secret and speedy proceeding and, depending on its findings, could censure either of the litigants or force reparations to be paid up to 10,000 lire. With regard to the duel, representatives would be expected to submit all *vertenze* to the new tribunals, and failure to do so not only would deprive them of the protection currently provided by the penal code but also would actually increase the existing criminal penalties by one-third. He concluded by affirming his belief that such sanctions would indeed resolve "a large part if not all of the question of the duel."[82]

Coming from the minister of justice, this extraordinary compromise of official and private justice was understandably cheered by much of

81. Gelli 1920, 268.
82. The proposal is appended to Ettorre 1928, 318–38.

the chivalric community.[83] Gentlemen would now have virtually their own courts, with legal sanction, where they might work out affairs of honor among themselves and even have the state impose hefty monetary penalties. Yet for all its cleverness and the substantial support that it generated, Orlando's project never became law. In fact, despite renewed efforts in 1909 and 1915, it failed to come to discussion before the full parliament: a result perhaps in part of bad timing within the legislative cycle.[84] The project also stepped on the toes of parliamentary immunity in some of its other particulars.[85] Equally likely, however, is that the project's failure stemmed from the fundamental inconsistency, evident throughout the controversy over the courts, of allowing certain individuals privileged legal status simply because they claimed adherence to a parallel code of chivalric honor. True, Orlando's proposed courts would not have openly discriminated against any sectors of society, but his attempt to co-opt the existing private juries of honor pointed to the social exclusivity of the new institution. His project further raised the old problem of somehow reinforcing the "legal" status of the duel itself by offering sanction to *vertenze* that went unresolved through the courts.[86] Unlike Zanardelli, Orlando had attempted to bulldoze through the legal paradoxes of such a strategy, but the time for such an abandonment of liberal principles was not yet at hand. It would become easier, as we shall see, once fascism had moved Italy into more authoritarian modes after World War I.

Conclusion

The history of the courts of honor reveals a constant struggle of elites seeking to justify their illegal behavior vis-à-vis society and, frankly,

---

83. Gelli dedicated the 1916, 1920, and 1923 editions of his code to Orlando and "his ideas on the courts of honor." Dissenting voices came from Di San Malato 1913, 10, and Brunetti 1916, 624–25, both of whom found simple censure and money reparations demeaning to the ritual.

84. "Per le corti d'onore," La Nazione, March 13, 1930, 1; "Un'importante sentenza del giudice Poggiolini in materia giornalistica," *La nazione,* Feb. 11, 1915, 3.

85. It would have made deputies and senators more vulnerable to investigation by judges seeking to ascertain the "facts" in cases of defamation.

86. Juridical repugnance to these problems was obvious in a lengthy legal commentary that supported Orlando's defamation law in theory but rather pointedly left out every single reference to the duel or judges of honor. Capello 1910, XIII–XIV, 283–91.

vis-à-vis themselves. On one hand, this meant providing a self-defense mechanism that aimed to limit the actual bloodshed needed to lubricate the gates that guarded gentlemanly status. If prickly sensibility and its armed defense determined one's belonging to the *ceto civile,* then some recourse had to be available to keep a lid on the violence. Juries and courts of honor offered a second line of defense after would-be duelists had exhausted their limited options of reconciliation through their representatives. Moreover, having embraced an illicit ritual as a legitimizing force, elites had to somehow protect themselves against those who would take advantage of the system, forcing men to fight for either monetary or social advantage. Proponents of the courts of honor, like authors of the dueling manuals, often obsessed over who was to be allowed the privilege of combat, and the chivalric community longed for some seemingly neutral source of selection that would allow them to refuse the unworthy or the unscrupulous. Needless to say, refusing a challenge from a swashbuckling scoundrel was a lot easier if a jury of honor backed you up. Such support was critical as well because the inner discipline of the chivalric community's dynamics was supposedly based on a collective judgment of qualification. Cheating at cards was grounds for disqualification, yet who could arbitrate such a charge without recourse to swordplay and thus prevent a man from "measuring" himself against a cheater? Failure to act like a gentleman or follow the precepts of the code meant that one could no longer seek satisfaction through the duel, but ultimate enforcement had to reside beyond the individual, and the juries and courts of honor, at least in theory, helped put teeth in chivalric sanctions.

On the other hand, state recognition of these institutions, no matter how tenuous, was seen as critical in validating their membership and influence, because, in reality, the juries and courts were self-fashioned by self-appointed experts and gentlemen. Their authority lay primarily in the status their members could muster as individual men of honor who demanded respect from their own communities and constituencies. The various tribunals that arose in Rome, Florence, Naples, and Venice depended on the organizing energy of local elites who took upon themselves the mantle of arbiters of regional honor. In this sense the courts ran parallel to the political culture of liberal Italy, where emerging groups clustered around strong individual personalities to create networks of informal power relations. Yet lacking the institutional gravity of parliament and bereft of legal sanction, the tribunals of honor naturally remained weak and ephemeral: a point reflected in the competing dueling manuals, each of which purported to represent the true essence of Italian chivalry and which more often than not backed up its claim with the signature of honorable men willing to attest to the contents.

All of this revealed reams about the sociology of power in the new nation. Contrary to its frequent portrayal as a period of stasis and continuity, the Risorgimento offered new forms of social and political organization that would have previously been impossible. Dueling offered an important means of access to such new groupings for men like Fambri or Gelli, who were willing to defend their honor according to collective rules that placed them above the law of the land but not above the social pressure of their acquaintances. More than just a willingness to fight, the culture of chivalry demanded that gentlemen participate in the larger organizational framework of the ritual. On one level it might mean offering one's services as a representative or *padrino,* but on another level it might include joining a jury of honor to help settle a *vertenza* or negotiate rules of combat—all actions which in theory could have life-or-death consequences for the participants. The point is that in its various attempts to create a "jurisprudence" of chivalry, the community of "gentlemen" was constantly struggling to get the state to recognize and affirm its right to such exclusive social power, even though the definition of "gentleman" was anything but certain.

Aside from bolstering the status (and protecting the lives) of men who manned and used them, however, the courts and juries of honor, like the dueling manuals, had the oft-unstated purpose of preserving the dignity of the entire culture of honor. The emphasis on proper procedure, strict rules, and disqualification for those who failed to behave in accordance with them, all worked to protect the chivalric community from charges of barbarism on the one hand and buffoonery on the other. The ability to adjudicate *vertenze* and allow only the most serious to end in carefully controlled conflict helped offset the image of a bloodthirsty ritual run amok and also protected the solemnity of an almost sacred act from being besmirched by neophytes and nonbelievers. The legalistic guise of the most popular codes and the deliberate formation of parallel legal structures such as juries, judges, and tribunals attempted to create an illusion of juridical legitimacy and rigor that reinforced the appropriateness of the practice among the participants themselves and offered a shield against the barbs of a variety of opponents. The many manuals and the mania for official courts betrayed a fundamental uneasiness about the role of the duel in a "civilized" and law-abiding society, even on the part of its adepts. In the context of the great dueling debate, to which we turn in the next chapter, this much-sought-after discipline and uniformity were in and of themselves arguments that supposedly spoke well for honorable men who were genuinely dedicated to law and order throughout the land, yet who broke the law on a regular basis.

V

The Great Dueling Debate

"LIKE THE DEATH PENALTY the duel has been so much discussed in school and in court, in academia and in parliament, that a new book, study, or dissertation can now only be just a mosaic of pallid contours and easy work."[1] As indicated by the lament of this legal scholar seeking to write something original about dueling in 1886, the continuing and constant presence of the ritual in the lives of Italy's elites was hard to ignore and engendered endless discussion, argument, and diatribe throughout the land. According to Zanardelli (who certainly should have known), the duel posed "the most arduous and delicate problem" facing modern legislators, and it is fair to say that the code of honor provided one of the main topics of journalistic, juridical, and literary commentary during the life of the liberal regime.[2] Antidueling forces would deliver sermons, collect signatures, publish tracts, draw cartoons, promote laws, write novels, and eventually organize at both the national and the international level. Lawmakers would wrangle with their own demons of honor as they sought to prosecute a practice in which they themselves often engaged and which some felt necessary to the health of the country. Defenders of the duel were less organized and less prolific in their publications because much of elite society already embraced the code of honor, and they could count on

1. Vico 1886, 422.
2. Zanardelli 1888, 371.

its general acceptance as automatic and "natural" behavior. Proponents of the duel did speak out in a more formal fashion, but they seldom defended the duel as a good thing in and of itself, preferring to portray it as a necessary evil that might one day no longer serve its current functions. This was an important ploy, particularly popular among authors of the many dueling codes published during the period, because it allowed duelists to admit the inherent dangers and inconsistencies of the practice while proceeding right ahead with one *vertenza* after another. In this manner proponents sought to disarm their antagonists and mitigate the contradictions of proudly trumpeting an illegal behavior in a country dedicated to the rule of law. Meanwhile, as the debate ensued, dueling manuals flooded the market, juries of honor offered their pronouncements, playwrights promoted the efficacy of honorable combat, and newspapers dished up a daily "propaganda of deed," in which prominent people, sword in hand, demonstrated what it truly meant to be a gentleman. In the end, the controversy betrayed the inherent contradictions of a regime that vaunted equality before the law and the end of corporate privilege, but that could not escape its own exclusive notions of honor and power.

The Duel as a Social Prejudice

One of the interesting aspects of the great dueling debate was the common tendency on both sides to define dueling as the result of a "social prejudice." Unfortunately, commentators pro and con were equally unanimous in their assumption that there was no need, given its apparent currency, to explain what they meant by the term, leaving the modern analyst somewhat in the dark. Carefully examining this widely accepted notion of "social prejudice" with regard to the duel, however, we begin to see that it generally referred to the network of pressures ranged throughout Italian society which forced men to defend their honor no matter how trivial the offense or how great the danger. In this way the idea of "social prejudice" became a shorthand for a complex set of assumptions concerning the nature of masculinity, bravery, and status, all of which needed no further discussion by either critics or supporters of the duel. Moreover, all involved in the discussion clearly understood how this prejudice operated on a practical level and how refusal to fight a duel could effectively "disqualify" a man from polite society and perhaps ruin him financially. Such was the pervasiveness of this "prejudice" that various opponents of the duel, be they Catholic, socialist, or progressive, were unable to withstand the public and private pressures of a challenge and eventually found themselves fighting on the field of honor. Even more interesting, perhaps, is the fact that most commentators agreed on the negative nature of the prejudice but considered it so deeply rooted in society as to defy eradication. It was the very pervasiveness of this belief that helped perpetuate the dueling ethic well into the twentieth century and, in contrast to other western European countries, even beyond the cataclysm of the First World War.

Attempting to unravel the concept of social prejudice is naturally frustrating because despite its ubiquity in the literature of dueling, or perhaps because of it, few authors actually ever bothered to explain it. For instance, in an 1839 tract against the duel, Michele Costi could claim that dueling was caused by an "almost general prejudice," without need for further details.[3] Likewise, in 1888 Giuseppe Leti, although an opponent of the duel, argued that the crime of dueling deserved lesser penalties because against "inveterate prejudices, every legislative action will fail no matter how serious or even ferocious it may be."[4] The Italian military was hardly more useful with its decree against dueling in 1908, which declared that "the duel does not constitute an act of courage, but rather an illogical coercion arising from an inveterate prejudice which today no longer has a motive to survive."[5] Apologists for the duel were just as obtuse in their use of the term: witness Costantino Cacchione, the author of an 1895 dueling code, who freely admitted that the duel was "an absurd social prejudice."[6]

So what exactly was this "social prejudice" that could be bandied about with such great frequency and so little fear of misunderstanding?[7] One clue can be found in a revealing short story written by an antidueling author, Luigi Dossena, in 1864. Dossena's protagonist sits about ready to commit suicide because he has been disgraced for having honored a promise to his future father-in-law not to engage in duels. His fiancée had initially supported his resolve, but, when faced with the public disdain that came after he refused to defend his honor, she abandoned him. In his parting letter, he writes to her: "I do not reproach you, I do not have the right; I only say that we were mad to

3. Costi 1839, 236
4. Leti 1888, 37–38.
5. Decree in Gelli 1926, 243.
6. Cacchione 1895, 7. Also see Salafia-Maggio 1895, x; Borgatti 1914, 4.
7. An early French usage of the term is in Rousseau 1960, 130–31.

want to fight against society, against public opinion. God grant that I be the last victim of this prejudice."[8] Amazingly, Paolo Fambri used exactly the same story to emphasize why men *had* to be allowed to duel, his argument being that an attempt to buck the prejudice could only lead to social death and ultimately suicide.[9] In short, the social prejudice surrounding the duel consisted of the assumption on the part of society that a man, once insulted, had *no choice* but to fight the transgressor so as to defend his honor. These assumptions thus formed the basis for what Ute Frevert has called in Germany the "social compulsion" to duel.[10]

But what was the nature of this compulsion, and what if one rejected the precepts of the prejudice or simply found the prospect of dueling unacceptable or unnerving? According to the published manuals on honor, refusing to fight a duel in the face of an insult or legitimate challenge was grounds for *squalifica,* or disqualification from the "prerogatives of chivalry." This meant that one was no longer guided or protected by the laws of honor, and thus one had forfeited honor itself. Likewise, since according to the Gelli's popular *Codice,* "The sentiment of honor in a gentleman must dominate all other hierarchies of duty," then one was no longer, by definition, a gentleman at all. At first glance this "disqualification" might appear both superficial and tautological—if one did *not* duel, then one was *not allowed* to duel. But having lost the right to duel meant that one could never request satisfaction for an insult, and one thus automatically entered—at least according to current codes of chivalry—the same category as criminals, lunatics, cheats, gamblers, bankrupts, and police spies, to say nothing of the generically disqualified sectors of women, workers, and peasants.[11]

On paper, such a pseudolegal reclassification appears abstract or even silly, but in practice it had devastating effects for anyone moving within the circles of polite society. In the first place, it was virtually impossible to counter the assumption that fear, not to say cowardice, had inspired a refusal to fight, no matter what the actual motive, and this assumption struck at the heart of a man's masculinity. This was a disaster for men in the military, where courage was seen as intrinsic to the profession, but it could be equally damaging for civilian gentlemen. Honor was by definition part of public behavior, and, within the close-knit

8. Dossena 1861, 24.
9. Fambri 1869, 37–41.
10. Frevert 1995.
11. Gelli 1926, 1–6, 27, 45–47.

communities of people who "counted," one simply could escape neither the stigma nor the implications of disqualification. Affairs of honor served as romantic and titillating topics of discussion at social functions, be they dances, dinners, or operas; and a refusal to duel for an offense—either received or given—set off a chain reaction of gossip, innuendo, disdain, and rejection that contemporaries compared to a public pillory or even a "social death."

What did such a living death entail? For Italy, at least, its consequences were minutely dissected by Marchese Crispolti in his novel *Un duello,* published in 1899. As his protagonist, Crispolti offered Count Ermenegildo Canetoli, a young roman nobleman who attempts to break free of the prejudice surrounding the duel after being publicly slapped in the face for no apparent reason by an arrogant army officer, Tornabuoni, at the racetrack. With the insult witnessed by a large crowd, Canetoli is immediately encouraged to challenge the assailant, and his best friend offers his services as a second. But Canetoli has serious religious scruples about dueling. Although willing to frequent "normal" society—including a men's club known for its liberalism—he is a scion of Rome's "black" ultra-Catholic aristocracy. After considerable reflection he decides that he must hold by the Church's condemnation of the duel and refuses to issue the much-expected challenge. He has few illusions about what trouble lies ahead or where it will come from: "His true enemy was not Tornabuoni, but rather the many people who had already profited from the occasion to threaten him [Canetoli] with the pillory; those who were pushing him to fight Tornabuoni if he wanted to justify himself to them."[12] Nevertheless, Canetoli feels that he can rely on his reputation as an honest and brave man, especially since he had previously made no secret about his religious opposition to the duel.

But Canetoli proves to be wrong. He immediately finds himself caught up in a whirlwind of gossip, accusation, and denunciation that rips through his many social circles. High teas, dinner parties, and family gatherings all vibrate with opinions on the case, most of them aimed against his masculinity and courage. He fears that his company will embarrass his friends, so he offers them the option of not inviting him to functions, and, to his surprise and dismay, they take him up on it. Both friends and acquaintances warn each other not to be seen with him until society has sorted out his fate. This seclusion quickly begins

12. Crispolti 1899, 18.

to erode his self-confidence as well as his informal influence in Rome. He finds, for instance, that his lobbying efforts for Catholic charities with members of parliament are curtailed because he no can longer see them socially.[13] Eventually his adversaries place an announcement in the local newspaper condemning him as "a person who, having in other circumstances refused to ask satisfaction for a physical insult, has put himself beyond the rights of chivalry and therefore has no means to fulfill his obligations honorably."[14] This attack opens the door for others, and Canetoli finds that he cannot attend social events without being snubbed by people he thought were his friends. In a particularly dramatic incident, he goes to his club where one of the members tells him he is no longer welcome. When he attempts to argue the point, he is called a coward to his face and discovers that he has no recourse to such an affront. He raises his hand to slap his opponent, but the latter steps back and reminds him "the same maxims that prohibit the use of the saber also prohibit the use of the hands." Caught between his convictions and his pride, Canetoli feels he can do nothing. His ostracism is complete when the various members of the club witnessing the encounter all simultaneously turn their backs on him and leave the room in a public act of shunning.

As the pressure continues to mount, Canetoli begins to crack. He feels trapped in a living death. "Day and night he passed between the horror of feeling buried and the hope and the fever of somehow lifting the stone of the sepulchre."[15] At a certain point he decides his only alternative is to go to Greece and die fighting the Turks—a Christian death of bravery that will squelch the charges of cowardice back in Rome. But in the end, Crispolti saves his hero through a Christian transfiguration that is nothing less than a personal resurrection. Having died the "social death" of honor, Canetoli is born again within the bosom of the ultra-Catholic community. With the help of his father confessor, he discovers his error in having cared for the opinion of liberal society, and through his fiancée (who is shamelessly compared to Dante's Beatrice) he discovers a brave *Vita Nuova* of Christian devotion.

We can hardly fault Crispolti for his happy resolution of Canetoli's situation or for his hero's relative willingness to give up the parties, dances, and dinners of "white" (read liberal) Roman society. After all, Crispolti himself was a member of the black Roman nobility, a leader

13. Ibid., 89–90.
14. Ibid., 156.
15. Ibid., 274.

of the intransigent Catholic *Opera dei Congressi,* and, most significantly, the founder and leader of Italy's Anti-dueling League.[16] In a very real sense, he himself had already relinquished those things that he forced his hero to sacrifice in his novel. But besides his dramatic and colorful catalogue of the pressures pushing Italian men to duel at the end of the nineteenth century, what is most revealing about Crispolti's account—especially considering his own biases and purposes in its creation—is the fact that his hero actually loses the struggle. No matter how deep Canetoli's convictions, he *must* withdraw from regular civil society into a much smaller social sphere of religious compatriots. Rather than suggest the weakness of the "dueling compulsion" as a social prejudice, Crispolti's book underlines its extraordinary vigor.[17]

That vigor was further witnessed by various cases of declared anti-duelists who eventually were forced into fighting duels for fear of being branded as cowards. "The world," declared Fambri with obvious relish in 1869, "is full of abolitionists who fight [duels]."[18] As proof positive, he would later cite the case of Federico Gabelli, who wrote to condemn Fambri's famous book in support of the duel and then two weeks later wrote back to ask him to serve as his *padrino.*[19] The most famous such *pentito* was undoubtedly Francesco Lorenzini, a major in the Piedmontese army, who published a lengthy tome condemning the duel in 1852. Lorenzini was well-known as an avid duelist, and his public about-face on the issue created a storm of derision in the press of Torino. Consequently, despite his many dramatic arguments against the practice, Lorenzini fought two duels within as many days against his journalistic critics, sending one to the hospital seriously wounded. Likewise, Captain Filippo Abignente was forced into a duel in 1894 by Ferruccio Macola, a newspaper editor, specifically because Abignente had written a treatise criticizing the duel as a barbaric social prejudice.[20] In another case, Ernesto Teodoro Moneta—winner of the 1907 Nobel Peace Prize—offered a series of arguments against the duel in an article in 1872 and was immediately pilloried as a coward and poltroon by an opposing newspaper. Within days, Moneta found himself not only attempting to provoke his opponent Carlo Righetti into a challenge,

---

16. For a short biography see Martire 1943.
17. A parallel portrait of social death from the produeling side is in Fambri 1869, 20–27.
18. Fambri 1869, 39.
19. Letter to Abignente, quoted in La Manna 1901, 24.
20. Gelli 1928, 208–9.

but eventually resorting to a court of honor to force Righetti to fight him.[21]

For some opponents of the duel these contradictory pressures simply proved too much and led to suicide. Such was the case of Bruno Crescitelli, brother of the Reverend Alberico Crescitelli who was later beatified after his martyrdom in China during the Boxer Rebellion. A fervent Catholic like his brother, Bruno had become an army officer, and in 1893, during a posting in Torino, he was personally insulted at a party by a civilian guest. Exhorted by his fellow officers to defend the honor of the corps, Bruno held true to his religious convictions and refused to fight. Facing expulsion from the army and the scorn of his colleagues, he gave way to despair and ended his own life. His brother, writing from China, angrily condemned the "anti-Christian, ungrateful and assassin" government "in the hands of free masons" for deliberately using the dueling compulsion against the Church and knowing full well how it would test the allegiance of Catholic officers.[22] Conspiracy charges aside, the case indicates the psychological power of the prejudice, which could run roughshod over strongly held religious beliefs and could lead from the rejection of one mortal sin to the commission of another, and this without hope of redemption. In short, as long as a man wanted to operate within the bounds of "normal" society, he had little choice but to obey the constraints of honor as they arose before him. And one must not forget that dueling as a prejudice was not only an external coercive device. The very strength and ubiquity of the code of honor derived from the fact that so many Italian men had internalized the precepts of chivalry and felt empowered rather than threatened by their operation.

The universally accepted notion that dueling resulted from a deeply rooted social prejudice on the part of the public was used in exactly opposite ways by proponents and opponents of the practice.[23] The latter argued that because dueling was caused by such an illogical prejudice, it should be eradicated immediately as part of a post-Risorgimento "civilizing" of Italian society. They viewed the duel as a barbarous atavism, similar to the superstitious persecution of witches or the pursuit of family blood feuds, which was simply incompatible with modernity and

---

21. See "Agli Onorevoli Membri del Giurì d'Onore," Aug. 3, 1872, a pamphlet in MRM. For other examples see Brunetti 1914, 80–81.

22. Criveller 2004, 44–45.

23. This ambiguity regarding the duel was cleverly encapsulated in Clemente Tomei's aptly named drama, *Il pregiudizio*, published in 1898.

progress. In contrast, defenders of the duel claimed that the prejudice was so deeply woven into Italy's social fabric that it was virtually impossible to legislate against it without a long period of preparation. Any attempt to do otherwise would only cause more problems than it could possibly solve.[24] There was, in fact, a general evolutionary conception among the advocates of the duel that eventually, sometime in the future, Italy would reach the same level of civilization as England and the duel would become unnecessary. At the same time, however, they argued that current conceptions of honor were so strong, the prejudice so deeply ingrained, that to abolish the duel would strike at the very heart of Italy's civility.[25]

To conclude this necessarily convoluted discussion of dueling as a public prejudice, it is important to point to two interesting and interrelated issues. First, the discourse that surrounded dueling in Italy after unification tended to a surprising degree to construe honor as a social construction rather than as an inherited or biological characteristic. Chivalric honor, for all its aristocratic overtones, was seen as an invention of society itself, which in turn could evolve. Second, although both sides of the debate acknowledged that the dueling prejudice was deeply woven into the matrix of Italian society, such an image was rather at odds with the fact that, except for Piedmont and Naples, dueling was relatively rare in preunitary Italy, and in some regions, such as the Papal States, it was virtually unknown. For many parts of the country, then, the much-vaunted prejudice that promoted the duel was a relatively recent phenomenon, yet no one seemed to doubt either its ubiquity or its force under the liberal regime.

A partial answer to this apparent paradox of the short reign yet pervasive power of the dueling prejudice can be found in the crucible of unification itself. The duel had been used as a metaphor and a mechanism to bring about the creation of the country, and, as we have seen, proponents of the practice considered the birth of the dueling ethic and the resuscitation of the point of honor as necessary and positive steps in the creation of a virile, patriotic people. In this sense, the duel and the social prejudice that surrounded it were indeed woven into the fabric of united Italy's elites' social conscience, and the spread of the Piedmontese military machine throughout the peninsula guaranteed that the red, white, and green colors of that fabric would be dyed in

---

24. For example, Coelli 1904, 178–79.
25. Fambri 1869, 30, 81.

the wool. On the other hand, understanding the patriotic regeneration of the duel also helps in turn explain the popular vision of the prejudice as a social construction: there were numerous people, including proponents of the duel, who had lived through the transition and who knew that issues of honor had not always led to the clanging of swords.[26]

Champions of the Duel: Fambri and Modugno

In Italy's long, involved debate over the duel, its most prominent and influential defender was unquestionably, although not surprisingly, Paolo Fambri, who remained active and outspoken until his death in 1892. Despite his enthusiasm for the code of honor, best summarized in his 1869 book, *Della giurisprudenza . . . del duello,* Fambri argued that in moral terms the duel was not in and of itself a good thing. On the contrary, he portrayed it as a necessary evil brought about by the country's recent and rapid attainment of unity and liberty. Freedom was an incalculable good, but it brought with it responsibilities that many Italian elites—whose general character had suffered from long years of domination by foreign powers—were simply not ready to handle. The duel was thus a "master of ceremonies of civilization" forcing people to treat each other with respect and circumspection. For Fambri, what appeared to be an anachronistic return to medieval chivalry was, in fact, a necessary step forward after the intervening centuries of decadence and abuse.[27] Once the duel had finished its civilizing mission, it would disappear by itself, as it had in the more advanced nation of England.

In the meantime, the duel not only set new standards of comportment, but it also limited the violent consequences when men did trespass across the boundaries of etiquette. With a duel, an altercation that might have turned a party or reception into an ugly shoving match, a bloody fistfight, or something even worse was now transported to a time and place far from the social arena of both polite and mixed company.[28] More serious still was the possibility that without a formal means of dealing with insults, individual disputes could fester into feuds,

26. Fambri 1869, 32–33; Gelli 1992, 56. Also see Brancaleoni's speech in Crispolti 1899, 159–60, 191.
27. Fambri 1869, xi, 16, 32.
28. Ibid., 21–22, 90.

and Fambri found little need to remind his audience that Italians had patented the word *vendetta* as a universal term of revenge and suffering. At heart he had little confidence in the ability of Italian gentlemen to act civilly over matters of honor without such a ritual intermediary, a point that later informed his popular aphorism set in a fictitious parliamentary debate:

>—The sword of the gentleman has its rights
>—Let's break it!—I was interrupted by a deputy.
>—Break it—I replied—and you will have four shards:
>these will be collected, sharpened, and instead of a noble sword you will have four assassins' daggers.[29]

Murder lurked in the minds of men, and the old forces of cowardly vengeance rather than virile chivalry lay just below the surface. Gradually this scenario would change: political progress had cleared the way for economic and moral progress, and, with the help of the code of honor, Italy's transition to civil society would come sooner rather than later.

While Fambri's defense emphasized the civilizing aspects of the duel, other authors would stress its inverse causal relationship to the inadequacies of the law, and specifically the way the courts dealt with issues of honor. The most sophisticated of these was Niccolo Modugno, a legal scholar whose 1880 treatise, *Il duello,* laid out a general theory of juridical evolution as a context for understanding the continuing necessity of the duel in Italian society. The history of positive law, he argued, represented a constant push for progress, which in its desire for reform and order could sometimes push beyond the sensibilities of certain groups within the community. Specifically, modern jurisprudence was necessarily based on the idea of equality before the law, but individual sensitivity to issues of honor differed widely and was determined by class, profession, upbringing, and personal susceptibility. Punishments for insult—whether written, verbal, or physical—all had to be aimed at a common audience and tended to be of a minimal nature, while, in contrast, certain people held their honor in higher regard than others. An accusation of conjugal infidelity constituted completely different offenses when directed at a scoundrel who sold his wife's favors as opposed to a man who "in his woman esteems and honors the clean

29. Fambri 1888C, 1.

and pure mother of his children." Yet the law applied the same minimal sanctions in both cases.[30]

Considering this and other faults in the law, Modugno thought it only logical that the duel should have continued to exert its power as a means of reestablishing bruised honor. It was not a social prejudice; rather it was a "law of opinion" which had evolved out of medieval juridical rituals to compensate for the contradictions of modern jurisprudence.[31] The duel was thus born out of inexorable legal necessity, and he unabashedly maintained that for certain serious insults or offenses, the law could never and would never offer adequate compensation. Some aspects of honor simply needed blood in their defense. Although based on an evolutionary notion of society and law, this view was a far cry from Fambri's contention that progress would render the duel a useless anachronism once it had served its civilizing function. Rather, the very nature of modern law determined that the code of honor would survive far into the foreseeable future.[32] This was not to argue that the state should legalize the duel, for such radical action would be contrary to the progress of the law itself. Rather, it should keep penalties low, assign dueling cases to juries in tune with public opinion, offer judges ample latitude for leniency, and, for much of the time, quite simply "close its eyes."[33]

For all their learning and logic, Modugno's arguments rather obviously indicated the degree to which he had internalized the precepts of the dueling code. They also propagated the belief that "real" issues of honor referred primarily to sexual discipline, that is, the defense of a woman's reputation and a man's right to her fidelity. Although he implied that there were serious nonsexual insults which the law could not assuage, virtually all of the examples designed to sway the reader to his point of view referred to adultery or accusations of other sexual impropriety. Who, for instance, would allow his daughter's or wife's name to be dragged through the mud of a regular court trial should someone slander her character: "The honor of a woman is like a sensitive plant, which, being touched is ruined. It is not possible to allow the honor of a sister to be placed in discussion in order to convict a scoundrel of mendacity. To discuss something is to put it in doubt; and

30. Modugno 1880, 32–42, 50.
31. Ibid., 76.
32. Abolition of the duel in England created a problem for Modugno who spent 20 pages trying to explain it away. Ibid., 80–101.
33. Ibid., 71.

one never discusses honor, especially that of a woman."[34] Men might equivocate on many matters, and friends or juries might compound many offenses away from the field of honor, but the bottom line for Modugno was protecting sexual propriety, and it would be the standard trope when one wanted to expose the helplessness of the law in the face of dishonor and reinforce the legitimacy of the dueling ethic. What good was judicial censure in the case of profound humiliation, when only blood and danger could restore honor and masculinity?

Literature as Legitimizer

Whatever the efficacy of their logic, Fambri's and Modugno's works were pretty heavy going, generally reserved for specialists seeking legitimacy for their dueling codes or for parliamentarians seeking to defend the duel in the face of abolitionist onslaughts. More accessible to the public palate were the various pieces of literature that presented the duel in a positive light.[35] The most blatant of these works was Paolo Ferrari's *Il duello,* a stage play first performed in Florence in 1868. Ferrari stresses that although the duel may seem cruel—especially to women—it serves the purpose of protecting honorable men against the slings and arrows of those who would seek to malign or insult them for fun or profit. Furthermore, he reflects the fascination that the duel exerted over Italy's civil classes and portrays the risks of rejecting the principles and practice of chivalric honor.

Set during an electoral campaign in Livorno, the play personifies these themes in characters that run the gamut of Italy's new elites: a democratic lawyer (and patriotic war hero of 1859) who is actually a Neapolitan nobleman in disguise; a respectable northern army officer; a conservative and upright Marchese running against the lawyer in the parliamentary elections; and a dastardly count (also from Naples) who has previously been a lackey of the corrupt Bourbon regime. The action revolves around the personal tragedy (including his wife's death by starvation and his exile to South America) that afflicted the lawyer/nobleman (and erstwhile antidueling author) when, under the old regime, he failed to defend his personal honor by dueling the evil count, who had set out to ruin him for his liberal politics. This already convoluted

34. Ibid., 58.
35. Fambri himself realized the importance of this approach, as witnessed by his *Novelle cavalleresche* (1888B), especially "I bimbi."

plot is further enlivened by the appearance of the lawyer's long-lost daughter who has been secretly raised by the evil count's estranged wife out of repugnance for her husband's wicked deeds. Needless to say, all is revealed and brought right again at the end of the play by no fewer than two duels, one of which leaves the villain cavalierly smoking a cigar as he bleeds to death on stage and the other which allows the lawyer to establish the honor of his true identity as he goes into the elections.

Beyond the social utility implied by these outcomes, however, Ferrari concentrates not on the combat, which occurs offstage, but on the preliminary discussion in which the lawyer/nobleman denounces his previous opposition to the duel and declares it instead "one of the provident wisdoms of society which governs the improvident prejudices of our passions."[36] He later explains to his recently recovered daughter, who is appalled that she might lose him so quickly to such a "barbaric" practice, that the duel is necessary because "[t]he law can protect life, property, and probity; it cannot protect honor, which is a case of conscience, which stands above the law, which the law cannot even define. A judge can punish a blow from a rock that has left a bruise, he cannot punish a glove that has been raised towards my face!"[37] Had he responded in the first instance to the villain's insults according to the rules of honor, he might have saved himself, his wife, and his daughter their respective travails. With this preamble he confronts her with the necessary choice, "either catcalls, or a brawl, or the duel." Despite her anguish, she rises to the occasion and commands him, "Go . . . go fight . . . it is the lesser of the evils." Thus the natural propensity of the woman to seek peace is once again brought round to the necessary and dangerous imperatives of honor. In the end, Ferrari's intent is obvious: the play is designed and executed as a piece of propaganda for the dueling ethic as a critical part of the new Italy's identity and as a facilitator of its moral and social regeneration.

Not all literary proponents of the duel were as obvious as Ferrari in the focus of their subject matter, but they could be equally if not more effective in portraying the code of honor as a positive force in society. Take, for instance, Achille Torelli's *I mariti*, which was first performed in Florence in 1868—the same year as Ferrari's *Il duello*. Set in Naples shortly after the fall of the old regime in 1861, the story revolves around the unhappy marriages of the Duke of Herrera's three

36. Ferrari 1928, 8–9.
37. Ibid., 159.

children, two of whom have married fellow aristocrats and the third who feels superior to her middle-class husband. At first blush, the play is a social commentary on the foibles of hereditary privilege. The current crop of noblemen—including a marchese, a baron, and the duke's heir, or duchino—variously reveal themselves as dissolute, unmannerly, and insecure. As husbands (hence the title), they drive their wives to distraction with their indifference, infidelity, and, in one case, excessive jealousy. The protagonists of the tale are Fabio Regoli, a successful lawyer (married to the duke's daughter), and Enrico di Riverbella, a handsome naval officer. Honest, hardworking, and honorable, they prove themselves far more suitable as husbands than the play's noblemen, and each in his own way helps make the point that talent, character, and upbringing are more important than pedigree, a point reinforced by the aging duke toward the end of the play: "I had to live seventy years to realize that race and blood are nothing but nonsense! Myself, I don't acknowledge blood anymore. I boast of a pedigree that is as pure as that of the count of Chambord; and have you seen my son? Have you ever seen more of a peasant (*bifolco*) than him. Education, education, has to be it, not blood."[38] Written in the first decade of unity by a bourgeois playwright who had won a battlefield commission after being wounded at the battle of Custoza in 1866, Torelli's play thus celebrates the fusion of the old aristocracy with the newly empowered elites of Italy. In the end, Regoli tames his aristocratic bride's haughtiness with forthright actions and kind words, and she appropriately informs him in the last line of the play that she is pregnant with their first child. On the other hand, di Riverbella wins the affection of the old duke and sets himself up to marry his true love, whose current husband—the duke's son—is terminally ill as a result of his dissipated lifestyle.

Digging a bit deeper, one finds that the play is essentially a treatise on honor, reputation, and manhood. The women offer themselves as weak and emotional creatures whose instruction and protection have been betrayed by their aristocratic husbands and brothers, and who thus must rely on the good offices of the "real men" of the world. Constantly in danger of being compromised in their decorum and reputation by their husbands' associations with fallen women and unscrupulous men, they bring the family to the brink of social disaster, only to have the situation saved by Regoli and di Riverbella who understand the importance of both proper comportment and public opinion. In this sense, the

---

38. Torelli 1954, 80.

lawyer and the soldier give the aristocracy lessons in matters of honorable behavior. This comes out most clearly when di Riverbella challenges the baron to a duel for having attempted to seduce the duke's daughter-in-law but then very cleverly manipulates the chivalric negotiations to hide the true cause of the *vertenza,* which would have embarrassed the duke's family. In the ensuing combat, di Riverbella permanently disfigures the baron's face with a saber slash—thus demonstrating the man's true nature as a *mostro* or monster—but finds himself challenged by the duke who fears that the duel has somehow compromised his daughter-in-law's reputation and revealed his son's weakness. Di Riverbella then reveals to the duke how he has actually saved the family's honor, and he shows him the *verbale di scontro* signed by the *padrini* which successfully hides any mention of his son's wife. The duke is astonished and delighted at di Riverbella's gentlemanly expertise, for he understands these things and declares to Regoli, "Do you perhaps believe that honor is the privilege of the young? . . . We are of the old generation, and we only tremble when we have become paralyzed." Honor now connects across generation and class, and the duke declares di Riverbella "a true gentleman" whom he sadly contrasts with his profligate son whose days are numbered.[39] Together Regoli and di Riverbella prove themselves perfect examples of true men, in stark contrast to the others and especially the overly jealous marchese who pathetically stumbles through the last act yelling to all, "But I am a man!"[40]

In all of this, the duel itself takes place offstage before the fifth act, but it provides a major turning point in the action, and the many conflicts are sorted out and settled in its aftermath: a sort of *deus ex duello.* Whatever the political or social message of *I mariti,* its affection for and affirmation of the code of honor are obvious and effective. Men who know the rules of proper comportment and have the courage to back them up with blood are those fit to rule the country. It was a popular point of view, at least gauging from public reaction to the play. Torelli was celebrated immediately after its first performance, with members of the prestigious Accademia della Crusca crowding onstage to shake his hand and the minister of education (Florence was currently the capital of Italy) calling for his immediate knighthood. Verdi and Manzoni both publicly praised the play, and one critic declared "in all that various and splendid manifestation of an idea there is something that forms part and

39. Ibid., 83–87.
40. Ibid., 73, 75. Consider as well the duchess's discourse (78) in which she berates him: "But who are you? What husband? What man? What obscene mixture of flesh and spirit?"

substance of ourselves." He consequently proclaimed it to be the start of a new national theater—an idea reiterated by Croce in 1904.[41] Obviously having struck a chord within Italy's cultured audiences, the success of *I mariti* constituted a continuing advertisement for the dueling code which, along with plays such as Felice Cavallotti's *Agatodemon* (1889), Francesco Garzes' *Bianca d'Oria* (1892), Clemente Tomei's *Il pregiudizio* (1898), and Marco Praga's *La crisi* (1904), constantly claimed to Italians that if they wanted to count, if reputation mattered, if they were to be real men and not poltroons, they would have to be ready to find their way to the field of honor.[42]

Treatises against the Duel

"Society is shocked, public tranquility is compromised, order is continuously disturbed, truth, liberty, and life and limb (*persona*) of the citizens is in danger."[43] Such a complaint, from the antidueling author Jacopo Nicoletti in 1864, characterized the frustration felt by many Italians as the code of chivalry became the order of the day in the newly united country. For all its apparent force, the dueling compulsion immediately gave rise to an extensive antidueling movement, which would eventually include three intertwined and overlapping activities: first, agitation for legislative reform against duelists and their compatriots; second, the organization of various antidueling committees, including an Italian chapter of the International Anti-dueling League; and third, the publication of numerous antidueling tracts intended to galvanize public opinion against the practice. Despite their common goal of reducing and eventually eliminating dueling, however, antidueling advocates were neither uniform in their composition nor united in their efforts. On the contrary, some of the most vociferous attacks on dueling came from opposite extremes of Italy's political spectrum, with the intransigent Catholics on the right and the nascent socialists on the left. Significantly, these were the very groups most critical of the way in which Italy had been united as a liberal, parliamentary monarchy, and their attacks on the duel demonstrate its important ties to the postunitary regime.

41. Introductory notes, ibid., 5–12.
42. Parallel to *I mariti,* Praga's 1904 play offers the positive image of an ex-colonel who saves his brother's marriage by dueling his sister-in-law's lover and manipulating the *verbale* to save her honor.
43. Nicoletti 1864, 50.

Even those friendly to the liberals, however, could use the campaign against dueling as a political stalking horse for other purposes, and they did not hesitate to do so.[44] Setting aside for the moment the legislative debate over penal sanctions and the organization of the Anti-dueling League, this section scrutinizes the various antidueling tracts that were printed in Italy before and after unification. It demonstrates how, despite the often-repetitious nature of the arguments invoked, such literature revealed a good deal both about dueling in general and about its many opponents, whose differences occasionally detracted from the effectiveness of the movement to abolish the practice.

Books and pamphlets against dueling were hardly new to Italy. A series of antidueling tracts had been written in the sixteenth century, the arguments of which had been reclaimed, repackaged, and expanded during the course of the next 200 years, although with diminishing frequency. The nineteenth century, however, saw a recrudescence of such propaganda, and between the Restoration and the First World War, scores of antidueling tracts were published in Italy, ranging from articles and pamphlets of 5 to 20 pages to full-length books complete with chapters and indexes. The very volume of tracts indicates the concern generated by Italy's new love affair with the duel, although their number was never matched by their creativity. As is the case perhaps with any long-enduring abolition campaign, one soon becomes struck by the repetitious nature of the rhetoric, a fact alluded to by the authors themselves who defended this redundancy as the nature of effective propaganda.[45] True as that may be, the standard list also becomes rather tedious, and one understands why Ute Frevert, when facing the barrage of antidueling literature that came out of Enlightenment Germany, attempted to clump the arguments according to their "typical characteristics." If one were to adapt her "abstracted" list somewhat to fit nineteenth-century Italy, it would include the following:

Dueling is irrational: it makes individual self-worth dependent on the opinion of others and subordinates questions of character to either luck or prowess.
Dueling is completely counter to Christian morality.
Dueling is a crime condemned both by society and by the laws of the state.

44. Cf. Frevert (1995, 17) for Germany.
45. For example, Parodi 1892, 7.

Dueling is exclusionary and based on class or caste privilege.
Dueling enjoys the protection of the state and thus perverts modern notions of justice such as equality before the law.[46]
Dueling runs counter to freedom of the press and speech.
Dueling turns public issues into personal squabbles.[47]

Although they would be enhanced, embellished, and exemplified, these basic arguments run like a litany through the antidueling literature of Italy, and as page after page rolls by, one looks with anticipation for something different, original, or exotic.

One such notable feature was the frequent attempt to distance Italy from the origins of the duel. With amazing monotony, and cutting widely across political lines, antidueling authors argued at length that dueling had not derived from classical culture and indeed had been unknown among either the Greeks or the Romans. Events that might have been presented to the contrary, such as the single combats found in the *Iliad,* were explained away as aspects of ancient warfare rather than real duels, just as countless examples were offered of how dueling, with its emphasis on individual private justice, had run counter to the essential legal principles of Roman citizenship.[48] On the contrary, opponents insisted that the duel had only arrived with the fall of the Roman Empire, a gothic import brought out of the forests of the north by Germanic invaders.

Whatever its historical merits, the affirmation of the duel's "gothic" provenance automatically provided Italy's antidueling advocates with three important pieces of ammunition. On the one hand they could stress the "barbarity" of the practice as being, quite literally, the invention of "barbarians." On the other hand, they could demonize dueling as something imposed from without, something uncivilized and foreign to the great cultures of Italy's past.[49] Thus dueling was simply un-Italian and even antithetical to the Italian character. Finally, the flip side of this argument could be used against the current notion of honor itself. Surely no one could doubt that the Romans had been both courageous and honorable, yet they had no tradition of the duel. Therefore, those who vaunted dueling as a proof of honor were both clearly mistaken and also out of touch with the historical roots of Western civilization.

46. Frevert 1995, 18–22.
47. I have added these last two to Frevert's list.
48. For example, Nicoletti 1864, 68–71; Minieri 1869, 5.
49. For example, Scaglione 1869, 7; Patroni 1881, 10–12.

Moreover, by focusing on the Romans' rejection of dueling, critics could offer a new definition of honor, one tied to civic virtue and service to the state. This concept particularly served those who wanted to break the military's close connection to the duel, for there was no arguing with the obvious valor and efficiency of the Roman army. Certainly, the Romans had had a strong sense of honor, but they had subordinated it to the needs of the community. Thus critics could point to stories from Roman history in which soldiers had had their personal disputes but, instead of dueling, redirected their competitive energies against the enemies of Rome. Time and again, then, the stalwart virtue of ancient Rome was vaunted over the individualistic and punctilious niceties of the "barbaric" code of honor.[50]

Such rhetoric, of course, played to the nationalist sentiments of the early Risorgimento, which portrayed Italy as a leader of world progress with Rome (whether Mazzini's or Gioberti's) as its capital. To proclaim the duel "uncivilized," "un-Roman," and "un-Italian" was to establish the patriotic credentials of those who had to counter the nationalist and militarist ethos of the produeling forces. Moreover, as unification progressed, the assertion that dueling had come from the Germanic North allowed opponents of the duel to marry their campaign with Italy's ongoing struggle with Austria. For example, Luigi Dossena wrote: "The duel is the last barbarian remnant to come to us from the forests of the North with those dear marauding friends, who like hungry locusts, fell upon our backs, and with the brutal supremacy of numerical force, turned us into their humble slaves, and began for us a long epoch of tears and humiliation."[51] Published in 1861 in Milan, which had only just been liberated from the Austrians, we should perhaps not be surprised that Dossena's diatribe reduced the Germanic tribes to insects that had robbed Italy of its freedom. Yet even as the Risorgimento ended, and Austria eventually shifted in the 1880s from enemy to ally, the tradition of blaming the duel on the barbaric hordes remained a constant for the antidueling movement, revealing the importance of somehow breaking the link between Italian nationalism and chivalric honor.

It also revealed an interesting blind spot on the part of the antidueling forces, which consistently failed to come to terms with Italy's close identification with the birth of the modern duel in the sixteenth century. Almost universally, opponents of the duel ignored the impor-

50. Ibid., 11, 24.
51. Dossena 1861, 43.

tant differences between the medieval trial-by-combat, or *giudizio di dio*, and the point-of-honor duel as it had developed during the Italian Renaissance. Thus Emilio Federici, a Catholic critic of the duel, could affirm that eventually the duel would disappear as was the case with "ritual proofs of fire, boiling water, and the other so called judgements of God."[52] Yet, by tying the duel so closely to medieval rituals, antiduelists opened themselves up to the charge that they did not understand the nature of modern honor. In fact, many opponents railed against the duel because it reduced the decisions of justice to chance or brute strength, and in so doing they missed the essential and most interesting aspect of what was going on around them: that is it did not matter who won and that honor was washed clean by blood, no matter whose blood it was. Nevertheless, to have acknowledged an Italian genesis for the modern duel would have struck at one of the common cornerstones of antidueling propaganda. Consequently, opponents of the practice for the most part simply skipped from the Middle Ages to the modern period with hardly a glance in between.[53] Dueling was un-Italian, end of story.

The popularity and ubiquity of this claim, however, certainly did not mean that all opponents necessarily supported the regime that had emerged with Italian unification. On the contrary, Catholic critics of the duel used the "barbarity" argument as splendid leverage against the government and ideology that had despoiled the papacy of its temporal holdings. Monsignor Giuseppe Patroni, for instance, could assert in 1881: "One notes the duel, a vestige of barbarous times, which current reformers seek to revivify by all means, thus setting our age back several centuries, while they continue to have on their lips the expressions: *civilization and progress.*"[54] The duel demonstrated, according to Patroni, the true hypocrisy of the liberals who praised themselves and their revolution as harbingers of rational modernity but who, in fact, had resurrected the barbarians' duel against all logic. Having divorced reason from religion, the liberals had lost their moral bearings and had even gone so far as to create chivalric rules to govern the savage practice which, if observed, provided impunity from prosecution.[55] The Risorgimento had embraced "the pronouncements of a vain and fallacious science,"

---

52. Federici 1903, 127.
53. In contrast Russo-Ajello (1906, 37–38) acknowledged an Italian genesis but then blamed the French for its perversion. Cf. Di Menza e Vella 1875, 3–4.
54. Patroni 1881, 6.
55. Ibid., 16.

and the increase in dueling clearly justified Pius IX's 1864 *Syllabus of Errors* which had condemned any truck with liberal ideas and, one might add, any recognition of the new Italian government.[56] Although some Catholic critics of the duel would gradually take a less antagonistic stance toward the Italian state as the battles of unification faded, others did not relent. As late as 1898 Salvatore Brandi would still maintain that dueling in Italy was "the natural product of sectarian liberalism."[57]

A different refrain of this same antiliberal theme was the argument that dueling was a form of indirect suicide or even a combination suicide/homicide. According to this point of view, exposing oneself to death in order to avoid the shame of dishonor and public derision was tantamount to complete despair and was thus analogous to suicide.[58] This was an old concept and may have been the reason that the Council of Trent had set forth basically the same penalties for dueling as it had for suicide: absolute excommunication and exclusion from Christian burial. But it had taken on new meaning in the second half of the nineteenth century as it came to light that proportionally more and more Italians were taking their own lives. It was thus easy to assert that these two plagues, dueling and suicide, were being visited upon Italy because the Risorgimento had embraced the forces of rationalism and materialism and rejected the moral anchor of Catholicism. Cut adrift in a rapidly changing and amoral society, people, according to one Catholic critic, became "disfigured in the slime of transitory pleasures, no longer believing in the future."[59] As such, they looked for meaning in their lives and, unable to find it, sought to hide behind the false precepts of chivalry or instead sought final escape through suicide. Whichever the case, there was little doubt in the minds of the Catholic critics as to the basic causes of these two "epidemic" problems, just as a solution was to be found in returning to a Christian concept of the state.[60]

Interestingly, however, Catholics were not the only ones interested in equating dueling and suicide. As Geltmaker has pointed out, criminal anthropologists also drew such a connection, with Enrico Ferri asserting that the duel consisted of a "generic and indirect consent of one's own death" as part of a desire for honor. Of course, they took a rather

56. Ibid., 6.
57. Brandi 1898, 6. Also see "Duelli parlamentari," *Il bastone,* March 20, 1910, 3.
58. This was a common trope, e.g., letters of the Archbishop of Pisa and Bishop of Frascati in Capretz 1926, 75, 138.
59. Tagliabue 1867, 30.
60. Geltmaker 2002, 49–61.

different approach than the Church as to why both dueling and suicide were on the rise in Italy. Although they agreed that suicide was tied to changes in society since unification, they argued that it was a natural reaction to the disruption of previous patterns of behavior and the shift from a rural agrarian economy to an urban industrial one. The quickening of the pace of life and the loss of familiar surroundings made people "nervous" and led those with innate and atavistic tendencies toward instability to react in a degenerate manner. Since societal pressure was growing against violence and toward greater "civilization," these individuals struck out against themselves either directly through suicide or indirectly through the duel.[61] Such actions were seen in part as a beneficial "safety valve" because they reduced the number of homicides, but there was also an assumption on the part of people like Ferri, who was a devoted socialist, that if living conditions were improved and people became more comfortable, fewer people with atavistic tendencies would be pushed to manifest them, although there would always be a core group of "degenerates" who would never really fit into society.[62] Consequently, as Italy evolved socially, both suicide and dueling would abate in due time.

The overlap of medicine and law, so clearly evident in the thinking of the criminal anthropologists, also affected regular physicians who opposed the duel, albeit in a somewhat different way. Doctors found themselves in a very ticklish position vis-à-vis dueling because in order for a duel to be "legal" a physician had to be in attendance. As with the other rituals of the "code of honor," failure to meet this obligation could disqualify the duel and open the participants to more serious legal sanctions.[63] Although many physicians only assisted duels with reluctance, they did so in order to provide immediate medical care if necessary. Even more important, they were able to limit the damage done in duels by declaring one of the opponents in a state of "inferiority" because of a wound, thus ending the combat.[64] On the other hand, attending physicians were obviously participating in a ritual designed by its very nature to injure or kill at least one of its participants, and this seemed to make them rather culpable.

61. Ibid., 37–43. For other examples of criminal anthropology's influence on discussion of the duel see Berenini 1889; Venturi 1898; Russo-Ajello 1906, 15–17; and Bruchi 1893, 4.
62. On Ferri see Gibson 2002, 30–35. In 1906 Lombroso suggested that one could "draw" an anthropological portrait of the typical duelist. Russo-Ajello 1906, xv.
63. On the legal aspects of doctors at duels see Benussi 1907.
64. "Il medico nel duello," *Cappa e spada,* March 15, 1888, 39–40.

This moral/legal dilemma was complicated by the gains of positivism in Italy and the growing professionalization of medicine in the last quarter of the nineteenth century. Doctors could now argue that it was their duty to actively and collectively counter the duel as part of their "sanitary mission" working toward the "hygienic progress" of mankind. Hence dueling became something akin to a microbe against which prophylactic action was necessary. The previous tradition of participating at duels had been only a reactive or "curative" process, but now doctors had to lead the way and find a proactive, "preventive" cure for the problem. Professor Gaetano Parlavecchio could therefore argue that the medical community, armed with the weapons of modern medicine, had the "right and duty to modify the environment" and protect their gentleman neighbors from the dueling contagion.[65]

His prophylactic scheme was eminently simple: doctors should *as a group* refuse to participate in duels. Without medical assistance and the legitimacy it provided to their actions, duelists would find other ways to settle their disputes. However, in order to implement this plan, Parlavecchio proposed that the government would have to give doctors greater power to police themselves. Thus he implored the parliament to "stop the worthless delays which it has previously interposed against the approval of the projected law for the juridical recognition of the Doctors Associations."[66] If such empowerment were not forthcoming, doctors would still be able to continue to participate at duels despite the general condemnation of the practice by the current medical organizations.[67] Clearly then, the campaign against the duel became part of a larger campaign on the part of the medical profession, or at least certain important sectors of it, to create an officially sanctioned guild that could discipline its members for the overall good of society and, one suspects, for themselves.

This blatant bid for professional power obviously transcended the issue at hand and once again underscored the often political nature of the antidueling movement in Italy. Thus, despite its common goal, the campaign did not have a common agenda, and arguments could be adduced from a wide variety of angles, interests, and factions. In this respect, the antidueling movement acted as a mirror to Billacois' adage that dueling was a "total social phenomenon by virtue of the richness

---

65. Parlavecchio 1907, 12–13.
66. Ibid., 7.
67. In fact, rival medical associations did not follow Palermo's example. See Federici 1909, 40.

of its meanings and implications."[68] Although diverse groups and individuals could be equally and honestly opposed to the practice, their assumptions, approaches, and desires often differed radically according to politics, profession, or confession. For instance, Russo-Ajello, a lawyer from Palermo, published over 300 pages in 1906 denouncing Italy's "duellomania" as antithetical to everything good, but he saved his concluding chapter to condemn the duel as symbolic of everything wrong with the Italian military, including the government's often tragic tendency to use soldiers for internal security. Thus he argued:

> The duel signals the degeneration of militarism: to use weapons sacred to the fatherland for killing companions instead of fighting enemies is the worst of faults.
> And we therefore criticize the government whenever it uses soldiers for police services or for the bloody repression and slaughter of innocent citizens [. . .].[69]

Dueling, like police work, undercut military prestige and efficiency, and it was no secret, Russo-Ajello chided, that Italy's army was famous for its duelists rather than its victories. Leaving aside his rather tortuous logic, we are struck by the ease with which the duel became a touchstone of political complaint against the liberal regime and its practices. In a sense, because of its multivalent nature, the duel invited critics to come from every corner, and the very exclusionary principle that lay at the heart of the point of honor only emphasized the isolation of "legal" Italy, dominated by "little writers, little publicists, and little officeholders, now raised by their positions and social dignities" from the real Italy of the people.[70]

The Socialist Dilemma

Such rhetoric naturally found favor among Italy's socialists. At the party's fourth national congress, which took place in Florence during the summer of 1896, a large majority of delegates voted to prohibit members from fighting in duels or even acting as seconds. In addition, they pledged to promote a propaganda campaign designed to disabuse

68. Billacois 1990, 1.
69. Russo-Ajello 1906, 352–53.
70. Bianchetti 1887.

the masses of the prejudice "that he is dishonored who when challenged does not fight and when offended does not challenge." They recommended as well that socialist deputies work to pass legislation that would punish crimes of violence committed in a duel with the same severity as those committed under normal circumstances.[71] Although some important figures opposed such a motion, the fundamental social inequalities inherent in the dueling ethic prompted easy passage of the condemnation. According to one delegate, "[I]t is precisely because proletarians are not considered gentlemen, to whom alone the honor of arms is accorded, that we, if we want to show the solidarity that ties us to the workers, must reject the duel." How, asked another, could the party ever ask workers to give up the violent culture of their knives if its bourgeois leaders were allowed to keep fighting with their swords? While the congress balked at expelling members who might get involved in a duel, delegates vented their ire against those who betrayed the socialist belief in an ideal future for the sake of medieval notions of honor. Collectivist principles demanded opposition to a prejudice that was by its very definition tied to rampant individualism.[72]

The party remained true to these precepts, and when the rest of Italy cheered the "triumph" of the Count of Turin in his defense of Italian honor against the Prince of Orleans in 1897, *Avanti*—the socialist newspaper—refused to be drawn into the celebration. Instead, it criticized the affair as simply a result of Savoyard monarchical pretensions.[73] Less than a year later, however, the party joined the chorus of outrage over the death of Felice Cavallotti, and the socialist deputy Giuseppe Berenini called on parliament to deprive the duel of its privileged *sui generis* status as a crime, thus increasing penalties against duelists who wounded or killed their opponents.[74] Respectfully consigned by the *Camera* to the oblivion of further study, the presentation of the project nevertheless allowed Berenini to point with pride to the fact that the socialists had openly and consistently opposed the duel in both word and deed.[75] Here he was referring to those comrades, such as Camillo Prampolini, Enrico Ferri, and Mario Todeschini, who on principle had publicly refused to fight when challenged and who had endured the

---

71. Text of the motion is in Pedone 1959, vol. 1, 81.
72. Partito Socialista 1897, 87–89.
73. "Vertenza Savoia-Orleans," *Avanti*, Aug. 16, 1–2. Also see Aug. 15 and 17.
74. *Atti parlamentari*, Leg. XX, 1st session, vol. 574, 5076–77, with discussion on 5814–19: April 10 and 16, 1898, respectively.
75. Ibid., 5805; also see Mazza 1904, 8.

resulting social pressure, including for Ferri a proclamation on the part of the *Tribuna* of his figurative death as a man.[76]

Despite Berenini's positive assertions, however, the socialist campaign against the duel remained sporadic and half-hearted. Some provincial sections attempted to expel members who dueled, but at the national level there was a notable lack of commentary or criticism.[77] By 1910, Giovanni Zibordi, in a special report prepared for the National Party Congress in October, declared the party's propaganda effort stillborn and chided the leadership for apathy and acquiescence in the face of the chivalric ethic. Key members had participated in various duels and *vertenze,* and the socialist press had more or less accommodated their activities. Had Zibordi looked back to the debates of 1896, he would have easily discerned the roots of the problem. Some of the most prominent figures in the movement, including both present and future editors of *Avanti,* had spoken out against the original condemnation of the duel on both theoretical and practical grounds. Filippo Turati had argued that most likely the phenomenon would simply disappear in the near future, and he had seconded a statement by Carlo Tanzi that since the proletariat did not duel, and since the party worked for the proletariat, there was no need to deal with the issue. Claudio Treves had criticized those who wanted an official condemnation of the duel as a means of fending off *sfide* from the opposition for being weak souls of vacillating conscience. He felt that it was a matter of private morality which the party should not attempt to legislate, and he invoked the memory of Ferdinand Lasalle, who had died in a duel, but who had been a great socialist and was still highly revered in Germany.[78]

Even more revealing were the comments of Bernardino Verro, founder of the Fasci Siciliani, who had only recently fought a duel and who defended his actions as necessary to his political efficacy. His opponents had accused him of cowardice, and, if he had not accepted the challenge, his working-class supporters would have agreed with them. Yes, he was against dueling as a barbaric custom, and he admitted that duelists were no more than marionettes going through the motions prescribed by society:

---

76. Ibid. Ferri's condemnation was mentioned at the 1896 congress. Partito Socialista 1897. On Prampolini's refusal as "propaganda" see "Contro il duello," in *L'Italia del popolo,* Milano, Oct. 27–28, 1891, 1.
77. On expulsions see Russo-Ajello 1906, 73–74; Mazza 1904, 8.
78. Partito Socialista 1897, 87–88.

But, you know, the crowd is a little fanatic for certain vestiges of barbarism, and when the opposing parties utilize such fanaticisms to discredit us, one just has to do something. If I had not accepted the duel, many others would have done it in my stead, and the *popolo,* irritated, might have resorted to acts of violence.

When I am not known, it is necessary to fight in order to make myself known. Our friends Ferri and Prampolini [who had refused duels] had already fought, and so no one could say that they were cowards. I had never fought before and so one could say it of me; and in that case I could not have remained in the midst of my people.[79]

This was a remarkable admission in front of a public meeting, and it was particularly piquant in its assertion that once a man had demonstrated his bravery on the field of honor, it was easier to then refuse for moral or ideological reasons. Above all, however, it laid bare the connection of power and honor on the public stage, where the physical courage of one's convictions was central to political action, and the need to prove one's manhood through ritual violence trumped other considerations.[80]

This tension created a real dilemma for the socialists. They opposed the duel, yet they sought to foster an image of revolutionary dynamism and virile force that was easily undercut by possible accusations of timidity.[81] For instance, Leonida Bissolati, prior to fighting a duel with Ferruccio Macola in the 1890s, reportedly proclaimed: "It is necessary to demonstrate that socialism is not a school of cowardice."[82] We see a later example of this tension in Anna Kuliscioff, the *grande dame* of Italian socialism, who in 1922 chastised Mario Missiroli for accepting a challenge from Mussolini, while her attitude toward him following the duel was couched in chivalric admiration: "Missiroli came here, lightly wounded, and for it being his first time fighting he magnificently did his part. He was cool, composed, deadpan; the other was madcap with the saber, anything but courageous and totally vulgar in everything."[83] The socialists' need to protect their masculinity also naturally raised questions about the duels they fought for reasons of intimacy, and even

79. Ibid. In 1886 Prampolini had spent 10 days in jail for dueling with the editor of *L'Italia centrale.* Andreucci and Detti 1975, vol. 4, 218.
80. See Addis Saba 1993, 125.
81. Nor was there any lack of critics willing to attribute the party's antidueling stance to a general spirit of cowardice; e.g., Morelli 1904, 240–41.
82. Rossi 1958, 60–61
83. Addis Saba 1993, 390.

the most vociferous opponents of the practice admitted this issue was almost impossible to deal with.[84]

These considerations naturally eroded the supposed solidarity of socialist resolve. When Walter Mocchi was wounded in a high-profile duel in 1905 over a private affair, he was taken to task by various local sections of the party, and the federation of Milan called for a special meeting, complete with advocates pro and con, to consider his expulsion. Yet the incident inspired an article by Vittorio Piva in *Avanti della domenica* which ran completely counter to the party's official position on the duel. He warned that the current attempt to create a "confraternity" that encroached on the moral liberty and intimate matters of its members would alienate good men who would shy away from such punctilious control.[85] Mocchi and Piva belonged to the more militant wing of the party, and the debate over the duel may have been more political smoke than moral fire as the moderates and maximalists struggled for control of the Milanese federation. Nevertheless, Piva's point fit his more general critique of the party's pacifist and antimilitarist policies, and it can be interpreted as a hedge against possible charges of effeminate weakness on the part of the left. Socialism needed men of fiber, but in Italy men of fiber had to be ready to duel.

The political nexus of honor, masculinity, and chivalry naturally impinged most directly on socialist deputies, and it was a parliamentary incident in 1910 that forced the party to admit and analyze the weakness of its previous policy. When Eugenio Chiesa's unbridled accusations against the ministry of war (examined in chapter II) resulted in no fewer than five *vertenze* and two duels within a week, two socialist deputies, Leonida Bissolati and Giufredda De Felice, figured prominently in the negotiations and encounters, with minute details of their involvement appearing in Italy's dailies, including *Avanti*. Turati, probably sensing a black eye for the party, tried to get the parliament to create a jury of honor to derail and pacify the various affairs, but he found no support for such intervention on the part of his fellow legislators.[86] In response to this startling contrast of socialist theory and socialist actions, the party leadership asked Giovanni Zibordi to prepare a position paper for the national congress to be held in Milan in October. Zibordi, who claimed to be about the only socialist journalist to have consistently written

84. Zibordi 1910, 7.
85. "I socialisti ed il duello," *Avanti della Domenica,* March 19, 1905.
86. "Una lettera di Filippo Turati," *Avanti,* March 9, 1910, 1. For an attack on the socialists over their part in the affair see "Duelli parlamentari," *Il Bastone,* March 20, 1910, 3.

against the practice, rose to the occasion and offered up a lengthy and sophisticated denunciation of the duel as being completely contrary to the antimilitaristic and humanitarian principles of the party. He also reiterated the main theme of the congress of 1896, which had focused on the social inequality inherent to chivalric honor, and he bitingly noted that no democratic or republican *borghese*, no matter how radical his politics, had ever deigned to duel with a member of the working class (a charge that he could have, in fact, extended to his own party).[87]

Zibordi went beyond these standard arguments, however, to interpret the acquiescence of some party leaders to the dictates of the dueling code as symptomatic of a larger problem: the gradual pollution of socialist faith by the bourgeois arena in which they were trying to operate. In the corrupting ethos of parliament, some socialists had acted like provincial innocents and had lost sight of their basic principles, bedazzled by the artificial individualism of power politics. They had been taken in by a ritual of false physical courage which was used—either consciously or unconsciously—to cover the many transgressions of the liberal regime. How many times, as had been the case with Chiesa's accusations against the ministry of war, had important questions regarding public policy been sidelined and silenced after being personalized as affairs of honor? The socialists should be, by definition, the party of opposition, the party of surveillance, but they gave up that role when they allowed themselves to be dragged like marionettes onto the chivalric stage: "The political duel is an alibi or a diversion; often calculatingly desired by interested parties, and always concluding in the same effect, that is that the right of control is circumvented and the higher good of the collectivity is obliterated thanks to a personal solution."[88]

In order to combat these seductions of the dueling ethic, Zibordi called on members of the party to recognize that the physical bravery supposedly demonstrated in a duel was already inherent in someone willing to risk the dangers of joining the militant avant-garde of socialism. Beyond such physical valor, however, socialists had to manifest the moral courage and civil virtue necessary to hold the course of right action leading toward truth and reason. They had to turn the logic of the duel on its head. By rejecting all participation in *vertenze* and resisting the resulting social pressure, they would demonstrate the meaning of true courage, which would be reinforced by their moral rectitude

87. Zibordi 1910, 5.
88. Ibid., 10.

and "virile frankness." Without the crutch of chivalry as a means of settling personal disputes, socialists would have to comport themselves in a truly virtuous and straightforward manner, and their example would elevate the notion of courage for all civilized men. It was, in fact, a call to construct a new form of socialist masculinity, which would embrace a revolutionary notion of honor and leave the pathetic and artificial rituals of the duel in the dust.

Nevertheless, Zibordi tempered this idealistic fervor with some pragmatic considerations, the most important of which was to make an exception for duels arising from affairs of the heart. He felt that in such cases no absolute prohibition could be applied by the party because matters of intimacy were "complicated and compelling." Given the current state of society, Italians were not ready for the "cold customs of other countries" by which a betrayed husband might turn to the regular judiciary. To offset such problems, he called on the party to push for civil reforms such as divorce and a more modern conception of marriage that would blunt the "tyrannical concepts" that forced husbands to risk their lives in the wake of being cuckolded.[89] These reforms were easy to project into the future, but Zibordi obviously still had to deal with the current tension between "rational" socialists and their sexual self-image as "real" men. Consequently, his final motion, which was presented to the 1910 congress, railed against the duel as an abominable bourgeois prejudice and prohibited socialists from participating in *vertenze* no matter what the issue; yet it conspicuously failed once again to provide for the expulsion of those party members who might actually do so.[90]

What the effect of such a draconian provision might have been is hard to tell, but, as it was, prominent socialists, including Claudio Treves, Emanuele Modigliani, Francesco Ciccotti, Pietro Nenni, and Leonida Répaci, would continue to duel up to the First World War and beyond. As with the other abolitionists, the socialists would thus come up against the frustrating reality of having their own fine words and arguments betrayed by the actions of their colleagues: actions that pointedly and counterproductively advertised the currency rather than the bankruptcy of the dueling compulsion. On the other hand, it is obvious that, overall, the socialists viewed dueling as an integral aspect of the class biases

89. Ibid., 7–9.
90. The motion was never discussed, and it is unclear whether it was ever formally adopted. See Direzione del PSI, *Resoconto stenografico dell XI Congresso Nazionale,* Roma: Officina Poligrafica, 1911.

of liberalism which would automatically disappear along with that regime. In consequence, they focused their attention on preventing people in the party from participating in duels, and one searches the antidueling literature in vain for any pamphlets written by socialists to a larger audience. Such an isolated approach, aimed purely at the party faithful, naturally proscribed participation with other groups and highlights a problem inherent in the antidueling movement as a whole: although vehement in their mutual denunciation of the duel, opponents of the practice were often at even greater odds with each other, especially the Catholics and the socialists. This antagonism, which mirrored the larger strategies of the two groups as they struggled to define their roles in Italy's changing political landscape, would naturally hamper widespread cooperation as a more formal antidueling movement began to emerge around the turn of the century.

Filippo Crispolti and the Anti-dueling League

The catalyst for such innovation came once again from Cavallotti's spectacular demise in 1898, which, as previously noted, helped revitalize the debate over the juries of honor. His death genuinely shocked public opinion, and at the news crowds of students reportedly marched through the streets of Rome yelling, "Down with the duel! Long live socialism!" while the masons issued a general denunciation of the practice.[91] According to Cavallotti's biographer, "For the first time in Italy, there were not just isolated voices rising up against the barbaric and absurd institution, but a wide movement of opinion, that finished by putting it in crisis."[92] He unquestionably overstated the case—the duel still had a long life to lead—but Cavallotti's death did raise awareness of the problem to a new level and also paved the way for the first voluntary societies devoted specifically to the eradication of the duel as a means of settling disputes among gentlemen. Such societies were an old idea in Italy; Clemente Pellegrini had published a lengthy treatise advocating their creation as early as 1868, but a general impetus to action had been lacking.[93] Now, before the fatal year 1898 had run out, Milan's International Society for Peace, under the direction of the pacifist Teodorico Moneta, began organizing an Italian antidueling society. It appears,

91. Lega 1930, 332–33; Galante Garrone 1976, 719.
92. Ibid., 720.
93. Pellegrini 1868.

however, to have immediately run afoul of the Lombard Press Association, which felt, given Cavallotti's journalistic roots in Milan, that it should lead the charge against the "grotesque and barbarous prejudice." Further confusion came when yet another committee in Milan formed for the same purpose in 1902.[94] Cavallotti's unfortunate end had certainly created a favorable climate of opinion, but some larger organizational structure seemed necessary for effective action to occur.

That structure and the energy requisite to its creation would come from Marchese Filippo Crispolti, whose name became synonymous with the antidueling movement after the turn of the century. Born into a well-heeled aristocratic family of the Romagna in 1857, he initially trained as a lawyer but abandoned the law for journalism and soon emerged as one of the bright lights of the Catholic intransigent movement as it came to grips with the evolving political situation in Italy. An editor of the influential *L'osservatore romano* from 1887 to 1895, he was a key player in the Opera dei Congressi and a faithful adherent of the careful and conservative policies of Leo XIII. Far from reactionary, he sought to integrate the Catholic movement into a wide spectrum of social and political activities, all the while renouncing any accommodation with liberalism or the Italian parliamentary system, both of which he considered doomed to eventual failure for their lack of moral center. He accepted (as some of his compatriots did not) the legitimacy of the Savoyard monarchy and the fact that Italy was a nation whose capital was in Rome. With these concessions in mind, he sought to prepare a sort of "Catholic patriotism" which looked to the traditions of the papacy as a source of cohesion for the upcoming day when the Church would return to power in a new political synthesis. In the meantime he used his journalistic skills to fight for those reforms that he thought appropriate and against those, such as the introduction of divorce, which he found contrary to Catholic doctrine.[95]

With regard to the duel, Crispolti may have taken his lead directly from Leo XIII. Although Pius IX had reiterated the Church's threat of excommunication against duelists and their accomplices in 1869 (a reaction perhaps against the perceived "plague" of duels sweeping the country), his successor felt compelled to publish a full-length diatribe against the practice in 1891.[96] Two years later, Crispolti outlined a campaign against the duel in a long treatise that promoted Leo's condemnation

94. Russo-Ajello 1906, 76–78.
95. Martire 1943; DBI, vol. 30, 813–18; Crispolti 2005.
96. "Costitutio Apostolicae Sedis" (Oct. 12, 1869) and "Pastoral officii" (Sept. 12, 1891).

as a fundamental weapon of propaganda and persuasion. Crispolti was convinced that the dueling prejudice was so deeply ingrained in liberal society that the standard apparatus of criminal justice was helpless in its repression. The bourgeoisie, he claimed, had overthrown the old regime and, lacking any religious compass to guide it, had grasped on to the old aristocratic point of honor as a source of moral legitimacy. Thus the duel was difficult to deal with because high society had internalized its basic precepts and transformed them into a set of morally coercive behaviors designed to assure compliance. One could perhaps convince Italian elites of the fundamental illogic of the duel, but when push came to shove, so to speak, Crispolti was convinced that they would bow to the pressure of their clubs and compatriots.[97]

Based on this analysis, Crispolti supported a campaign of conferences and pamphlets aimed at creating a countervailing public opinion that rejected the false and flattering precepts of chivalry. Yet he offered an important caveat to such propaganda. One might easily win the war of words, but the battles of behavior would be consistently lost because the duel offered not only honor but also a dramatic sense of struggle and self-sacrifice that appealed to young people of spirit. Combined with the psychological compulsions of elite society, this was a seductive and dangerous package, and Catholic energies should be directed first and foremost toward protecting the faithful, and especially the young, from its enticements. Previous attempts in this direction had been overly defensive rather than offensive according to Crispolti. They had adopted the liberals' own arguments of logic and reason, which lacked real moral clout, and consequently Catholic youth had been ill-prepared to stand up to the pressure of public opinion. In contrast, the Church needed to act "fiercely" on the issue of the duel and offer a virile program that stressed strict obedience to papal command, calling on the very spirit of self-sacrifice and bravery that fueled the duel itself. The strictures of Leo's 1891 prohibition should be sold to Italy's Catholic youth as an onerous and difficult task, requiring courage and fortitude in the face of social adversity. From that perspective, the very challenge of resistance would reinforce its effectiveness. "Remember," rang the last line of his project, "that only the strong understand the glory of obedience."[98] Such muscular Catholicism lay at the heart of Crispolti's battle against the duel, and it helps explain, along with his

97. Crispolti 1893, 18–39.
98. Ibid., 45–47.

obvious leadership in the Catholic movement, why the league which he inspired had to consistently combat accusations of confessionalism.[99]

With public sentiment primed by Cavallotti's death, Crispolti felt he had an opportunity to launch a broad-based crusade against the duel, but he was also well aware that his clerical connections might limit the scope of his success. Looking beyond the Catholic community, he understood that a proactive campaign, which might have a general effect on the behavior of all Italian elites, would have to assert some authority other than papal pronouncement. He conveniently found his inspiration in Don Alfonso di Bourbon, pretender to the throne of Spain, who currently resided in Vienna. In the summer of 1900, Don Alfonso had been shocked by a notorious case in which an Austrian officer had refused to fight a duel out of religious conviction and had been cashiered from the army and excluded from polite society. He began corresponding with his many acquaintances throughout Europe in hopes of starting an international wave of protest and soon attracted adherents to his cause across the continent.[100] A formal association emerged in 1902, and national branches soon appeared in Germany, France, and Spain. In June of 1808, delegates from the different countries attended a three-day international congress in Hungary and adopted a 13-point plan of action, including the creation of a permanent headquarters, provisionally located in the host city of Budapest.[101]

Italy joined this movement relatively early. Crispolti had been recommended to Don Alfonso as the perfect person to push the new crusade, and in November 1902 he published an article in *Nuova antologia,* one of liberal Italy's most prestigious journals, trying to create enthusiasm for the league. Keeping his intransigent Catholic fervor at bay, he described dueling primarily as a sociological problem, and, rather than attack the moral credentials of liberalism, he pushed for the creation of courts of honor to handle insults and libels. On a more ominous note, he hinted that the glaring class bias, obvious in the legal immunity afforded duelists, might help bring the proletariat to power, and then the duel would surely disappear—along with bourgeois society in general![102] In dealing with the international antidueling movement, he emphasized Don Alfonso's stature as a king-in-exile and his military valor, proven under fire during Spain's recent power struggles,

---

99. For example, Russo-Ajello 1906, 4; Gelli 1920, xvii.
100. De Bourbon 1908, 3.
101. Crispolti 1902; Federici 1909.
102. Crispolti 1902, 139.

rather than the depth of his religious beliefs. This was to be a campaign open to civil courage as well as Catholic conviction. Equally important from a tactical point of view, Crispolti argued that Italy's branch of the Anti-dueling League should be named after General Ettore Perrone di San Martino, a Piedmontese officer who had gone into exile in France after the revolution of 1821. San Martino had become the poster child of Italy's abolitionist movement because he had written an impassioned denunciation of the duel (which he presented to the French legislature) and also because he had returned to Piedmont during the revolutions of 1848 and had bravely died fighting against the Austrians.[103] Crispolti co-opted the cachet of this Risorgimento war hero, whom he cleverly dubbed the "Beccaria of the abolition of the duel," as a perfect political foil to the monarchical, Bourbon, and Catholic background of Don Alfonso, under whose auspices the league was about to be born. The Bourbons had been traditional enemies of Italian unification, but adopting the name of a Piedmontese revolutionary and "constant liberal" like San Martino helped balance the symbolic scales.[104]

Crispolti's ecumenical approach apparently struck a chord, and within 15 days of the article's publication he received some 475 letters of adherence, including 21 from retired generals. An organizing meeting was held on December 21, 1902, in Rome, and the National Anti-dueling League "Ettore Perrone di San Martino" was born under the presidency of Prince Doria Pamphili, in whose villa the event took place.[105] A second meeting held the following June approved a platform pushing for the revision of the penal code and the use of juries of honor to settle disputes.[106] The league was self-funded, with founding members paying a one-time fee of 50 lire and contributing members paying annual dues of 2 lire, a sum easily affordable to a wide spectrum of the middle class. Women were allowed to join, as were resident foreigners, and members were expected to promulgate the league's goals without prejudice to politics or religion. While Crispolti stressed the primacy of winning over retired military officers and the old aristocracy, whom he called the true *arbitri elegantiarum* in Italy, he happily reported receiving affirmations from judges, politicians, academics, and journalists.[107]

Despite this early enthusiasm, the league failed to produce much

103. Perrone's petition against the duel is in Abignente, second edition (1898).
104. For his concern on such issues see Crispolti 1905.
105. "Il movimento internazionale contro il duello," *Civiltà Cattolica*, Feb. 6, 1909, 333.
106. For the league's constitution see Mazza 1904, 59–62.
107. Russo-Ajello 1906, 79.

practical action during its first few years, in part because when it came time for the members to do real work, Crispolti was forced to rely on his personal contacts, hence reinforcing the group's conservative Catholic identity.[108] It gradually gained momentum, however, and 1906 saw a flurry of new organizing activity that produced affiliate committees and juries of honor in Pisa, Genoa, Florence, Turin, Venice, Bologna, Naples, and Casale, as well as a women's league in Lombardy that could boast 300 members.[109] In June of that year, Crispolti wrote a letter pressing the issue at the Congress of Retired Officers meeting in Rome, and it reportedly sparked that association's public call for the creation of courts of honor on the part of the high command.[110] One of the founding members, Count Emiliano di Paravicino, successfully persuaded a national conference on the family to adopt a resolution calling for the incorporation of antidueling propaganda at the high school level and encouraging eighteen-year-olds to join the league.[111] Eventually, the league embraced the international 13-point platform that came out of the 1908 congress, including a call for doctors to stop attending duels and the promotion of antidueling essay contests among students.[112]

The big news came at the end of 1907 when, in rapid succession, the minister of war Viganò informed Crispolti in an open letter of his vigorous opposition to the duel in the army, and on the next day—and probably not without connection—King Victor Emmanual III declared that he had decided to become the high patron of the Italian Antidueling League.[113] This was a major coup. The monarchy seems to have previously maintained a studied silence on the duel, and any argument to the contrary was undercut by the fact that successive kings had consistently cranked out pardons for convicted duelists. Now Victor Emmanuel III had declared royal support for the Anti-dueling League, and on December 17, 1907, he invited a delegation, including Crispolti, to discuss the details of its program.[114] One can only assume that

---

108. See Russo-Ajello 1906, 4, 80–81. In contrast see Crispolti 1905 and Di Paravicino 1906, 7.
109. Russo-Ajello 1906, 80–81; "Il movimento intenazionale contro il duello" in *Civiltà cattolica*, Feb. 6, 1909, 333.
110. De Bourbon 1908, 23–24.
111. Di Paravicino 1906, 8.
112. Federici 1909, 38–41.
113. The king apparently did not write directly to Crispolti but rather to General Count di Revel, who was acting deacon of the army and a founding member of the league. "Il movimento," in *Civiltà cattolica*, Feb. 6, 1909, 334.
114. De Bourbon 1908, 25–26.

these developments helped set the stage for the decree of October 8, 1908, establishing the courts of honor within the military, and Crispolti was congratulated by the Catholic hierarchy for having brought that particular reform into port.[115] Reporting on the general progress of the movement in the fall of that year, Don Alfonso predicted that Italy would soon no longer need an antidueling league because the king and the army had begun to set an example for the rest of society.[116] Crispolti was equally optimistic. By the time the First World War had brought the International Anti-dueling League to an abrupt end, he felt that the tide had turned against the duel, and he had focused his attention on other issues.[117] Little did he know that he would have to return to the problem after the war as the duel rebounded in a completely different political context.

We must also be careful in giving Crispolti's organization too much credit. Virtually all of the glowing reports on the league's achievements came from abolitionist sources or their allies such as *Civiltà cattolica*. The very act of proclaiming varied and widespread antidueling activity was seen as effective propaganda on their part, whatever the practical results on the ground. Nor was Crispolti able to co-opt the antidueling energies of the socialists, hardly surprising for an organization that drew over half its original executive council (13 of 24) from the nobility.[118] Nevertheless, it is fair to say that the league helped focus much of the energy resulting from Cavallotti's shocking death and provided a pan-Italian forum for gentlemen to at least consider rejecting the dueling compulsion without losing face, especially once the king came on board as an official patron.[119]

Crispolti's success came in part because he understood the tie between the dueling ethic and nationalism, not surprising for the man who had created the concept of "Catholic Patriotism" as a means of healing the rancorous rift between church and state in Italy. His grasp of the problem was most obvious when he tied the Italian League to the memory of a Risorgimento war hero who had publicly opposed the duel and died fighting for Piedmont. Yet it is also hard not to notice

---

115. See the letter of Cardinal Agliardi in Martire 1943, 77.
116. De Bourbon 1908, 26.
117. Martire 1943, 31–32. Crispolti's nephew, Giovanni B. Crispolti, confirmed this in a private conversation with the author.
118. Membership list in Mazza 1904, 62. On the socialists see Crispolti's senate speech in Capretz 1926, 153.
119. Premoli 1910, 4–7.

his constant emphasis on the fact that the Italian League was part of a grand European-wide project, backed by elites across the continent. Part of this pitch came naturally from his "lower-case" catholic concept of universal morality, but it also sprang from his grasp of the duel as a purveyor of symbolic courage for both individuals and Italian men as a group—a concept which he had dissected and attempted to co-opt in his own project of virile obedience to the pope back in 1893. If Italy had unilaterally and effectively embarked on the path to abolish the duel, it might have raised the old specter of an effeminate country lacking in martial fiber. If, however, the French, Germans, Austrians, and others were equally involved, then there could be no hint of cowardice or national weakness in Italian opposition. Understanding the need for Italian elites to appear strong and courageous, his international approach was a clever way of getting around the old bugaboos. Moreover, it would be, at least in some ways, more successful than the attempts of Italy's lawmakers, who in their extended debates over the duel would often run aground on their own identities as men of honor.

The Legal Conundrum of the Duel

The rapid growth of dueling after Italy's unification certainly did not go unnoticed by the country's legislators, and they consistently decried the proliferation of the practice as antithetical to the rule of law and to Italy's image as a civilized nation. They felt that at least part of the responsibility for the increase could be attributed to the new country's dueling laws, which were complex, contradictory, and obviously inefficient. In fact, united Italy had two penal codes, one for Tuscany and one for the rest of the country, and their widely divergent sanctions against the duel were respectively regarded as either overly severe or overly lenient. As a result, a Bolognese convicted of a duel resulting in a minor wound faced a maximum of six months' confinement and no minimum, while his Florentine counterpart had to spend three months to five years in prison.[120] The two codes had been allowed to stand together as one of the political compromises of the Risorgimento on the assumption that a unified code for all of Italy would soon be forthcoming. For a variety of reasons such a code did not appear, and the

---

120. Article 589 of the Piedmontese Penal Code (1859) and Article 345 of the Tuscan Penal Code (1853).

dueling issue got caught up in the confusion and delay that affected the overall reform of the country's penal code. As we have seen with the debate over the juries of honor, that process finally ended with the creation of the Zanardelli code of 1889, and in the intervening period Italy's dueling laws (like the rest of the criminal code) would be the focus of no fewer than three major parliamentary commissions and would evolve through some eight widely divergent draft versions, each appropriately vetted by the legal community. As frustrating as this process may have been for legislators and citizens alike, the many drafts of the law and the extended discussion they prompted provide a gold mine of insights into elite perceptions of honor and their impact on the political landscape of liberal Italy.[121]

Above all, the commentary and debate clearly revealed the numerous difficulties that Italian lawmakers encountered in dealing with the duel, which, it was suggested, engendered more discussion than any other penal issue except perhaps for the death penalty.[122] One legal wag complained in 1876: "The argument of the duel is the rock of Sisyphus. The more you roll it the more it stays where it is."[123] Almost 20 years later, an Italian judge reiterated that the legal ink spilled over the duel had exhausted "the minds of intelligent men."[124] Dueling proved an especially thorny problem for lawyers and legislators alike because it was a crime committed primarily by members of their own class and because it was based on precepts of chivalry which they tended to embrace. In short, the lengthy legal discourse on penal reform clearly demonstrated the intimate ties between dueling, honor, and Italy's liberal elites, who frankly found it hard to legislate against themselves. Yet their own conception of the rule of law, their belief in the equality of justice, and their desire to have Italy appear as a civilized and modern country led them to try to find effective ways of preventing the practice. In the end, this tension would result in legislation that would generally increase penalties against the duel but at the same time would thoroughly reinforce the ethos of chivalry in Italy, bolster the privileges of the "honorable" classes, and offer unofficial sanction to a parallel system of both legislation and adjudication that ran counter to their own legal imperatives.

---

121. All of the draft versions, commission reports, and parliamentary debates regarding the duel up to 1884 were collected and published in Crivellari 1884.
122. See Lo Manna's introduction to Salafia-Maggio 1895, ii; Facchinetti 1890, 7–8.
123. *Rivista penale,* vol. 5, 1876, 98.
124. Sost. Proc. Gen. Prampolini in *Rivista penale,* vol. 20, Sept.–Oct. 1884, 237.

There were, of course, people who felt that the duel should not be treated as a crime at all.[125] Some argued that because of its extensive roots in society, any law against it was unenforceable. Prosecutors would not bring dueling cases to trial, juries would not convict, parliament would not deprive its deputies of their legal immunity, and, in the end, the king would probably pardon those who were sentenced, especially if they were in the army. So what was the point of passing dead-letter laws? Others, such as the criminal anthropologists, suggested that neither dueling nor its violent results constituted crimes at all, because the participants entered the affray by their own free will and thus constituted no threat to society.[126] Some took a different approach and argued for the "French model," which, after 1837, allowed for the punishment of homicides or serious wounds arising from dueling, although not for the practice itself.[127] Later proponents of this policy argued that it was actually more effective than having special provisions against the duel, because the offending duelist was held fully responsible for a violent crime. A murder in a duel became just another murder.

In general, Italian legislators did not buy these arguments. Rather, they felt very strongly that dueling was a crime that should be punished in and of itself, and that the goal of such punishment was to end the practice as soon as possible for a wide variety of reasons. First, despite its supposedly honorable roots, dueling caused pain and suffering not only to the individuals involved but especially to their families. It also kept the "best" citizens in a high state of anxiety from which they could not escape and, in the case of death or permanent injury, deprived the nation of their talents.[128] Likewise, it replaced public justice with private vengeance, offering a bad example to the lower classes and offending the prerogatives of the state. Moreover, it smacked of premeditated murder or assault because the principal players had had time to cool down from their affront—whatever it might be—before taking action against each other. Such logic could lead to some rather strange places, and in one piquant exchange in parliament, the Royal Commissioner of Italy, Senator Eula, proclaimed that he felt better disposed to a man who killed his wife's lover in the hot blood of the betraying bedroom than toward a man who had the *sang-froid* to kill the interloper later in a duel.[129]

125. A good synopsis is in Crivellari 1884, 35–45.
126. For a synopsis see Bruchi 1893, 4.
127. Nye 1993, 134–35.
128. For a summary see Crivellari 1884, 47–49.
129. Session of April 26, 1875, in Crivellari 1884, 171.

Less romantic, but perhaps more important, was the leitmotif that ran through the entire discussion, and that was the rather simple idea that dueling was unworthy of a civilized country. This accounts for the constant vilification of the duel as a barbaric rite, an atavistic horror, a medieval vestige, all of which flew in the face of the progress and modernity that Italy had hoped to enjoy after unification.[130] Yet the case against dueling ran deeper than that. Rather, the duel struck at one of the heartstrings of the Risorgimento: the rule of law itself. Constitutional guarantees and equality before the law had been keynotes of the campaign against the tyranny of the preunitary governments, just as respect for public order and property had been a rallying cry of moderates as they had adopted unity under Piedmont as the key to social stability. How damaging, then, was the image, reported on an almost daily basis in the newspapers, of Italy's leading citizens flouting their own laws against dueling? Senator Chiesi railed against this "scandal" in 1875: "In Italy you can see important functionaries and politicians pass from the field of combat to the halls of parliament where they discuss laws and measures of public order in the general interest."[131] The legal considerations of such hypocrisy were compounded by an undercurrent of uneasiness regarding the lower classes. Unable to appreciate the hypersensibilities of honor that might excuse the need to duel, the *volgo* could only take the message that the law was less than sacred, that public order was negotiable, and that social position could dictate impunity: all disturbing conclusions for elites who considered the working classes as dangerous classes.

But legislating against the duel was difficult. Most lawmakers felt that it constituted a special, *sui generis,* crime that deserved lighter penalties compared to "regular" acts of violence. The assumption for such special treatment was that the duelists, although seeking to harm each other, were doing so by mutual consent and for what ultimately was a legitimate or at least a positive reason—the defense of their honor. Moreover, they were forced into this action by the weight of the "social prejudice" which both explained and excused their behavior. To not take that constant and powerful pressure into account when dealing with the legal sanction of the duel was to reject the reality within which the law had to operate.[132] Likewise, legislators reiterated the common arguments which maintained that the dueling compulsion was to a

130. For example, Senator Chiesi, session of April 24, 1875, in ibid., 152.
131. Session of April 16, 1875, in ibid., 134.
132. See, for instance, Senator Ambrosoli in ibid., 122.

certain extent justified, especially considering the weakness of Italy's current laws regarding both verbal and written insults. Even trickier were the minor physical insults which virtually escaped sanction under the penal code but which if unanswered could wreck a man's reputation and career. Thus Senator Pantaleoni argued that a man who was publicly slapped in the face but failed to seek satisfaction could never stand for public office, while the aggressor at most might get a minor fine from the courts.[133] And, of course, there were affairs of the heart. How could the legal system compensate the loss of a sister's virginity or restore a wife's fidelity? All of these problems might one day be resolved by improving the press laws, punishing minor assaults more firmly, introducing divorce into Italy, or, in the end, hopefully educating people to act more civilly. In fact, the final version of the code did substantially increase Italy's penalties for defamation and insult, and it clarified that some physical acts, such as a slap, constituted offenses against one's honor as opposed to one's body.[134] But these reforms were unproven, and in the meantime one had to take it easy on those who gave way to the prejudices around them and followed the dictates of chivalry and society.

Some lawmakers also adopted the arguments of Fambri and others that dueling had had a positive effect on Italian society, and, although deplorable as a crime, it had to be given special consideration that took its "honorable" role into account. Thus Senator Gallotti described in 1875 how dueling served as an antidote to vendetta by restricting and structuring the violence commonly associated with feuding in certain areas of the country.[135] His colleague Pantaleoni went even further and argued that there were nations of swords and nations of knives, with Corsica and Sicily serving as examples of the latter, where vendetta took the place of chivalry. Dueling, he claimed, limited conflicts, set rules, allowed reconciliation, and individualized offenses to honor rather than spreading them to entire families. But dueling, he claimed, went beyond the control of personal violence. Rather, it appealed to the best sentiments of men and had thus played an important role in helping the Italians find their way to freedom and independence:

---

133. Session of April 16, 1875, in ibid., 141. On the extraordinary gravity attributed to slapping see Morelli 1904, 266–68.
134. For an explanation of the changes in laws against honor see Zanardelli 1888, 568–601, and 1889, 148–51.
135. Session of April 24, 1875, in Crivellari 1884, 154.

The nations that had the duel were the greatest and the strongest; and those of the knife, of the assassin's poison, were the conquered and the enslaved. And why is that? Because the duel is founded on the sentiment of dignity, on courage, on strong convictions, while the secret vendetta, which takes its place, includes treason, vileness, cowardice. If for many centuries we did not have the duel, from the barbarians we had in its stead servitude, slavery, tyranny; and if now for some years we have had a great vogue for the duel they have been the first years of regeneration, of our emancipation, of our liberty.[136]

Once again the intimate tie of Risorgimento and chivalry manifested its attraction, and to simply demote the duel to the status of a common crime, on a par with murder or theft, bordered on the unpatriotic.

This nationalist theme was cleverly elaborated in 1888 during final discussions of the Zanardelli code by Luigi Indelli, a deputy from Bari working on the chamber's revision committee. Indelli, like most other legislators, agreed that "in theory" the state had to punish the duel, but in reality it had to tread very softly because dueling was close to the hearts of Italians and to the destiny of the country. Harking back to the revolutionary traditions of unification, he compared dueling (which was not committed by common criminals and had noble honor as its cause) to the "political crimes" that had struck at despotism and oppression under the old regime. So much for the past: but the duel according to Indelli was also important to the future. The chivalric code had become engrained in Italy's associations and institutions, and it deserved to stay there because it served the nation's ambitions. As European society embraced a "general armament," Italy needed stalwart men for its armed forces. Could the parliament, he asked, really expect an officer, like Christ, to turn the other cheek to a slap in the face and still be capable of defending the country's borders?[137] Such invective lay at the heart of the dueling dilemma for Italian lawmakers. They had to acknowledge the position that the duel and the point of honor had come to play in their own regime, yet they all believed mightily in the rule of law. Consequently they had to thread the juridical needle of treating the duel with greater leniency than other crimes, all the while providing penalties that would affirm the prerogatives of the state and eventually lead to its diminution.[138]

136. Session of April 16, 1875, in ibid., 144.
137. Indelli 1888, 1.
138. Leniency was also counseled by the difficulty of getting judges and juries to enforce

Having made the decision rather early on to treat the duel as a special crime with lesser consequences, however, Italy's lawmakers quickly found themselves facing another conundrum that only seemed to reinforce the code of chivalry and its imperatives. How was one to recognize a duel as being a duel, and what constituted a "legal" duel? Was there even such a thing since dueling was, by definition, illegal? Although they did not openly admit it, the logical consequence of such questions was to strengthen the juridical position of various experts in the field of chivalry. One could be assured of fighting a correct duel by relying on the instructions of a dueling manual, written by a recognized authority, such as Angelini or Gelli, and, as we have seen, there would eventually be over 20 manuals to choose from. In this sense Italy's lawmakers came to legitimate the autoregulation of honor and its defense as controlled by the duelists, and thus they indirectly recognized a parallel legislation created by private parties.[139] It was just this compromise that led to the interminable approach/avoidance response that the regime manifested toward the courts of honor as it flirted with a mechanism that offered another layer of chivalric expertise to the process.

Nowhere was this connection between the code of honor and "official" Italy clearer than in the consideration of penalties. Although much debate ranged over the amount of fines and length of prison sentences, the real controversy raged over the proposal to punish duelists and their accomplices with "civil disqualification," or *squalifica civile*—that is, the revocation of the right to vote, hold government office, or sit in parliament. Proponents of this penalty considered it poetic justice that men claiming to protect their honor should be struck directly in their *amour propre* as citizens. Curtailing their ambition and declaring to the public that they were unfit for service, it constituted a perfect punishment for dueling, which found its adherents among the "educated and well off" sectors of society.[140] Such arguments carried considerable weight, and of the seven draft versions of the dueling law before 1889, no fewer than six carried penalties incurring various forms and lengths of civil disqualification

Opponents, however, were adamant in their criticism of such proposals and mustered impassioned pleas that easily demonstrated how close to home *squalifica civile* came. Dueling, they claimed, might be

---

severe sanctions. Crivellari 1884, 31, 82, 140, 144.
  139. This parallel legislation was celebrated by dueling advocates such as Morelli 1904, 255.
  140. Crivellari 1884, 83, 148.

many things, but it was based on concepts of honor, and in the rest of the penal code, civil disqualification was reserved only for dishonorable crimes. To lump duelists with cheaters, perjurers, and embezzlers was to miss the point of honor entirely. It also jeopardized the administration of justice, because most people did not consider dueling as dishonorable, and to have it punished as such would only put the law at odds with public opinion and thus condemn it to dead-letter status. Moreover, everybody was aware that dueling was prominent among, if not restricted to, the *classe civile* from which Italy recruited its best and brightest political talent. What a sad state, protested Senator Gallotti, the country would be in now if such a penalty had been around before: "How many soldiers, how many ministers who fortunately offer service and create honor for Italy, with this law, if it had been passed and placed in action earlier, would have not been able to serve the land of our birth, Italy."[141] Such arguments eventually won the day, and when the Zanardelli code was finally finished, it prescribed *squalifica* only for those duelists who had attempted to use fraud or trickery to gain unfair advantage or for those who had failed to carry out a "legal" duel.[142] Once again this prescription followed from the logic of chivalry: only those who had dishonored themselves in violating the ritual rules of combat deserved a dishonorable punishment.

Indeed, a careful examination of the Zanardelli code, which was the result of all the debate and discussion, reveals just how consistently the legislators accepted the basic precepts of the dueling ethos in their deliberations. The most obvious case was the aforementioned elimination of *squalifica*, which specifically protected the new political class in its economic and social opportunities. But there were other examples. While it was true that the new code increased fines and prison terms compared to the Sardinian Code of 1859, it was substantially more lenient than the Tuscan Code of 1853. The new code also made issuing and accepting challenges a crime unto itself, something the Sardinian Code had neglected, and this fit the new description of the crime which was now categorized as being against the administration of justice rather than against persons or property. This definition was seen as more sophisticated than those of the past because it recognized the roots of dueling in the desire—or rather the need—to take the law into one's own hands when it came to matters of insult and honor.[143] But, at

141. Quoted in ibid., 1884, 153; also ibid., Ambrosoli and Pantaleone, 125, 157–59.
142. Article 243, Italian Penal Code, 1889.
143. Morelli 1904, 241.

the same time, the new definition also indirectly reinforced the semi-legal nature of the dueling code as an alternative to sanctioned judicial procedure. However, what was most remarkable about the Zanardelli code, compared to the two codes that it replaced, was its attempt to adjudicate cases according to the severity and particulars of the affront to the defendant's honor. True, issuing a challenge was a crime, punishable by a fine of up to 100 lire or detention up to two months. Yet if the defendant were "induced to the challenge by grave insult or serious disgrace," he was exempt from penalty altogether. Similarly, penalties for injuring or killing an opponent in a duel could be reduced by one-sixth to one-third if the guilty party could show that he had been "seriously" insulted.[144]

These "loopholes" were mirrored in the rest of the code, which constantly hedged its strictures with distinctions, exceptions, and reductions, all drawn from a common conception of honor. Seconds might pay between 100 and 1,000 lire or spend up to 18 months in jail, but not if they attempted to reconcile the combatants. Whoever was determined to be the party provoking the duel was subject to greater penalties than the person insulted, but no means of determining this difference were mentioned. No one could fight a duel for another person, unless, of course, he happened to be a close relative. And the longest article, #243, spent its time determining the various conditions by which a duel could be declared fraudulent or improper and would thus incur penalties that were far higher than those accorded to "legitimate" duelists. In short, the new code had embraced the duel wholeheartedly as a socially nuanced legal force, begging for commentary from dueling experts and courts of honor alike. And this accommodation naturally fit the tensions of the long debate from which the new code had evolved, the result of which had been to further inculcate the new dueling law with the ethos of the dueling tradition itself.

The great debate over the dueling law demonstrated just how close this "crime" lay to the heart of the liberal regime. Proud of their honor and inhabiting the drawing rooms and social clubs where the compulsion of chivalry held sway, Italy's ruling elites were conflicted as they attempted to legislate against what in reality constituted a privilege of their class and a manifestation of their supposed superiority. Countless times senators and deputies inadvertently referred to a dichotomy between themselves and the *volgo,* the *volgari,* and the *plebe,* who could

144. Articles 237 and 240, Italian Penal Code, 1889.

not share their conception of honor or utilize the chivalrous mechanisms to defend it. Ironically it seemed as if an entire legislation had been set up for a crime specific to a privileged group of people—and pointedly it was the group making the laws for everyone else. Italy's legislators were not unaware of this paradox, but they could not get beyond their own "prejudices." Their convoluted attempts to curb their own honor only underscored the political/social rift that dogged the new country, once again exacerbating the unfortunate image of an "official" Italy of ruling cliques and sabers as opposed to the "real" Italy of the people and stilettos: an image that would eventually help lead to the demise of liberalism and the rise of fascism.

Rhetoric and Reality: Effects of the Great Debate

On the eve of World War I, opponents of the duel could point with some justification to the success of their various efforts. Although the duel was certainly not yet eliminated from the Italian social scene, its reported numbers steadily declined between 1890 and 1915. According to the last major set of statistics compiled by Iacopo Gelli, as illustrated in table 12, yearly averages of duels dropped some 60% during the 1890s and another 50% in the first decade of the century.[145] This trend continued during the five years before the war, with another 30% drop in the average number of duels per year. The decline was all the more impressive considering that Italy's population was growing rapidly throughout the period, and thus rates adjusted per capita would be even more dramatic.

Gelli attributed the gradual but steady decrease after 1890 to a number of factors, including a new sense of self-worth based on honesty and hard work in Italy's growing urban areas; the spread of socialist ideas which condemned the duel; and the increased use of new dueling manuals (his own being the most successful), which helped adjudicate more disputes without the shedding of bloods. Even more important was the implementation in 1890 of the new Zanardelli penal code (approved in 1889), the impact of which seems overwhelmingly obvious when we illustrate Gelli's original statistics (see table 2 in chapter III) as a line graph as shown in chart 2. So as not to skew the data line, I have extrapolated 1879, 1889, and 1895 from partial data for those years.

145. Gelli 1928, 17 footnote.

Table 12
Yearly averages of reported duels in Italy, 1879-1925

Period	Number of Duels
1879–1889	276
1890–1900	116
1901–1910	65
1911–1915	45
1916–1918	3
1919–1925	74

Chart 2
Reported duels in Italy, 1879-95

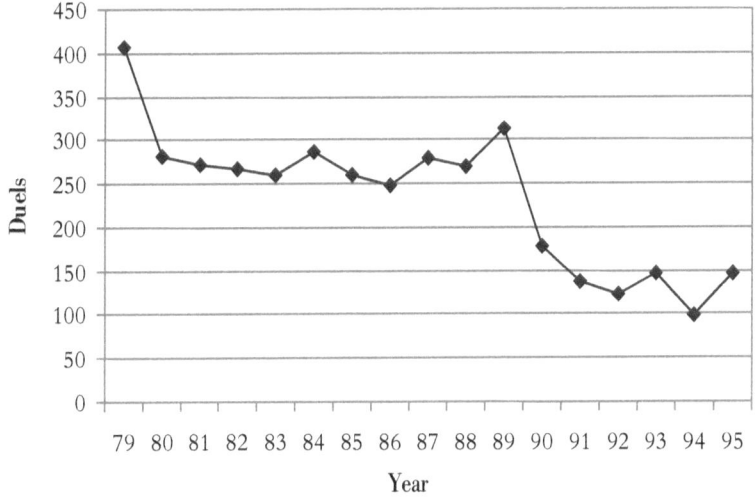

Why the promulgation of the code had such a dramatic effect is something of a mystery, especially given its previously described regard for the precepts of chivalry. Also, although the code set higher penalties for duelists and their seconds, it was noted that actual sentences remained very low. Case in point: when Giovanni Coppola and Emilio Solari were convicted in October 1891 for fighting a duel in which one was wounded, they could have been punished with up to four months'

detention; instead they each received three days.[146] Nor did the new code bring a massive wave of enforcement against the duel. Referring to the relative number of prosecutions listed in chapter III, one notes from the somewhat spotty data that the percentage of known duelists who ended up in court did rise after 1890, from 11.3% between 1880 and 1885 to 17.4% between 1890 and 1895. But these figures hardly constituted a serious crackdown on the practice, and a duelist still had less than a one-in-five chance of facing any legal penalty for his actions. Gelli, who was the closest observer, felt that the threat of greater penalties under the Zanardelli code had had some effect, but he warned that only about half of the statistical decrease was real; the rest was due to people hiding their duels more effectively from the public eye.[147] Gelli also credited the new code with improving the laws regarding personal defamation, which he thought had led to a tripling or even quadrupling of court cases that previously might have inspired *vertenze*.[148] Whatever the exact cause, there seems little denying that duels were becoming less frequent. Even taking Gelli's caveat about actual numbers versus apparent statistics, one can use the year 1890 as a baseline of visibility and suggest that the diminution that followed over the next 15 years probably mirrored reality fairly accurately, especially given the relative political calm of the Giolittian period after the turn of the century.

Such assertions seem to be borne out by yet another set of statistics, shown in table 13, reportedly released by the Italian military, which Fredrick Robertson Bryson reproduced in his 1938 study on Renaissance dueling.[149] Representing the number of duels fought by Italian officers between 1901 and 1910, this table shows a steady diminution that is generally consistent with the pattern portrayed by Gelli's statistics. The data do not indicate whether this included only duels between officers or also those between officers and civilians, although one suspects the former. Whatever the case, the downward trend is rather obvious and suggests that within the traditional bastion of the chivalric ethic, duels were becoming increasingly rare, a trend apparently hastened by the the1908 decree demanding that an official court of honor be convened prior to any combat. Thus in September of 1909,

---

146. See "Idee di Parmenio Bettoli" and "Processi per duello," in *Scherma italiana*, Oct. 1891, #20, 157–59.

147. Ibid. Compare to Gelli 1903, 2, and La Manna 1901, 20.

148. Gelli 1901A, 5–7. He further mentioned the recent frequency of deaths from duels, a reference perhaps to the six dueling fatalities that occurred between 1895 and 1898.

149. Bryson 1938, 209.

Table 13
Reported duels per year in the Italian military, 1901–10

Year	Number of Duels
1901	60
1902	56
1903	57
1904	54
1905	51
1906	35
1907	29
1908	29
1909	14
1910	13

Giuseppe Prezzolini reported in the influential Florentine journal, *La Voce,* that "officers, before fighting [a duel], have to pass through so many inquests, verdicts, and judges, that it would blunt the desire to duel of a revivified d'Artagnan."[150] The dramatic drop in 1909 and 1910 suggests that Prezzolini was correct in his appraisal and that the policy was having the intended effect.[151]

Returning to Gelli's more general statistics, it is worth noting that Italy was at war with Turkey over Libya between September of 1911 and October of 1912, and it was traditional that soldiers not duel when the country was actively engaged in armed conflict. This fact also helps account, of course, for the extraordinary decline of duels during the First World War, as reported in table 12 of yearly averages and illustrated in chart 3 as a columnar graph. In this case the single largest influence was the Italian high command's decision in 1915 to order the postponement of all military affairs of honor until the war was over. Other gentlemen may have followed the army's example, putting off their personal grievances while the country was in danger, although the stringent press controls of the period may have been equally important

150. "Usi e costumi dell'Egregio Collega: il duello," *La Voce,* Sept. 1909.
151. A military commentator, Borgatti (1914, 5, footnote) noted that the number of duels had fallen primarily because people were not fighting as many frivolous duels.

Chart 3
Yearly averages of reported duels in Italy, 1879–1925

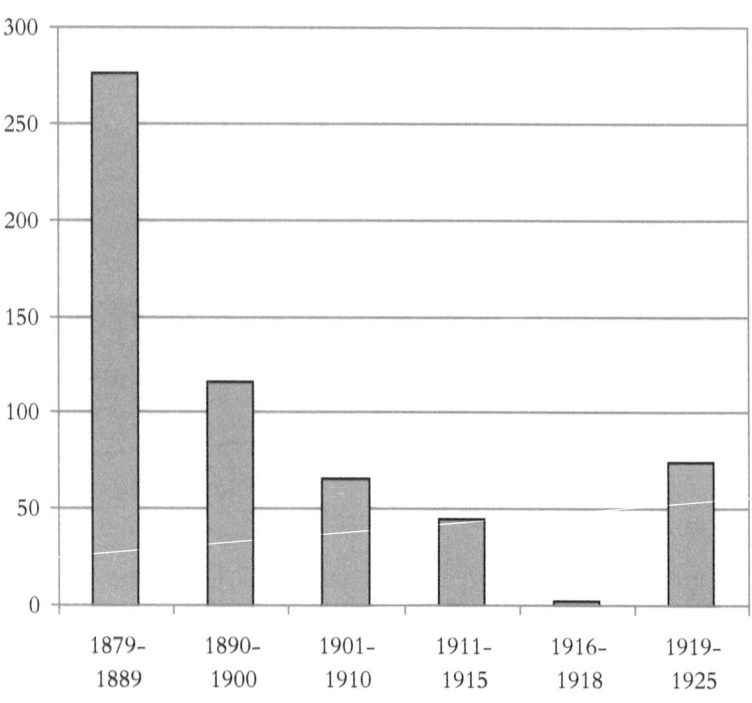

in that they perhaps limited both insulting debate between journalists and the public announcement of duels.

Yet even before Italy joined the Great War, general sentiment seemed to be that the duel was indeed beginning to lose much of its vigor.[152] Gelli himself prefaced a 1906 antidueling tome by Antonio Russo-Ajello with the confession that he had lost much of his faith in the duel and that chivalry had become a refuge for scoundrels and blackmailers.[153] By 1912 he admitted in the eleventh edition of his famous *Codice cavalleresco* that "public opinion today is no longer inclined towards the duel."[154] Similarly, one contemporary opponent of the duel, Orazio

---

152. See, for instance, Aldo Valori (2001, 137), a journalist working for the *Resto del Carlino* in Bologna in 1911 who compared his experience to that of his predecessor who "bore the scars of a large number of duels."
153. Introduction to Russo-Ajello 1906, 4.
154. Gelli 1912, xiii.

Premoli, argued in 1910 that the Anti-dueling League had produced a real effect among Italy's elites and that the tide had turned against the "prejudice of honor":

> [N]ot accepting a duel is no longer, as it was twenty years ago, considered an injurious derogation of social conventions, against which society, *comme il faut*, had the right, or perhaps the duty, to react, closing, if necessary, the golden doors of their clubs in the face of the disgraced person, but now [not accepting a duel] is a declaration of principles that, although not universally accepted, must be by everyone, society included, *comme il faut*, respected.[155]

His report was later echoed by the president of the Lombard Anti-dueling Society, Lieutenant Generale Giulio Manzoli, who boasted at a conference in June 1914 that, although duels were still occurring, more *vertenze* were being resolved peacefully than ever before.[156] Confirmation of these claims, although understandably without the attending enthusiasm, came from the other side of the debate when, also in 1914, the radically produeling author Carlo Mario Brunetti decried the "incontestable" diminution of the duel as an incontrovertible sign of the growing weakness, effeminacy, and vileness of Italian society.[157]

Across the board, then, commentators just prior to the war reflected on the gradual demise of the duel, and one postwar author would look back with considerable frustration (and some exaggeration) to that time when the duel had become a "source of ridicule and humor" and "a mere shadow of its former vital self, utilized only for wayward affairs of the heart which could be settled no other way." His frustration, of course, derived from the fact that, as he was writing in 1924, chivalric combat had regained much of its previous sway in Italy, and "slaps, challenges and duels" had become once again *la musica di moda*.[158] As indicated by Gelli's own statistics, portrayed in chart 2, this was no chimera. The duel was back, and considerable time would pass before it began to recede again. By the time it did, the liberal regime with which it had had such a symbiotic relationship would be long gone, and fascism would be the order of the day.

155. Premoli 1910, 4; also see Crispolti 1926, 2.
156. *Conferenza sul duello tenuta al R. Liceo Cesare Beccaria il 6 giugno 1914*, Milano: Turati, 1914, 59–60.
157. Brunetti 1914, 89.
158. "Duelli 'primavera 1924,'" in *La giustizia*, Milano, May 21, 1924.

VI

The Duel and Fascism

THE RECRUDESCENCE of the duel after the Great War, which appears so obvious in Gelli's statistics, coincided with the coming to power of the fascists and the end of the liberal regime. Although partly provoked by the backlog of *vertenze* postponed by the military during the war, the increase drew continuing strength from the press, which, free of its wartime trammels, entered into the most politically volatile period of united Italy's history. In newspapers, in parliament, and in the streets, fascists, liberals, and socialists literally fought for control of the country, and many were the challenges exchanged and the duels fought as insult and aggression became the norm of public life. In this mêlée, the fascists were noted as particularly quick to resort to the sword, and, not surprisingly, the renaissance of the duel persisted even after the mass political struggle ended and Mussolini began to consolidate his dictatorship in 1925. The fascist journalist Silvio Maurano thus recalled in his memoirs that there had been a new "epidemic" of duels in the latter half of the 1920s, during which the staff of his newspaper, *L'Impero,* had alone accounted for some 67 encounters.[1] The dash, courage, and danger of the dueling ethic harmonized well with fascism's emphasis on virility, action, and violence. At the same time, it served the traditional functions of promoting status and buffering conflict as new elites, many from lower-middle-class backgrounds, scrambled for position and prestige within the new bureaucracies of the regime. At

---

1. Maurano 1973, 51.

the end of the decade, however, as fascism moved ever further away from its revolutionary roots and became increasingly concerned with hierarchy, conformity, and obedience, the new "epidemic" would begin to abate.

As in so many other aspects of Mussolini's rule, the regime would maintain a contradictory stance toward the chivalric code and its enforcement. Although fascism based its rhetoric on conflict, energy, and national honor, the ideology of state power eventually came to dominate, and it found dueling too individualistic and too blatant in its flouting of the government's monopoly over coercion. While many of the early fascists, including Mussolini, prided themselves on having fought various duels during their rise to power, the regime would gradually and subtly direct its policies against the practice. Paying homage to the traditions of chivalry by finally giving legal status to some courts of honor, it would increase penalties and pressure members of the party and militia not to fight. Rhetoric would shift from honor defined as personal sensibility to honor as personal duty to the regime. Affairs would arise and duels would occur in the 1930s, but always in shrinking numbers. In this sense, fascism managed to maintain the virile myth of the duel while undercutting its reality.

Equally important, when fascism destroyed liberalism and its freedom of discourse in parliament and press alike, it restricted the public debate and publicity that often made duels worth fighting. This was even the case among fascist journalists who were increasingly expected more and more to toe the party line. Gradually after 1930 they too would lose the force of dialogue and dissent that might give rise to *vertenze* within their ranks. Coupled with the fact that Italy's military became increasingly engaged in conflicts abroad, first in Ethiopia and then in Spain, limiting the opportunities for *vertenze* and duels between officers, these factors determined that the duel would once again become "a mere shadow of itself" as the second great war of the century began. In short, as the fascists killed off the liberal regime, so too would they help kill off the dueling ethic, and this time—as the shock of war, defeat, occupation, and resistance took hold—the traditions of honorable individual combat would disappear for good.

A "Harder" Approach to Italian Honor

The reflowering of the dueling ethic in Fascist Italy would find its ideological and literary roots in the decade preceding the First World War, as an aggressive and virulent attraction to violence permeated a new generation of elites. Ranging from the revolutionary syndicalists on the left to the antiparliamentarian nationalists on the right, a fascination with danger, risk, and destruction as creative spiritual forces took hold of some of Italy's brightest young writers. Inherent to this movement was a bitter criticism of Italy's lackluster history since the Risorgimento—inherited from disgruntled intellectuals such as Giosuè Carducci, Angelo Sommaruga, Gabrielle d'Annunzio, Pasquale Turiello, and Alfredo Oriani—and a rejection of the rational and pluralistic assumptions of liberalism and democracy.[2] Although the voices of this strident call for a violent regeneration of Italian society would sometimes disagree over the legitimacy of chivalric honor—and some would even denounce dueling as inappropriate for literati defending their ideas—they all stressed courage, action, and conflict as a means of forging a new "real" Italy that would rightfully take its place among the superior nations of the world. Imbued as well with heavy misogynistic overtones that condemned the current political system and its assumptions as weak and effeminate, writers such as Enrico Corradini, Giovanni Papini, and Luigi Ambrosini all expressed a disdain for women and domesticity that emboldened previous prejudices, hyperemphasizing the manly virtues of aggression and conflict, both private and public.[3] Issuing a common call for a new aristocracy that would bridge the much-maligned gap between Italy of the people and Italy of the state, these *Avanguardisti,* as they called themselves, put forth a pattern of ideas and rhetoric that would help resurrect a chivalric ethos of combat after the war. Combined with the Futurists—whose own manifesto of 1909 called for the disdain of women, the love of danger, and the exaltation of war as the "world's only hygiene"—they offered a new and militant virile vision of Italy's future.

How that vision might be applied directly to the dueling ethic came to fruition just before Italy entered World War I in a lengthy book written by a Genovese lawyer, Carlo Maria Brunetti. Assertively entitled *A loro* (a word play on "*a voi,*" the command to attack in a duel), Brunetti's tome promoted the duel as a means of pulling Italy out of the doldrums of poltroonish timidity into which it had supposedly fallen. Reenergizing the dueling ethic, according to Brunetti, would cultivate Italians'

2. For specifics see Drake 1980 and Thayer 1964.
3. See Adamson 1993.

"warrior spirit, sang froid, self control, resistance to pain" and would rehabilitate "nature, life, the superior man, the gentleman." Although familiar with the works of the nationalists, *Avanguardisti,* and Futurists, Brunetti's true hero was Friedrich Nietzsche, and he used the tenants of Nietzsche's *Beyond Good and Evil* to reject the standard argument that "blood washes honor clean" and instead offered the duel as an egoistic affirmation of a man's resentment: "an affirmation of the real *I,* which proclaims all knowledge of the instincts, and says *Yes* to the total, full, complete, exuberant life" [Brunetti's emphasis]. All of these ideas fit an individualistic notion of the will to power that had, according to Brunetti, been consistently blocked by those who lacked it: the moralists, the dog-men, the *non-vir,* the men of modern times, who were all dominated by their women.[4]

Within this general framework, Brunetti took to task those who attacked the duel as immoral, those who wished to legislate against it, and those who condemned it as barbaric, because this was all philosophical smoke covering their secret motivation: "the madness of impotence festooned with virtuous words."[5] Cowardly, commercial, materialistic: such were the liberal "non-men" and the socialist "eunuchs" who did not feel the force of their own manhood and thus misunderstood and misrepresented the duel. Nor did Brunetti spare the previous defenders of the duel, such as Gelli and Fambri, who he claimed had been half-in-bed with its opponents and had mistakenly accommodated an image of the practice as a necessary evil, as a vestige of the past that would serve a temporary civilizing function, and, of course, as a "social prejudice" that would fall by the wayside with society's progress. Liberal poppycock! So what, he demanded, if dueling is the result of a prejudice? Most of society and morality is a prejudice; what counts is that real men feel their own essential force and dignity and assert them without limitations, without categorical imperatives.

He naturally affirmed the old argument that dueling helped maintain a martial spirit among the people, but now he exalted war as a critical creative force that each nation had to embrace. To live is to fight, for both individuals and nations alike, and to deprive Italians of the right to duel, to deprive them of "the pleasure of combat" and to fail to inculcate in them "a certain contempt for death" was to hold them back while suppressing "glory, tradition, power, prestige, life."[6] True,

4. Brunetti 1914, 2, 39, 42–44.
5. Ibid., 36.
6. Ibid., 71–75.

dueling had been in decline for a while, but not because of the efforts of its opponents. Rather, it was the result of the general degeneration and emasculation of modern society, which was "of a soft, vile, prosaic nature: self interested and utilitarian to the point of nausea." Society had been at peace too long, and too much concern had been lavished on the timid, the weak, and the poor. In the grip of utilitarian commerce and industry, and seduced by sentimentalism and pity, Italy had lost its fighting edge, and people no longer enjoyed fencing, not even in the military.[7] This sad state of affairs, according to Brunetti, was equally evident in the growing power of women in society. Abandoning their natural feminine instincts, they were now demanding new rights and seeking to exert their subtle mastery over men, who for the most part were growing correspondingly "weak, ulcerous, and prematurely impotent."[8]

In contrast to these weaklings, Brunetti ended his book with yet another description of a "true gentleman," or rather a "true man," for they were one and the same, to the exclusion of the rest. These men were, in fact, superior beings who knew they were somehow special. Such a gentleman had *individualità,* a sense of self that refused to countenance the mediocrity and uniformity of society, and consequently he would return "often and gladly" to the field of honor. Italy, whose race was strong and chivalrous and recognized the value of great deeds, could only hope that the number of such punctilious and pugnacious men would multiply, "even if they might occasionally practice the cult of force, even if they might occasionally glorify the exaltation of power."[9] Although Brunetti did not say it, these gentlemen were, for all their positive traits, different from their earlier liberal brethren, for they were men who had to live outside the bounds of normalcy, who had to eschew conventional morality, and who had to force their will upon the rest of society. It was an image that would soon become all too concrete.

With regard to the growth of dueling after the war, Brunetti's book was probably more a symptom than a cause.[10] Although he won the praise of some journalists and fencing masters, as well as a Grand Gold Medal conferred by the Italian Fencing Federation, neither his book nor his new *Codice* was republished, and Gelli's work would continue

7. Ibid., 89–98.
8. Ibid., 99.
9. Ibid., 265
10. Cf. Di San Malato 1913.

to dominate the chivalric scene well into the 1930s. Rather, Brunetti demonstrated how the literary, philosophical, and political obstreperousness popular before the war, and obvious in the *avanguardisti* and the *futuristi,* could be applied to a practice that had begun to lose its hold on the ruling elites. The war and its aftermath would soon offer an opportunity for that rhetoric to work its way into reality, as massive social and political forces came to loggerheads across Italy. Yet Brunetti's book had already caught the essential paradox of a group of violent and forceful men—whose will to power, rejection of convention, and disdain for danger would prefigure the *me ne frego* (I don't give a fig) motto of the *squadristi*—but who still needed to adhere to the dictates of a code, a set of rules determined by a collective. Soon, this same tension would be written large as the fascists came to confront their own paradoxes of personal honor in the course of the 1920s.

Fascism and the Postwar Plague of Duels

In March 1925 a young idealistic professor, Giuseppe Capretz, put the finishing touches on a lengthy collection of letters, essays, and documents entitled *The Shame of the Duel,* attacking the renewed popularity of chivalric combat in Italy. Capretz's hope was to demonstrate support for his cause against the duel from a wide variety of Italian professionals and academics, in order to counter the image that it had again become universally accepted. He was incensed that there had been so little public outcry at the current "paroxysm" of dueling, and he was particularly enraged that the Italian parliament had recently placed its seal of approval on the new "duellomania" by voting on January 3, 1925, to not move against four deputies who had blatantly violated the dueling laws of the nation.[11] Capretz had launched this campaign in 1924, and it stands out as the year when it became obvious to many Italians that the duel was truly back in fashion, with the number of encounters consistently increasing, despite the supposed political stability provided by Mussolini's march on Rome two years earlier. Thus the *Corriere del Mattino* reported from the capital in June of 1924 that the number of parliamentary *vertenze* had been rising at an alarming rate,[12] and in July, *Il cittadino* of Genova complained that the dueling "mania"

11. Capretz 1926, 16–17.
12. Ibid., 1926, 270–71.

had returned in a "frightening manner": "Everyday one reads news of at least one saber encounter, with the usual touches and almost always with embraces and the formal shaking of hands; [e]verything that has been written and said against the duel—with the usual debates, competitions, volumes etc.—has not served and does not serve for anything."[13] Somewhat capriciously, the newspaper went on to blame the duel's current popularity on the increasingly warmer weather. The Italian military had a rather less whimsical explanation of the trend. Aside from the backlog of *vertenze* left over from the war, the high command noted in March of 1924 that the huge number of officers who had served during the war years had simply created an expanded pool of men in Italian society more disposed to duel.[14]

Substantial blame also fell on Mussolini and his followers. For instance, the liberal journalist Piero Gobetti specifically accused the fascists in 1922 of poisoning Italy's political system and promoting the duel as the "ultimate and perfect exaltation of individual activity."[15] Gobetti was echoed two years later by Giovanni Vidari, a professor of philosophy in Turin, who derided the "adoration of force" and the propagation of "fierce" doctrines that had brought new vigor to the dueling ritual.[16] Meanwhile, Marchese Crispolti, erstwhile head of the defunct Anti-Dueling League and now a senator, specifically took the fascists to task in parliament for embracing and promulgating the dueling ethic.[17] Capretz himself alluded to the fascists in his book and argued that the duel's current vogue had derived from the war, which had unleashed a form of political immorality that praised both ferocity and cynicism as virtues.[18] Having reduced politics to combat, embraced the love of danger, heaped scorn upon their opponents, and overturned traditional patterns of power, the fascists had helped reinvigorate the duel as an acceptable and even laudable means of settling disputes in the public sphere.

Mussolini, of course, had offered his adherents an early advertisement for the dueling ritual. According to his wife's memoirs, he fought at least a dozen duels, and she soon complained of the expenses incurred for fencing lessons, gifts for his seconds, and the new shirt he seemed

13. *Il Cittadino,* July 11, 1924—"Quando si era coraggiosi senza batersi in duello," BNCR, Levi.
14. "Le *vertenze* cavalleresche," CDS, Nov. 3, 1920, 2.
15. Piero Gobetti, "Uomini e idee," *La rivoluzione liberale,* May 28, 1922, 56.
16. Letter in Capretz 1926, 214.
17. Speech of Dec. 3, 1924, *Atti parlamentari,* vol. 1091, Senato, Discussioni, 1924, 349.
18. Capretz 1926, 22–25.

to require for each encounter.[19] Although Rachele's recollection of a dozen duels is surely exaggerated (I can only substantiate five), there is no denying that Mussolini came to embrace the duel as part of his public persona, and the timing of his earliest encounters is revealing. In fact, prior to his break with the socialists in 1914, he had obeyed the party's ban on dueling, even though he had not necessarily agreed with it.[20] With his move to interventionism and his subsequent expulsion from the PSI, he quickly changed his ways. In February 1915, he found himself involved in a *vertenza* with the anarchist Libero Merlino, who had publicly scorned Mussolini's new-found patriotism and accused him of not having the courage to face his neutralist opponents. Meeting by chance in the law courts of Milan, the future *Duce* flew into a rage and assaulted Merlino, who responded by sending his seconds with a challenge. The notoriety of the event was such that the police put surveillance on Merlino and even managed to frustrate a first attempt to fight, confiscating the men's sabers and issuing rather meaningless citations. Conspiring against the state's interference, the dueling party broke up into four different cars and managed to regroup at a predetermined spot outside one of the city's gates.[21] Having successfully eluded the police, a saber duel transpired in which both men fought furiously and were simultaneously wounded in the arm after only two "assaults." They parted by shaking hands, although, according to one account, there was no formal reconciliation.[22]

The encounter with Merlino seems to have been a revelation to Mussolini, appealing as it did to his taste for action, his eye for political drama, and his need as an interventionist to show his martial spirit.[23] Consequently, within a month, he had begun a campaign designed to force Claudio Treves, a leading socialist who had been attacking Mussolini's "betrayal" of the party and its policy of neutrality, into an affair of honor. Cleverly, Mussolini began with a journalistic assault in *Il popolo d'Italia* that accused Treves of supporting neutrality not out of conviction but because it ran to the financial advantage of his wife's wealthy family in Venice. More clever still, he maintained that such

---

19. Mussolini 1974, 34–36.
20. Rossi 1958, 60–61.
21. "La vertenza Mussolini-Merlino risolta con un duello," in Mussolini 1964, vol. 7, 474–75.
22. Rossi 1958, 62–63.
23. Rachele would remember that his first duels directly coincided with his shift to the interventionist camp. Mussolini 1974, 34.

motivation and circumstances automatically disqualified Treves from seeking satisfaction through a duel. He thus simultaneously slurred his socialist opponent for making a marriage of convenience, for living off the money of a woman, and for bending morality to opportunity. For good measure, he added that Treves was a "rabbit" who had undercut the revolutionary energy of the socialists and who "loves not risks but only stipends." More important, however, he had from the start managed to focus the public's attention on the chivalric question of disqualification and whether Treves had a right to even fight him in response to the accusations.

Mussolini continued his provocations. On March 24 he reiterated Treves' supposed cowardice by calling him "Claudio Tremens," and on March 28 he claimed to have finally revealed to the world the socialist's true nature: "perfidious, wicked, vulgar, disgusting." By this point, Treves had had enough and took the chivalric bait. He responded in print, calling Mussolini "canaglia," "invidious bum," and (my personal favorite) "a shoeshine brush," while affirming that Mussolini himself was the coward for trying to disqualify him as a gentleman while in the process of insulting him. "What," he asked, "is to be done with a man who begins a campaign of slurs with the premise that a chivalric affair is impossible?"[24] Apparently, the answer was to challenge him to a duel, and Treves sent his emissaries almost immediately to make contact with Mussolini.

The encounter took place in a villa outside of Milan at 3:00 in the afternoon. By that point, emotions between the two men ran so high that they jumped the command to start and had to be brought to order by the director, an accountant named Leonardo Pracchi. When they finally began in a proper fashion, the two men rushed at each other with enormous fury, and one of the attending physicians, Dr. Ambrogio Binda, who had already seen some 40 duels, reported it to be the most violent in his experience. By the third assault, Mussolini's saber was bent beyond use and had to be replaced. Five more assaults produced wounds to both men's arms, Treve's forehead, and Mussolini's ear. At that point, the doctors did their job and stopped the fight before somebody got really hurt.[25] Needless to say, the two antagonists were not to be reconciled, and both sides claimed victory for their respective causes. From the beginning, however, it was Mussolini who had orchestrated

24. Matteoti 1987, 30–32.
25. Ibid., 34; Rossi 1958, 65.

the event. He had laid out the most damaging insults, both personal and political, by questioning the sincerity and courage of the neutralist forces, and he had gained public revenge for his expulsion from the Socialist Party. He had also dramatically demonstrated his own physical courage and willingness to fight—important credentials for a man who was actively pushing his country into war.

As was the case for all of Italy, Mussolini's chivalric career was put on hold as the war unfolded, but he would soon make up for lost time. Between the armistice in 1918 and the March on Rome in October of 1922, he was involved in at least six bloodless *vertenze,* including one with Gaetano Salvemini, and three actual duels. His opponents in these latter encounters ranged across the political spectrum and included, in chronological order, his old socialist comrade, Francesco Ciccotti; his fellow fascist and founder of the blackshirted *arditi,* Lieutenant Colonel Cristoforo Baseggio; and the left-leaning liberal journalist, Mario Missiroli. Significantly, the only one of these duels to end with the traditional reconciliatory handshake was that with Baseggio, which helped heal a potentially damaging breach in the movement and symbolically reinforced Mussolini's co-optation of the *arditi*'s traditions.[26]

The duel with Missiroli, which occurred in May 1922, would be Mussolini's last. The success of the March on Rome radically changed his status within the movement and placed him in a position of power that demanded a different decorum. He truly had become the Duce and psychologically may have put himself above the equality implied by the dueling ethic. Be that as it may, the rapidity with which he adopted the duel in 1915 and dropped it upon achieving power in 1922 suggests that Mussolini viewed the code of chivalry as simply another arrow in his quiver of political combat—useful but expendable as circumstance demanded. Certainly his challenges and duels had the ring of orchestrated tactics as opposed to outraged honor, although such ambiguity had always been part of the practice's success throughout the liberal period. The line between personal honor and practical politics was a porous one, and Mussolini had certainly taken the politics of personality to a new height on his way to becoming prime minister.

There is also evidence that Mussolini was not totally cynical about the mechanisms of honor as a means of settling disputes between "real" men. Cesare Rossi, a journalist who worked for him at *Il popolo d'Italia,* remembered what he called Mussolini's "passion" for the duel: "There

---

26. Rossi 1958, 76; "Il duello Mussolini-Baseggio," CDS, March 28, 1922, 2.

was a period in which, not content to duel on just his account, he forced his editors, even the sedentary and good-natured ones, to resolve their little political and personal differences with four sabre-blows; some top fascist journalists owed their success with the [now] defunct dictator to a certain scribbling arrogance using the threat of chivalric combat."[27] The duel, Rossi claimed, appealed to Mussolini's sense of exhibitionism and taste for conflict, the latter perhaps a product of his upbringing in the traditions of the Romagna. Rachele, his wife, remembered his recalling his duels with fondness and remembered that he had liked to regale her with the details of combat.[28] Galeazzo Ciano noted in his diary that the Duce had complained to him in 1939 that 17 years in power had cost him "the pleasure of fighting several dozen duels."[29] One must also keep in mind that chivalry offered the upstart Mussolini a sense of legitimacy. Particularly once he had become a deputy in parliament, the duel provided a traditional means of asserting authority and also of diverting attention away from his more illegal activities. The *onorevole* Mussolini thus played the part of the *gentiluomo* in parliament while his squads wreaked havoc in the streets, part of a general pattern by which he consistently offered the promise of domesticated force to the old liberal establishment while acting against its essential institutions.

Blackshirts and Sabers

Mussolini's example in this regard was taken to heart by his fellow fascists, who throughout the movement engaged in *vertenze* and duels with various political adversaries. For example, Gino Calza Bini, head of the fascio of Rome, battled Alberto Giannini, editor of the antifascist newspaper *Il paese* in November 1921.[30] A few months later, Dino Grandi, future fascist Foreign Minister, fought two saber duels on consecutive days in Bologna: one against the liberal lawyer Giuseppe Cangini and the other against a certain Professor Osti.[31] Back-to-back duels occurred again in 1922, when the fascist newspaper *Giovinezza*

27. Rossi 1958, 59.
28. Mussolini 1974, 36. Cf. Mussolini 1958, 72–74.
29. Entry of Feb. 15, 1939, Ciano 1946, 29.
30. CDS, Nov. 18, 1921, 2.
31. CDS, Feb. 5, 1922, 2. Cangini would fight yet another fascist, the Centurione Oreste Roppa, in Sept. 1923. CDS, Sept. 26, 1923, 5.

of Empoli provoked the democratic journalist Athos Gaston Banti into fighting first the secretary of the local Fascio on June 20 and then its managing editor on the following day.[32] Italo Balbo, *ras* of Ferrara and soon-to-be *quadrumvir* during the March on Rome, was wounded three times in a sword duel with Colonel Pavone of the *arditi* in May 1922 in Bologna over an article published in *La balilla*.[33] The *arditi* figured in another incident in August of that year, when Captain Padovani, a fascist in Naples, had to face an opponent chosen at random from a group of Fiume's Legionaires who were incensed at unfortunate comments he had made about Gabriel D'Annunzio.[34] In Trieste, the secretary of the National Fascist Syndicate of Architects and Engineers dueled with the socialist communal counselor, Nicola Cupolo, with whom he was reconciled after both were lightly wounded.[35] In Sicily, a fascist newspaper, *Messina Fascista*, so thoroughly insulted five local men in April 1925 that four duels immediately resulted.[36] Any slight toward the fascists as individuals or as a group could become grounds for a *sfida*, and in 1923, Lieutenant Carmelo Garagozzo forced a fellow officer in Udine into a duel simply because he had not risen fast enough to his feet when the fascist anthem, *Giovanezza*, had played in their local café.[37]

Such encounters, which ranged from one end of Italy to the other, included some of the brightest lights of the movement. Apart from those mentioned above, they included Francesco Giunta (secretary of the Fascist Grand Council), Galeazzo Ciano (future foreign minister and Mussolini's son-in-law), Giovanni Giurati (future president of the Fascist Chamber of Deputies and secretary of the PNF), Renato Ricci (founder of the fascio of Carrara and future head of *Ballila*, the fascist youth organization), Augusto Turati (secretary of the Partito Nazionale Fascista from 1926 to 1930), Leandro Arpinati (ras of Bologna and early confidant of Mussolini), Aldo Finzi (fascist deputy, interior undersecretary, and head of Mussolini's assassination squad), Achille Starace (vice-secretary and then secretary of the PNF), Ezio Maria Gray (fascist deputy, founder of the fascio of Novara, and member of the Fascist Grand Council), Carlo Scorza (founder of the fascio of Lucca, fascist

---

32. CDS, June 21, 1922, 5; June 22, 1922, 5. Interestingly Banti was reconciled with the first opponent but not the second.
33. CDS, May 26, 1922, 5.
34. CDS, Aug. 27, 1922, 2.
35. CDS, Aug. 19, 1923, 2.
36. *Vertenza, Lo Presti—Manci*, BNCR, Levi.
37. CDS, Jan. 4, 1923, 2.

deputy, and eventually commander of the Young Fascists), Alfredo Rocco (organizer of the fascist state, president of the Chamber of Deputies, and minister of justice), and Giuseppe Bottai (founder of *Critica fascista* and future minister of corporations).[38]

Although some of these men dueled for purely personal causes— Arpinati, for instance, fought a captain with whom he had had a *contretemps* on the beach at Rimini—the vast majority of their encounters were obviously political and journalistic in nature.[39] In this respect it must be remembered that between the March on Rome in October 1922 and the declaration of Mussolini's dictatorship in January 1925, Italy remained a country with a functioning parliament and a relatively free press. The fascists thus availed themselves of the dueling traditions of those liberal institutions to enhance their status, protect their public reputations, and keep their opponents, who ranged across the political spectrum from *arditi* to anarchists, off balance and on the defensive.

What was strikingly different about duels and *vertenze* in the postwar period was how often their description in the papers appeared alongside reports of fascist beatings, punitive expeditions, and street battles. In this sense the fascists engaged in a constant counterpoint of legal, semilegal, and illegal political combat that generally and effectively muddied the division between honor and brutality. Take, for instance, the case of Augusto Turati (future secretary of the Partito Nazionale Fascista) who, as ras of Brescia, ordered the beating of local Catholic activists in 1922 while simultaneously challenging one of their leaders, Leonzio Foresti, to a duel.[40] On the receiving side of such "mixed" violence was the example of Alberto Giannini, a democratic journalist whose mordant wit proved particularly infuriating to the fascists. He recalled with his typical brio how he had set up a successful opposition newspaper in 1921: "For me it was really a triumph. After only 106 issues I had taken a saber blow to the side, a stab wound to the right forearm, and a club to the head.... I then suffered a second attack: twelve days in bed."[41]

Equally revealing of such tactics was the experience of Randolfo

---

38. These offices, taken primarily from Cannistraro 1982, indicate only the highlights of their careers. Ciano fought Leonardo Repaci, a socialist turned communist in 1924, over a polemic concerning an actress, Maria Melato. Santini 1989, 172. Bottai fought the *On. Viola* in 1925 in Rome. CDS, April 5, 1925, 2.
39. On Arpinati see CDS, Aug. 23, 1922, 5.
40. Fappani 1985, 18.
41. Giannini 1934, 113–14.

Pacciardi, a republican lawyer, who, in April 1923, was supposed to deliver a talk on the Risorgimento at the Popular University of Grosseto. Aware of his anti-fascist principles, the local fascio sent a warning to Pacciardi that "to avoid possible incidents" he should not stray from his topic of national unity during the Risorgimento to criticize the current regime. Pacciardi naturally balked at this restriction, refused to hold the lecture, and took the fascists to task in *La voce republicana*. Umberto Pallini, the political secretary of Grosseto's local Fascio, took umbrage at Pacciardi's complaints and sent his emissaries with a challenge. A saber duel ensued on a farm north of Grosseto, and after 34 assaults, the seconds called a halt when Pacciardi, having received numerous blows to his sword arm, could no longer maneuver his weapon effectively. According to the *verbale*, the two men had demonstrated "superlative courage and ardor," and after the bout "they professed for each other the maximum esteem and consideration, and they cordially shook hands as a sign of their complete reconciliation."[42] This was, of course, all very chivalrous, but the fact remained that Pacciardi had been successfully muzzled by the fascists, and then he had validated their gentlemanly right to satisfaction, including a friendly reconciliation, after he had complained of their repressive tactics.

This imbroglio of honor and intimidation intensified during the tumultuous electoral campaign of 1924: the year when critics began to complain about a new plague of duellomania in Italy. Having unleashed the violence of the squads in their attempt to win the three-quarters majority necessitated by the Acerbo electoral law, the fascist leadership had thoroughly confounded the traditional rules of parliamentary competition with the reality of raw force. Consequently, the *Corriere della sera* could report side-by-side stories on February 12, 1924 (page 4) that Francesco Giunta, current secretary of the PNF, had dueled in Rome with the journalist Mario Baseggio over "injurious words" printed in a social-democratic newspaper, while the Socialist deputies, Di Vittorio and Vela, were being informed by a "fascist commission" that they had been banned from Bari for the entire electoral campaign and had only hours to leave the city under the threat of death. The confluence of club and saber in 1924 was again obvious when Luigi Bellini, a maximalist socialist from Emilia, complained of the fascists' *squadristi* tactics in March and was quickly challenged to a saber duel by Alberto

---

42. Documents in *La Risveglia* (Jan.–April; May–Aug., 2000) at www.geocities.com/soho/den/7257/numero3/paccia1.html#link0.

Montanari, a *seniore* in the Fascist Militia. Within minutes of the command to start, both men were so badly cut up they had to stop the fight.[43]

The prize for 1924, however, went once again to the liberal journalist Alberto Giannini, who had just founded the *Becco Giallo,* a satirical and bitingly anti-fascist weekly. Attacked in mid-March by *squadristi* during the electoral campaign, he subsequently fought two duels within two weeks: one with Mario Carli, editor of the fascist *L'impero,* and the other with Amerigo Dumini, the fascist enforcer who would soon become internationally infamous for his part in the murder of the socialist deputy, Giacomo Matteotti.[44] As usual, Giannini recounted the events with sardonic wit in his memoirs, published in Paris, where he eventually went into exile.

> Between one issue and another, I calculate on average [I had] two beatings a week and one duel a month.
> Speaking of duels, I noted that, in my haste to take saber blows and sword pricks, I gained fame as a great fencer.
> Speaking of beatings, I noted as well that, in my haste to collect wounds and contusions, people would say of me: Don't tangle with that guy, he's trouble for sure.[45]

Nothing could better testify to the confusion that had come to reign within rituals utilized in the world of liberal discourse but that now faced the challenge of illiberal action. As with their leader Mussolini, chivalry for the fascists was on a continuum of violence that could be invoked to justify, to intimidate, to retaliate, or to warn. Simply telling the truth about fascist excesses became an insult worthy of a challenge, and in this regard the nightmare, which had so frightened both opponents and proponents of the duel, of cynical *spadaccini* abusing the rituals of the sword to hamper freedom of speech was finally being played out, and on a very large stage.

However, the power of the chivalric ethic for the fascists was not just in maintaining silence but rather, as for Mussolini, in creating legitimacy. Their many *vertenze* constantly renovated their status as gentlemen, while their opponents kept being pulled into the double bind of

43. CDS, March 18, 1924. For similar duels that spring see Rossi 1958, 60–61, and CDS, March 20, 6, and April 17, 1924, 2.
44. CDS, March 27, 1924, 4; April 1, 1924, 5.
45. Giannini 1934, 121–22.

fighting or losing face. The fact that a number of the duels listed above ended in reconciliation illustrates how easily intimidation and thuggery could be washed away by the blood of manly ritual. In the postwar period personal transgressions had far exceeded the liberal sphere of operations—a whole new political game was afoot that transcended the dishonor that a duel could exonerate. The point was brought home in November 1924 by Vittorio Vettori of the *Giornale d'Italia* who had been challenged to a duel by Roberto Farinacci for some journalistic transgression. After a stinging condemnation of the fascists, he categorically refused to accord the rights of chivalry to Farinacci who was, he claimed, no gentleman in either his person or his politics. He continued: "You have to choose: either the club or the sword."[46] Yet less than two months earlier, Farinacci had been accorded just such status by no less a person than Prince Pignatelli, a celebrated war hero and aristocratic *ardito*. Severely wounded in his right arm, Farinacci had managed to continue the encounter with his left, simultaneously broadcasting both his courage and his chivalric credentials.[47] Clearly, despite Vettori's invective, Farinacci and many other Italians did not find the club and the sword mutually exclusive as tools of political action.

Honor and Fascism

We must be careful, however, not to let the jarring juxtaposition of *squadrismo* and *duello* reduce our understanding of the fascists' penchant for chivalric combat purely to cynical opportunism. Early fascism had particularly appealed to demobilized young officers, and especially members of the *arditi*, who, one assumes, had all been exposed to the Italian military's traditions of honor. According to Adrian Lyttelton, Mussolini sought to capitalize on the militant energy generated during the war and give it an "internal social content" which would prevent a "demobilization of the spirits."[48] The raw material for such a "spiritual" conversion could be seen already in d'Annunzio's expedition to Fiume in 1919. In a propagandistic panegyric, published while the city was still occupied, the futurist "legionnaire" Mario Carli portrayed the entire episode as a "chivalric deed" designed to save Italian honor in the face of the Versailles treaty. Combined with images of the attempted

46. *Giornale d'Italia,* Nov. 11, 1924, in Capretz 1926, 278–89.
47. CDS, Sept. 28, 1924, 2.
48. Lyttelton 1973, 47–48.

"castration" of Italy's veterans by postwar politicians, who had to be combated with "the overwhelming ostentation of our bronzed virility," such rhetoric appealed to men who had recently risked their lives on the front lines and who, like Carli, proudly proclaimed themselves to still be "in the trenches." Carli, who was the founder of the postwar *arditissmo* movement and the first *fascio di combattimento* in Rome, felt that Fiume offered a perfect moment of politics, art, and action in which the blackshirted *arditi*—who had, he claimed, been scorned and dispersed by the regular army to the cheers of the socialists and "defeatists"—were appropriately honored by d'Annunzio as "Cavaliers of Death": that is, nothing less than a new order of knights forged in the defiant struggles following the defeat of Caporetto. Together with the other legionnaires, and led by the indomitable poet/warrior d'Annunzio, their daring and patriotism would, Carli claimed, help push Italy into that new era of spiritual regeneration and glory so easily predicted by the nationalists and *avanguardisti* prior to the war. As befit these themes, he ended his book on Fiume with a description of a duel that he had recently fought with a *carabiniere*, whose corps he had insulted for acting against the legionaries. A lieutenant aviator presented himself as the "paladin of the corps' honor" and offered a pistol duel to settle the matter. Bravado prevailing over custom, the two agreed that they would use the same pistol in sequence and thus unflinchingly face each other's fire unarmed. On the fourth shot Carli wounded the lieutenant in the chest and the men parted with honor satisfied but personally unreconciled. Combining courage, theatricality, and a rivalry between licit and illicit military activities, the event nicely summed up Carli's call for honorable action in the name of the new "ardent" and artistic Italy.[49]

Expanding this élan beyond Fiume into the mainstream of Italian public life, the fascists quickly militarized the political process—which generally left their liberal and socialist opponents overwhelmed—and often co-opted the language of chivalry as a justification of their actions. Consequently, much of the struggle against the socialists, who were portrayed as internationalist backstabbers, was couched in the rhetoric of protecting Italy's national honor during the tumultuous postwar period.[50] Even a liberal journalist like Aldo Valori, who worked for *Il Resto del Carlino* in the early 1920s, remembered approvingly in his memoirs that "fascism presented itself as defender of the honor and right of the

---

49. Carli 1920, 40, 65–68, 89–93.
50. "Honor" could also specifically refer to military honor; e.g., De Bono 1931, 384.

fatherland. It opposed the iniquitous devaluation of the victorious war. It spoke in the name of the combatants."[51] Such tropes would eventually find their way into Mussolini's mass "oceanic" dialogues, one of which pointedly asked "To whom the honor" to the group response "To us to us."[52] Combined with Italy's desire to save face in reaction to the "mutilated peace" of Versailles, this could all be parlayed into chivalric images of national regeneration, and *Il Duce* did not hesitate to do so. Thus in the June 25, 1922, issue of *Gerarchia*, Mussolini talked about the fascists as a new elite, or hierarchy, which had come to take the place of the old liberal regime and rejuvenate the blood of the Italian nation. He then compared the battle with the liberals and the socialists to a duel which had begun after the war.[53]

The extent of these images as they impinged on the issue of honor was probably best exemplified in the affirmations contained in the regulations of the Fascist Militia as published in October 1922:

> The Fascist Militiaman has a morality all his own. For him honor is, as it was for the knights of old, a law that seeks, without ever reaching its goal, the peak of a limitless perfection, even if he falls into error; it is all-powerful, absolutely just, even outside, and always superior to, written and formal law. Absolute honor is the law of discipline for the militiaman and is defended not only by the political organ but by the leaders of the hierarchy.[54]

Considering such rhetoric and the martial spirit of the squads, one should not be surprised to find that the blackshirts occasionally utilized the language of chivalric *vertenza* as they confronted their opponents in the streets.

We see this in an incident involving the honorable Benedetti, a liberal deputy who ran afoul of the fascists for not displaying the Italian flag during a political rally in Pescia, a small town in Tuscany. The secretary of the local fascio had been arrested for "outrageous insult" (technically a crime) against Benedetti, who proceeded to testify in court against him and print an account critical of the fascists in the Florentine newspapers. In retaliation, a crowd of fascists surrounded Benedetti's house

---

51. Valori 2001, 240.
52. An idea from Phil Cannistraro who felt that it went back to Mussolini's early rapport with the *arditi* of Milan.
53. "Stato, anti Stato e Fascismo," *Gerarchia*, June 25, 1922.
54. Quoted in Gentile 1996, 19.

and scuffled with the police who were guarding him inside. More serious confrontations were avoided by the arrival of two fascist deputies, Ciano and Luiggi, who agreed to get Benedetti to "explain" his actions. As violence threatened, the two deputies, acting like classic chivalric representatives, helped Benedetti write out a *verbale* explaining that his injurious words in the article were perhaps excessive and possibly based on faulty information. This was a textbook retraction of a journalistic insult, implying that no intentional harm had been done and that it was all a big misunderstanding beyond the control of the principals. It did the trick, and following the signing of the *verbale,* an accord was reached and the fascists gave orders for demobilization. The scene offers an important insight into how issues of honor and its defense could become embroiled with the actions of the fascist squads. The fascists felt that they and the Italian flag had been insulted, and the two fascist deputies, who shared characteristics of both "principals," were able to bring the *vertenza* to an honorable conclusion. It was not, however, a completely bloodless solution, because during the turmoil of the day supporters of Benedetti had mixed it up with some of the fascists, and one "Benedettiano" had been shot with a revolver. The ambiguity of the semilegitimate chivalric ritual and illicit political action of the fascists could hardly be better illustrated.[55]

Mussolini himself revealed this connection in his famous speech of January 5, 1925, when he took responsibility not only for the murder of Giacomo Matteotti but for all fascist violence during the postwar period:

> If I had founded a Cheka, I would have founded it following the criteria that I have always placed in command of that violence that cannot be expelled from history. I have always said, and here those who have followed me in these five years of battle will remember, that violence, to be resolute, must be surgical, intelligent, chivalric. But the acts of this so-called Cheka have always been unintelligent, disorderly, stupid.[56]

The key here is the concept of "resolution" in that the violence is intended to be effective and finite. The use of the term "chivalric" is not accidental but rather can be construed as referring to the functions of the duel as a means of ending conflict, just as the term "surgery"

---

55. Episode in CDS, Sept. 27, 1922, 5.
56. Quoted in Spackman 1996, 136.

counteracts images of random butchery.[57] At the same time, "chivalric" offered honorable status to all fascist violence and could even confer a certain honor to its victims (as we have seen in the case of Benedetti). Indeed, in the same speech, Mussolini offered a grudging admiration to Matteotti as a worthy opponent "that I held in esteem because he had a certain *crânerie*, a certain courage that sometimes resembled my courage and my obstinacy in defending my positions."[58] Matteotti might have been a man worth dueling, but not murdering, and hence the specific crime was supposedly beyond the scope of the Duce's vision of violence.

Despite the obvious ambiguities involved in such cases, there seems little denying the early fascists' genuine affinity for the duel. Renato Ricci (future leader of Balilla, the fascist youth organization) reportedly went so far as to argue in the early days of the movement that all personal disputes between fascists should be solved through the laws of chivalry.[59] In fact, the recrudescence of dueling in the 1920s was as much a product of inter-fascist conflicts as it was of challenges aimed at their political opponents. Time and again, newspapers would proclaim duels "fra fascisti" ranging across all levels of the hierarchy. Such was the frequency of chivalric combat among the fascists of Alessandria, in Piedmont, that in March 1923, the city's fascio held a plenary session and voted that its members could not duel with each other upon penalty of expulsion. All *vertenze* within the fascio had to be submitted to a jury of honor, and permission to duel would be granted only in "extraordinary and extremely serious cases."[60] A similar prohibition might have been useful in Naples where, also in 1923, the three Scarfoglio brothers, Paolo, Antonio, and Michele, were all wounded across the course of a week in duels with a rival faction of fascists.[61] The fascist deputy Alfredo Misuri actually fought two pistol duels within an hour of each other in 1922, one against his fellow fascist deputy Guido Pighetti, and the other against Felice Felicioni, Secretary of the fascio of Perugia.[62] Pighetti and Felicioni were both lightly wounded in the chest.

Of course, many of the inter-fascist encounters derived from purely personal antagonisms amongst men thrown together in new and unfa-

---

57. Mussolini used similar terms (*aristocratic, surgical*) about violence in 1921. See Gentile 1989, 191.
58. Quoted in Spackman 1996, 138.
59. Zanzanaini 2004, 46, 51.
60. CDS, March 28, 1923, 2.
61. CDS, Oct. 31, 1923, 6, and Nov. 6, 1923, 2.
62. CDS, Feb. 1, 1922, 2.

miliar political circumstances.⁶³ The situation was exacerbated by the rather raucous and unruly nature of the fascist movement itself as it sought to incorporate and coordinate the energy and efforts of a wide variety of actors, from syndicalists and futurists to *arditi* and nationalists, into a cohesive organization capable of effective action.⁶⁴ Early fascist meetings seem to have been rather tumultuous, and individual egos often clashed as controversies arose over tactics, strategies, and goals, at both the national and local levels. Thus in December of 1922, the provincial secretary of the fascio of Torino, "following an incident which erupted a couple of evenings ago in the headquarters of the fascio," battled a lieutenant of the *arditi* in a saber duel, after which "the adversaries hugged each other repeatedly."⁶⁵ Such individual tensions were heightened by the major divisions within the early movement which set "centralizers" who supported Mussolini's "normalizing" parliamentary maneuvers against the more independent and action-oriented "revolutionaries" of the provinces.

That particular conflict was played out in a duel in October 1923 between Massimo Rocca, who represented the moderate "revisionist" branch of the movement, and Ferruccio Lantini, an "intransigent" ally of the provincial leaders. The two had vied for top positions in the executive committee (*Giunta Esecutiva*) of the party hierarchy, and their rivalry had come to public attention in a letter, published by Rocca, attacking the intransigents as disloyal to Mussolini and the nation. The attack inspired a challenge from Lantini, and they subsequently fought with sabers at a villa outside of Genova. The duel ended quickly when Rocca was wounded in the arm during the second "assault," and the men refused to be reconciled. However, their seconds arranged a meeting later in the day, and this time they not only shook hands but ended up in each others arms as Rocca apologized for his letter being caught up in the "ardour of the polemics."⁶⁶ Their chivalric *rapprochement,* in fact, mirrored the compromise between the two sides that had recently been arranged by the Fascist Grand Council.⁶⁷

The point is that as fascist politics became Italian politics and gradually replaced the old liberal system, the dueling code still provided a number of important functions by which men could assert their right

63. For example, "Duello fra due fascisti mantovani," CDS, Aug. 17, 1923, 2.
64. For example, CDS, Sept. 29, 1925, 2.
65. CDS, Dec. 9, 1922, 6.
66. CDS, Oct. 20, 1923, 2.
67. Lyttleton 1973, 180–83.

to belong to and operate within the new elite. Moreover, the fascist "revolution" opened up an avenue for men who previously might have been beyond the pale of chivalric honor to enter a rapidly changing social and political matrix, often devoid of previous markers of adhesion, while previous elites sought to defend their own "turf" as the situation evolved around them. Party discipline was necessarily weak in the beginning, and Achille Starace, future favorite sycophant of the Duce, fought a duel in 1922 with Ugo Questa, the editor of *La nazione,* for simply reporting problems in the internal affairs of the Florentine fascio. Who was a good fascist, who was a better fascist, and how did these definitions fit with the old patterns of privilege allocation? All of this gave rise to the kind of fluctuation and social shifting that reinforced and reinvigorated the role of the duel as a demarcator of success, identity, and ability. Moreover, the duel could still be used to solve traditional conflicts of honor which now arose between fascists. Thus when the head of the Bolognese fascio, Gino Baroncini, accused the fascist editor of the *Resto del Carlino,* Nello Quillici, of profiting from his ties to the party, Quillici was able to call him out and defend his honor at the expense of a wound to his arm.[68]

In a sense, fascism exacerbated the personalized nature of Italian politics of the liberal period, infusing it with armed muscle and intolerant illegalities as the movement went through a series of identity crises that set many different factions and individuals at odds. Heavily leavened with men recently returned from the trenches and familiar with military honor, the fascio offered new social convergences that were overwhelmingly male, loose on rules, and charged with potential violence. This all reflected the central paradox of the fascist movement towards violence in general, in that men were supposed to be assertive, combative, and even reckless, yet acting on such principles amongst themselves sometimes made it difficult to achieve discipline and unanimity of purpose. In this context the duel offered the early fascists a disciplined means of settling disputes amongst men for whom violence had become a way of life and who might otherwise have resorted to rifles rather than sabers.[69]

An excellent example comes from the fascist journalist Silvio Maurano, whose memoirs relate a duel arranged by Augusto Turati, secretary of the PNF from 1926 to 1930. Turati, whom Mussolini promoted

---

68. CDS, March 28, 1923, 2. For details see Valori 2001, 265, and Malatesta 1978, 335.
69. See, for instance, Farinacci vs. Arangio-Ruiz, CDS, Jan. 15, 1924, 5.

with the purpose of creating a more disciplined party, found himself faced with two fascists from Sardinia whose history of family vendetta had already led to one killing and promised further retaliation. Turati prompted a duel between the two men to end the conflict permanently and went so far as to assign each of them *padrini* of proven value. In addition, a particularly stern (not to say brutal) "director" was chosen to oversee the combat and thus assure that enough blood would flow to satisfy the purpose at hand. The *padrini,* one of whom was Maurano, quickly discovered that neither of the men had ever handled a sword, and consequently they were given a month to prepare for the event. A capable swordsman and proven duelist, Maurano tried to impose prudence on his "primo," teaching him a defensive technique that might get him through the ordeal with minimal damage. Unfortunately, his advice fell on deaf ears, for his pupil had his blood up and demanded to be taught only how to skewer his opponent. The folly of this approach became quickly apparent during the duel when, as he unsuccessfully dove to drive his saber home, his adversary slashed his face so badly as to reveal both rows of teeth through his cheek. One of his seconds, General Sanna, confided to Maurano that he was sickened by the spectacle, but he understood its logic: "Fortunately there is a 'good result,' this little bit of spilled blood will save a lot more in Sardegna."[70]

If the fascist hierarchy countenanced the duel within its ranks, fascist journalists embraced and promoted it as a given tradition of their trade. Lando Ferretti, who served as head of the fascist Press Office from 1928 to 1931, proclaimed shortly before taking office that he felt "the pen and sword" offered the "synthesis of fascist journalism," and he elaborated: "to have ideas and know how to express them: [that's] the pen; to know also how to defend them against everyone and everything, [that's] the sword."[71] Even as the regime tightened its control over the mass media, editors and reporters of the major fascist news organs delighted in duels and *vertenze* amongst themselves and with others. For instance, as editor of the fascist *L'Impero,* Mario Carli—erstwhile futurist, *ardito,* and cofounder of the first fascio in Rome—was a notorious *bretailleur,* whose pugnacious belief in the cult of force helped contribute to the 67 duels reportedly fought by himself and his staff in the latter half of the 1920s. According to his colleague Maurano, "Amongst the editorial staff of the *L'impero,* dueling was necessary like eating and

---

70. Maurano 1973, 76–80.
71. Quoted in Ferretti 1930, 247.

sleeping. . . ."; and he recalled with fondness the many encounters that eventually ended with a bit of blood followed by friendly reconciliation, usually over a plate of spaghetti and a bottle of Frascati.[72] Maurano claimed in explanation that the many duels among fascists and against their enemies were not really important in any political sense but rather "[t]hey were only ventings of vitality, which served to render public life less incandescent." In other words, they were natural manifestations of the fascists' will-to-power as they came to rule all of Italy. What Maurano and his dashing fellow fascists did not know, of course, was how quickly this romantic image of "white-hot" public life would disappear into the maw of fascist conformity. For Mussolini and Italian fascism were already making their way out of the postwar muddle toward a new brand of dictatorship, and in that mutation from revolutionary movement to totalitarian regime, the virile traditions of individual honor would give way to the mass virility and duty of the "new fascist man."

Fascism versus the Duel: The Rocco Law

The transition from macho man of action to dutiful servant of the regime would be neither rapid nor complete, and, for the most part, the fascists would finesse rather than force issues regarding the duel and its role within the new Italy. In some ways the iconography of the early dueling days would become part of fascism's public image, just as the Duce's encounters became part of his public myth.[73] Mussolini loved to be seen in fencing garb or skirmishing with sabers, and the Italian fencing team became a jewel in the crown of fascist sports propaganda.[74] At the 1936 Berlin Olympics, Italian fencers swept four of the six top prizes, and the coach, Nedo Nadi, was appropriately honored by the regime.[75] In creating the monumental Foro Italico sports complex, the "Casa delle Armi," or fencing hall, was lavishly appointed and became a focal point for public receptions and exhibitions.[76] Meanwhile, Mussolini's fencing lessons with Maestro Rodolfi (sometimes called Ridolfi) during his later dueling days were purported to be the catalyst for his

72. Maurano 1973, 51.
73. For example, Cervi 1992, 141.
74. See Rossi et al. 1983, 11, 163.
75. Santini 1989, 169–72.
76. See Archivio Centrale dello Stato 2005. Also see the portrait of Giuseppe Bottai in the Palestra di Scherma, Bottai 1982, photosection 5.

general interest in sports, which would become famous in the proliferation of his photo-ops as a *uomo sportivo*. Rodolfi, in fact, became one of Mussolini's most common public companions, offering continuing instruction in fencing and riding. He was made head of the new Fascist Fencing Academy in 1934, and on one state visit to the facility, he and the Duce pulled off a secretly rehearsed "impromptu" saber match without benefit of protective masks. The event was filmed and photographed by the Istituto Luce for popular consumption and may have been staged in part so as to impress Hermann Goering, who was in attendance.[77] Given such myth-making fodder, the regime would find it difficult to simply dump its chivalric traditions and would thus occasionally send mixed messages about its attitude toward the duel, especially when it concerned the military, where honor was considered critical to fascism's international aspirations.

In the main, however, the fascist state would undertake a series of actions designed to weaken the culture of individual honor and reduce the number of duels, oftentimes using the formal mechanisms of chivalry as a ploy to undercut the actions of would-be *bretailleurs*. Specifically, the fascists encouraged the proliferation of juries and courts of honor and offered them semi-official recognition in ways that the liberal regime had steadfastly rejected. This allowed the regime to embrace the traditions of chivalry, while simultaneously enforcing discipline and delay among potential duelists, who talked their conflicts into the ground rather than carrying them to the field of honor. Combined with a stricter legal code and a clamp down on liberal discourse, these efforts gradually eroded the impulse to duel while still trumpeting the virile nature of fascism in particular and Italians in general.

The first major evidence of a rift between the dueling ethic and the fascist hierarchy came in September 1927 with an article in *Il Tevere,* a newspaper generally regarded as an unofficial vehicle for Mussolini's personal views.[78] Commenting on the project for a new "fascist" penal code, the paper celebrated the harsher penalties to be levied against the duel and its "propagandists." Rather than fall back on weak "moral" arguments against personal violence, which would not have been appropriately fascist, the article simply satirized the dueling ritual as both silly and venal, and, in anticipation of the impending force of the new law, it concluded by already putting the duel into the past tense:

77. Mancini 2003, 24–28.
78. Cannistraro 1982, 281.

In sum, the duel was no longer a school of courage in Italy. It was a school of equivocal pseudo-chivalric formulae, a school of low dialectics, a ridiculous parade, of which the most impressive part was the large packages of cotton-wool lined up to repair an imaginary fainting fit. The fascist life, intense, adventurous, full, offers a thousand occasions to demonstrate courage and, where it is necessary, to multiply courage.[79]

The critical message here was that a repudiation of the duel had nothing to do with a repudiation of courage. By painting duelists as bumbling clowns waiting to swoon at the sight of blood, the article isolated the practice from the seriousness of real, fascist, men who could find many other ways to manifest their mettle.

Actually the law for which *Il Tevere* had such high hopes in 1927 would turn out to be less forceful than the newspaper predicted, and its relative leniency clearly reflected the regime's ambivalence on the issue. The contradictions of the duel for fascist legislators could already be seen in the commentary collected from various authorities on the first draft of the law, which was circulated in 1928. For instance, the Royal Commission of Attorneys in Padova defended the practice in light of fascism's own values: "Since the Regime is taking the race back to the height of its magnificent virtues, among which shines bravery, one should not set a challenged man between the generous impetus of his soul and respect of the law." In contrast, however, other authorities argued that the triumph of the fascist movement automatically dictated a harsher attack on the duel. The University of Urbino, for instance, demanded the end of the practice's privileged *sui generis* status because "the old outfit of challenge, of carriers of challenge, of *padrini* or seconds, of the use of arms in duel, of insult for refusal to duel, etc. breaks across the animating spirit of the regime." The lawyers and prosecutors of Cagliari also wanted harsher penalties, arguing that fascism's new "ethical conception of the state" put it more in line with the Catholic faith which had always condemned the duel.[80]

Responsibility for reconciling such divergent visions of the duel under fascism fell on the shoulders of Alfredo Rocco, minister of justice from 1925 to 1932. Although the bulk of the fascist penal code was written by a commission of experts dominated by his own brother, Arturo, who was (like himself) a professor of law, Alfredo Rocco had the

79. Quoted in CDS, Sept. 3, 1927, 2.
80. Ministero della Giustizia 1928, 244–48.

final say over its contents, and it was he who explained its various provisions to the fascist parliament. An integral nationalist with a profound sense of historical purpose, Rocco mixed the ideas of Vico, Mazzini, and others to interpret fascism as part of an almost cosmic cycle of rising and falling civilizations. The keynote of this cycle was the competition between forces of integration and disintegration in which progress was made when private and group interests became subordinate to those of the nation as a whole. Rejecting what he perceived as the selfish and destructive individualism of liberalism and democracy, he argued for the totalitarian organization of society so as to serve the Italian state in its own struggle on the world stage. He thus embraced and promoted Mussolini's famous adage, "everything in the State, nothing outside of the State, nothing against the State," but he combined it with a firm conviction in the rule of law as the basis of society: hence his work to codify and institutionalize the historical dynamic of fascism, moving beyond the "sentiment and action" of the early years.[81]

With regard to the duel, one would assume that Rocco's subordination of the individual to the state, combined with his rigid formal legalism, would have militated against a practice rooted in private honor and illicit activity. Indeed, in his comments introducing the code, Rocco explained that he considered the duel to be a crime because "[w]ithout doubt, the political argument must prevail that it is not allowed to resolve conflicts with individual force and private violence." Moreover, he had increased the penalties against it because "the citizen must put these personal qualities to the service of the collectivity and to the interests of the fatherland, and not waste them in private struggles which give a dangerous and mischievous example of the triumph of force and violence over Justice. Such arrogance of private force can be tolerated only in times of irrepressible and anarchic individualism." In its very essence, then, the duel was antithetical to Rocco's conception of the well-ordered fascist nation.

Rocco admitted, however, that while regarding the duel as illegal, he had followed the lead of the liberal state and resisted the extreme position of simply treating it as a common crime with regular (read higher) penalties for any bloodshed incurred. Such a course, he suggested, would have been inconsistent with Italy's traditions of honor and ignored the social importance of the "inveterate" customs of chivalry. Moreover, he felt it necessary to explain that, even though he was increasing the

---

81. Gentile 1980, 322–35; Cannistraro 1982, 460–61.

penalties for dueling. he in no way wanted to discourage "that exaltation of the sentiments of energy, honor, and courage, which the fascist regime considers one of its major tasks."[82] Having fought a duel himself in 1921 against General Roberto Bencivenga, and well aware of the chivalric exploits of his fascist brethren, Rocco had to be careful not to throw the baby of virile honor out with the bathwater of private combat.[83] He was, in fact, convinced that until Italian customs changed, and a new means of dealing with insults was found, men would continue to fight for honor no matter what the penalties invoked.[84]

Such leniency in fact marked much of the new dueling legislation, despite Rocco's claims to the contrary and his code's overall reputation for rigor.[85] It was true that the new law closed the old liberal loophole which allowed duelists who had been "gravely" insulted to avoid prosecution for the simple act of dueling. Now all duelists and all *padrini*, no matter how serious the offense involved, were subject to legal sanction. Rocco also raised the minimum prison sentence for homicide during a duel from six months to a year while keeping the maximum at five years, and he substantially increased the fines applicable at all levels. Still, as some critics pointed out, the increases in fines either only kept up with inflation since 1889 or constituted something of a tax on honor, which could be easily borne by the well-to-do.[86] Indeed, the new law actually weakened the minimum penalty for dueling, which previously was subject to some jail time, but which could now be paid off with a fine between 1,000 and 10,000 lire.[87] In addition, the new law maintained all the chivalric escape clauses and exemptions for representatives, *padrini*, and doctors, just as it maintained all of the justifying explanations about what did and did not constitute a "legal duel." For all the talk of the power of the state, the parallel private jurisdiction of the dueling code remained intact, integrated, and forceful.

Rocco could afford a certain leniency regarding the penalties for dueling, because his most innovative moves against the ritual were to be of a more indirect nature. The first of these was aimed at the public face of honor and punished the publication of any news or *verbali* concerning a duel with a fine up to 500 lire. This provision, which ultimately did not

82. Ministero della Giustizia 1929, 185.
83. On Rocco's duel see CDS, Oct. 8, 1921, 5, and Oct. 26, 1921, 5.
84. Ministero della Giustizia 1929, 186.
85. For commentary see Scalfati Fusco 1930; Lembo 1933; Lovati 1939, 99–107.
86. Scalfati Fusco 1930, 7.
87. Articles 396 and 238 of the 1930 and 1889 codes, respectively.

make it into the code, had a very revealing history. It had originally been suggested by Catholic Action, but the fascist parliament had rejected its inclusion, with Roberto Farinacci, who was an avid duelist, leading the resistance on the grounds that it singled the duel out for special obscurity among all the crimes.[88] Rocco stood up to Farinacci, but eventually the produeling forces prevailed. The code that went into effect July 1, 1931, did not mention the publication of "dueling news." Yet Rocco's revenge was rapid. In December of that same year the new head of the fascist press office, Gaetano Polverelli, simply forbade newspapers *tout court* to report any aspect of *vertenze cavalleresche*.[89] This preventive censorship was actually far more effective than Rocco's reactive fines, because—as some critics had noted—the latter system allowed editors the latitude to "say and pay" as the occasion demanded. In this sense Rocco had lost the battle but won the war over chivalry's public face.

Rocco's second innovation was even more oblique in its approach. In fact, it did not appear in the same section as dueling at all but rather came under crimes of personal insult and defamation. Here in article 596 the code took the revolutionary step of offering official recognition to the jury of honor as a valid legal institution in certain cases. Provided that both sides agreed, it allowed judges to appoint such juries from "lists" of suitable gentlemen—and it also gave legal status to juries attached to certain "moral entities," such as the Naples Fencing Academy or the *Nastro Azzurro* Veterans' Association.[90] Specifics on how these juries could be set up by the courts were contained in *Regulations of Criminal Procedure,* and the official nature of their duties was reaffirmed in the fact that they would have access to the same documents and witnesses as the regular courts.[91] The intention of the legislators appears to have been to resolve at least part of the cases involving defamation in an amicable fashion through the good offices of other gentlemen, while maintaining the personal privacy of the people involved—the latter being impossible in a regular court of law.[92]

---

88. Ministero della Giustizia 1928, 249. Also see *Atti della commissione parlamentare chiamata a dare il proprio parere sul progetto di un nuovo codice penale,* Roma: Senato, 1930, vol. 6, 246–47, 617.

89. See number 19, "Direttive per stampa," in Cannistraro 1975, 423.

90. The idea of the courts in a fascist context was effectively argued by General Giuseppe Ettorre (1928) who appears to have had an influence on Rocco's law, which did not include the courts in earlier drafts.

91. Lembo 1933, 46–47. Also see Tedesco Castelnuovo, "Il nuvo codice di procedura penale," *La nazione,* June 28–29, 1931, 1.

92. Giovanni Maresca di Serracapriola, "Delle corti di onore e dei codici cavallereschi,"

This was a controversial maneuver and one that the liberal government had consistently rejected despite (as we have seen) constant and sometimes powerful pressure from the chivalric community. It was also confusing, perhaps intentionally so. While some existing permanent juries were now recognized, Gelli's prestigious *Corte permanente* in Florence—which had been revivified in 1922 and had been doing a land office business as the postwar duellomania continued—was rejected as a "moral entity."[93] Furthermore, whatever their provenance, the actual force of such juries was highly ambiguous. Agreement to take a case to a jury of honor automatically eliminated the possibility of penal sanctions, but the juries had no official sanctions to use against possible slanderers or libelists. And what code would be applied? The famous jurist Piero Calamandrei argued that the state should drop its hypocrisy on the duel and accept the norms of chivalry as real law—but which ones?[94] Others claimed in the same vein that since the state now recognized courts of honor, it would have to offer one of the various dueling codes official sanction in order to have consistent decisions.[95]

The ambiguity of the law concerning the courts and juries was not lost on its authors, as was revealed by Rocco's immediate subordinate, Giuseppe Morelli, during discussion of the code in parliament. On the one hand, according to Morelli, all crimes of honor could be logically assigned by the presiding judge to a jury of honor if the parties mutually agreed. However, since a jury of honor could lead to a duel, which was a crime defined by the code itself, the judge could do nothing to impel the disputants to accept a jury, nor could he sanction any of its decisions—this despite the fact that all legal evidence had to be made available to its members. By keeping the juries of honor "facultative" or optional, the law gained the advantages of the chivalric tradition without having to admit the legal possibility of a duel. The twist came in the legislators' own recognition of the validity of the duel, especially in the fascist setting. Thus Morelli argued that the duel was still deeply rooted in the traditional customs of the country and that the upper classes in

---

Echie commenti, Nov. 25, 1932, 32.
93. "Chiaramenti circa 'della 'corte d'onore permanente,'" *La nazione*, June, 13, 1929. There is some evidence that the fascists may not have trusted Gelli, who was labeled by the prefecture of Livorno in 1927 as an anti-fascist who had attempted to cover his early opposition to the regime. ACS, Ministero dell'Interno, P.S. A1, 1929, busta 16, Prefettura Livorno a Ministero dell'Interno, DGPS, Feb. 18, 1927. Thanks to Claudio Mancini for this citation.
94. "Regole cavalleresche e processo," cited in Lovati 1939, 122.
95. Lembo 1933, 29–38; Sangiovanni 1937, 10–11, 22–23, 63–67.

particular still felt that certain offenses had to be resolved with an armed encounter. He continued in his comments to the chamber:

> Whence, from the strictly legal point of view the speaker can augur that the day will come when the Italian people will be able to definitively abandon the custom of the duel; without passing judgement however on the subject, either as a man or a fascist. Certain it is that our mentality, which is neither too quietist nor too pacifist, does not see close the day when every offense, even the most intimate and atrocious, can be washed away with a verdict from a regular judge or a special judge.[96]

Thus Morelli, as a fascist and as a man, obviously approved of the duel as a symbol of Italy's dynamic militancy, but at the same time, as undersecretary of justice, he worked to segregate its criminal essence from the new dictates of the state.

The Bureaucratization of Honor

Despite such rhetoric, however, and the apparent sanction given the culture of chivalry by the code, the new law aided and abetted a general movement in the fascist regime to try to reduce the number of duels. The keynote of this campaign was the proliferation of juries of honor through an ever greater number of Italy's institutions, and it clearly coincided with the emphasis that Rocco's code put on such semiformal mechanisms of adjudication. As one might expect, the military was of primary concern, and with Regio Decreto #1875 of July 11, 1929, the government issued "Norms for the definition of *vertenze cavalleresche* among soldiers."[97] This was actually a restatement of the decree of 1908 which forced all *vertenze* between soldiers to be reviewed by a jury of honor, but it now extended the rule to the air force and the navy. To that end, it offered precise details on the composition of such juries in each of these branches as well as rules regarding interagency confrontations. For officers not in active service, use of a jury was optional but considered a "moral obligation," whereas "mixed" *vertenze* with civilians could be adjudicated by a military jury, but only with the consent of both parties. The decree served the function of restating a pre-fascist

---

96. Morelli, quoted in "Per le corti d'onore," *La nazione,* March 13, 1930, 1.
97. *Leggi e decreti del Regno* 1929, 5289.

policy in a fascist context, while making it easier, and necessary, for all military men to try to resolve their conflicts.

The decree also served as a model for other institutions. Less than two months after the decree's promulgation, the head of the fascist militia, General Attilio Teruzzi, issued an exact duplicate for members of his organization, changing only the corresponding titles and grades of seniority.[98] The Guardie di Finanza, Italy's treasury police, followed suit on January 16, 1930. The Fascist National Party included a shortened version of the decree, requiring obligatory juries of honor for *vertenze* among its members, in its revised constitution of 1932, but the provision was not officially adopted until 1939.[99] Nevertheless, combined with the now-official juries of honor residing in the National Fencing Academy and the National Veterans' Association, this flurry of chivalric legislation, crowned by Rocco's law, created a network of obligation and control at the beginning of the 1930s that could be used to derail, defuse, or at least delay *vertenze* before blades and blood could be drawn.[100]

That this bureaucratization of honor under the fascists was effective in reducing the number of duels was indirectly evidenced by the military's eventual decision to add yet another layer of review to the process. In February 1938, Minister of War Alberto Pariani submitted to the fascist council of ministers a new law regarding *vertenze* between members of the military. Already approved by the other branches of the service and the Consiglio di Stato, the project would have forced potential duelists to submit their cases to a two-tiered system consisting of a jury of honor and then, if a peaceful resolution were not reached, to a higher court of honor, with an appeals process at each stage. More comprehensive than previous decrees, it would have expanded its purview to any affair including a member of the military or the militia, even those involving civilians. The authors of the bill made no secret as to its intent, which was to further decrease the number of duels in the country. The earlier juries of honor had had a positive effect, but there had been too many loopholes. Consequently, a number of duels had been allowed to occur, and, having gone through the jury process, they carried the semi-official blessing of the hierarchy.[101] The new proposal

---

98. "Le norme per le *vertenze* cavalleresche fra appartenenti alla milizia," *La nazione,* Sept. 25, 1929, 2. The provision would later become law with RD 279, on March 5, 1935.
99. See Article 27 in Lembo 1933, 5–7, 15; and Article 126, "Regolamento del PNF" 1939 in Missori 1986, 443.
100. Rules of the Corte d'Onore del Nastro Azzurro in Gelli 1943, 249–50.
101. On the general success of the juries see Ettorre 1928, 188.

was designed to reduce to only an absolute minimum the cases that might actually end in bloodshed, and the details of the decree were such that—if adopted and enforced—it would have most likely sounded a death knell for dueling within the Italian military.[102]

It was also too bold a move for Mussolini's government. The council of ministers, of which he was president, postponed the measure indefinitely in the spring of 1938, apparently because, according to the attending commentary, it clashed too openly with the "antimony" currently reigning between the "necessity of keeping high the sentiment of honor among the members of the armed forces" and the continuing illegality of the duel as recently defined by the Rocco law. Therefore, the government preferred to continue its policy of avoiding "in both its consultative and jurisdictional activity the solution of a problem that can be considered immature for a definitive solution."[103] By postponing rather than rejecting the decree, the government reinforced its own ambivalence between admiring the positive military aspects of the chivalric tradition while deploring its obvious infringement of state power.

Meanwhile the fascists' dilemma of the duel for the military was being played out in other ways. In October 1934, the IVth section of the Consiglio di Stato emphatically stated: "Refusing a duel, for the simple reason that this constitutes a crime, is not allowed to officers, who in wanting to maintain their rank, must accept the military traditions, even if these present themselves as clashing with the dispositions of the Penal Code."[104] Thus the old informal rule that an officer had to either duel or lose his commission was openly sanctioned by a branch of the administration, and similar, albeit somewhat less blunt, rulings would follow through the 1930s.[105] Yet all of them ran counter to the government's ongoing project to create a new, fascist, military penal code that would deal with the perceived problems of the old 1869 code, including its total lack of reference to the issue of dueling.[106] This internal conflict

102. ACS, Presidenza del Consiglio dei Ministri, 1937–39, Busta 2148, Fascicolo 1/2–2, n4123.
103. Ibid.; Consiglio as quoted in note from Ministero della Guerra, Feb. 10, 1938, #7412.
104. Oct. 5, 1934, Siracusa—Ministero della Guerra, quoted in Gelli 1943, 244.
105. Gelli 1943, 243–49.
106. It bears observing that by the 1930s it would have been obvious to Italy's military establishment that its counterparts in Germany, France, and England—in short, its closest points of reference—had all abandoned the duel as incompatible with modern notions of discipline and efficiency. Indeed, even prior to the First World War there had been calls for the reform of the military's penal code, and as Mussolini consolidated power in 1925, he set up a commission in July to do so. See Manzini 1943, introduction.

300 / Chapter VI

clearly influenced the final version of the code, which appeared in 1941 and which proved a revealing masterpiece of exemption and false rigor when it came to chivalric combat.

True, the new code declared for the first time that dueling between officers of the same rank was a crime to be handled by the military courts, and punishments could go as high as three years' imprisonment. But there were no minimum sentences, there was no connection between penalties and physical damage inflicted (not even death), and a sentence could be reduced by one-sixth of its severity if the duel had been caused by a grave insult. *Padrini* were never to be punished, and no officer should ever suffer removal from his rank for having been convicted of a crime connected to dueling. Obviously, there could be no dishonor attached to a crime of honor. To top it off, judges had the power, in consideration of "circumstances of particular moral value," to not send cases to trial, to not condemn sentenced officers, and to reduce punishments from one-third to two-thirds. Such discretion rivaled the notorious *ad arbitrium judice* of the *ancien régime* that had so incensed Beccaria, and it revealed the extent to which the military was afraid to challenge its own ties to chivalry. Nevertheless, the code closed the old loophole inherited from the Piedmontese army that had helped protect officers who dueled, and in its most innovative measure it threatened prison for up to a year to those representatives who allowed fellow officers to fight without first submitting the *vertenza* to an official jury of honor. Such severity stood in stark contrast to the more lenient treatment of representatives under the Rocco code, and its intent was obvious: the military wanted to repress the duel with honorable and chivalric prevention rather than with reactive criminal prosecution.[107] Thus while the new code clearly demonstrated the paradoxical relationship of fascism to the dueling tradition, it also showed the continuing willingness of the military to reduce the practice to a slowly vanishing minimum.

The Decline of the Duel and the "New Fascist Man"

That the duel was incompatible with the totalitarian nature of the fascist state became clear as it steadily diminished in frequency through the course of the 1930s. Already by 1934, Niccolò Molinini would

---

107. Military Code of 1941 in Manzini 1943, 81–85.

assert, "The duel, struck by the new moral and social dispositions, and rendered impossible by the new development of western civilization and by the more severe sanctions of fascist law, has lost that halo of legend that still in the last century raised it up to vainglory and heroism, and has disappeared from the present life of the nation."[108] Antidueling authors, such as Filippo Crispolti and Carlo Lovati, agreed by the end of the decade that the dueling ethic had lost most of its adherents, while the penultimate edition of Gelli's *Codice,* published in 1935, could declare success in settling most *vertenze* amicably.[109] Indeed, when Gelli died in December of that year, his obituary in the *Corriere della Sera* recalled his broad erudition and bibliographic skills, while mildly degrading his much-vaunted code as being tied to antiquated notions of honor: "For us his already retrograde conception of chivalry and chivalric discipline was surpassed, and his name rather than representing an innovator remained as a sign of a great scholar."[110] The trend was particularly obvious in memoirs and diaries from the period. For instance, Giovanni Comisso, Giuseppe Bottai, Galeazzo Ciano, and Aldo Valori do not mention any duels in their accounts of the 1930s.[111] Especially revealing in this regard was Silvio Maurano's *Memorie,* which had happily reveled in its descriptions of duels in the 1920s but did not mention a single encounter during the following decade. Looking back from 1947, another journalist recounted that the fascists had placed the duel "in the attic" for the last 20 years.[112]

One must be careful here not to overstate the case. Challenges were issued and duels were fought during the second decade of fascism, as was evidenced by the testimony of a fencing master who admitted to having trained seven duelists to fight in the 1930s, including one after the Spanish Civil War.[113] A high ranking fascist could still openly duel and even privately publish the results, as was the case of the hierarch Gino Rocca, who was wounded by a lawyer, Rino Valdameri, over a disputed government appointment in March of 1936.[114] Also, from a

108. Molinini 1934, 31.
109. Lovati 1939, 200; Crispolti 1939, 171. The preface of Gelli's 1935 edition is in Gelli 1943, xviii–xix.
110. CDS, Dec. 16, 1935, 5.
111. Likewise, the memoirs of Alvaro (1950) and Baron Pompeo Aloisi (1957).
112. Adone Nosari, "Quando I deputati si sfidavano a duello," *Il tempo,* Feb. 26, 1947. http//www.palermoedintorini.it/ilfoglio-pag5.html.
113. Personal interview in 1992 with Maestro Enzo Musumeci Greco of the Accademia d'Armi Aurelio Greco in Rome.
114. *Vertenza cavalleresca Rocca/Valdameri,* ACS, Fondo S.B.D.—Co, #1788.

methodological point of view, one must bear in mind that, as we have seen, after December 1931, fascist press censorship specifically blocked any and all mention of chivalric disputes. Thus the best historical source for keeping track of *vertenze* and duels disappeared, along with a free press, although some *verbali*, such as that regarding the Rocca and Valdameri duel, were printed for private distribution. Nevertheless, all evidence indicates that the diminution of the duel was not just a reporting error; and the archenemy of the practice, Filippo Crispolti, declared pointedly in 1939 that it was, in fact, the fascist state's prohibition on dueling news that had had the greatest impact. Blocking the publication of the *verbali*, he claimed, had broken the "mainspring of the duel" which had been the vanity of the participants.[115]

Growing regulation of the press had other serious consequences for the dueling tradition. Having first eliminated the socialist newspapers and then co-opted the liberal ones, the regime used a variety of laws and professional organizations to turn the press corps into what Ermanno Amicucci, president of the press union, praised as "a weapon at the disposition of the Duce and the Party."[116] As Mussolini consolidated his dictatorship, and the PNF became ever more bureaucratized under its vexingly punctilious secretary, Achille Starace, journalists had to increasingly adhere to a strict party line, while serious debate or criticism, even among the fascists themselves, faded from public view.[117] Words as well as topics were dictated from the top because, as a journalist turned politician, Mussolini believed almost mystically in the force of rhetoric and constantly checked the Italian papers for proper vocabulary and style.[118] Those writers who failed to conform sufficiently in either form or content were soon out of a job or marginalized.[119] The fascist journalist Silvio Maurano, who had been both an *ardito* and a *squadrista*, bitterly described the process in 1943:

> For years and years, beginning with the cursed reign of Starace, it has been prohibited to write and to speak: all of a sudden we came to the paternalistic regime in which only the elect had the right to have a brain and everybody else, including those of us who had something to say between 1919 and 1930, were put to the side or confined to secondary

---

115. Crispolti 1939, 171.
116. Quoted in Matteini 1945, 23.
117. Murialdi 1996, 131–81; Cannistraro 1975, 173–224.
118. Koon 1985, 9–10.
119. On other forms of intellectual conformity see Ben Ghiat 2001, 23.

newspapers.... With the new system, I was not a *"simpatico"* and therefore ended up in the provinces, where my abilities were perfectly unutilized, especially after the Prefects had the possibility of ferociously strangling any mention of criticism or control over local life.[120]

Such a system, where news became propaganda and editorials became adulation, soon extinguished the old fires of controversy and insult that had led men to put steel behind their words.

A parallel process affected parliament, the other great arena of political discourse and chivalric challenge during the liberal period. Marred by fascist violence and coercion, the last "free" elections had been held in the spring of 1924, and a new law in 1928 arranged for the selection of deputies by the Fascist Grand Council from a list prepared by the fascist syndicalist federations. Eventually the old chamber of deputies disappeared completely in 1939, to be replaced by a Chamber of Fasces and Corporations, but it was only window dressing for the fact that all real legislative power had long fallen to Mussolini and his advisors. The successful establishment and articulation of his dictatorship limited any real debate to the secret realms of the Fascist Grand Council and the Council of Ministers, thus depriving politics of the public space that had been so important for the dynamics of private honor. Even for high ranking fascists this process was stultifying, and Giuseppe Bottai, an early fascist who served in a variety of posts, complained in a diary entry of January 1936 about the complete sterility of discussion in the Fascist Grand Council, a fault it shared with "all the organs of the Revolution." "Unanimity," he remarked dryly, "is now presupposed in the unfolding of our political life."[121] With political conformity so rigidly enforced, personal slights that might previously have occasioned a *vertenza* could now become criminal acts. For example, according to Galeazzo Ciano, when, in 1939, the honorable Egilberto Martire accused him behind his back in the corridors of the parliament of having the "evil eye," he was overheard by Achille Starace, reported to the police, and taken to jail. Pointedly, Mussolini's comment on the case was that it was a pity he had not been able to personally challenge Martire to physical combat in Ciano's name and, more generally, that he regretted his having had to forego dueling since coming to power.[122]

120. Maurano 1973, 327–28.
121. Bottai 1982, 73.
122. Ciano 1946, 29.

With political polemics and a free press sacrificed to the cult of authority and repressed by a police state, the totalitarian pretensions of the fascist regime as it evolved in the 1930s became ever more antithetical to the individual notions of honor that had fed the dueling compulsion. Reacting to the economic pressures of the depression, the increased fear of working-class opposition, and the continuing agitation of its own "intransigent" party members—who wanted more "revolution" and less accommodation with the institutions and assumptions of the old liberal regime—Mussolini and his supporters embarked on a massive program to reorganize Italian society and culture. The task was a complicated one since the regime lacked the ideological clarity of dictatorship in Communist Russia or Nazi Germany and had to be careful not to alienate the elite capitalist classes whose interests it had come to power defending. Nevertheless, once overt political opposition had been muzzled, co-opted, exiled, or executed, the way was clear for a broad series of measures that changed the style of many people's lives if not necessarily their relative positions on the social ladder.

The most telling feature of this movement was the creation of pan-Italian institutions and programs designed on one hand to "make the masses adhere to the state" and on the other to create a race of "new Italians" who would be capable of meeting the demands of a young and vital nation.[123] Large bureaucracies, such as the Opera Nazionale Dopolavoro (OND), the Opera Nazionale Balilla (ONB), and the Opera Nazionale Maternità e Infanzia (ONMI), were created to organize the leisure time of workers, shape the character of young people, and promote the health and number of babies born to the regime. The party itself became the most prominent feature of Italy's public life, and membership was a critical prerequisite of employment within the government or its ever-expanding parastate agencies. Likewise, the party dominated public space and filled it with ceremonies that often mirrored Catholic rituals but served a new secular religion of fascism, particularly the cult of the Duce.[124]

What was especially important about all of this mass "organization" for the dueling ethic was the insidious uniformity that cut across class lines and lumped Italians together bureaucratically, politically, and spatially. As the regime articulated its power, it pushed the social matrix of Italy into interactive modes, often in a common functional landscape

---

123. De Grazia 1981, 6.
124. Gentile 1996.

such as sports fields or movie theaters. That is not to say that it broke down class boundaries; on the contrary, scholars agree that fascism only widened the disparity between rich and poor, and opportunities to attend university became even more exclusive under the reforms of Giovanni Gentile. Yet children of all classes wore the distinctive uniforms of their cohort in the Balilla youth organizations, members of the lower middle classes joined the haute bourgeoisie in the blackshirts of the party, university students were recruited and regimented in the Gruppi Universitari Fascisti, and fascist women's groups recruited widely across the social spectrum.[125] Cheap tickets to theaters and concerts obtained through the OND brought workers into spheres previously privileged to the upper middle classes, and mass sports events came to include a wide variety of people in their participants and spectators. Party-organized spectacles and Mussolini's "oceanic" speeches deliberately sought mass audiences and attempted to catch them up in the collective identity of the moment. Fascism did not seek to obliterate hierarchy; indeed it celebrated the concept and actively vaunted its desire to recruit and train new elites through party structures. Yet all such social ranking of a "new aristocracy" fell within the guidelines of the "ethical state" and beneath the discipline of the omniscient Duce. Hence, as Emilio Gentile has pointed out, the regime became increasingly obsessed with enforcing standard dress codes as each echelon and branch of the party and its far-flung organizations came to share uniformity despite their place in the hierarchy.[126]

Within this social logic, according to Gentile, conformity was consistently validated through "parallel processes of regimentation, indoctrination, and integration" and depended on the "total subordination of all those values belonging to the private sphere (religion, culture, morality, love, and so forth) to the supreme political value which was embodied in the state alone."[127] To this list of "private" values he might well have added "honor," for there was little room for a traditional sense of personal honor in this collective geography. The energy, indeed the body, of the individual belonged to the greater purposes of the "ethical state" and was not to be thrown away on frivolous or "haughty" conceptions of chivalric honor.[128] Such was the message of a pamphlet

125. By 1939 about one-fourth of Italy's women were in some party organization. De Grazia 1992, 265.
126. Gentile 1996, 94.
127. Gentile 2002, 162.
128. Cf. Spackman 1996, 146–47; also see Ettorre 1928, 222.

entitled "Suicide and the Duel in the Fascist Conception" printed in 1934: "The duel is contrary not only to the ethical and social principle of conservation and perfection, but it is an arbitrary fact, because the individual has a mission, an end that supercedes his individual existence: as part of an everything he cannot for personal matters and for a misunderstood sense of honor put himself under the risk of death."[129] In this sense, honor and its defense had to be subsumed by the larger purposes of the nation.

The ultimate goal of all this energy, regimentation, and organization was nothing less than an "anthropological revolution" capable of creating a "new fascist man" who would fulfill the destiny of Italy as a great power.[130] Italy had purportedly started this process with its intervention in the Great War, which had created a battle-hardened and selfless "aristocracy of the trenches" ready to take on the internal and external enemies of the *patria*. With fascism triumphant, the role of the regime was to inculcate future generations with that same spirit of self-sacrifice, daring, and patriotism so as to assert Italy's rightful place in the Mediterranean as the heir of Roman imperial tradition. Italians had to be ready for the physical challenge as well, in terms of both fertile reproduction and military action—hence the regime's heavy emphasis on sports and physical education for Italy's youth, which was aimed at preparing them for the battlefield.[131] This was made clear by Lando Ferretti, first fascist head of Italy's Olympic committee, in his 1930 treatise, *Examples and Ideas for the New Italian:* "Without qualification, sports are a militia[;] they are a militia of peace that knows, however, how to do their duty in war."[132] From this perspective, then, mass spectacles, in which athletes of both sexes performed synchronized maneuvers, symbolized not only dynamic and youthful agility but also the group discipline and coordination necessary for effective modern combat.

The fascist approach to sports corresponded to the general militarization of Italian society, and the martial rhetoric of Mussolini and Ferretti also brought to the fore the regime's ambiguous relationship to the duel. Honor, chivalry, virility, and combat all obviously figured in the creation of the "new fascist man," but the cult of individual honor manifested in the code *duello* clashed mightily with the images of mass

129. Molinini 1934, 30.
130. Gentile 2002, 167–68; Ben Ghiat 2001, 1–15, and 2005, 340–44.
131. Ferretti 1928, 225; Koon 1985, 99–102; in general see Rossi et al. 1983.
132. Ferretti 1930, 173.

mobilization, integral nationalism, and the all-powerful, all-absorbing, "ethical state." This clash was a result of the more general contradiction, noted by George Mosse, inherent in the masculine ideals of the fascist regime "between the revitalized, active, individual and the duties of the 'citizen soldier.'"[133] Men had to be aggressive, daring, and dynamic, yet adhere consistently to the dictates of discipline. Such contradictory demands became increasingly more problematic for fascism as Rocco's legal apparatus of dictatorship arose out of the conflict, and the party focused on organizing, mobilizing, and militarizing the masses. The regime's conundrum was to promote honor (even utilizing the chivalric images of Italy's past) as a motivator of the new Italian man, while regimenting those new men into a cohesive, spiritual totality capable of carrying out the wishes of the Duce, who presided over all as the ultimate man of honor.

This was hardly a new problem; the military had long understood the dilemma of promoting the courage and élan of chivalric combat while expecting men to obey orders and fight together as a disciplined collective. Fascism had only raised the stakes by glorifying aggression, praising romantic adventure—e.g., better one day as a lion than a thousand as a sheep—and militarizing society to the point of routinely placing uniforms on children starting at the age of six. Not surprisingly, then, the means by which the fascist regime solved the conundrum of the duel reflected those used by the military, more or less successfully, in the recent past. The first of these was the system of courts of honor which, as we have seen, proliferated starting in the late 1920s and then became enshrined in Rocco's legal code. Forcing members of the militia, the military, and eventually the PNF to take their issues of honor through laborious formal procedures, while empowering various "moral entities" to adjudicate *vertenze* for the rest of society, offered the regime the advantage of trumpeting its concern for chivalric honor while bringing its conflicts constantly under greater control. As with so many of their other problems, the fascists simply attempted to bureaucratize the duel to death.

The other military tradition that acted against the duel, although it was probably not a conscious policy on the part of the fascists, was the postponement of all *vertenze* during times of active war. In this regard, Mussolini militarized society, but he did so as part of a permanent state of war in which the fascists constantly fought the regime's enemies

133. Mosse 1996, 164.

both inside and outside the nation. This went far beyond the simple fact of first fighting the socialists and then rooting out anti-fascist activities.[134] Rather, it was related to the portrayal of Italy as being in a series of crises that took the mass mobilization of the people to resolve. The "battle of the baby" against the degeneration of the race, the "battle of the lira" against the devaluation of the currency, "the battle of the grain" against the country's dependency on foreign imports: all of these placed the Italians in a state of constant symbolic combat that demanded the subordination of the individual to the needs of La Patria. The exigencies of individual honor therefore had to give way to mass duty to the nation.[135] This transformation resonated quite nicely with the fascist regime's attempt to resurrect and capitalize on the traditions of the Roman Empire, whose armies had often been at war to protect the internal *Pax Romana*. As antidueling propagandists had never tired of saying, the Romans had not dueled and had instead saved their virile energies for the battlefield. This was perfectly summed up in the ancient Roman aphorism, *MOLTI NEMICI—MOLTO ONORE* (many enemies—much honor), and it was no accident that those words appeared in large mosaic letters at the entrance of Mussolini's giant sports arena in Rome (1934–38). Of course, Italy's *nemici* became all too numerous as the metaphors of war switched to the realities of conflict in a series of military adventures designed to establish its place in the sun and among the great powers. Ethiopia (from 1935 to 1936), Spain (from 1936 to 1939), and Albania, Libya, Greece, Russia, etc. (from 1940 to 1943), all saw Italian soldiers and fascist militiamen on the battlefield and under fire. All of these forces militated against the duel in Italian society as the regime claimed symbolic and then physical allegiance over the honor and blood of Italy's men. Significantly, Mussolini's last word on the duel was a directive, dated May 29, 1941, postponing all *vertenze* between military men until after the end of the war.[136]

---

134. Consider the 1926 Statuto of the PNF: "il Fascismo si è sempre considerato in istato di guerra: prima per abbattere coloro che soffocavano la volontà della Nazione, oggi e sempre per difendere e sviluppare la potenza del popolo italiano" ("Fascism has always considered itself in a state of war: first to defeat those who were suffocating the will of the Nation, today and for always to defend and develop the power of the Italian people"). In Missori 1986, 355.
135. The fascist ideologue of honor, General Achille Ettorre (1928), devoted the entire sixth chapter (139–52) to the relationship between *onore* and *dovere*. Also see 53, 63–68, 76.
136. ACS, Presidenza Consiglio Ministri, 1940–41, Fasc. 1, sottofasc. 2.2 #16807.

Conclusion: The Sword and the Dagger

Generally speaking, the trajectory of the duel under the fascists paralleled the rapid rise and gradual decline evident in both the Renaissance and Risorgimento periods. Emerging from the devastation and disruption of the First World War, the fascists promoted the duel to prove their martial merits, assert their aggressive political credentials, and keep their opponents off balance. The war had accelerated and exacerbated many of the economic and social conflicts of the liberal regime, and the resulting confusion allowed a new elite to come to power backed by a violent paramilitary movement. Like the *gentiluomini* of the sixteenth century and the liberals of the nineteenth, these elites (generally co-opting elements of the old) laid claim to the chivalric tradition and modified its supposedly universal precepts to fit their particular social and political needs. The duel was thus one mechanism, among others, by which the fascists laid claim to legitimacy as they consolidated their power. However, as the regime eliminated all opposition, controlled public communication, and created a civil religion based on a cult of the *Duce,* the duel lost much of its usefulness and was relegated, like the revolutionary energy of the fascist squads, and with all the appropriate platitudes, to the realm of recent myth rather than current reality. At heart, the monopoly of coercion demanded by the totalitarian regime was inconsistent with the private yet public combat of the duel.

Likewise, the duel embraced a notion of personal honor that ran counter to the organic, integralist theories of nationalists such as Rocco, who claimed excessive individualism to be the "congenitive Italian illness" that had held the country back under atomistic liberalism.[137] The uniforms, the marching children, the gymnastics exhibitions, all denoted a mass movement in which the individual was swept away to higher spiritual purposes. At the same time, the regime had to make itself popular, in both senses of the word, and attempted to create a mass culture that would unite the peninsula and the islands, all the while celebrating the rural roots and peasant traditions of the "true" Italy. Mussolini, in particular, was portrayed as a "man of the people" who could—threshing wheat or riding tractors—hark back to his rustic beginnings, all the while leading Italy forward.

One aspect of this populism manifested itself in the portrayal of the dagger as an icon of power projected by the fascist party. Admittedly,

---

137. Ben Ghiat 2001, 18.

this interpretation takes an intellectual leap of faith, but for someone sensitized to the long-standing denigration of the "perfidious stiletto" to the advantage of the "loyal sword" by elite proponents of the duel, the images of blackshirts constantly saluting the Duce with rows of drawn daggers virtually crackle with meaning (see image 7). As with so many fascist "innovations," the original emphasis on the dagger rather than the sword came from the *arditi*, who had prided themselves on attacking the enemy at close quarters. After the war, it became part of a consciously anti-elitist ideal that was described by Giovanni Comisso, an *ardito* and a legionnaire in Fiume, in a conversation he had with Guido Keller, Gabriele d'Annunzio's quartermaster in 1920: "We spoke of making a revolution that would begin to change the structure of the army by abolishing the ranks above captain, by recreating the old Italian tradition of companies of adventure, by taking the *ardito* as the typical example of the true Italian soldier, and by modifying the uniform, abolishing the closed collar and the *useless sword*" [my italics].[138] In fact, the symbolism of the dagger became intricately tied to the redemption of Italian honor at Fiume, as postcards and photos from the period attest (see image 8).

From these roots, the fascists embraced the image of the dagger along with the blackshirt and deathshead symbol (see image 9) of the *arditi*, and it became part of the standard uniform of the militia as it evolved in the 1920s.[139] Although military in its origins, the iconic dagger could only appeal to the popular traditions of Italy's knife-carrying lower classes. Here is not the place to elaborate the details of that pervasive "blade-culture," but one need only cite the introduction to Giancarlo Baronti's exhaustive *Coltelli d'Italia* to grasp the concept:

> There is no man of the people who, in his own personal knife, chosen carefully by weighing, hefting and trying at the moment of acquisition, sees not just a versatile instrument of work, useful for a thousand daily needs, [but] the tangible sign of his humanity, his virile solidity, and his personal pride and dignity. The knife is a faithful companion—light in weight yet instilling assurance in one's step—a friend of the night—always diligently ready for those exciting moments during which one can, and indeed must, place one's life on the line in order to maintain the respect of others.[140]

138. Comisso 1951, 59.
139. The dagger was consistently used to salute Mussolini by his honor guard. To complete the transfer of chivalric honor, they were called the "Musketeers" of the Duce.
140. Baronti 1986, 9–10.

Image 7
Mussolini's Honor Guard

Image 8
Propaganda postcard for Fiume invasion

By taking the dagger rather than the sword as fascism's iconic weapon of honor, the party reached out not only to the trenches of World War I but also to the honor traditions of the popular classes, which the liberal regime had so often ignored or disparaged. Yet the fascist dagger-*cum*-bayonet was, in fact, uniform; it was controlled and disciplined, and it became part of the mass display designed to subordinate individual honor to that of the collective (see image 10). Popular, potent, and obvious, it symbolized a bellicose tie between the Duce (who, one remembers, was dismissed from school for stabbing a fellow student with a knife) and the people. It thus offered an environment in which the elite traditions of the sword and the ritual of the duel no longer held the upper hand. By the time World War II shook Italy to its core and betrayed the dangers of Mussolini's virile rhetoric and military daring, the duel was already mortally wounded. It would not rise again.

Image 9
Mussolini's office with deathshead symbol

Image 10
Postcard, "Befana fascista anno XIX (1941)"

Conclusion

ALTHOUGH PERHAPS easily dismissed as a quirky "side issue" of history affecting only a small number of people, the duel, as portrayed in the preceding pages, figured prominently in the construction of men's social and political identities during much of Italy's modern history.[1] In the Renaissance, during the Risorgimento, after unification, and with the rise of fascism, new groups vied with old for power and prestige and found the armed defense of honor both a talisman and a touchstone of legitimacy. As a general pattern, a period of frequent "plague-like" combat gave way to gradual decline as publications and institutions adjudicating affairs of honor tended to mitigate and pacify previously explosive encounters of personal insult and injury. The *scienza cavalleresca* of the sixteenth century, the dueling manuals of the nineteenth, and the honor courts of the twentieth, all worked to restrict the membership of those capable of seeking satisfaction and to discipline the violence among them. Overall, the actual combat involved was relatively limited—nothing compared to war, brigandage, or revolt—but it always provided the possible threat and occasional reality of the ritual blood necessary to sustain the system as it proliferated and matured in each phase. Most members of the chivalric community would never face another man's sword, but they generally lived as though they might, and in consequence the dueling ethic helped shape

---

1. Thanks to Elizabeth Cohen for giving focus to this point.

behavior in both the public and the private sphere. Gentlemen often participated tangentially in duels as representatives, *padrini,* or jurors of honor, while the many *vertenze* that never came to bloody fruition still offered them the legitimizing semblance of ritual combat. At the very least they might own a dueling manual or two and remain secure in the knowledge that they were "in the know" when it came to matters of honor.

Having virtually disappeared from most of Italy during the eighteenth century, the duel returned with the French occupation and became inextricably entwined with the movement toward, first, liberation and then unification. Whereas aristocratic continuity of the chivalric tradition seems to have informed much of the dueling sentiment in countries such as England, France, Ireland, and Germany, in Italy it was specifically the *breakdown* of the compulsion during the many years of foreign occupation under the *ancien régime* that helped promote the practice as the ultimate arbiter of honor. For dueling experts like Paolo Fambri and fencing masters like Cesare Enrichetti, the Italians had been cut off from their Renaissance roots of chivalric dominance by a period of poltroonish subservience to tyranny and foreigners. Consequently the regeneration of honor was tied to the regeneration of Italy, and the duel became intrinsic to the identity of the country.

The role of France in this process of rediscovery and reaffirmation is particularly revealing. It is an old debate about how much credit should be given to the Napoleonic experience in shaping Italian nationalism, but the history of the duel comes down foursquare on the side of the little corporal. While historians, including me, have played up the economic, administrative, and political changes that occurred under French hegemony, the reintroduction of the dueling ethic suggests a social/psychological dimension that penetrated to some of the most fundamental cultural attributes of what it meant to be a man who counted. In providing a military experience for hundreds of thousands of men, including 222,000 in the Kingdom of Italy alone, the French offered a model of armed honor that would reverberate throughout the peninsula following the restoration. Officers who had fought under the flags of the empire would orchestrate the revolutions of 1820 and 1821, and their influence was still evident in those of 1831 and 1848.[2] Their important political role, as exemplified in the duel of the revolutionary exile Pepe, would assure an identifying link between the recrudescence

---

2. Ceva 1999, 16.

of the dueling ritual and the resurgence of Italian manhood in the defense of the honor of *Italia*, who was generally and effectively portrayed as a woman. Thus the "rearmament" of Italian honor determined attitudes and aptitudes for generations to come and played a critical role in the *risveglio militare*, or military reawakening, that swept up Italian elites during the Risorgimento. As John Whittam has suggested, the period from the restoration to 1848 saw a sea change in public opinion, from "Italians don't fight" to "Italians do fight," and this shift saw its individual analogue in the gradual proliferation of dueling throughout the peninsula.[3] Overall, then, our portrait of the duel's resurgence offers yet another example of how deeply Italian society was affected by Napoleon's policies and how the very definition of what it meant to be a man, or at least a gentleman, could be altered by a mass military experience.

It bears mentioning in this regard that the history of Italian dueling reinforces the causal connection between changing conceptions of honor and warfare in general. The Renaissance chivalric ethic matured in Italy and then spread to France (and beyond) during the Italian wars (1494–1559), only to fade in the former as demilitarization bolstered other factors, such as papal condemnation, militating against it. The Napoleonic incursion reintroduced the dueling ethic to Italy, which then received a major boost from the Risorgimento wars of independence, and a third lease on life from the "aristocracy of the trenches" coming out of the First World War. But warfare, and especially mass warfare, could also have the opposite effect. The American Civil War is generally credited for ending the practice of dueling in the United States, as did the First World War in France and Germany. As discussed below, Italy did not follow their example, but in the end it was the Second World War that definitively finished the job of killing off the duel which had been begun by the fascist regime. The point is that cultural habits are not so deeply engrained that they can necessarily resist the psychological and social dislocations of extreme events in the collective lives of a community.

Shifting to a different register, the marriage of the masculine duel and national honor forged during unification only became more complex as the new country emerged from the Risorgimento, and Italy's history of the duel clearly confirms the viability of current studies that link

3. Whittam 1977, 11–41.

gender and nationalism in the nineteenth century.[4] In fact, issues of gender ran rampant throughout the construction of the dueling ethic among Italy's elites and consistently conditioned the resulting debate over its continuing hold over society. Respectability became a key ingredient of status and translated into ever-greater control over elite women, who were increasingly isolated from the public sphere where men handled the business of the nation in both an economic and a political sense. Proper behavior in maintaining these social distances figured heavily in the dueling codes as they regulated the actions of men in both mixed company and the all-male settings of private clubs and electoral politics. As seen in the fictional literature regarding the duel, women were generally regarded as emotional countertypes whose inherent sentimentality prohibited their immediate grasp of chivalric honor, but with proper patriarchal guidance they could be brought to not only accept but reinforce the ethic among their offspring. Enshrined in terms of Italian regeneration, female sexual conformity trumped all other conceptions of honor, and the duel was consistently seen as the ultimate arbiter of offenses so intrinsically injurious, such as the adultery of wives or the seduction of daughters, that no official court could ever offer alternative recourse, an argument that consistently stymied opponents of the practice through the years. All of these factors and forces add up to a prime example of what R. W. Connell describes as "hegemonic masculinity" in which a reinvigorated gendered hierarchy advertises and undergirds the realigned power structures of a new regime emerging from a period of crisis.[5] In the Italian case dueling placed elite women's unidimensional honor under the control and tutelage of their male relations while conspicuously denying complete masculine identity to lower-class men. Only those who understood and embraced the dueling code as a guide to proper behavior could be considered *real* men to whom the affairs of the nation could be entrusted.

The great dueling debate likewise indicated the potency of gender pressures even for those who rejected the nationalist precepts of the liberal state. Socialists and Catholics alike faced the difficulty of working against the duel without opening themselves to charges of feminine weakness. The muscular religiosity of Crispolti, who tried to inject a crusading image of young men suffering for their beliefs into the abolitionist campaign, in some ways mirrored the general deficiency of

---

4. Aside from Patriarca, De Grazia, Ben Ghiat, Spackman, and Mosse, one gets an idea of the variety of topics open to this line of analysis from Blom et al. 2000.

5. Connell 2002, 102–8.

the socialists in policing their comrades who dueled in direct defiance of party policy. Indeed, some socialists, despite the obvious class basis of dueling, simply argued that private matters of manhood should stay beyond the pale of party discipline, while others stressed revolutionary violence as a manly substitute for the duel, and still others feared that energetic recruits might be lost to a party that rejected the dictates of honor. By the same token, liberals who argued against the duel had to emphasize over and over again the martial and masculine traditions of the Romans who had not engaged in duels and who had relegated one-on-one combat to condemned slaves for the enjoyment of others. Across the board, then, opponents as well as proponents of the ritual had to keep their discourse within rather narrow parameters of what it meant to be a man.

Gender also permeated the discourse on dueling by asserting the virility of Italian men as the country sought to establish itself as a serious player in the European community and eventually in the world. This assertion became increasingly manic after Italy performed poorly in the Austrian-Prussian War of 1866, thereby giving lie to the martial myths so easily created around Garibaldi and Victor Emmanuel II during the earlier wars of unification. Fencing schools and chivalric conflict were the elite analogue of gymnastics for the masses, and defenders of the duel argued that the ritual kept officers on their toes, prepared them to lead upon the battlefield, and offered concrete evidence of Italian courage in the face of danger. Defeat in Africa at Dogali and Adua only heightened concerns about Italian weakness and effeminacy and led to an increasingly shrill rhetoric of redemptive violence that prompted dueling manuals, such as those of Barbasetti, Brunetti, and San di Malato, to become ever more petulant and bloodthirsty. Informed by the growing scientific tendency to "sex" everything, the discourse of both national and individual honor became more radically gendered, and promotion of a more violent dueling ethic offered a means of reclaiming Italy's true masculinity—a pattern that Robert Nye has examined for other European countries.[6] Following World War I, Italian fascism served up the most virulent form of modern male identity with its glorification of impetuous violence and disdain for "womanly" prudence, all of which found their honorable counterpart in the recrudescence of dueling in the 1920s. Eventually, however, the individualistic manhood of the chivalric ethic ran afoul of the evolving totalitarian concept of the "new fascist man," and the regime actively,

6. Nye 1995, 77–78.

albeit carefully, began to draw the teeth of the dueling ethic. In general, then, the history of the duel enhances our understanding of elite conceptions of gender and points up how critical issues of masculinity were to Italian leaders throughout the course of the liberal and fascist regimes.

Beyond its confirmation of virility, the duel offered practical advantages to the new Italian state. Alberto Banti has discussed how nationalism provided a crucial form of identity for Italy's new elites and indeed formed one of the few common denominators that papered over the many fragments and strata of the mutating multi-*borghesie*.[7] The same might easily be said of the dueling code. Given its Risorgimento roots and ties to continuing national regeneration, the chivalric ethic supplied an important pan-Italian set of assumptions that helped bind the disparate elites of Italy together under the rubric of "gentlemen" as they struggled to create a workable polity. Hence, the supposedly universal aspects of male honor offered a lexicon of behavior, comportment, and redress that helped forge a portrait of what it meant to be an Italian who mattered. If, as everyone points out, d'Azeglio was correct in his famous dictum that "we have made Italy, now we must make the Italians," he was referring not only to the lower classes but also to the upper echelons of society as well—and the reintroduction of chivalric combat offered them a readily understandable model with historical roots in the Renaissance which could be handily appropriated as intrinsic to the national character.[8] This paradigm was especially important in the realm of post-Risorgimento politics, and the dueling code allowed for the honorable settlement of disputes between men who radically disagreed about how the country had been created and where it should be going. It set limits over how far one might go in political and journalistic discourse and then enforced those limits with blood or, ever more frequently, polite negotiations backed by the threat of blood.

Socially, it offered a handy and restrictive tool for the definition and legitimization of new notables, all the while assuring previous elites of their place in the changing order of things. Indeed, no better case for the new chivalry's potential for social mobility can be found than Iacopo Gelli, who became the ultimate arbiter of honor in Italy, rising from an artisan background in the Tuscan provinces to marry his daughter off to a member of the aristocracy. On a different level, one

---

7. Banti 1996, 214. Also see Lanaro 1988, 70–81.

8. Thus Fambri in an article on the courts of honor would claim, "Making Italians is the second and as yet unsolved part of the problem of making Italy." Fambri 1888A, 267.

could argue that the duel helped stimulate the growth of a fencing "industry" that became a source of national pride as Italian masters and champions competed for jobs and prizes on the international stage, a tradition that remains vibrant even today.[9] Combined with potent patriotism and masculine symbolism, such functions make it anything but astonishing that the liberal regime consistently failed in its attempts to end the practice of dueling. On the contrary, the track record of legislature, police, and courts was consistently one of accommodation rather than confrontation.

There was, however, a heavy price to be paid for the favors granted by the chivalric ethic. First, as bemoaned by such disparate critics as the socialist Zibordi and the *avanguardista* Prezzolini, the mechanisms of personal honor could cloud the transparency critical to a liberal society. Frequent recourse to *sfida* and *duello* were allowed to sidetrack real debate as politicians lost sight of issues for the *vertenze* they sparked. For instance, during a parliamentary session in 1889, Felice Cavallotti accused the undersecretary of war, General Corvetto, of lying about current circumstances in Sicily. This charge went beyond the pale of reasonable discourse, and Corvetto sent General Pelloux (the future prime minister of Italy) and General Mocenni to request satisfaction. Cavallotti agreed to a duel but demanded that the *verbale* specifically guarantee that he be able to return to the facts at issue back in parliament. However, after Corvetto was seriously injured in the head and arm, Cavallotti let the matter drop. The personal had triumphed over the political import of the moment. In the proper circumstances, then, the chivalric code could allow the obfuscation of charges of malfeasance, and it fit handily into the general pattern of informal barter and civil illegalities that undergirded the system of *trasformismo*.

The most impressive of those illegalities was, in fact, the extraordinary toleration of the crime of dueling by the Italian state over the course of the liberal period. High crime rates and the attending fear of disorder had been one of the major weak points of the preunitary governments, and one of the major goals of the Risorgimento had been to achieve the "rule of law" as a panacea for the problems incurred by the old regime's "absolutist inefficiency" and its corporate concepts of privilege and power.[10] The duel, however, seemed to fly in the face of good government. It broke the liberal covenant of impartial juridical

9. For example, Biblioteca Nazionale 2005.
10. See Davis 1988 and Hughes 1994.

equality and determined that a new, albeit amorphous, aristocracy had the right to flout the word of the law in an incredibly open fashion, as long as it was in the name of chivalric honor. The almost daily spectacle of duels being reported in the newspapers with little or no action on the part of police or prosecutors clearly enhanced the prestige of elites as well as broadcasting to the others the importance of staying within their hierarchical range of influence. Yet it also had a negative effect on society in general. Italian legislators often bemoaned the possible consequences of allowing such obviously illegal activity to be carried out in the open with virtual impunity, and they were not wrong. The whole juridical approach to the duel in Italy reinforced "a wink and a nod" approach to the strictures of the law and suggested that personal power and status could consistently override any notion of equality before the law or even of the importance of the law itself. This attitude in turn reinforced the worst aspects of *trasformismo*, which was based on a culture of clientelism that promoted what Amalia Signorelli has called "the mass socialization in the practices of illegality."[11] This tradition of honorable impunity came home to roost with a vengeance when, after the First World War, the liberals faced the fascists who explained their crimes—chivalric and otherwise—in terms of defending bruised Italian honor.

It was, however, the paradox of liberal "men of order" consistently breaking the law that helps account for the voluminous and sometimes tortured debate about the duel under the liberal regime. As much as legislators and jurists might denounce the duel as an evil example to the lower classes and a barbaric prejudice unfit for a progressive country, they simply could not relinquish the mechanism that sanctioned their status and their virility in society and in the world. Honor was a positive force for the country, and honor had to be defended, even if by illegal means. It was in order to mitigate this paradox that Fambri, Angelini, Gelli, and other promoters of the duel all couched their support of the practice in terms of a necessary evil whose rapid disappearance was to be hoped for in some not-too-distant future. Their obsession with finding a "national" dueling code and creating a parallel system of chivalric courts symbolized their desire to seem to be acting legally, knowing full well that they were not. The same paradox led them through a variety of projects to seek state recognition for the courts and juries of honor, but the parliament, led by the legal community, consistently

11. Quoted in Ginsburg 2003, 101.

refused to do so. Liberal legislators might be willing to create a *sui generis* category of crime for those who dueled according to the rules, but they would not fall into the self-contradiction of sanctioning an illegal act, no matter how indirect the connection. Significantly, it was finally the fascist government, which could afford to look askance at the troubling liberal sensibilities of consistency and equality before the law, that allowed the courts of honor to finally come into the legal realm, albeit in a very limited fashion.

The obvious juridical impunity of the duel ran parallel to its other significant consequence for united Italy, which was that it socially and symbolically broadened the gulf between the people and the ruling elites. Contemporary commentators as diverse as the Catholic Stefano Jacini and the Marxist Antonio Gramsci pointed out (and later historians have consistently echoed them) that the liberal period was dogged by a split between "legal Italy," represented by the official institutions of the parliament, the bureaucracy, and the military, and "real Italy," which consisted of almost everybody else. Failure to bridge this gap created a resounding dissonance in Italian society that undermined allegiance to the state and even the basic precepts of liberalism, eventually contributing to the rise of fascism. As demonstrated by the current study, perhaps no clearer line could be drawn between "legal" and "real" Italy than the distinction between those who could and those who could not defend their honor through the code *duello,* and the very assumptions of the ritual reinforced an elitist worldview that made communications across the gap all the more difficult.

Such should have been the role of parliament and the press, but, as we have seen, they were both institutions caught up in the blatant distinctions between *popolo* and *gentiluomini* that fed the dueling phenomenon. In a sense, this was a natural product of the way in which Italy was united. With the failure of the revolutions of 1848 and 1849, much of the Italian democratic movement shifted toward a "sterner plan" based on Piedmontese hegemony that aimed at the limited goals of liberation and unification.[12] The process played into the hands of the moderates who were interested primarily in creating an "administrative revolution" that would avoid popular participation and allow necessary reforms and economic progress without threatening the social order.[13] Italy was to be made by a cultured and politically aware minority,

12. See Grew 1968.
13. See Lyttleton 1979 and Davis 1988, 145–69.

backed by the Piedmontese army, with the rest of society only tangentially involved in the process. The dueling ethic mirrored this partition of participation and offered a legitimizing social aesthetic whose military and masculine imagery appealed, like the monarchy, across divisions of left and right while excluding the majority. Consequently, we must consider that the code of honor was not just a symptom of Italy's postunitary real/legal political dichotomy: rather, it was a critical set of assumptions that allowed the system to work the way it did, constantly reinforcing the gulf between men of honor and those below.

In so doing, it often denied honor to the vast bulk of Italy's population. One of the most striking aspects of the various dueling codes and the discussion that surrounded them was their general disregard for forms or manifestations of honor that did not fit the definitions or patterns of chivalry and heraldry. Students of Italian culture today emphasize that Italy's peasant classes set great store by the idea of honor (perhaps because they had precious little else).[14] Yet one gets the sense that Gelli, Angelini, and the others had no conception of this fact, or at least chose to ignore it. Indeed, Angelini affirmed, "Public opinion does not consider an honest day-laborer, a servant, or an artisan to be dishonored even if they are slapped."[15] This comment might have been true of Angelini's "public," but one doubts very much if it held for these peoples' own communities. Even honest members of the *popolo* were generally portrayed in the dueling literature as lacking the self-control and rationality to adjudicate insult honorably, and their knives and daggers were denigrated as both pedestrian and perfidious. No wonder that Italy's growing collection of elites failed to understand the mafia or *omertà* or high homicide rates or even peasant culture in general. They were self-absorbed in their own struggle for self-validation through honor as defined by their fellow "gentlemen" and adjudicated by the sword.

The study of the duel in united Italy equally offers an interesting adjunct to current theories of how Italian elites functionally defined themselves and their country by representing the Mezzogiorno, and especially Sicily, as an African "other" or "oriental" countertype. Jane Schneider (1998), Nelson Moe (2002), and others have analyzed how language and illustrations were consistently selected and manipulated, both consciously and unconsciously, to reinforce a negative image of

---

14. For example, Fiume 1989, and for the earlier period see Hanlon 2000, 26–30.
15. Angelini 1888, 4.

southern barbarism and irrationality that contrasted with the modernizing Euro-centric north. With regard to the duel, this analysis applies nicely in that the sword/dagger binary was more often than not aligned geographically on a north-south axis. As John Dickie has demonstrated, southern peasants eventually could be used to represent all Italian peasants, and the violence of postunitary brigandage in the Mezzogiorno reinforced a continuing stereotype of the bestial and savage dark side that underlay later "picturesque" portrayals of rural life. In that world of conflict, the peasant/brigand had no honor, and Dickie provides an insightful analysis of how real or putative brigands slated for execution were shot in the back rather than the front by firing squads: a traditional military symbol of disgrace and dishonor.[16]

More broadly, however, Dickie's central themes provide an informative perspective on the duel as part of the discursive "problematic" of creating a national identity on the part of Italy's elites. While acknowledging the importance of inclusive concepts such as those laid out generally by Benedict Andersen (1983), and more specifically by A. M. Banti, Dickie emphasizes as well the internal exclusionary boundaries of the "imagined community," at least for those elites engaged in its construction. Thus the "slippery" nature of defining the nation empowered elites to assert, maintain, and justify their privileged position as part and parcel of the patriotic enterprise, all the while claiming to include everyone.[17] They justified their leadership in terms of a morality that implied "both a civil competence, which one must achieve through such skills as literacy and the capacity to reason impartially, and a social sphere from which one may be excluded."[18] In a similar fashion Italy's elites embraced the duel in a spirit of patriotism that projected martial courage and personal honor as vital to the health of a young nation, yet it clearly served their social and political purposes of exclusion and self-definition. In the end this tension helps explain the constant anxiety that surrounded the dueling ethic during the life of the liberal regime, even among its proponents. Their own inclusive notions of nationhood and their belief in the liberal project of good government sat poorly with their practice of legally privileging gentlemen over issues of honor. Angst over who was allowed to duel; fear of unscrupulous *spadaccini;* endless legislative and juridical wrangling; to say nothing of Gelli's "democratization" of the duel and Fambri's

16. Dickie 1999, 44–47.
17. Also see Bollati 1983, 42.
18. Dickie 1999, 57–61.

justification of it as a transitory and necessary stage in the progress of the country, all betrayed the fundamental paradox of men who touted the totality of the nation but based their own social identities on exclusion.

※ ✝ ※

Looking beyond the borders of Italy, our study offers an obvious opportunity for comparison with dueling in other countries. In an early treatment of the topic, Robert Nye suggested that Italy represented a sort of middle way of dueling in the nineteenth century between France and Germany—both well-known for their affinity for the cult of honor. Having gone through an early liberal phase, France became more democratic in its dueling practices, with a rhetoric of egalitarian honor that fed the patriotism of the republic as a nation in arms looking forward to revenge after the "humiliation" of the Franco-Prussian War. As befit this model, the French dueled with high frequency and relatively low mortality rates using the traditional *épée*, with civilians rather than soldiers serving as the most common combatants. In contrast, the Germans maintained a more military, and some would say aristocratic, ethos of honor marked by a higher death toll, the latter assured primarily by the use of rifled pistols rather than swords.[19] Unlike its French counterpart, the German army (along with the reserve officer corps) provided the critical epicenter of chivalric combat. Italy, according to Nye, offered aspects of both styles.[20] The Italian army, backed by the Savoyard monarchy, unquestionably supported the dueling compulsion throughout its duration. Officers constituted the single largest group of duelists, and the overwhelming use of the saber rather than the *épée*—notwithstanding Italy's primacy in developing Renaissance rapier techniques—can be interpreted as carrying a military message that went back into the roots of the Risorgimento. On the other hand, Italian duels with their high frequency and relative lack of severity mirrored the French experience and made the ritual more useful for journalistic and

---

19. In contrast to Frevert, McAleer has stressed the overwhelming primacy of the aristocratic/military ethos of German dueling. Frevert does not dispute the importance of the military in the German dueling tradition, but she sees the bourgeoisie as redefining it to suit its own social purposes through the nineteenth century. Cf. Frevert 1995 and MacAleer 1994, especially 183–212.

20. Nye 1995, 74–77. For the sake of full disclosure I would add that Nye used my early work for his information on Italy.

parliamentary purposes. This mélange of traditions would seem to flow, on one hand, from the key importance of the Piedmontese military and monarchy in the unification of Italy and afterwards, but it was combined with the growing need to settle disputes arising from the political complexity and controversy reigning in the new country. Piedmont was not Prussia, unification was both messy and contested over a couple of decades, and things had to be sorted out with minimum damage and maximum honor. Moreover, Italy had regained its taste for the duel from the French, not the Germans, and even in the 1860s Chatauvillard's dueling manual was still the reference of choice among some of Italy's gentlemen.

Where Italy primarily differed from both Germany and France was in the recrudescence of dueling after World War I. Nye has effectively argued that for France the extraordinary bloodletting occasioned by the war simply put the personal combat of honor into a negative light. From the perspective of the trenches the *terreno* seemed petty, and the war required a "new standard of masculine courage" that made the *sang-froid* demonstrated in a duel seem "a Tinkertoy" in comparison.[21] Frevert has made much the same case for Germany, where the mechanized industrial nature of the war's violence dissipated the duel's heroic individualism, but she also stresses the massive reduction of the officer corps that came out of defeat and that weakened the clout of the army and its chivalric traditions within society. Moreover, the destruction of the empire and the abdication of the kaiser deprived the duel of its official backers and replaced them with politicians, many of whom, like the socialists, had consistently opposed the practice. Staged student duels or *Mensur* would survive and even thrive in the 1920s, and the military would offer a stream of pronouncements upholding the old way of things, but compared to its earlier currency, the point-of-honor duel in Weimar Germany became an increasingly rare occurrence.[22]

In contrast, the duel returned with renewed vigor to Italy during the postwar period, and the reasons seem obvious enough. First, although one should never underestimate the impact of the war on Italian society, the raw devastation of the army was less drastic than in France or Germany. Italy joined the fray a year later than the other two and thus enjoyed a corresponding reduction in its casualties, with signifi-

21. "The End of the Modern French Duel," in Spierenburg 1998, 92–93.
22. Frevert 1995, 200–219.

cantly fewer than half the number of dead and even fewer wounded.[23] Furthermore, the Savoyard monarchy remained in power, as did the old parliamentary system, and although they would both soon prove unequal to the challenges wrought by the war, they still represented traditional bastions of honor. Finally, and most important, when revolution did come, it was carried out by the fascists who, as we have seen, embraced the dueling ritual as both an instrument of legitimacy and a symbol of their martial virility. Thus, far from coming to power as they did in Germany, the socialists (complete with their antidueling attitudes) were soon forced into submission or exile, and the Catholics acquiesced in the face of fascist pressure. The new regime promoted and tolerated the duel, and only later would they decide to alter its course. Even then, the delicacy with which the fascists handled the dueling issue provides a new example of how the regime dealt with inveterate institutions such as the army, the Church, or the bureaucracy as it compromised its way toward a supposedly totalitarian state.

While such contrasts are highly interesting, they primarily prove the chameleonlike nature of the chivalric code as it adapted to fit the needs of elites in different social and political environments. In this regard they underscore the consistency of the core values of masculinity and courage attached to the late-eighteenth-century construction of the "Image of Man," so carefully delineated by George Mosse, all the while demonstrating their high cultural valence in both time and place. The Italian example, however, emphasizes to a high degree the affinity of the dueling ethic with the political structures of liberalism and leads us to look for parallels in other countries. As noted, France fits the model particularly well, with the duel serving the purposes of politicians and journalists as they created a society based on the open exchange of information and public debate.[24] The rise of new elites into realms of political power naturally coincided with these changes, and the elastic definition that could be applied to the term "gentleman" increased the number of men who would seek satisfaction through either the duel or its auxiliary mechanisms such as the *vertenza* or jury of honor. Developmental timing seems to be important, for dueling flourished in the United States between the Revolution and the Civil War and in England at the end of the eighteenth century and prior to the Reform Bill, both periods in which new elites struggled for power

---

23. The total proportion of casualties per number of men mobilized was 39.1 for Italy, 76.3 for France, and 64.9 for Germany. See Gilbert 1994.

24. Nye 1993, chapters 7–9; Reddy 1994.

using the rhetoric and the devices of liberal government, free speech, and individual achievement.[25] Can one then postulate a period of "liberal" development in which up-and-coming elites "learned" how to handle their new freedoms and used dueling as a means of both setting limits on behavior and legitimizing their own status in society?

Three national examples, Ireland, Belgium, and Portugal, taken in chronological order clearly illustrate the argument. First let us consider Ireland, a country that enjoyed a widespread reputation for aggressive and ubiquitous duelists up through the early nineteenth century. Relying on a variety of sources, James Kelly has clearly demonstrated that starting in the 1750s the frequency of dueling increased (and its danger declined) as economic growth encouraged the number of would-be gentlemen and as politics became an increasingly common source of conflict. Pamphlets and newspapers expanded in number, offering greater coverage to affairs of honor and quickening the pace and publicity of political discourse. These trends accelerated in the 1760s to become a veritable "plague" of dueling, similar to that in Italy after unity, and Kelly makes no bones about attributing the phenomenon to the "emergence of a younger generation of more aggressive politicians who aspired to make government in Ireland more responsive to the wishes and needs of Protestant opinion at large."[26] Intrinsic to this change was the imposition of a new electoral law in 1768 which established regular parliamentary elections every eight years. Suddenly members of the emerging factions had a chance to gain or lose power on a regular basis, which raised "the political temperature in the country at large. . . ."[27] With increasing ideological divisions between nationalist reforming "Patriots" and conservative "Castle" supporters and the eventual granting of legislative independence, the 1770s and 1780s would see twice as many duels as occurred in the previous five decades. Kelly interprets increased political dueling in Ireland as the result of flaring tempers and clashing ideological animosities, but he is surprised at how so few of the duels ended in death or even serious injury. It is here that the Italian case offers an extra layer of interpretation and allows us to suggest that the dueling "fever" that gripped Ireland was not just about confrontation and ire but also about allowing Irish elites to come to

---

25. Simpson 1988, 106–7. Cf. Shoemaker 2002, 542–45. Shoemaker argues that dueling became less violent in the "long" eighteenth century and suggests this may have allowed it to flourish as it became increasingly tied to print culture. Also see Andrew 1980.
26. Kelly 1995, 97.
27. Kelly uses the barometric metaphor throughout; see, for example, 94, 98, 128.

terms with their often emotional interchanges in a sphere of civil power and personal politics.

An even closer parallel with the Italian case can be found in Belgium, where nationalism and liberalism also arrived on the scene at the same time. Dueling had become a relatively limited phenomenon in the Southern Lowlands under Austrian control during the eighteenth century.[28] Like Italy, the Lowlands were then sucked into the French orbit after the revolution and came into direct contact with the recently revamped and more inclusive chivalric code of the republic. Such exposure was then reinforced by mass participation in Napoleon's armies, which by 1813 included 160,000 Belgian troops.[29] These influences only came to full fruition, however, following the revolt against the Dutch in 1830 and the eventual establishment of a parliamentary monarchy under the watchful eye of the European powers. At that point observers began to mark a "plague" of duels involving officers, journalists, and politicians which would rage throughout the decade and beyond.[30] The setting for this "most remarkable paroxysm" of dueling, as the contemporary Fougeroux called it, is highly instructive. Having broken away from the Kingdom of the Netherlands, Belgium established the most liberal constitution on the continent, based primarily on the English model. Freedom of speech, press, and religion undergirded a representative monarchy in which suffrage was tightly limited by property qualifications to a small percentage of adult males.

Overall, the new system represented an extraordinary compromise between Catholic and liberal elites, who were willing to accommodate controversial settlements regarding education, marriage, and the status of the clergy, so as to offer a united front against the Dutch Crown, which did not recognize Belgian independence until 1839. Despite this uneasy truce, however, politicians and journalists were unaccustomed to unrestricted public debate and pulled no punches in their discussions. Observing from France, Fougeroux found French parliamentary debate a model of decorum in comparison to its Belgian counterpart.[31] At the same time, the Belgian army had to be fashioned from a muddle of military components, including a number of French soldiers who

28. Fougeroux 1835, 54.
29. Cook 2002, 53.
30. For contemporary complaints see "Du Duel," in *Journal de Flandres,* Jan. 1, March 13 and 15, 1836.
31. Fougeroux 1835, 54–56.

had intervened against the Dutch and then stayed to compete for preferment and promotion within the new system.[32] In short, it was a situation rife with possibilities for personal insult, bruised honor, and armed satisfaction as new political and military leaders demonstrated their bravery to each other, to their constituents, and to the rest of the world—especially the Dutch and the French. Likewise it allowed strategies of settling potentially disastrous disputes among elites coming from radically different ideological and professional directions.

Similar forces were at work in Portugal, although later in the century. According to Mário Matos E Lemos, dueling was not fashionable in Portugal in the first half of the nineteenth century, but it began to increase after the chaotic reign of Maria II ended in 1852, and parliament began to play a more viable role in running the country. By the 1880s it had become a more common practice, especially among politicians and journalists who were operating in an extremely complicated and highly contested political environment. Harsh words and recriminations both in print and in parliament led to challenges which had to be sorted out using French and later Italian dueling manuals because there were no native sources. Despite the government's adoption of antidueling legislation, the practice continued into the next century and apparently increased in intensity with the creation of the republic in 1910. In fact, one of the first acts of the new government was to set up tribunals of honor in hopes of adjudicating the many affairs affecting the top ranks of society, but it met with little success. Despite the duel's popularity during the republic, which filled the newspapers with exciting tales of chivalric negotiations and bloody encounters, its lifespan as a practice would be relatively short. Following the military coup d'état in 1926, the liberal regime ended, and public notices of duels began to decline rapidly. The coup de grâce came with the consolidation of Salazar's dictatorship around 1930. A jurist with a Catholic corporativist approach to government, Salazar found dueling antithetical to his morality and his regime, and he did not hesitate to use his ever-growing police power to enforce its extermination.[33]

The death of the Portuguese duel at the hands of its dictator effectively points up again the complex relationship between dueling and liberal politics in modern European society, a relationship that is further evidenced by Sandra Gayol (1999), Pablo Piccato (1999), and David

32. Leconte 1949, 250.
33. Matos E Lemos 1993, 561–97.

Parker's (2001) various studies on dueling in Latin America between 1870 and 1920. Piccato has shown, for instance, how duels (which had previously been rare events) notably increased in Mexico after 1880:

> The code of honor became a guide for the behavior and speech of public men during a key period in the construction of a modern political legitimacy. A national ruling elite was trying to establish its primacy after conflicts—such as the Reforma war (1857–1860), and the French intervention and Second Empire (1861–1867)—which generated deep and often bloody political cleavages. In this context of recent factional strife, the practice of dueling coexisted with other elements of the Mexican state's and upper classes' embrace of European progress.
>
> Dueling reveals, perhaps better than any other cultural product, the contradictions of Mexican ruling elites' embrace of modem politics. They construed the duel as a prestigious gesture of modernization, because it echoed the uses of other political elites in contemporary Europe.[34]

According to Parker, much the same process took place in Uruguay and Argentina as these nations embraced a troubled liberalism in the wake of anarchical postindependence. Although he agrees with Piccato that there was a strong demonstration effect coming from France, Germany, and Italy, he stresses the inherent usefulness of the duel as it "filled a need created by the destruction of the colonial consensus and the explosion of modern competitive politics within a legitimacy vacuum."[35]

Such parallels leave us only to reiterate the reasons for such a consistent connection. Obviously, the code of honor functioned in a variety of ways to provide stability and status to elites trying to consolidate power in times of transition. In this sense it is anything but the "cultivation of eccentric identities and behaviors" suggested by Geltmaker in his efforts to see it as a form of suicide.[36] Rather, it offered a supposedly universal set of norms governing male behavior that could actually be quite flexible in dealing with local conditions, and it helped govern public conflict among men with sometimes radically different visions of how the world should operate. As the public sphere became an open forum of personal opinion, reputation had to be increasingly defended

---

34. Piccato 1999, 331.
35. Parker 2001, 10.
36. Geltmaker 2002, 82. However, Geltmaker's other comments on the duel in liberal Italy are quite cogent.

as men sought to gain credibility for their words and actions. Critical to that forum, however, was an understanding and acceptance of the loyal opposition by which men agreed to disagree and continued to play by the rules of "civil society" and parliamentary process. The duel provided a constant dramatic reiteration of this political ritual at the personal level, for—in theory—neither man ever admitted his fault in a *vertenza* that ended on the *terreno*. Both remained adamant in their words or actions, but by carefully following the script of chivalric combat each was vindicated as a gentleman who acknowledged the worth and loyalty (however oppositional) of the other.

On the other hand, when new patterns of political power consolidated, dueling helped demarcate membership in an honor group that allowed for the rise of a limited number of new men armed with talent, élan, or luck while keeping the rest of society at bay. The duel offered what Piccato calls a "technology of honor" that laid out rules and rituals that only literate elites could internalize and articulate, while lower-class forms of interpersonal honor conflict were relegated to barbaric or at least criminal status.[37] The truthfulness and self-control supposedly sanctioned by the ritual spoke directly to the public ability of special men who wanted others to place power in their hands. Courage might be proven by martial *sang-froid,* but in the public realm it denoted a strength of conviction and a willingness to take responsibility for collective decisions. In short, it demonstrated a man's willingness and ability to lead and accept the consequences of his decisions, after older justifications of entitled power, such as birth, had disappeared. Nevertheless, the strength it drew from its class exclusivity and its ties to individual freedom would also prove its weakness, and the duel of liberalism would fade in the face of either disciplined democracy or preemptory dictatorship.

Shifting toward a more philosophical tone, what is most striking in all the examples above is what they reveal about modalities of masculinity in the modern world. It is an axiom of the new gender studies that notions of manhood are malleable and socially constructed, but the vicissitudes of the duel in Italy (as well as Ireland, Belgium, and Portugal) tend to surprise us with the rapidity with which those notions and their attending actions can mutate. On one hand, we might bemoan the obvious currency and ubiquity that the virile and violent "image of man," so aptly illustrated by Mosse, has enjoyed since the eighteenth century. But, on the other hand, watching the relative speed with which

37. Piccato 1999.

groups of men could adopt and then abandon assumptions and behaviors that they felt essential to their very existence—indeed worth dying and killing for—should give us all hope that perhaps with a little luck and a lot of reason we might be able to head things in the right direction.

Works Cited

Note: Newspaper articles, many of which were unsigned, are given full citation in the footnotes.

Abba, Giuseppe. 1907. *Cose Garabaldine.* Turin: Nazionale.
Abignente, Filippo. 1894. *Il duello.* Verona: Drucker. 2nd ed. 1898.
Adamoli-Castiglioni Branda, Contessa A. M. 1900. *Cenni biografici del Generale Achille Angelini.* Firenze: Seeber/Loescher.
Adamson, Walter I. 1993. *Avant-Garde Florence: From Modernism to Fascism.* Cambridge: Harvard University Press.
Addis Saba, Marina. 1993. *Anna Kuliscioff: vita privata e passione politica.* Milano: Mondadori.
Aloisi, Baron Pompeo. 1957. *Journal.* Paris: Plon.
Alvaro, Corrado. 1950. *Quasi una vita: giornale di uno scrittore.* Milano: Bompiani.
Anderson, Benedict. 1983. *Imagined Communities: Relections on the Origin and Spread of Nationalism.* London: Verso.
Andre, Emile. 1903. *Les Duels Franco Italiens.* Paris: Flammarion.
Andreucci, Franco and Tommaso Detti. 1975–1979. *Il movimento operaio italiano: dizionario biografico 1853–1943.* 6 vols. Roma: Riuniti.
Andrew, Donna. 1980. The Code of Honour and Its Critics: The Opposition to Duelling in England, 1700–1750. *Social History* 5: 409–34.
Angelini, Achille. 1867. *Riforme per l'esercito italiano.* Florence: Cassone.
———. 1888. *Codice cavalleresco italiano.* 3rd ed. Roma: Vercellini.
Angelozzi, Giancarlo. 1996. La proibizione del duello, Chiesa e ideologia nobiliare. In *Il concilio di Trento e il moderno*, ed. Prodi e Reinhard, 283–97. Bologna: Il Mulino.
Angelozzi, Giancarlo and Cesarina Casanova. 2003. *La nobiltà disciplinata.* Bologna: Clueb.
Anglo, Sydney. 1990. How to Kill a Man at Your Ease. In *Chivalry in the Renaissance*, ed. Anglo, 1–12. Woodbridge: Boydell.

Anonymous. 1837. *Della questione.* Napoli: n.e.
Archivio Centrale dello Stato. 2005. *Luigi Moretti: La casa delle armi le sue opere e il suo archivio.* Roma: ACS.
Arista, Salvatore. 1884. *Del progesso della scherma in Italia.* Bologna: Compositori.
Artieri, G. 1957. *Il vesuvio col pennacchio ovvero funiculì funiculà.* Milano.
Associazione della Stampa Periodica in Italia. 1877. *Atti costitutivi.* Roma: Popolo Romano.
Banti, Alberto. 1996. *Storia della borghesia Italiana: L'età liberale.* Roma: Donzelli.
———. 2000. *La nazione del Risorgimento: parentela, santità e onore alle origini dell'Italia unita.* Torino: Einaudi.
Banti, Athos Gaston. 1926. Preface to Gelli, *Codice Cavalleresco.*
Barbasetti, Luigi. 1898. *Codice cavalleresco.* Milano: Gattinoni.
Barbèra, Gaspero. 1930. *Memorie di un editore: 1818–1880.* Firenze: Barbèra.
Barbiera, Raffalele. 1919. *Il salotto di contessa Maffei.* Milano: Treves.
Baretti, Giuseppe. 1768. *An account of the manners and customs of Italy.* 2 vols. London: Davies.
Baronti, Giancarlo. 1986. *Coltelli d'Italia: rituali di violenza e tradizioni produttive.* Padova: Muzzio.
Bellassai, Sandro and Maria Malatesta. 2000. *Genere e mascolinità.* Roma: Bulzoni.
Ben Ghiat, Ruth. 2001. *Fascist Modernities: Italy, 1922–1945.* Berkeley: University of California Press.
———. 2005. Unmaking of the Fascist Man: Masculinity, Film and the Transition from Dictatorship. *Journal of Modern Italian Studies* 10 (3): 336–65.
Benussi, Fermo. 1907. Della responsabilità penale dei medici che assistono al duello. *La giustizia penale* (13): 1244–54.
Berenini, Augusto. 1889. *Sul duello.* Torino: Bocca.
Bergando, Alfonso. 1888. *Sulle convenienze sociali e sugli usi dell'alta società.* Milano: Dumolard.
Besenzanica, Ernesto. 1886. *Come il sistema Redaelli fu esautorato.* Milano: Dumolard.
Besso, Marco. 1970. *Autobiografia,* ed. Luigi Rava. Rome: Fondazione Besso.
Bianchetti, Carlo. 1887. *Il duello: saggio popolare esposto agli operai cattolici di Torino.* Torino: Subalpina.
Bianchi, Paola. 2002. *Onore e mestiere: le riforme militari nel Piemonte del settecento.* Torino: Zamorani.
Bianco, N. A. 1848. *Sul duello.* Napoli: Dell'Araldo.
Biblioteca Nazionale Centrale di Roma (BNCR). 2005. *A fil di spada: il duello dalle origini . . . agli ori olimpici,* ed. Alda Spotti. Roma: Colombo.
Billacois, François. 1986. *Le Duel dans la société française des XVI–XVII siécles. Essai de psychosociologie historique.* Paris: École des hautes études.
———. 1990. *The Duel: Its Rise and Fall in Early Modern France.* New Haven: Yale University Press.
Bixio, Nino. 1939–1954. *Epistolario.* 4 vols. Ed. Emilia Morelli. Roma: Vittoriano.
Blengini, Cesare Alberto. 1864. *Trattato della moderna scherma italiana.* Bologna: Muse.
———. 1868. *Duello e sue norme prinicpali per effettuarlo.* Padova: Prosperini.
Blom, Ida et al. 2000. *Gendered Nations, Nationalism and Gender Order in the Long Nineteenth Century.* New York: Berg.

Bolis, Givoanni. 1871. *La polizia e le classi pericolose della società*. Bologna: Zanichelli.
Bollati, Giulio. 1983. *L'Italiano: il carattere nazionale come storia e come invenzione*. Torino: Einaudi.
Bonetta, Gaetano. 1990. *Corpo e nazione: l'educazione ginnastica, igienica e sessuale nell'Italia liberale*. Roma: Angeli.
Borgatti, Mariano. 1914. *Saggio di codice cavalleresco militare*. Torino: Schioppo. Originally compiled for his regiment in 1898.
Boschi, Daniele. 1998. Homicide and Knife Fighting in Rome: 1845–1914. In Spierenburg, 1998, 128–58.
Bossi, Giacomo. 1827. *Del duello; conseguente dal volgare sistema d'onor militare*. Torino: Stamperia Reale.
Boswell, James. 1955. *Boswell on the Grand Tour: Italy, Corsica, and France*, ed. Frank Brady and Frederick A. Pottle. New York: McGraw-Hill.
Bottai, Giuseppe. 1982. *Diario (1935–1944)*. Milano: Rizzoli.
Botteri, Inge. 1999. *Galateo e Galatei*. Roma: Bulzoni.
Bottrigari, Enrico. 1961. *Cronaca di Bologna*. 4 vols. Bologna: Zanichelli.
Brachet Contol, G. 1977. La formazione di Francesco Faà di Bruno. In *Francesco Faà di Bruno: Miscellanea*. 5–77. Torino: D'Erasmo.
Branchi, Andrea. 2005. La virtù puntigliosa. I filosofi del duello. *Giornale di storia contemporanea* 8 (2): 28–51.
Brandi, Salvatore. 1898. *La deformità del duello, studio giuridico*. Roma: Civiltà Cattolica.
Brantôme, Pierre Bourdeille de. 1887. *Discours sur les duels*. Paris: Bibliophiles.
Brioist, Pascal, Hervé Drévillon, and Pierre Serna. 2002. *Croiser le fer: violence et culture de_l'épée dans la France moderne, XVIe–XVIIIe siècle*. Paris: Presses universitaires de France.
Broers, Michael. 2001. Noble Romans and Regenerated Citizens: The Morality of Conscription in Napoleonic Italy, 1800–1814. *War in History* 8 (3): 253–56.
Bruchi, Arturo. 1890. Il delitto di duello e il futuro codice penale militare. *Rivista Penale*, 31: 434–47.
———. 1893. *Il duello nel codice penale e nella società*. Roma: Bertero.
Brunetti, Carlo Maria. 1914. *A loro! Note giuridico/cavalleresche sul duello*. Genova: Spiotti.
———. 1916. Le corti d'onore. *Il Filangieri* (Sept.–Oct.): 609–37.
Brusa, Emilio. 1871. Del duello nel progetto di codice penale italiano riveduto e modificato. *Archivio giuridico* (Feb.–March): 398–400.
Busimo, G. 1977. *Vilfredo Pareto e l'industria del ferro nel Valdarno*. Milano: Banca Commerciale.
Brydone, Patrick. 1901. *Viaggio in Sicilia e Malta*. Messina: Oliva.
Bryson, Frederick Robertson. 1938. *The Sixteenth-century Italian Duel: A Study in Renaissance Social History*. Chicago: University of Chicago Press.
Cacchione, Costantino. 1895. *Scherma e codice per duello*. Sarzana: Tellarini.
Cagnano, Antonio. 1837. *Sul duello*. Napoli.
Cannistraro, Philip. 1975. *La fabbrica del consenso: fascismo e mass media*. Bari: Laterza.
———, ed. 1982. *Historical Dictionary of Fascist Italy*. Westport: Greenwood.
Capello, Maggiorino. 1910. *Diffamazione e ingiuria: studio teorico-pratico*. Milano: Bocca.

Capone, Alfredo. 2000. Il corpo maschile. In Bellassai and Malatesta, 195–221. 2000.
Capretz, Giuseppe. 1926. *La vergogna del duello*. Padova: Zannoni.
Cardoza, Anthony. 1989. An Officer and a Gentleman: The Piedmontese Nobility and the Military in Liberal Italy. In Deputazione, vol. 1, 1989, 185–200.
———. 1997. *Aristocrats in Bourgeois Italy*. Cambridge: Cambridge University Press.
Carli, Mario. 1920. *Con D'Annunzio a Fiume*. Milano: Facchi.
Carpi, Leone. 1878. *L'Italia vivente: aristocrazia di nascita e del danaro, borghesia, clero, burocrazia, studi sociali*. Milano: Vallardi.
Carrillo, Ercole. 1837. *Pensieri sul duello*. Napoli: Tasso.
Casati, Gianni. 1914. Il duello nella storia. In *Conferenza sul duello tenuta al R. Liceo Cesare Beccaria il 6 giugno 1914*. Milano: Turati.
Castelli, Michelangelo. 1888. *Ricordi*, ed. Luigi Chiala. Torino-Napoli: Roux.
Castronovo, Valerio. 1973. *La stampa italiana dall'unità al fascismo*. Bari: Laterza.
Cavalleria e tribunale: documenti di un processo. 1889. Bologna: in BNCR, Levi.
Cavina, Marco. 2003. *Il duello giudiziario per punto d'onore*. Torino: Giappichelli.
———. 2005. *Il sangue d'onore: storia del duello*. Bari: Laterza.
Cavour, Camillo. 1982. *Epistolario*, 19 vols., ed. Rosanna Roccia. Firenze: Olschki.
Cervi, Mario. 1992. *Mussolini, album di una vita*. Milano: Rizzoli.
Cesana, Giuseppe. 1874. Il primo *duello* (dalle memorie di un giornalista). *Almanacco di Fanfulla*, 141–60. Roma: Dell'Italie.
Cesarano, Federico. 1874. *Trattato teorico-pratico di scherma della sciabola*. Padova: Penada.
Ceva, Lucio. 1999. *Storia delle forze armate in Italia*. Turin: UTET.
Ciano, Galeazzo. 1946. *The Ciano Diaries: 1939–1943*. Garden City, NY: Doubleday.
Cicirelli, Pasquale. 1873. *Riflessioni sul duello*. Reggio Calabria: Lipari e Basile.
Clark, Anna. 1995. *The Struggle for the Breeches: Gender and the Making of the British Working Class*. Berkeley: University of California Press.
Coelli, Angelo. 1904. *Il duello attraverso i secoli*. Milano: Nazionale.
Cohen, Richard. 2002. *By the Sword*. New York: Random House.
Comisso, Giovanni. 1951. *Le mie stagioni*. Treviso: Treviso.
Connell, R. W. 2002. *Gender*. Cambridge: Polity.
Cook, Bernard. 2002. *Belgium: A History*. New York: Peter Lang.
Corradini, Enrico. 1923. *Discorsi politici*. Firenze: Vallecchi.
Corsi, Adone. 1877. *Considerazioni storiche e giuridiche sul duello*. Florence: Fioretti.
Costi, Michele. 1839. *Progetto di una processura criminale e dei mezzi per estirpare il duello*. Padova: Minerva.
Crispolti, Filippo. 1893. Il duello. In *A Leone XIII nel suo giubileo Episcopale*. Siena: San Bernardino.
———. 1899. *Un duello*. Milano: Fratelli, Treves.
———. 1902. L'Italia e il moto internazionale contro il duello. *Nuova antologia* 186: 141–46.
———. 1905. La lotta contro il duello. In *Il momento*, March 30.
———. 1926. Un nuovo moto contro il duello: ricordi di un cattolico. *Corriere della sera* (Nov. 13): 2.
———. 1939. *Politici, guerrieri, poeti: ricordi personali*. Milano: Treves.
Crispolti, Giovanni B. 2005. Filippo Crispolti e la lega antiduellistica. In Biblioteca Nazionale Centrale di Roma, *A fil di spada*, 57–58.

Crivellari, Giulio. 1884. *Il duello nella dottrina e nella giurisprudenza: studio sui progetti del nuovo codice penale.* Torino: Unione Tipografico.
Criveller, Gianni. 2004. *The Martyrdom of Alberto Crescitelli, Its Context and Controversy.* Hong Kong: Holy Spirit Study Centre.
Croce, Benedetto. 1963. *A History of Italy from 1871 to 1915,* trans. C. M. Ady. New York: Russell.
Daniels, Elizabeth. 1972. *Jessie White Mario: Risorgimento Revolutionary.* Columbus: The Ohio State University Press.
Davis, John. 1988. *Conflict and Control: Law and Order in Nineteenth-Century Italy.* Atlantic Highlands, NJ: Humanities Press International.
De Amicis, Edmondo. 1887. *Military Life in Italy: Sketches.* New York: Putnam.
D'Amico, Franz Andrea. 1894. *Nuovo codice sul duello e procedura cavalleresca.* Catania: Giannotta.
Davis, John. 2006. *Naples and Napoleon: Southern Italy and the European Revolutions, 1780–1860.* Oxford: Oxford University Press.
D'Azeglio, Massimo. 1833. *Ettore Fieramosca o la disfida di Barletta.* Milano: Ferrario.
———. 1987. *Epistolario.* 5 vols. Torino: Piemontesi.
De Bono, Emilio. 1931. *Nell'esercito nostro prima della guerra.* Milano: Mondadori.
De Bourbon, Don Alfonso. 1908. *Résumé de l'histoire de la creation et du dévelopement des ligue contre le duel.* Vienna: Jasper.
De Brosses, Charles. 1991. *Lettres Familières,* ed. Giuseppina Cafasso. Naples: Bérard.
De Dominicis, Emilio. 1864. *Pensieri sul duello.* Turin: Unione Tipogr.-Editrice.
De Grazia, Victoria. 1981. *The Culture of Consent: Mass Organization of Leisure in Fascist Italy.* Cambridge: Cambridge University Press.
———. 1992. *How Fascism Ruled Women: Italy, 1922–1945.* Berkeley: University of California Press.
Della Peruta, Franco. 1991. War and Society in Napoleonic Italy. *Society and Politics in the Age of the Risorgimento,* ed. Davis and Ginsborg. 26–48. Cambridge: Cambridge University Press.
Della Rocca, Enrico. 1898. *The Autobiography of a Veteran: 1807–1893.* New York: Macmillan.
Del Negro, Piero. 1979. *Esercito, stato, società: saggi di storia militare.* Bologna: Cappelli.
De Lorenzo, Giuseppe. 1999. *Memorie,* ed. Paola Russo. Napoli: Vivarium.
Deputazione di Storia Patria per L'Umbria. 1989. *Esercito e città dall'unità agli anni trenta.* 2 vols. Perugia: Deputazione di Storia Patria per L'Umbria.
De Rosis, Luigi. 1865. *Codice Italiano sul duello.* Rpt. 1868 and 1869. Napoli: de Angelis.
De Rossi, Eugenio. 1927. *La vita di un ufficiale italiano sino all guerra.* Milano: Mondadori.
De Sanctis, Francesco. 1872. *La scienza e la vita.* Naples: Morano.
De Simone, Eduardo. 1906. *L'anima della donna nel pregiudizio cavalleresco.* Roma/Torino: Roux and Viarengo.
———. 1921. *La scuola magistrale militare di scherma.* Rome: Italia.
Dickie, John. 1999. *Darkest Italy: The Nation and Stereotypes of the Mezzogiorno, 1860–1900.* New York: St. Martins.
Di Giorgio, Generale Antonino. 1938. *Scritti e discorsi vari (1899–1927).* Milano: Società Dante Alighieri.

Di Menza e Vella, Giuseppe. 1875. *Il duello leale e il duello sleale: Memorie del Socio Consigliere G. Di Menza, letta nella tornata del 4 ottobre 1875*. Palermo, n.e. Copy in BNCR, Levi.
Di Paravicino, Emiliano. 1906. *Dell'educazione dei giovani contro il pregiudizio del duello*. Como: Ferrari.
Di San Malato, Athos. 1913. *La partita d'onore e le sue leggi*. Napoli: Detken and Rocholl.
Di Simplicio, Oscar. 1994. *Peccato, penitenza, perdono, Siena 1575–1800*. Milano: Franco Angeli.
Dizionario storico dell'Italia unita. 1996. Roma: Laterza.
Donati, Claudio. 2001. A project of 'Expurgation' by the Congregation of the Index: Treatises on Duelling. *Church, Censorship and Culture in Early Modern Italy*, ed. Gigliola Fragnito. 134–62. Cambridge: Cambridge University Press.
Dossena, Carlo Luigi. 1861. *Il pregiudizio del duello racconto seguito da riflessi morali e notizie storiche sulla monomachia*. Milano: Sanvito.
Drake, Richard. 1980. *Byzantium for Rome: The Politics of Nostalgia in Umbertian Italy, 1878–1900*. Chapel Hill: University of North Carolina Press.
Enrichetti, Cesare. 1871. *Trattato elementare teorico-pratico di scherma*. Parma: Grazioli.
Erspamer, Francesco. 1982. *La biblioteca di Don Ferrante: duello e onore nella cultura del Cinquecento*. Roma: Bulzoni.
Ettorre, Giuseppe. 1928. *Questioni d'onore*. Milan: Hoepli.
Evangelista, Nick. 1995. *Encyclopedia of the Sword*. Westport: Greenwood.
Faà di Bruno, Francesco. 1854. *Manuale del soldato cristiano*. Torino: Marietti.
Facchinetti, Giuseppe. 1890. *Duello e legge*. Rimini: Malvolti.
Fambri, Paolo. 1869. *Della giurisprudenza e della tecnica del duello*. Florence: Barbèra.
———. 1874. Il duello e la riforma del codice penale. *Nuova Antologia* 26 (8): 893–99.
———. 1884. Discorso Fambri. In *La domenica letteraria*, June.
———. 1888A. Le corti d'onore. *Nuova Antologia* 16 (14): 234–67.
———. 1888B. *Novelle cavalleresche*. Torino: Loescher.
———. 1888C. Fra la legge e l'onore. *Capitan Fracassa* (151): 1.
Fappani, Antonio. 1985. *Un vescovo di fronte al Fascismo: Mons. Giacinto Gaggia*. Brescia: Tedeschi.
Federici, Emilio. 1903. *Guerra al duello*. Venezia: Emiliana.
———. 1909. La storia delle leghe anitduellistiche e il congresso internazionale di Budapest. *Rivista internazionale di scienze sociali e discipline ausiliarie* 49: 31–44.
Ferrara, Patrizia. 1992. *L'Italia in palestra: storia documenti e immagini della ginnastica dal 1833 al 1973*. Rome: La Meridiana.
Ferrari, Costante. 1942. *Memorie postume*, ed. Mario Menghini. Milano: ISPI.
Ferrari, Paolo. 1928. *Il duello*. Milano: Treves. Original version 1868.
Ferretti, Lando. 1928. *Il libro dello sport*. Rome: Tip. Del Littorio.
———. 1930. *Esempi e idee per l'Italiano nuovo*. Rome: Tip. Del Littorio.
Ferriani, Lino. 1897. *Delinquenti scaltri e fortunati: studio di psicologia criminale*. Como: Omarini/Longutti.
Filangieri Fieschi Ravaschieri, Teresa. 1902. *Il generale Carlo Filangieri*. Milano: Treves.
Fiume, Giovanna, ed. 1989. *Onore e storia nelle società mediterranee*. Palermo: La Luna.
Fontana, Severina and Paola Subacchi. 1991. Il mutamento guidato. *Quaderni storici* 26 (77): 508–9.

Forte, Luigi. 1878. *Sul metodo di scherma Radaelli: lettera critica*. Catania: Galatola.
Fougeroux de Campigneulles, M. 1835. *Histoire des duels ancien e modernes*. Paris: Tessier and Cherbuliez.
Fozzi, Daniela and Mario da Passano. 2000. Uno 'scabroso argomento': Il duello nella codificazione penale Italiana. *Acta Histriae* 8: 243–95.
Freeman, Joanne. 1996. Dueling as Politics: Reinterpreting the Burr-Hamilton Duel. *William and Mary Quarterly* 53 (2): 289–318.
———. 2001. *Affairs of Honor: National Politics in the New Republic*. New Haven: Yale University Press.
Frevert, Ute. 1995. *Men of Honour: A Social and Cultural History of the Duel*. Cambridge: Cambridge University Press.
Gabelli, Federico. 1869. *Il duello e la giurisprudenza del duello per l'onorevole Paolo Fambri*. Foggia.
Galante Garone, Alessandro. 1976. *Felice Cavallotti*. Torino: UTET.
Galati, Domenico. 1879. *Gli uomini del mio tempo*. Bologna: Zanardelli.
Gambarella, Tito. 1898. *Padrini e testimoni del duello*. Napoli: Pierro e Veraldi.
Gandolfi, Giovanni. 1876. *Metodo teorioco-pratico per la scherma di sciabola*. Turin: Borgarelli.
Garibaldi, Giuseppe. 1870. *Clelia: il governo del monaco*. Milano: Rechiedei.
Garzes, Francesco. 1892. *Bianca d'Oria*. Genova: Sordo-muti.
Gaugler, William. 1998. *The History of Fencing: Foundations of Modern European Swordplay*. Bangor: Laureate.
Gayol, Sandra. 1999. Duelos, honores, leyes y derechos: Argentina 1887–1923. *Anuario* 14: 313–30.
Gelli, Iacopo. n.d. *Statistiche del duello*. Milan: Lombardi.
———. 1888A. Codice e duello. *Cappa e Spada* 1 (4): 61.
———. 1888B. *Corte d'Onore Permanente in Firenze: note e regolamento*. Firenze: DeAngelis.
———. 1888C. *Responsibilità penale dei duellanti*. Firenze: Loescher and Seeber.
———. 1890. *La scherma italiana nell'esercito*. Florence: Ademollo.
———. 1891. Zanardelli e il duello. *Scherma italiana* 17 (Sept. 9): 131.
———. 1892. *Codice cavalleresco italiano*. Milano: Dumolard.
———. 1894. *Manuale del duellante*. Milano: Dumolard.
———. 1901A. Il duello in Italia nell'ultimo ventennio. *Nuova antologia* 1: 3–12.
———. 1901B. *Scherma italiana*. Milano: Hoepli.
———. 1902. A traverso la scherma, le sfide e i maestri. *Illustrazione italiana* (Dec. 7): 447–53.
———. 1903. La parabola del duello in Italia. *Il giornale d'Italia* (Jan. 4): 2.
———. 1912. *Codice cavalleresco italiano*. Milano: Hoepli.
———. 1920. *Codice cavalleresco italiano*. Milano: Hoepli.
———. 1926. *Codice cavalleresco italiano*. Milano: Hoepli.
———. 1927. Livorno nell'arte della scherma. *La rivista di Livorno* 2 (2): 73–93.
———. 1928. *Duelli celebri*. Milano: Hoepli.
———. 1934. Da Torino a Palermo—cinque morti in duello. *Armi* (Sept.): 17.
———. 1943. *Codice Cavalleresco Italiano con massima di giurisprudenza dell IV Sezione del Consiglio did Stato*, ed. Paolo Lepanto Boldrini. Milano: Hoepli.

———. 1992. *Duelli Mortali del Secolo XIX*. Milano: Suger. Originally published in 1899.
Geltmaker, Ty. 2002. *Tired of Living: Suicide in Italy from National Unification to World War I, 1860–1915*. New York: Peter Lang.
Gentile, Emilio. 1980. Alfredo Rocco. In *Uomini e volti del fascismo*, ed. Ferdinando Cordova. Roma: Bulzoni.
———. 1989. *Storia del partito fascista*. Bari: Laterza.
———. 1996. *The Sacralization of Politics in Fascist Italy*. Cambridge: Harvard University Press.
———. 2002. Fascism in Power: The Totalitarian Experiment. In *Liberal and Fascist Italy*, ed. Adrian Lyttelton. Oxford: Oxford University Press.
Giannini, Alberto. 1934. *Le memorie di un fesso: l'anteguerra, la guerra, l'esilio*. Paris: self-published.
Gibson, Mary. 2002. *Born to Crime*. Westport: Praeger.
Gigli, Lorenzo. 1962. *Edmondo De Amicis*. Torino: UTET.
Gilbert, Martin. 1994. *The First World War*. London: Weidenfield and Nicolson.
Ginsburg, Paul. 2003. *Italy and Its Discontents 1980–2001*. London: Penguin.
Gorn, Elliott J. 1985. "Gouge and Bite, Pull Hair and Scratch": The Social Significance of Fighting in the Southern Backcountry. *American Historical Review* 90 (1): 18–43.
Grew, Raymond. 1968. *A Sterner Plan for Italian Unity*. Princeton: Princeton University Press.
Hanlon, Gregory. 1998. *The Twilight of a Military Tradition: Italian Aristocrats and European Conflicts, 1560–1800*. New York: Holmes and Meier.
———. 2000. *Early Modern Italy, 1550–1800: Three Seasons in European History*. London: Macmillan.
Hobsbawm, Eric and Terence Ranger, eds. 1983. *The Invention of Tradition*. Cambridge: Cambridge University Press.
Hughes, Charles. 1967. *Shakespeare's Europe: A Survey of the Condition of Europe at the End of the 16th Century: Being Unpublished Chapters of Fynes Moryson's Itinerary (1617)*. New York: Blom.
Hughes, Steven C. 1994. *Crime, Disorder, and the Risorgimento: The Politics of Policing in Bologna*. Cambridge: Cambridge University Press.
———. 1998. Men of Steel: Dueling, Honor, and Politics in Liberal Italy. In Spierenberg, 1998, 64–81.
———. 2001. Deadly Play: Napoleon, Dueling and the Rearmament of Honor in Italy. *Rivista Napoleonica* (2): 27–58.
———. 2005A. Una storia tra due codici. In Biblioteca Nazionale Centrale di Roma, *A fil di spada*, 51–56.
———. 2005B. Società e duello nella mente di un collezionista. In Biblioteca Nazionale Centrale di Roma, *A fil di spada*, 19–33.
———. 2007A. "Soldiers and Gentlemen: The Rise of the Duel in Renaissance Italy." *Journal of Medieval Military History* 5: 99–152.
———. 2007B. Swords and Daggers: Class Conceptions of Interpersonal Violence in Liberal Italy. In *Cultures of Violence*, ed. Stuart Caroll. London: Palgrave/Macmillan, 212–35.
Hurd, Madeleine. 2000. Class, Masculinity, Manners, and Mores. *Social Science History* 24 (1): 75–100.

Indelli, Luigi. 1888. Il duello nel codice. *Il popolo romano* (Nov. 4): 304.
Iviglia, E. F. 1907. *Il vero gentiluomo moderno.* Torino: Cassone.
Jannone, Giovanni. 1912. *Il duello Pepe-Lamartine su documenti inediti.* Terni: Visconti.
Johnson, Lyman L. and Sonya Lipsett-Rivera, eds. 1998. *Sex, Shame, and Violence: The Faces of Honor in Colonial Latin America.* Albuquerque: University of New Mexico Press.
Kelly, James. 1995. *That Damn'ed Thing Called Honour: Dueling in Ireland 1570–1860.* Cork: Cork University Press.
Kiernan, V. G. 1989. *The Duel in European History: Honour and the Reign of Aristocracy.* Oxford: Oxford University Press.
Koon, Tracy. 1985. *Believe, Obey, Fight: Political Socialization of Youth in Fascist Italy, 1922–1943.* Chapel Hill: University of North Carolina Press.
La Manna, Biagio. 1901. *Il duello e il codice penale.* Palermo: Vena.
La Marmora, Alfonso. 1881. *Ricordi della Giovinezza,* ed. Luigi Chiala. Roma: Botta.
Lanaro, Silvio. 1988. *L'Italia nuova: identità e sviluppo 1861–1988.* Turin: Einaudi.
Langella, Paolo. 1989. Cultura e vita dell'ufficiale italiano (1878–1911). In Deputazione, 1989, vol. 1, 201–18.
Laven, David. 1992. Liberals or Libertines. Staff, Students, and Government Policy at the University of Padua, 1814–1835. In *History of Universities,* 123–64. Oxford: Oxford University Press.
Leconte, Jacque Robert. 1949. *La Formation historique de l'armeé belge.* Paris: Ed. Universitaires.
Lega, Gioacchino. 1930. *Cinquant'anni di giornalismo.* Roma: Della Stampa.
Lembo, Giuseppe. 1933. *Il duello nella logica e nel diritto.* Bari: Cressati.
Leti, Giuseppe. 1888. *Il duello nella sua evoluzione storica nella filosofia e nella giurisprudenza.* Roma: dell'Opinione.
Levi, Giorgio Enrico and Iacopo Gelli. 1903. *Bibliografia del duello.* Milano: Hoepli.
Lo Cicero, Silvia. 1929. *Athos di San Malato.* Palermo: Sanzo.
Lo Monaco-Aprile, G. 1898. *Vertenze cavaleresche nell'esercito.* Milano: Pirola.
Longo, Antonio. 1891. *La quistione ardente: il duello.* Brescia: Codignola.
Lorenzini, Francesco. 1852. *Il duello in generale. Analisi.* Torino: Economica.
Lovati, Carlo. 1939. *Il duello: conversazioni di un avvocato.* Milano: Corticelli.
Lucianelli, Alma Serena. 1994. Il viaggio in Italia. In *Ranieri Inedito: Le notti di un eremita and Zibaldone scientifico e letterario.* Napoli: Macchiaroli.
Luigia Caglioti, Daniela. 1996. *Associazionismo e sociabilità d'élite a Napoli nel XIX secolo.* Napoli: Liguore.
Lyttelton, Adrian. 1973. *The Seizure of Power, Fascism in Italy: 1919–1929.* London: Weidenfield and Nicolson.
———. 1979. Landlords, Peasants and the Limits of Liberalism. In *Gramsci and Italy's Passive Revolution,* ed. John A. Davis, 104–35. New York: Barnes and Noble.
———. 1991. The Middle Classes in Liberal Italy. In *Society and Politics in the Age of the Risorgimento: Essays in Honour of Denis Mack Smith,* ed. Davis and Ginsborg, 217–50. Cambridge: Cambridge University Press.
Mack Smith, Denis. 1968. *The Making of Italy, 1796–1870.* New York: Harper.
———. 1989. *Italy and Its Monarchy.* New Haven: Yale University Press.
Malatesta, Maria. 1978. *Il resto del Carlino, potere politico ed economico a Bologna dal 1885 al 1922.* Milano: Guanda.
Malvica, Ferdinando. 1826. *Epistola sopra il duello.* Roma: Salviucci.

Mancini, Claudio. 2003. Camillo Rodolofi, maestro di scherma e di equitazione. *Per la Val Sasanta,* 24–28 (Mancini private collection).
Mancini, Luigi. 1986. Sale di scherma e schermitori a Rome fra le due guerre *L'Urbe* (Sept.–Dec.): 208–13.
Mancini, Pasquale Stanislao. 1853. *Imputabilità de' padrini ne'duelli.* Torino: Benedetto.
Manzini, Vincenzo, ed. 1943. *Codici penali militari.* Padova: Cedam.
Marchionni, A. and C. Enrichetti. 1863. *Norme sui duelli e attribuzioni dei padrini.* Firenze: Fioretti.
Marcucci, Vincenzo. 1836. *Della legittimità positiva e negativa delle pene, con un trattato del duello e dei mezzi di estirparlo.* Lugano: Ruggia.
Mariotii, Temistocle. 1897. *Comemorazione di Paulo Fambri.* Roma: Voghera.
Marselli, Niccola. 1984. *La vita del reggimento: osservazioni e ricordi.* Roma: Stato Maggiore.
Martire, Egilberto. 1943. *Amicus Filippo Crispolti: Note biografiche.* Milano: Pro-Familia.
Martucci, Roberto. 1999. *L'invenzione dell'Italia unita.* Milano: Sansoni.
Marzano, Filippo. 1907. *Del duello nella storia e nella legislazione.* Bari: Palasciano.
Matos E Lemos, Mário. 1993. O Duelo em Portugal depois da Implantação da República. *Rituais e Cerimónias, Revista de História das Ideias* 15: 561–97.
Matteini, Claudio. 1945. *Ordini alla stampa.* Roma: Polilibraria.
Matteoti, Matteo. 1987. *Il duello Treves-Mussolini.* Milano: Sugar.
Maurano, Silvio. 1973. *Ricordi di un giornalista fascista.* Milano: Ceschina.
Mazza, Giacomo. 1904. *Che cosa è oggi dì un duello?* Novara: Miglio.
Mazzonis, Filippo. 1989. Usi della buona società e questioni d'onore. In Deputazione, 1989, vol. 1: 229–53.
McAleer, Kevin. 1994. *Dueling: The Cult of Honor in Fin-de-Siècle Germany.* Princeton: Princeton University Press.
Melina, A. 1888. *La nuova scherma mista e la vera italiana.* Napoli: Bellisario.
Melzi, Gaetano. 1838. *Bibliografia dei romanzi e poemi cavallereschi italiani.* Milano: Tosi.
Menet-Genty, Janine. 1989. L'immagine dell'ufficiale nel teatro borghese. In Deputazione, 1989, vol. 1: 255–72.
Meriggi, Marco. 1989. L'ufficiale a Milano in età liberale. In Deputazione, 1989, vol. 1: 273–96.
———. 1992. *Milano borghese: circoli ed elites nell'Ottocento.* Venezia: Marsilio.
———. 1993. The Italian Borghesia. In *Bourgeois Society in Nineteenth-Century Europe,* ed. Mitchell and Kocka. Oxford: Berg.
———. 1996. Borghesie. In *Dizionario storico dell'Italia unita.* Roma: Laterza.
Messori, Vittorio. 1998. *Il beato Faà di Bruno. Un cristiano in un mondo ostile.* Milano: Rizzoli.
Minieri, Vincenzo. 1869. *Il duello. Pensieri. . . .* Napoli: dell'Industria.
Ministero della Giustizia. 1928. *Lavori preparatori del codice penale,* Vol. 3, *Osservazioni e proposte,* part 3, Articoli 246–518. Roma: Mantellate.
———. 1929. *Progetto definitivo del codice penale,* Vol. 5, "Relazione," part 1, Roma: Mantellate.
Ministero della Guerra, 1899. *Regolamento di disciplina militare.* Rome: Voghera.
Minuzzi, Giovanni. 1998. *Memorie storiche nella scherma.* Private edition from collection of Claudio Mancini.

Missori, Mario. 1986. *Gerarchie e statuti del P.N.F.* Roma: Bonacci.
Modugno, Nicola. 1880. *Il duello.* Giovinazzo: Ospizio. Revised edition 1898.
Moe, Nelson. 2002. *The View from Vesuvius: Italian Culture and the Southern Question.* Berkeley: University of California Press.
Molinini, Niccolò. 1934. *Il suicidio e il duello nella concezione fascista.* Bari: La Disfida.
Montanelli, Indro. 1973. *L'Italia dei notabili: 1861–1900.* Milano: Rizzoli.
Morelli, Ercole. 1904. *Lame incrociate.* Bari: Losasso.
———. 1907. *La scherma nell'esercito.* Rome: Voghera.
Morton, E. D. 1988(?). *A–Z of Fencing.* London: Macdonald, Queen Anne.
Mosse, George. 1985. *Nationalism and Sexuality: Respectability and Abnormal Sexuality in Modern Europe.* New York: Fertig.
———. 1996. *The Image of Man: The Creation of Modern Masculinity.* Oxford: Oxford University Press.
Muir, Edward. 1993. *Mad Blood Stirring: Vendetta and Factions in Friuli during the Renaissance.* Baltimore: Johns Hopkins University Press.
Murialdi, Paolo. 1996. *Storia del giornalismo italiano.* Bologna: Il Mulino.
Mussolini, Benito. 1964. *Opera Omnia.* 36 vols. Ed. Edoardo and Duilio Susmel. Firenze: La Fenice.
Mussolini, Rachele. 1958. *Benito il mio uomo.* Milano: Rizzoli.
———. 1974. *Mussolini: An Intimate Biography by His Widow.* New York: Morrow.
Nadi, Aldo. 1955. *The Living Sword: A Fencer's Autobiography.* Sunrise, FL: Laureate Press.
Nasalli Rocca, Amedeo. 1946. *Memorie di un prefetto.* Roma: Mediterranea.
Nash, Thomas. 1592. *Pierce Penilesse, His Supplication to the Devil.* London: Jones.
Nicoletti, Jacopo. 1864. *Del duello civile e militare ed argomenti atti a distruggerlo.* Firenze: Nazionale.
Nicolini, Fausto. 1962. *Benedetto Croce.* Torino: UTEP.
Nievo, Ippolito. 1973. *Le confessioni di un Italiano.* Milano: Garzanti.
Nye, Robert A. 1993. *Masculinity and Male Codes of Honor in Modern France.* Oxford: Oxford University Press.
———. 1995. The Modern Duel and Masculinity in Comparative Perspective. *Masculinities* 3: 3.
———. 1998. The End of the Modern French Duel. In Spierenburg, 1998, 82–95.
———. 2000. The Transmission of Masculinities. Paper presented at the European Social Science History Conference in Amsterdam, April 12.
Oriani, Alfredo. 1943. *Fino a Dogali.* Bologna: Cappelli. Originally published in 1889.
Palanca, Lino. 2001. Attilio Valentini, giornalista. *Potentia: Archivi di Porto Recanati e dintorni* 2 (5).
Papini, Giovanni. 1994. *Passato Remoto 1885–1914.* Florence: Ponte alle Grazie.
Parise, Masaniello. 1884. *Trattato teorico-pratico della scherma di spada e sciabola preceduto da un cenno storico sulla scherma e sul duello.* Roma: Nazionale.
———. 1897. *Manuale cavalleresco.* Rome: Voghera.
Parker, David S. 2001. Law, Honor, and Impunity in Spanish America: The Debate over Dueling, 1870–1920. *Law and History Review* 19 (2).
Parlavecchio, Gaetano. 1907. La lotta dei medici contro il duello. *Gazzetta siciliana di medicina e chirurgia* 6: 1–13.

Parodi, Giuseppe. 1892. *Il duello, conferenza*. Avellino: Pergola.
Partito Socialista Italiano. 1897. *Congresso socialista: rapporti della direzione del partito, etc.* Milano: "Lotta di classe."
Pascale, Emilio. 1848. *Sulla dottrina del duello*. Napoli: Gazzetta dei Tribunali.
Pateale, Emanuele. 1837. *Il duello*. Capolago: Elvetica.
Patriarca, Silvana. 2005. Indolence and Regeneration: Tropes and Tensions of Risorgimento Patriotism. *The American Historical Review* 110 (2): 380–408.
Patroni, Giuseppe (Mons.). 1881. *Il duello. Ragionamento letto nella Romana Accademia degli Arcadi*. Siena: S. Bernardino.
Pedone, Franco, ed. 1959. *Il Partito Socialista Italiano nei suo congressi*. 5 vols. Milano: Avanti.
Pellegrini, Clemente. 1868. *Considerazioni sulla razionalità e punibilità del duello*. Venezia: Visentini.
Peltonen, Markku. 2003. *The Duel in Early Modern England: Civility, Politeness and Honour*. Cambridge: Cambridge University Press.
Pepe, Gabriele. 1980. *Epistolario*, vol. 1. Ed. De Lisio. Naples: Napoletana.
Pepe, Gugliemo. 1847. *Memorie del Generale Gugliemo Pepe intorno alla sua vita e ai recenti casi d'Italia*. Paris: Vaudry.
Pesaro-Maurogonato, Isacco. 1839. *Intorno al duello: Dissertazione*. Venezia: Alvisopoli.
Pesci, Ugo. 1907. *I primi anni di Roma Capitale*. Firenze: Bemporad.
Petrosino, Dario. 2000. Crisi della virilità e 'questione omosessuale.' In Bellassai and Malatesta, 317–43, 2000.
Piaggia di S. Marina, Francesco Antonio. 1908. *La scherma di ieri e la scherma di oggi*. Palermo: del Povero.
Piccato, Pablo. 1999. Politics and the Technology of Honor: Dueling in Turn of the Century Mexico. *Journal of Social History* 32 (2): 331–54.
Pignatelli, Francesco. 1927. *Memorie de un generale della Repubblica e dell'Impero*, ed. Nino Cortese. Bari: Laterza.
Praga, Marco. 1926. *La crisi*. Milano: Treves. First performed in 1904.
Premoli, Orazio. 1910. Il duello nella pubblica opinione. *Rivista internazionale* (April 19): 4.
Premuti, Costanzo. 1924. *Felice Cavallotti: Cenni Biografici, Il duello Cavallotti-Macola*. Santa Maria Capua Vetere: S.I.T.A.
Puoti, Luca. 1835. *Ragionamento intorno a'duelli indirizato a sua Maestà il Re delle due Sicilie*. Napoli: Ariosto.
Ranzi, F. 1897. Il duello nel costume e nella legge. *Armi e Progresso, Rivista Militare Sociale* 1 (1): 20.
Reddy, William. 1994. Condottieri of the Pen: Journalists and the Public Sphere in Postrevolutionary France (1815–1850). *American Historical Review* 99 (5): 1546–70.
Regno di Sardegna. 1859. *Codice penale del Regno*. Torino: Stamperia Reale.
Reyfman, Ivan. 1999. *Ritualized Violence Russian Style. The Duel in Russian Culture and Literature*. Stanford: Stanford University Press.
Ristori, Oreste. 1872. *Dei duelli: regole cavalleresche*. Turin: Foa.
Rizzi, Filippo. 1836. *Osservazioni sul duello*. Napoli: Trani.
Rizzo, Domenico. 2004. *Gli spazi della morale*. Roma: Biblink.
Romanelli, Raffaele. 1979. *L'Italia liberale*. Bologna: Il Mulino.

———. 1991. Political Debate, Social History, and the Italian *borghesia:* Changing Perspectives in Historical Research. *Journal of Modern History* 63 (4): 717–39.
———. 1994. Il casino, l'accademia, e il circolo. In *Fra storia e storiagrafia: scritti in onore di Pasquale Villani,* ed. Macry and Massafra. Bologna: Il Mulino.
———. 1998. *Il comando impossibile: stato é società nell'Italia liberale.* Bologna.
Rossi, Cesare. 1958. *Trentartre vicende mussoliniane.* Milano: Ceschina.
Rossi, Gianni et al. 1983. *Atleti in camicia nera.* Roma: Volpe.
Rousseau, Jean Jacques. 1960. *Jullie ou La Nouvelle Héloïse.* Paris: Garnier Frères.
Russo, Renato. 1993. *La disfida di Barletta: L'epoca e i suoi protagonisti.* Barletta: Rota.
Russo-Ajello, Antonio. 1906. *Il duello secondo i principii, la dottrina, la legislazione.* Città del Castello: Lapi.
Salafia-Maggio, Ernesto. 1895. *Codice cavalleresco nazionale: sua procedura.* Palermo: Sandron.
Sangiovanni, Luigi. 1937. *Il duello fra militari, saggio critico giuridico cavalleresco.* Napoli: La Toga.
Santini, Aldo. 1985. *Mascagni viva e abbasso.* Livorno: Belforte.
———. 1989. *Nedo Nadi: personaggi, retroscena, e duelli della grande scherma italiana.* Livorno: Belforte.
Scaglione, Giuseppe. 1869. *Riflessioni e consigli sul duello ed osservazioni sul giurì d'onore.* Bologna: Monti.
Scalfati Fusco, Giovanni. 1930. *Il duello nel progetto definitivo del nuovo codice penale.* Naples: Majolo.
Schneider, Jane, ed. 1998. *Italy's "Southern Question": Orientalism in One Country.* New York: Berg.
Senior, Nassau William. 1871. *Journals Kept in France and Italy 1848–52, with a Sketch of the Revolution of 1848.* London: King.
Serbelloni, Fabrizio. 1756. *Bando generale della Legazione di Bologna e suo contado.* Bologna: Stamperia Camerale.
Seton-Watson, Christopher. 1967. *Italy from Liberalism to Fascism.* London: Metheun.
Settembrini, Luigi. 1934. *Ricordanze della mia vita,* ed. A. Omodeo. Bari: Laterza.
Sharp, Samuel. 1766. *Letters from Italy, describing the customs and manners of that country in the years 1765 and 1766.* London: R. Cave.
Shoemaker, Robert B. 2002. The Taming of the Duel: Masculinity, Honour and Ritual Violence in London, 1660–1800. *The Historical Journal* 45 (3): 542–45.
Simpson, Anthony. 1988. Dandelions and the Field of Honor: Dueling, the Middle Classes, and the Law in Nineteenth-century England. *Criminal Justice History* 9.
Smollett, George Tobias. 1979. *Travels through France and Italy,* ed. Frank Felsenstein. Oxford: Oxford University Press.
Spackman, Barbara. 1996. *Fascist Virilities: Rhetoric, Ideology, and Social Fantasy in Italy.* Minneapolis: University of Minnesota Press.
Spierenburg, Pieter, ed. 1998. *Men and Violence: Gender, Honor, and Rituals in Modern Europe and America.* Columbus: The Ohio State University Press.
Staglieno, Marcello. 1973. *Nino Bixio.* Milano: Rizzoli.
Steward, Dick. 2000. *Duels and the Roots of Violence in Missouri.* Columbia: University of Missouri Press.
Stewart, Frank Henderson. 1994. *Honor.* Chicago: University of Chicago Press.
Tagliabue, Antonio. 1867. *Il duello. Considerazioni filosofiche.* Milano: Lombardi.

Thayer, John. 1964. *Italy and the Great War: Politics and Culture, 1870–1915.* Madison: University of Wisconsin Press.
Toeplitz, Ludovico. 1963. *Il Banchiere.* Milano: Nuova.
Tomei, Clemente. 1898. *Il pregiudizio.* Torino: Aliprandi.
Torelli, Achille. 1954. *I mariti.* Milano: Rizzoli. First performed in 1867.
Tosh, John. 1999. *A Man's Place: Masculinity and the Middle Class Home in Victorian England.* New Haven: Yale University Press.
Ulloa, Pietro Calà. 1876. *Di Carlo Filangieri nella storia de'nostri tempi.* Napoli: Tornese.
Valeri, Nino. 1975. *Dalla "belle époque" al Fascismo.* Bari: Laterza.
Valori, Aldo. 2001. *I miei tempi.* Roma: Graphic.
Vassallo, L. A. (Gandolin). 1918. *Gli uomini che ho conosciuto, seguito dalle memorie d'uno smemorato.* Milano: Treves.
Venturi. 1898. *Sul duello: discorso.* Roma: Della Camera.
Vergani, Paolo. 1776. *Dell'enormeza del duello.* Milano: Galeazzi.
Veronesi, Giovanni. 1862. *Sul duello: requisitoria.* Torino: Derossi and Dusso.
Vertenza fra S. A. R. il Principe Vittorio Emanuele di Savoia-Aosta, Conte di Torino ed il Principe Enrico d'Orléans; Relazione riservatissima. 1969. In *Il duello fra il conte di Turin e il Principe Enrico d'Orleans.* Milano: Mondadori.
Vico, Pietro. 1886. Del duello fra militari di grado eguale o diverso. *Rivista penale* 23: 422–40.
Vigeant, A. 1883. *Un maître d'armes sous la restauration.* Paris: Motteroz.
Visconti Venosta, Giovanni. 1906. *Ricordi di gioventù: Cose vedute o sapute, 1847–1860.* Milano: Cogliati.
Viti, Giovan Battista. 1884. *Codice del duello commentato.* Genova: Ciminago.
Weinstein, Donald. 1994. Fighting or Flyting? Verbal Dueling in Mid-sixteenth-century Italy. In *Crime, Society, and the Law in Renaissance Italy.* 204–20. Cambridge: Cambridge University Press.
White Mario, Jessie. 1894. *In memoria di Giovanni Nicotera.* Florence: Barbèra.
Whittam, John. 1977. *The Politics of the Italian Army.* London: Croom Helm.
Wyatt Brown, Bertram. 1982. *Southern Honor: Ethics and Behavior in the Old South.* Oxford: Oxford University Press.
Zanardelli, Giuseppe. 1888. *Progetto del codice penale per il Regno d'Italia.* Roma: Stamperia Reale.
———. 1889. *Relazione . . . per l'approvazione del testo definitivo del codice penale.* Rome: Stamperia Reale.
Zanzanaini, Giuseppe. 2004. *Renato Ricci: fascista integrale.* Milano: Mursia.
Zibordi, Giovanni. 1910. *I socialisti ed il duello.* Roma.
Zucchi, Carlo. 1861. *Memorie del Generale Carlo Zucchi,* ed. Nicomede Bianchi. Milano/Torino: Guigoni.

Index

Abba, Giuseppe, 60–61
Abignente, Filippo, 118, 219
abolitionists. *See* antidueling
abolitionists who dueled, 219–20
Accademia della Crusca, 228
Adamoli-Castiglione (Countess), 72
administrative revolution, 323
Adua, 88, 99, 106, 107, 109, 319
affairs of the heart, 150–51, 223–25, 240–41, 255
Agnetta, Carmello, 57–58, 194
Airaudi, Gioacchino, 45–47
Albanese, Fedele, 123
Aldrovandi, Luigi, 1–2
Alessandri, Carlo, 75
Alfieri, Vittorio, 25, 34
Ambrosini, Luigi, 269
Amicucci, Ermanno, 302
Anderson, Benedict, 9, 325
Angelini, Achille, 9, 10, 71–72, 78, 91, 141, 147, 199, 257, 322, 324; dueling code author, 179, 187–89; and National Congress of Chivalry, 195–96
Angioletti (Senator), 99
antidueling, 4–5, 6, 24–25, 66–67, 108; 213–22; and gender, 318; as patriotic, 231–32; treatises, 229–37; tensions among abolitionists, 244, 247, 250. *See also* socialists
Anti-dueling League, 83, 193, 205, 219, 229, 230, 244–51, 265; International, 247, 251
arditi, 276, 278, 279, 282, 283, 302, 310
Argentina, 332
aristocracy, 15, 101, 138–39, 217, 227–28; and Anti-dueling League, 248; chivalric images in dueling manuals, 141–43, 322; new aggressive (fascist), 269, 284; new "spiritual," 139–41; of the trenches, 306, 317
Arnoaldi, Cesare, 1–2
Arpinati, Leandro, 278, 279
Aspromonte, 59, 62, 64
Asproni, Giorgio, 51
associational life. *See* clubs
Attendoli, Dario, 189
Austria, 232
Avanguardisti, 269, 272, 283
Avigdor, Enrico, 43–44

Bakounine, Alessandrina, 151
Balbo, Italo, 278

349

Banti, Alberto Maria, 7, 32–34, 116, 325
Banti, Athos Gaston, 116, 278
Baratieri (General), 106
Barbasetti, Luigi, 90, 182
Barbiera, Raffaele, 38
Baretti, Giuseppe, 17, 18–19, 102
Barletta, 26
Baroncini, Gino, 288
Baronti, Giancarlo, 310
Baseggio, Cristoforo, 276
Bazzoni, Giovan Battista, 25
Beccaria, Cesare, 300
Becchi, Stanislao, 74
Belcredi, Giacomo, 118
Belgium: liberalism and dueling, 329
Bellini, Luigi, 280
Bellini, Vincenzo, 41
Bencivenga, Roberto, 294
Benedetti (Deputy), 284–85
Berenini, Giuseppe, 238
Bertani, Agostino, 62
Bertolé-Viale (Minister of War), 91
Besso, Marco, 68–69
Bianco, N. A., 31–32
Billacois, François, 4, 17, 19
Binda, Ambrogio, 275
Bismarck, Otto van, 55, 98
Bissolati, Leonida, 240, 241
Bixio, Nino, 60, 194; duel with Agnetta, 57–58; and National Congress of Honor, 195–96
Bizzoni, Achille, 98, 118, 134, 172
Blengini, Cesare Alberto, 87–88, 164, 183, 184
Blondel, Luisa, 29
blood: baptism of, 32, 33, 36, 82, 144; patriotic images of, 33, 41, 105, 109
Bodio, Luigi, 112, 113
Bolis, Giovanni, 152
Bollati, Giulio, 86
Bologna, 1–3, 15
Bonajuto, Giuseppe, 148–49
Bonaparte. See Napoleon
Bonghi, Ruggero, 121
Bordoni, Ernesto, 67

Borgatti, Mariano, 182
Boschi, Daniele, 10n12
Bossi, Giacomo, 24
Boswell, James, 18
Bottai, Giuseppe, 279, 301, 303
Botteri, Inge, 152
Bottoni, Luigi, 45–47
Bottrigari, Enrico, 66, 119
bourgeoisie, 7, 101. See also *ceto civile*
Brandi, Salvatore, 234
Brantôme, Pierre Bourdeille de, 13
brigands, 325
Broglio, Emilio, 104
Bruchi, Arturo, 85
Brunetti, Carlo Maria, 182, 265, 269–72
Bryson, Frederick Robertson, 262
bureaucratization of honor (under fascists), 297–300, 307
Burr, Aaron, 175

Cacchione, Costantino, 141, 215
Cagnano, Antonio, 24
Cairoli, Benedetto, 124
Cairoli, Giovanni, 98
Calamandrei, Piero, 296
Calderini (General), 50
Calza Bini, Gino, 277
Cammarano, Salvatore, 34
Camperio, Manfredo, 38–39
Cangini, Giuseppe, 277
Caporetto, 283
Capretz, Giuseppe, 272, 273
Carafa d'Andria, Riccardo, 141
Carcano, Alfonso, 40
Cardoza, Anthony, 7
Carducci, Giosue, 97, 98, 103, 122, 269
Carli, Mario, 281, 282, 283, 289
Carpi, Leone, 101–3, 109, 138
Carrara, Francesco, 154
Carrascosa, Michele, 30
Casana, Severino, 206
Casati, Gianni, 108
Castelli, Michelangelo, 43
Catholic Action, 295

Catholic Church, 16, 217
Catholic patriotism, 245, 250
Catholics, 6, 127, 132, 133, 134, 138, 170, 182, 215, 217–19, 229, 233–34, 244, 318, 328
Cavallotti, Felice, 105, 118, 126, 127, 134, 205, 229, 321; biography, 171–76; impact of death, 238, 244, 250
Cavour, Camillo Benso, 40, 55, 64, 66, 127; duel with Avigdor, 43–44
ceto civile, 9, 134–39, 147–48, 156, 159, 176, 178
Chatauvillard (Comte de), 189, 327
Chiesa, Eugenio, 126–27, 241
chivalric community, 8–9, 10, 177, 178, 180 192, 193, 200, 208–11, 315
chivalric titles, 86
chivalry, 8, 9, 15; and fascism, 283–86; imagery in dueling manuals, 141–43; national congress (1868), 188, 195–96; national congress (1889), 94, 204; and nationalism, 32–33, 256; science of, 13, 19, 315
Cialdini, Enrico, 66
Ciani (Baron), 38
Ciano, Costanzo, 285
Ciano, Galeazzo, 277, 278, 301, 303
Ciccotti, Francesco, 243, 276
Cicirelli, Pasquale, 183
cicisbeismo, 18, 35, 36, 102
Cingia, Pietro, 73
civil class. See *ceto civile*
class. See honor, class notions
clubs, 137, 198; fencing, 92–93; men's 145–47
code *duello,* 22, 54, 63, 126, 136, 139, 328; importance of knowing and obeying rules, 129, 130, 144–45, 148–49; importance for united Italy 324; rules designed to reduce risk, 163, 180–81. See also dueling: codes (manuals); national dueling code
codice cavalleresco. See code *duello*
Comisso, Giovanni, 301, 310

Compagna (Baron), 150
Compignano, Lataneo di, 1–2
Congress of Vienna, 2
Connell, R. W., 318
Consalvi, Ercole, 2, 3
Coppola, Giovanni, 261
Corradini, Enrico, 106, 269
Corsica, 255
Corvetto (General), 321
Costi, Michele, 215
Council of Trent, 16, 18, 234
Count of Turin, 88, 106–8, 238
Counter-Reformation, 16, 17, 36
countertypes, 151–60. See also women; honor, class notions
courage, 144–45, 292; and Catholicism, 246–47; and liberalism, 333; and socialism, 242–43. See also military
courtesy, 143–46
courts (juries, tribunals) of honor, 8, 57, 78, 94, 171, 181, 191–211, 257; under fascists, 291, 295–296, 307, 323; functions, 193; of National Fencing Academy, 193, 198; Permanent Court in Florence, 190, 192, 193, 200–204, 296; of Press Association, 124–25, 198, 199, 200; in Prussia, 83, 196; state recognition, 195, 198–211, 322. See also military
Crescitelli, Alberico, 220
Crescitelli, Bruno, 220
criminal anthropology. See positivism
criminal code. See penal code
Crispi, Francesco, 105, 123, 133–34, 174
Crispolti, Filippo, 217–19, 244–251, 273, 301, 302, 318
Crivellari, Giulio, 154, 155
Croce, Benedetto, 122, 140–41, 144, 229
Cupolo, Nicola, 278

d'Adda, Luigi, 40
dagger. See knives

d'Amico Franz, Andrea, 183
Dandolo, Emilio, 39
d'Annunzio, Gabrielle, 103, 122, 269, 282–83, 310
Dante (Alighieri), 26
Da Passano, Mario, 161
Darwinism, 99, 105
d'Azeglio, Massimo, 25, 29
de Amicis, Edoardo, 79–81
de Dominicis, Emilio, 53
de Felice, Giufredda, 241
dei Tirreni, Calabritto, 129
de Lamartine, Alphonse, 26–28, 30, 107
della Porta, Luigi, 37
Del Negro, Piero, 80
De Lorenzo, Giuseppe, 23
De Martino (Deputy), 205
demilitarization, 17
Depretis, Agostino, 130, 133
de Rosis, Luigi, 183
de Rossi, Eugenio, 73, 76, 98
de Sanctis, Francesco, 104
Dessa (Colonel), 60
DeWitt, Eugenio, 116–18, 161
de Zerbi, Rocco, 105
di Bourbon, Alfonso, 247, 248, 250
Dickie, John, 325
di Paravicino, Emiliano, 249
di Salasco (Count), 60
di San Malato, Athos, 93, 94, 182, 319
di San Malato, Turillo, 59
di San Martino, Ettore Perrone, 248
disqualification, 58, 139, 140, 197, 210, 214; civil, 257–58; literary description, 216–20
di Vittorio (Deputy), 280
doctors (medical), 164
Dogali, 98, 100, 105, 106, 109, 319
Donizetti, Gaetano, 26
Doria Pamphili (Prince), 248
Dossena, Luigi, 41, 215, 232
drinking: and lower classes, 155–56
duel: interfascist, 283–86; "legal," 180, 198–99, 257; "perfect," 27, 65, 106–9, 164; types (*ad oltranza,* first blood, *ultimo sangue*), 181–82

dueling: abuses of, 177–78, 192, 197, 203; arranged by weapon, 88–89; against Austrians, 28, 37–42; as barbaric, 231; against Frenchmen, 22–28; as civilizing force, 222–23; codes (manuals), 13, 16, 42, 72, 179–92; debate over, 213–60, 322–23; decline after Renaissance, 16–19; early legitimization, 58,63, 65, 67–68; and fascism, 267–313; and fencing, 86–96; frequency, 4–5, 28–29, 53–54, 67–69, 113–15, 221, 260, 300–302; historiography, 4, 5; interfascist, 283–86; lack of continuity in Italy, 8–9, 316; and the law, 31, 44, 54, 66, 99, 193–203, 251–60; 321; and legitimacy, 15, 277, 281, 309, 315, 321, 323, 328, 332; and liberalism, 64, 111, 115, 329–34; and military, 69–86; and nationalism, 21–42; pan-Italian nature, 170–71, 177; participants, 69–70,117, 135; penal sanctions against, 2, 8, 25 48, 160–63, 251, 257–59, 294; plague image, 4, 24, 54, 69; proponents of, 213–14, 216; provincial differences, 164–71; reasons for decline, 260–65; recrudescence after WWI, 267–68; terminology, 11–12; and unification, 53–69; and warrior spirit, 83–84, 256; and women's fidelity, 150–51, 223–25, 255. *See also* national dueling code; courts of honor; social prejudice
duellomania, 4, 29, 237, 272
Dumas, Alexander, 63
Dumini, Amerigo, 281

editore gerente, 120
educazione (as manners), 145
elites, 111–76
emasculation (effeminacy), 35, 100–101, 251, 265, 270–71, 283, 319
emigration, 103

England: and early abolition, 221, 222; and liberalism, 328
Enlightenment, 17
Enrichetti, Cesare, 95, 96, 316
Erspamer, Francesco, 17
etiquette books, 92, 152
Eula (Senator), 253
Eusebio (Captain), 60

Faà di Bruno, Francesco, 48
Fambri, Paolo, 9, 29, 54, 88, 91, 97, 100, 101, 116, 125, 139, 219, 255, 270, 316; biography, 49–52; and courts of honor, 195–98; defense of duel, 178, 222–23, 224, 225, 325; and dueling manuals, 188–89, 322; and social prejudice, 216
Fanti, Manfredo, 71
Farinacci, Roberto, 282, 295
Fasci Siciliani, 239
fascism, 265; and conformity, 302–4; contradictory view of dueling, 291; and eventual decline of dueling, 300–302; and honor, 282–90, 328, 322; and increase in dueling, 272–82; and journalism, 267, 268, 294–95; and militarization of society, 306–8; new fascist man, 290, 304–7, 319–20; pressure against dueling, 297
Fascist Fencing Academy, 291
Fascist Grand Council, 287, 303
Fazari (Captain), 60
Federici, Emilio, 233
Felicioni, Felice, 286
fencing, 13, 15, 35, 55, 86–96, 319; and dueling codes, 93–94, 189; and fascism, 290–91; and military, 76, 89–92, 199
Ferrari, Costante, 23
Ferrari, Paolo, 83, 120, 225–26
Ferrero (General), 76
Ferretti, Lando, 289, 306
Ferri, Enrico, 234, 235, 238, 239
Ferriani, Lino, 82, 113, 115, 120
Filangieri, Carlo, 23, 30

Finzi, Aldo, 278
Fiume: as chivalric deed, 282–83, 310, 312
Fongi, Enrico, 148–49
Foresti, Leonzio, 279
Foro Italico (sports arena), 290, 308
Foscolo, Ugo, 25
Fourgeroux, de Campigneulles, 330
Fozzi, Daniela, 161
Francavilla, Federico, 1–2
France: attitudes toward Italians, 18, 22, 26–28; compared with Italy and Germany, 326–28; impact on dueling, 22–24, 44, 316; law code, 253
Franchetti, Leopoldo, 5
Freeman, Joanne, 128, 131
Frevert, Ute, 4, 216, 230
Futurists, 269

Gabelli, Federico, 219
Galante Garrone, Alessandro, 133, 172
Gallant, Thomas, 10
Gallotti (Senator), 255, 258
Gandolfi, Giovanni, 94
Garagozzo, Carmello, 278
Garibaldi, Giuseppe, 34, 55, 56, 60, 62, 66, 68, 97, 98, 103, 127, 171, 172, 319; attitude toward duel, 58–59; *vertenza*, 61
Garibaldini (Redshirts), 55, 56, 59–61, 63, 68, 172
Garzes, Francesco, 156–59, 229
Gayol, Sandra, 331
Gelli, Iacopo, 5, 9, 10, 69, 70, 81, 82, 94, 206, 216, 257, 270, 271, 301, 320, 322, 324, 325; and courts of honor, 190, 191–92, 200–204, 296; dueling code author, 178, 186–92; and fencing, 189; and statistics 112–17, 134–35, 138, 151, 162, 163, 164, 260–65
Geltmaker, Tye, 234, 332
gender, 35–37, 100–105, 145–47, 156–60, 318–20
Gentile, Emilio, 305

gentleman (gentlemen), 9, 51, 139–49, 177, 190–91, 193, 208, 210, 320, 324, 328; as "superman" beyond normal morality, 271–71
geography and honor, 164–71
German dueling, 216, 230; compared to Italy and France, 326–28
Giacomini, Eugenio, 201
Giannini, Alberto, 277, 279, 281
Gioberti, Vincenzo, 35, 232
Giulay (General), 39, 41
Giunta, Francesco, 278, 280
Giurati, Giovanni, 278
Gobetti, Piero, 273
Goering, Hermann, 291
Gorn, Elliott, 10
Gramsci, Antonio, 125
Grandi, Dino, 277
Gray, Ezio Maria, 278
Greco, Agesilao, 93
Grossi, Tommaso, 25
Gruppi Universitari Fascisti, 305
guantone (dueling glove), 174, 175
Guardie di Finanza, 298
Guerrazzi, Francesco Domenico, 29, 62
Guglielmi (Garibaldino), 68–69

Habermas, Jürgen, 159
Hamilton, Alexander, 175
Hanlon, Gregory, 17
Hoepli manuals, 191
honesty, 139–40
honor, 14–15; class notions, 7, 9, 52, 112, 151–56, 259–60, 324–25; heightened sense of, 147; institutions of, 117–211; and the law, 223–25; and nationalism, 33, 41, 47, 53–109; and politics, 126–34; regional differences, 164–71; and social mobility, 288; and virility, 96–109; of women, 150–51. *See also* courts (juries, tribunals) of honor; chivalric congress
Hurd, Madeleine, 159

immunity (leniency) for duellists, 44, 66–69, 131, 160–63, 259, 321; political dangers of, 322. *See also* seconds
impunity, physical, 163–64
Indelli, Luigi, 256
individualism: fascist opposition to, 293, 304–9, 319
Ireland: liberalism and dueling, 329–30
Italian Fencing Association, 94
Italy: disappointments, 98–99; dueling compared to France and Germany, 326–28; fencing successes, 95–96; legal vs. real, 237, 260, 269, 309, 323–24. *See also* stereotypes

Jews and dueling, 43–44, 160n136, 191
Johnson, Lyman, 10
journalism, 115–26, 320; fascist, 289–90, 302–3; truth claims, 119
juries of honor (contingency), 194–95

Keller, Guido, 310
Kelly, James, 329
knife-fighting, 10, 153–54. *See also* knives
knighthood, 76. *See also* chivalry
knives, 18, 19, 27, 42; as countertype to swords, 153–55, 223, 238, 255–56, 260, 309–13, 324–25
Kulisciof, Anna, 240

La Fayette (Marquis de), 31
La Marmora, Alfonso, 85
Lantini, Ferruccio, 287
Lasalle, Ferdinand, 239
La Scala (opera house), 41
Latin America: liberalism and dueling, 332
law code. *See* penal code
Leo XIII (Pope), 245–46
Leopardi, Giacomo, 25

Leti, Giuseppe, 215
libel laws, 119, 121, 255, 262
liberalism, 7, 61, 111, 115, 120, 122, 159–60, 265; Catholic criticism of, 220, 233–35, 245–46; destruction under fascists, 268, 293; and dueling elsewhere, 328–33; in Piedmont, 42–44, 64
literature: antidueling fiction, 215, 217–19; produeling fiction, 25–26, 225–29
Livorno, 168–69
Lombard Press Association, 245
Lombardy, patriotic duels, 37–42
Lombroso, Cesare, 152
Lorenzini, Francesco, 219
Louis XIV, 201
Lovati, Carlo, 301
lower classes. *See* honor, class notions; knives
Lovito, Francesco, 130–31
Luiggi (Deputy), 285
Luzzati, Luigi, 132
Lyttelton, Adrian, 282

Machiavelli, Niccolò, 18, 34
Macola, Ferruccio, 118, 173–75, 219, 240
Maffei (Countess), 38
Maffei, Scipione, 17
Magrini, Giuseppe, 90
Malvica, Ferdinando, 24
Mancini, Claudio, 141n79, 296n93
Mancini, Eugenio, 161
Mancini, P. S., 46–47, 161
Manzoli, Giulio, 265
Manzoni, Alessandro, 34, 228
Marchionni, A., 96
March on Rome, 276
Marcucci, Luca, 24
Maria II (Queen), 331
Mario, Alberto, 63
Marselli, Niccola, 77, 78
Martire, Egilberto, 303
masculinity, 6, 10, 64, 100–101, 227, 328; and clubs, 145–46; and fas-

cism, 288, 304–7; and fencing, 95; "hegemonic," 318; hypermasculinity, 270; and liberalism, 159–60, 333; and nationalism, 35–37, 317–20; and socialism, 243. *See also* virility
Matos E Lemos, Mário, 331
Matteotti, Giacomo, 285–86
Maurano, Silvio, 267, 288–90, 301, 302
Maximillian (Archduke), 39
Mayer, Enrico, 29
Mazzacorati, Giovanni Giuseppe, 68
Mazzini, Giuseppe, 34, 56, 63, 97, 103, 127, 232, 293
McAleer, Kevin, 4
medical doctors (and duel), 235–37
Menabrea, Federico Luigi, 85
Menelik (Emperor), 106
Menet-Genty, Janine, 150
Mentana, 98
Meriggi, Marco, 7, 136, 146
Merlino, Libero, 274
Mexico: liberalism and dueling, 332
Mezzogiorno, 165–67, 324–25
middle classes: ambiguity of, 137. *See also* ceto civile
Milan, 28, 37–42
military: character and efficiency, 78–81, 256; and chivalry, 76; concept of courage, 77–79; courts of honor, 84, 193, 206–7, 250, 262–63, 297–300, 308; creation of a national army, 56–61; criticism of, 237; decline in duels, 262; and dueling manuals, 187; high frequency of duels, 69; compulsion to duel and influence, 69, 74–75, 80–81, 82–85, 216; different ranks and dueling, 81–82; and fencing, 76, 89–92; general immunity from prosecution, 73, 83–85; hypersensitivity and "automatic" response, 80–81; "legal" compulsion to duel, 48; notions of honor, 75–77; penal code, 73, 299–300; Piedmontese dominance, 70–71, 81–82,

221–22, 327; recrudescence, 273; reticence to report duels, 70; and social prejudice, 215; traditions, 54, 70–72, 282; and virile education, 104–5
militia, fascist, 384, 310
Minghetti, Marco, 34; duel with Rattazzi, 64–67
misogyny, 269, 271, 319
Missiroli, Mario, 240, 276
Misuri, Alfredo, 286
Mocchi, Walter, 241
Mocenni (General), 321
Modigliani, Emanuele, 243
Modugno, Niccolò, 223–25
Moe, Nelson, 324
Molinini, Niccolò, 300–301
monarchy: and Anti-dueling League, 249, 250; and Catholics, 245; as national institution, 86, 138, 327; royal pardons, 74, 86, 188
Moneta, Ernesto Teodoro, 119, 219, 244
Montanari, Alberto, 280–81
Mordini, Antonio, 62
Morelli, Ercolo, 203
Morelli, Giuseppe, 296–97
Mosse, George, 104, 149, 307, 328, 333
Murat, Joachin, 30, 35
Mussolini, Benito, 240, 267, 268, 272, 281, 282, 285–91, 302, 303, 306, 308, 309, 312; honor guard, 310, 311, 313; oceanic dialogues, 284, 305; personal duels, 273–77
Mussolini, Rachele, 274, 277
Muzio, Girolamo, 189

Nadi, Nedo, 290
Naples: city, 40; Kingdom of, 25, 28, 31–32; National Fencing Academy, 94, 193, 198, 295, 298
Napoleon (Bonaparte), 1, 22, 34, 42, 83, 189, 316, 317

Napoleon III, 84
Nastro Azzurro. *See* National Veterans' Association
national dueling code, 178–92
National Fencing Federation, 271
nationalism, 6–7, 21–42, 221, 256, 320, 324–26; and antidueling movement, 231; hypernationalism, 269
National Society, 55, 57
National Veterans' Association, 295, 298
Nenni, Pietro, 243
newspapers. *See* journalism
Nicoletti, Jacopo, 111, 229
Nicotera, Giovanni, 62–63, 120, 129–31, 152
Nietzsche, Friedrich, 270
Nye, Robert, 4, 113, 326, 327

Obermann, Rudolfo, 103, 104
offenses: certain beyond law, 223–25
Olympics: Italian successes, 96, 290
opera (musical), 21, 26, 41
Opera Nazionale Balilla, 304, 305
Opera Nazionale Dopolavoro (OND), 304, 305
Opera Nazionale Maternità e Infanzia, 304
Oriani, Alfredo, 98, 103, 105, 269
orientalism, 324
Orlando, V. E., 207–8
Osti (Professor), 277

Pacciardi, Randolfo, 280
Padova, 169
Padovani (Captain), 278
Palermo, 40, 50, 52
Pallini, Umberto, 280
Pancrazi, Carlo, 117, 120
Panettoni, Carlo, 128–29
Pantaleoni, Maffeo, 151
Pantaleoni (Senator), 255
Papal States, 1–3, 28
Papini, Giovanni, 106, 269

Pareto, Vilfredo, 140, 151
Pariani, Alberto, 298
Parini, Cesare, 116–17, 161
Parise, Masiniello, 91, 94, 141
Parker, David, 332
Parlavecchio, Gaetano, 236
parliament, 43–44, 126–27, 130–31, 322–23; debate over duel, 251–60
Pascale, Emilio, 31–32
Patriarca, Silvana, 35–36
patriotism. *See* nationalism
patronage and clientelism, 132, 133–34
Patroni, Giuseppe, 233
Pavia, 37
Pavoni (Colonel), 278
peasants, 152, 155–56. *See also* honor, class notions
Pellegrini, Clemente, 244
Pellico, Silvio, 25
Pelloux, Luigi, 85, 321
penal code: of 1839 (Albertine), 45, 47, 66, 160; of 1853 (Tuscan), 251, 258; of 1859 (Sardinian/Italian), 48, 66, 160; of 1889 (Zanardelli Code), 99, 114, 162, 199–203, 251–62; of 1930 (Rocco), 291–97, 307. *See also* military, penal code
Pepe, Gabriele, 26–28, 30, 42, 107, 316
Pepe, Gugliemo, 23, 30–31
Peruzzi, Ubaldino, 140
Pesaro-Maurogonato, Isacco, 25, 28, 29, 44
Pettiti, Agostino Luigi, 62
Petruccelli della Gattina, Ferdinando, 63
Petrus (Austrian officer), 37
physical fitness movement, 103–5; under fascism, 306
Piccato, Pablo, 331
Piedmont, 17–19, 22, 28–29, 39, 41, 102, 323, 326–27; law code (1859) 48; political duels in, 42–49
Pierantoni, Augusto, 122

Pighetti, Guido, 286
Pignatelli, Francesco, 30
Pignatelli (Prince), 282
Pinelli (Minister of War), 50
Pini, Eugenio, 93
Pisacane, Carlo, 63
Pius VII (Pope), 2
Pius IX (Pope), 65, 132, 234, 245
Piva, Vittorio, 241
Pizzardi, Francesco, 68
police, attitude toward duel, 67–68
political parties, lack thereof, 125, 132–34. *See also trasformismo*
politics and reputation, 126–34, 174–75. *See also* liberalism
Polverelli, Gaetano, 295
populism (and fascism), 309
Portugal: liberalism and dueling, 331
positivism, 234–35, 236, 253
posting, 129
Pozzi (General), 50
Pracchi, Leonardo, 275
Praga, Marco, 229
Prampolini, Camillo, 238
Prampolini (public prosecutor), 83
Premoli, Orazio, 265
Press Association of Rome, 100, 116, 122–25
Prezzolini, Giuseppe, 122, 321
Prince of Orleans, 88, 106–8, 238
Prinetti, Carlo, 39
Prinetti, Giulio, 5
produeling: defenders, 213–14, 216; treatises, 222–29
Prudente (General), 126–27
Prussia, 83
public versus private power, 197–211, 252–53, 257, 259–60, 294, 305, 309, 321

Questa, Ugo, 288
Quillici, Nello, 288

Radetsky (General), 39

Ranieri, Antonio, 27
Rattazzi, Urbano, 64–67
reconciliation, 30; political after unity, 54–69; with and among fascists, 280, 282
regeneration (national), 40, 47, 316, 320
remilitarization, 35, 71, 316–17
Renaissance, 4, 8, 13–15, 196, 197, 233, 316, 317, 320, 326; fencing masters, 14
Répaci, Leonida, 243
republicans (democrats): penchant to duel, 62–64, 97, 134, 172–73
respectability, 36, 149–50, 223–25; and nationalism, 318
Restoration, 24, 27
Revolution: of 1820 and 1821, 316; of 1831, 316; of 1848 and 1849, 37, 38, 49, 316; of Naples (1848), 31–32; in Venice, 49
Riboli, Antonio, 60–61
Ricasoli (Baron), 206
Ricci, Renato, 278, 286
Righetti, Carlo, 119, 219–20
Risorgimento, 9, 21–52, 64, 88, 97, 127, 149, 232, 234, 251, 254, 256, 269, 317, 321, 326; as a masculine act, 102
rissa: as countertype to dueling, 154–55
Rocca, Gino, 301, 302
Rocca, Massimo, 287
Rocco, Alfredo, 279, 292–98, 307, 309
Rocco, Arturo, 292
Rodolfi (Maestro, also Ridolfi), 290–91
Romanelli, Raffaelli, 7, 135, 146
Romans (did not duel), 231–32, 308, 319
romanticism, 21, 25
Rome, imperial tradition, 306
Rossi, Cesare, 276
Rossini, Gioacchino, 26
Rousseau, Jean Jacques, 18
Russo-Ajello, Antonio, 237

saber. *See* swords
Salafia Maggio, Ernesto, 183, 185–86, 204–5
Salvemini, Gaetano, 276
Sanna (General), 289
Santelli, Italo, 90
Sardinia, 289
Savoy, House of, 17, 59, 85
Sbarbaro, Pietro, 103
Scaglione, Giuseppe, 54, 84
Scarfoglio, Antonio, 286
Scarfoglio, Edoardo, 103
Scarfoglio, Michele, 286
Scarfoglio, Paolo, 286
Schneider, Jane, 324
Schönhals (Baron), 38–39
Sciacca, Salvatore, 160–61
scienza cavalleresca. *See* chivalry, science of
Scorza, Carlo, 278
Scott, Walter, 25
Scuola Magistrale di Scherma (fencing school), 92
seconds (*padrini*): defense of and legal exposure, 45–46
Seldon, John, 14
self-control, 147–49; as different from lower classes, 153–56; and liberalism, 159
Selmi, Pier Alberto, 160–61
Senior, Nassau William, 43
Serbelloni, Fabrizio, 2, 15
Settembrini, Luigi, 40
Sharpe, Samuel, 16, 18
Sicily, 255, 324
Signorelli, Amalia, 322
Simonelli, Ranieri, 128–29
Simonetti, Rinaldo, 66
Sismonde de Sismondi, Jean Charles, 35
slapping, 255
Smollet, George Tobias, 16
socialists, 6, 108, 159, 182, 215, 229, 260, 270, 283, 308, 327, 328; and Anti-dueling League, 250; dilemma of duel, 237–44; affairs of the heart, 240–41; and

socialist masculinity, 242–43, 318
social mobility, 15, 111–76, 288, 320; in military, 81–82
social prejudice, duel as, 214–22, 254, 270
Solari, Emilio, 261
Sommaruga, Angelo, 103, 269
spadaccino (unscrupulous duelist), 178, 192, 281, 325
Spaventa, Silvio, 125
Spierenburg, Pieter, 10
Spina, Giuseppe, 1–3
Spirito, Ottavio Francesco, 200
squadristi (squads, blackshirts), 272, 277, 280, 284, 285, 302
Starace, Achille, 278, 288, 302–3
statistics of dueling, 112–14
stereotypes: of Italians, 22–23, 35–36, 98–99, 102, 251; male beauty, 104
stiletto, 260. See also knives
suffrage (franchise), 131, 135, 136, 137
suicide, 220, 234–35
sui generis (duel as crime), 254–55, 292
swords, 11, 15, 19, 33–35, 41, 310; special role of sabers, 76, 86, 88–90, 92, 95, 107, 163, 260, 326. See also knives

Tanzi, Carlo, 239
Tarde, Gabriel, 113
Tecchio, Sebastiano, 66
Teruzzi, Attilio, 298
Todeschini, Mario, 238
Tomei, Clemente, 229
Tommaseo, Niccolò, 49
Torelli, Achille, 226–29
trasformismo, 7, 133, 321, 322
treatises: antidueling, 24–25; produeling, 31–32
Treaty of Berlin, 98
Treves, Claudio, 239, 243; duel with Mussolini, 274–76
trials: percentage of duels prosecuted, 161–62, 262

Troya, Carlo, 27
Turati, Augusto, 279, 288
Turati, Filippo, 239, 241
Turiello, Pasquale, 269
Turn and Taxis (Prince), 182

Umberto I (King), 75, 88, 106, 124
unification, 136; difficulties lead to duel, 53–69
United States of America, 128, 131, 328
Uruguay, 332

Valdameri, Rino, 301–2
Valentini, Attilio, 122
Valeri, Nino, 106
Valori, Aldo, 283, 301
Vela (Deputy), 280
vendetta, 15, 165, 166–67, 223, 255, 289
Venturini, Aristide, 67
Verdi, Giuseppe, 21, 26, 228
Vergani, Paolo, 16
Verro, Bernardino, 239–40
Versailles, 282, 283
Vettori, Vittorio, 282
Vico, Giambattista, 293
Victor Emmanuel II (King), 34, 42, 56, 72, 85–86, 319
Victor Emmanuel III (King), 249
Vidari, Giovanni, 273
Viganò (Minister of War), 249
Vigliani, Paolo Onorato, 198
violence, as a positive force, 269
virility, 6, 78; and fascism, 267, 283, 306; and nationalism, 35–37, 96–109, 173, 319
Visconti, Sebastiano, 120
Visconti Venosta, Emilio, 37
Visconti Venosta, Giovanni, 35, 37–42

War of 1866: effects, 98, 319; and fencing, 91–92
White Mario, Jessie, 63

Whittam, John, 78, 317
women: as countertype, 156–60; and respectability, 36, 149–51, 223–25, 318–19; as symbol of Italy, 33, 183, 185, 317
World War I (impact on dueling), in France and Germany, 327; in Italy, 263–64, 267, 273, 317, 320, 327–28
wounds (relative lightness), 163–65

Zanardelli, Luigi, 125, 199–203, 208. *See also* penal code (1889)
Zibordi, Giovanni, 239, 241–43, 321
Zucchi (General), 77

History of Crime and Criminal Justice
David R. Johnson and Jeffrey S. Adler, Series Editors

The series explores the history of crime and criminality, violence, criminal justice, and legal systems without restrictions as to chronological scope, geographical focus, or methodological approach.

Certain Other Countries: Homicide, Gender, and National Identity in Late Nineteenth-Century England, Ireland, Scotland, and Wales
    Carolyn A. Conley

Prison Work: A Tale of Thirty Years in the California Department of Corrections
    William Richard Wilkinson. Edited by John C. Burnham and Joseph F. Spillane

Cops and Kids: Policing Juvenile Delinquency in Urban America, 1890–1940
    David B. Wolcott

Gender and Petty Violence in London, 1680–1720
    Jennine Hurl-Eamon

Pursuing Johns: Criminal Law Reform, Defending Character, and New York City's Committee of Fourteen, 1920–1930
    Thomas C. Mackey

Social Control in Europe: Volume 2, 1800–2000
    Edited by Clive Emsley, Eric Johnson, and Pieter Spierenburg

Social Control in Europe: Volume 1, 1500–1800
    Herman Roodenburg and Pieter Spierenburg

Policing the City: Crime and Legal Authority in London, 1780–1840
    Andrew T. Harris

Written in Blood: Fatal Attraction in Enlightenment Amsterdam
    Pieter Spierenburg

Crime, Justice, History
    Eric H. Monkkonen

The Rule of Justice: The People of Chicago versus Zephyr Davis
    Elizabeth Dale

Five Centuries of Violence in Finland and the Baltic Area
Heikki Ylikangas, Petri Karonen, and Martti Lehti

Homicide, North and South: Being a Comparative View of Crime against the Person in Several Parts of the United States
H.V. Redfield

Rethinking Southern Violence: Homicides in Post–Civil War Louisiana, 1866–1884
Gilles Vandal

Prostitution and the State in Italy, 1860–1915. Second Edition.
Mary Gibson

Violent Death in the City: Suicide, Accident, and Murder in Nineteenth-Century Philadelphia. Second Edition.
Roger Lane

Controlling Vice: Regulating Brothel Prostitution in St. Paul, 1865–1883
Joel Best

Race, Labor, and Punishment in the New South
Martha A. Myers

Men and Violence: Gender, Honor, and Rituals in Modern Europe and America
Edited by Pieter Spierenburg

Cops and Bobbies: Police Authority in New York and London, 1830–1870. Second Edition.
Wilbur R. Miller

Murder in America: A History
Roger Lane

www.ingramcontent.com/pod-product-compliance
Lightning Source LLC
Chambersburg PA
CBHW021846300426
44115CB00005B/31